SAMUEL RICHARDSON IN CONTEXT

G000137522

Since the publication of his novel *Pamela; or, Virtue Rewarded* in 1740, Samuel Richardson's place in the English literary tradition has been secured. But how can that place best be described? Over the three centuries since embarking on his printing career the 'divine' novelist has been variously understood as moral crusader, advocate for women, pioneer of the realist novel, and print innovator. Situating Richardson's work within these social, intellectual, and material contexts this new volume of essays identifies his centrality to the emergence of the novel, the self-help book, and the idea of the professional author, as well as his influence on the development of the modern English language; the capitalist economy; and gendered, medicalised, urban, and national identities. This book enables a fuller understanding and appreciation of Richardson's life, work, and legacy and points the way for future studies of one of English literature's most celebrated novelists.

PETER SABOR holds the Canada Research Chair in Eighteenth-Century Studies at McGill University, where he is Director of the Burney Centre. His publications include, as co-author, *'Pamela' in the Marketplace* (Cambridge, 2005) and, as editor, *Juvenilia* in *The Cambridge Edition of the Works of Jane Austen* (Cambridge, 2006), *The Cambridge Companion to Emma* (Cambridge, 2015), and *The Correspondence of Samuel Richardson with Lady Bradshaigh and Lady Echlin* (3 vols., Cambridge, 2016).

BETTY A. SCHELLENBERG is Professor of English at Simon Fraser University. Her publications include *Literary Coteries and the Making of Modern Print Culture* (Cambridge, 2016), an edition of Samuel Richardson's *Correspondence Primarily on 'Sir Charles Grandison' (1750–1754)* (Cambridge, 2015), *The Professionalization of Women Writers in Eighteenth-Century Britain* (Cambridge, 2005), and *The Conversational Circle: Rereading the English Novel, 1740–1775* (1996).

SAMUEL RICHARDSON
IN CONTEXT

EDITED BY

PETER SABOR

McGill University

BETTY A. SCHELLENBERG

Simon Fraser University

CAMBRIDGE
UNIVERSITY PRESS

University Printing House, Cambridge CB2 8BS, United Kingdom

One Liberty Plaza, 20th Floor, New York, NY 10006, USA

477 Williamstown Road, Port Melbourne, VIC 3207, Australia

314-321, 3rd Floor, Plot 3, Splendor Forum, Jasola District Centre, New Delhi - 110025, India

79 Anson Road, #06-04/06, Singapore 079906

Cambridge University Press is part of the University of Cambridge.

It furthers the University's mission by disseminating knowledge in the pursuit of education, learning and research at the highest international levels of excellence.

www.cambridge.org
Information on this title: www.cambridge.org/9781316604526
DOI: 10.1017/9781316576755

First published 2017
First paperback edition 2019

A catalogue record for this publication is available from the British Library

ISBN 978-1-107-15012-6 Hardback
ISBN 978-1-316-60452-6 Paperback

Contents

Contents

Illustrations

Notes on Contributors

EVE TAVOR BANNET is George Lynn Cross Professor Emeritus at the University of Oklahoma and editor of *Studies in Eighteenth-Century Culture*. Her monographs include *Transatlantic Stories and the History of Reading* (2011), *Empire of Letters: Letter Manuals and Transatlantic Correspondence* (2005), and *The Domestic Revolution: Enlightenment Feminisms and the Novel* (2000). She has edited *British and American Letter-Manuals, 1680–1810* (2008), Samuel Jackson Pratt's novel *Emma Corbett* (2011), and, with Susan Manning, *Transatlantic Literary Studies, 1640–1830* (2012). Her latest monograph is in press: *Eighteenth-Century Manners of Reading: Print Culture and Popular Instruction in the Anglophone Atlantic World*.

KATHERINE BINHAMMER is a Professor in the Department of English and Film Studies at the University of Alberta, where she specialises in eighteenth-century literature, feminist studies, and narrative theory. She has published *The Seduction Narrative in Britain, 1747–1800* (2009), co-edited *Women and Literary History: 'For there she was'* (2003), and contributed essays to venues such as *The Cambridge Companion to Women's Writing in Britain, 1660–1789*, *Feminist Studies*, *GLQ*, *Women's Studies*, *ELH*, *Eighteenth-Century Fiction*, *Studies in the Novel*, *Narrative*, and *Journal of the History of Sexuality*. Her most recent project focuses on downward mobility in the sentimental novel.

TONI BOWERS is Professor of English and Gender Studies at the University of Pennsylvania. Her publications include *Atlantic Worlds in the Long Eighteenth Century: Seduction and Sentiment* (co-edited with Tita Chico, 2012), *Force or Fraud: British Seduction Stories and the Problem of Resistance, 1680–1760* (2011), *Clarissa: An Abridged Edition* (co-edited with John Richetti, 2011), *The Politics of Motherhood: British Writing and Culture 1680–1760* (1996), and dozens of scholarly essays and reviews.

She lectures frequently in North America and Europe, and has taught at the University of Edinburgh and King's College London.

JOE BRAY is Professor of Language and Literature at the University of Sheffield. He is the author of *The Epistolary Novel: Representations of Consciousness* (2003), *The Female Reader in the English Novel: From Burney to Austen* (2009), and *The Portrait in Fiction of the Romantic Period* (2016), and co-editor of *Ma(r)king the Text: The Presentation of Meaning on the Literary Page* (2000), *Mark Z. Danielewski* (2011), and *The Routledge Companion to Experimental Literature* (2012). *The Language of Jane Austen* will be published in 2018.

LINDA BREE is Senior Executive Publisher and Head of Humanities at Cambridge University Press, and a Senior Member of Wolfson College Cambridge. She has written widely on novelists of the eighteenth and early nineteenth centuries, and has edited a number of works of the period from Daniel Defoe's *Moll Flanders* (2011) to Henry Fielding's *Amelia* (2010) and Jane Austen's *Persuasion* (2000). She is co-editor with Janet Todd of the *Later Manuscripts* volume (2008) in *The Cambridge Edition of the Works of Jane Austen*.

EDWARD COPELAND is Professor Emeritus of English at Pomona College. His publications include, as co-editor, *The Cambridge Companion to Jane Austen* (1997, 2011), *Clarissa and Her Readers* (1999), Catherine Gore's *Cecil; or, The Adventures of a Coxcomb* (2005); as editor, *Sense and Sensibility* (2006) in *The Cambridge Edition of the Works of Jane Austen*; and as author, *Women Writing about Money: Women's Fiction in England 1790–1820* (1995) and *The Silver Fork Novel: Fashionable Fiction in the Age of Reform* (2012).

BRIAN CORMAN is Professor Emeritus of English at the University of Toronto. His publications include *Genre and Generic Change in English Comedy 1660–1710* (1993), *Women Novelists before Jane Austen: The Critics and Their Canons* (2008), and *The Broadview Anthology of Restoration and Eighteenth-Century Comedy* (2013). He edited the *University of Toronto Quarterly* from 1996 to 2009.

LOUISE CURRAN is Lecturer in Romanticism and Eighteenth-Century English Literature at the University of Birmingham. She is the author of *Samuel Richardson and the Art of Letter Writing* (2016) and co-editor of *Correspondence Primarily on 'Pamela' and 'Clarissa'* in *The Cambridge Edition of the Correspondence of Samuel Richardson*, and has written articles on Samuel Johnson, Alexander Pope, and women's satire.

SIMON DICKIE is Associate Professor of English at the University of Toronto. He is the author of *Cruelty and Laughter: Forgotten Comic Literature and the Unsentimental Eighteenth Century* (2011), which won the 2012 Snow Prize from the North American Conference on British Studies. He is now writing a book about biblical and liturgical allusion in eighteenth-century culture, to be called *Sporting with Sacred Things*.

DARRYL P. DOMINGO is Associate Professor of English at the University of Memphis. He has published widely on eighteenth-century literature, including the works of Samuel Richardson, and is the author of *The Rhetoric of Diversion in English Literature and Culture, 1690–1760* (2016).

MARGARET ANNE DOODY, John and Barbara Glynn Professor of Literature at the University of Notre Dame, has edited works by Richardson, Burney, and Austen. She is the author of *A Natural Passion: A Study of the Novels of Samuel Richardson* (1974), *The Daring Muse: Augustan Poetry Reconsidered* (1985), *Frances Burney: The Life in the Works* (1988), *The True Story of the Novel* (1996), *Tropic of Venice* (2006), and *Jane Austen's Names: Riddles, Persons, Places* (2015). Her fiction writing includes *The Alchemists* (1980) and nine 'Aristotle Detective' novels (1978–2013), plus 'The Fable of the Two White Crows'.

MARKMAN ELLIS is Professor of Eighteenth-Century Studies in the School of English and Drama at Queen Mary University of London. He is the author of *The Politics of Sensibility: Race, Gender and Commerce in the Sentimental Novel* (1996), *The History of Gothic Fiction* (2000), and *The Coffee House: A Cultural History* (2004), and is co-author of *Empire of Tea* (2015). He is the general editor of *Eighteenth Century Coffee-House Culture* (4 vols., 2006) and *Tea and the Tea-Table in Eighteenth-Century England* (4 vols., 2010). He has also written on the history of natural history, georgic poetry, slavery and empire, literary coteries, and library history.

CHRISTOPHER FLINT, Professor of English at Case Western Reserve University, is the author of *The Appearance of Print in Eighteenth-Century Fiction* (2011), *Family Fictions: Narrative and Domestic Relations in Britain, 1688–1789* (1998), and articles on eighteenth-century literature and art.

IAN GADD is a Professor of English Literature at Bath Spa University. He is a General Editor of *The Cambridge Edition of the Works of Jonathan Swift*, and was the President of the Society for the History of Authorship, Reading and Publishing (SHARP) for 2013–17. In 2013, he co-edited the first volume of *The History of Oxford University Press*.

SÖREN HAMMERSCHMIDT is an Instructor of English at Arizona State University, where he mainly teaches first-year composition, second-language writing, and developmental writing. His other hat is a powdered wig: whenever he can tear himself away from commenting on thesis statements, transitions, and APA citation style, he returns to work on eighteenth-century correspondence networks, media culture, portraiture, and authorship. His work has previously appeared in *Word & Image, Eighteenth-Century Fiction, Journal for Eighteenth-Century Studies*, and *The Edinburgh History of Scottish Literature*, and he is co-editor (with Louise Curran) of a special issue for *Eighteenth-Century Fiction* on 'Mediating Richardson'.

HILARY HAVENS is Assistant Professor of English at the University of Tennessee. She is the editor of *Didactic Novels and British Women's Writing, 1790–1820* (2017), and her recent articles have appeared in *Studies in English Literature, Journal for Eighteenth-Century Studies*, and *Digital Humanities Quarterly*. Her research has been supported by fellowships from the National Endowment for the Humanities, the Huntington Library, and the New York Public Library.

CATHERINE INGRASSIA is Professor of English at Virginia Commonwealth University. Her publications include *Authorship, Commerce, and Gender in Early Eighteenth-Century England* (1998), '*More Solid Learning': New Perspectives on Pope's 'Dunciad'* (co-editor, 2000), and the *Companion to the Eighteenth-Century Novel and Culture* (co-editor, 2005). A past editor of *Studies in Eighteenth-Century Culture*, she has edited Eliza Haywood's *Anti-Pamela* (2004), co-edited *British Women Poets of the Long Eighteenth Century* (2009), and published essays on the literature and culture of eighteenth-century England. Most recently she edited the *Cambridge Companion to Women's Writing in Britain, 1660–1789* (2015).

THOMAS KEYMER is University Professor and Chancellor Jackman Professor of English at the University of Toronto. His work on Richardson includes *Richardson's 'Clarissa' and the Eighteenth-Century Reader* (1992) and, with Peter Sabor, *'Pamela' in the Marketplace: Literary Controversy and Print Culture in Eighteenth-Century Britain and Ireland* (2005). His most recent books are, as editor, *The Oxford History of the Novel in English*, Volume 1: *Prose Fiction in English from the Origins of Print to 1750* (2017), and as author, *Poetics of the Pillory: English Literature and Seditious Libel 1660–1820* (in press), in the Clarendon Lectures in English series.

BONNIE LATIMER is Lecturer in Eighteenth-Century Literature at Plymouth University. She is the author of *Making Gender, Culture, and the Self in the Fiction of Samuel Richardson* (2013), and an associate editor of *The Encyclopedia of British Literature 1660–1789* (2015). She has published essays on Richardson, Wollstonecraft, and Pope, amongst other things.

KAREN LIPSEDGE is Associate Professor in English Literature at Kingston University. Her research focuses on eighteenth-century domestic space and its representation in the British eighteenth-century novel. Her publications include '"Enter into thy closet": Women, Closet Culture and the Eighteenth-Century Novel', in John Styles and Amanda Vickery (eds.), *Gender, Taste and Material Culture in Britain and North America in the Long Eighteenth Century* (2007), '"I was also absent at my dairyhouse": The Representation and Symbolic Function of the Dairy House in Samuel Richardson's *Clarissa*' (2009), and *Domestic Space in Eighteenth-Century British Novels* (2012).

APRIL LONDON is Emeritus Professor at the University of Ottawa and editor of *The Cambridge Guide to the Eighteenth-Century Novel, 1660–1820* (forthcoming). Her publications include *The Cambridge Introduction to the Eighteenth-Century Novel* (2012), *Literary History Writing, 1770–1820* (2010), and *Women and Property in the Eighteenth-Century English Novel* (1999).

MARY HELEN MCMURRAN is Associate Professor of English at Western University. She is the author of *The Spread of Novels: Translation and Prose Fiction in the Eighteenth Century* (2009) and several articles on translation, the history of the novel, and cosmopolitanism. She has co-edited, with Alison Conway, *Mind, Body, Motion, Matter: Eighteenth-Century British and French Literary Perspectives* (2016).

HEATHER MEEK is Associate Professor of English in the Department of Literatures and Languages of the World at the University of Montreal. She has published several essays on the subject of eighteenth-century hysteria; her more recent work includes an article on Dorothy Wordsworth, illness, and authorship, and a forthcoming essay in *Literature and Medicine* on Frances Burney's mastectomy narrative and discourses of breast cancer. She is currently working on a book about the medical wisdom of eighteenth-century women writers.

LISA O'CONNELL is Senior Lecturer in English at the University of Queensland. She has published articles on the eighteenth-century novel, theatre, and travel writing, and co-edited *Libertine Enlightenment:*

Sex, Liberty and Licence in the Eighteenth Century (2004). Her book
Proper Ceremony: The Political Origins of the English Marriage Plot is
forthcoming.

KATHLEEN M. OLIVER is author of *Samuel Richardson, Dress, and Discourse*
(2008), and her essays on Daniel Defoe, Sarah Fielding, Samuel
Richardson, Frances Sheridan, Charlotte Smith, and William Wycherley
have appeared in peer-reviewed journals and scholarly collections.
In 2002, she received the Emilie du Châtelet Award for Independent
Scholarship, bestowed by the Women's Caucus of the American Society
for Eighteenth-Century Studies.

CAROL PERCY is Professor of English at the University of Toronto. Author
of an article on orthographical reformers in *The Age of Johnson* (2004),
she specialises in the codification of grammar by reviewers, editors, and
grammarians, male and female, and on the (meta)language of individuals including James Cook, George III, and Thomas Jefferson. Surveys
of issues and texts appear in *Eighteenth-Century English: Ideology and
Change* (2010), *English Historical Linguistics* (2012), and *The Oxford
Handbook of the History of English* (2012). Co-edited collections include
Languages of Nation: Attitudes and Norms (2012) and *Prescription and
Tradition: Language Norms across Time and Space* (2017).

ALBERT J. RIVERO is Professor of English at Marquette University. His
publications as editor include *New Essays on Samuel Richardson* (1996),
as well as *Pamela; or, Virtue Rewarded* (2011) and *Pamela in Her Exalted
Condition* (2012) in *The Cambridge Edition of the Works of Samuel
Richardson*.

PAT ROGERS is Distinguished University Professor Emeritus at the University
of South Florida, having served as DeBartolo Chair in the Liberal Arts
from 1986 to 2015, and having held posts at Cambridge, London, Wales,
and Bristol. He has written books on Pope, Swift, Fielding, Johnson,
Boswell, Austen, and others. Works on the bookseller Edmund Curll
include (with Paul Baines) a biography and a bibliography nearing completion. He has also written on topics ranging from weight-watching, the
evolution of modernity, gout, and the breeches role, to the history of sur-
veying, the Venus flytrap, the quest for the longitude, and gaol-breakers.

PETER SABOR, a Fellow of the Royal Society of Canada, holds the Canada
Research Chair in Eighteenth-Century Studies at McGill University,
where he is Director of the Burney Centre. His publications include,

as co-author with Thomas Keymer, *'Pamela' in the Marketplace: Literary Controversy and Print Culture in Eighteenth-Century Britain and Ireland* (2005) and, as editor, *Juvenilia* in *The Cambridge Edition of the Works of Jane Austen* (2006), *The Court Journals and Letters of Frances Burney*, Volume I: *1786* (2011), *The Cambridge Companion to Emma* (2015), and *The Correspondence of Samuel Richardson with Lady Bradshaigh and Lady Echlin* (2016).

BETTY A. SCHELLENBERG is Professor of English at Simon Fraser University. Her interests in the Bluestocking movement, the novel, women's writing, and print and scribal cultures inform numerous essays as well as her most recent book, *Literary Coteries and the Making of Modern Print Culture* (2016). Other publications include an edition of Samuel Richardson's *Correspondence Primarily on 'Sir Charles Grandison' (1750–1754)* (Cambridge, 2015), *The Professionalization of Women Writers in Eighteenth-Century Britain* (2005), *Reconsidering the Bluestockings* (2003, co-edited with Nicole Pohl), and *The Conversational Circle: Rereading the English Novel, 1740–1775* (1996).

NORBERT SCHÜRER is Professor in the English Department at California State University, Long Beach. His teaching and research focus on eighteenth-century book history, women's writing, and Anglo-Indian literature. His recent publications include *Charlotte Lennox: Correspondence and Miscellaneous Documents* (2012) and *British Encounters with India, 1750–1830: A Sourcebook* (with Tim Keirn, 2011). He was section editor on the novel for *The Encyclopedia of British Literature 1660–1789* (2015). In 2012, he curated the exhibition 'Jane Austen's Bookshop' (with Chris Mounsey and Debbie Welham) at Chawton House Library.

LYNN SHEPHERD is the author of *'Clarissa's Painter: Portraiture, Illustration, and Representation in the Novels of Samuel Richardson* (2009). Since completing her D.Phil. at Oxford, she has pursued a career as a writer and published four literary-historical novels. But her enthusiasm for Richardson has never waned: she wrote the afterword for a new, abridged edition of *Clarissa*, and discussed *Pamela* and its legacy as part of the 2015 BBC series *A Very British Romance*, with Lucy Worsley.

SIMON STERN teaches law and English at the University of Toronto. His research focuses on the evolution of legal doctrines and methods in relation to literary and intellectual history. Recent and forthcoming publications include articles and book chapters on legal fictions, obscenity law, early conceptions of criminal fraud, and the historical process by which the law/fact distinction developed. He is co-editor of *The Routledge Companion to Law and Humanities in Nineteenth-Century America* (2017) and *The Oxford Handbook of Law and Humanities* (forthcoming), and is co-editor (with Robert Spoo) of the book series Law and Literature.

E. DEREK TAYLOR is Professor of English at Longwood University (Farmville, VA). Along with a monograph, *Reason and Religion in 'Clarissa': Samuel Richardson and the 'Famous Mr Norris, of Bemerton'* (2009), he has published essays on Richardson in *Eighteenth-Century Fiction, Notes and Queries*, and *Theology and Literature in the Age of Johnson*. He co-edited Mary Astell and John Norris's *Letters Concerning the Love of God* (2005) and *Swiftly Sterneward: Essays on Laurence Sterne and His Times in Honor of Melvyn New* (2011), and has served for over a decade as the Samuel Richardson editor for *The Scriblerian and the Kit-Cats*.

JAMES GRANTHAM Turner holds the James D. Hart Chair of English at the University of California, Berkeley. His publications include 'Lovelace and the Paradoxes of Libertinism', 'Richardson and His Circle', and 'Novel Panic: Picture and Performance in the Reception of Richardson's *Pamela*'. The most recent of his five monographs is *Eros Visible: Art, Sexuality and Antiquity in Renaissance Italy* (2017).

PETER WALMSLEY is Chair of English and Cultural Studies at McMaster University and a past editor of *Eighteenth-Century Fiction*. His books include *The Rhetoric of Berkeley's Philosophy* (1990) and *Locke's 'Essay' and the Rhetoric of Science* (2003). His current research attends to cultures of death in eighteenth-century Britain, and to representations of skilled work in English literature between 1660 and 1750.

HOWARD D. WEINBROT, a reader at the Huntington Library, is Ricardo Quintana Professor of English Emeritus and William Freeman Vilas Research Professor in the College of Letters and Science Emeritus at the University of Wisconsin, Madison. His books include *Britannia's Issue: The Rise of British Literature from Dryden to Ossian* (1993), *Menippean Satire Reconsidered: From Antiquity to the Eighteenth Century* (2005), *Aspects of Samuel Johnson: Essays on His Arts, Mind, Afterlife and Politics* (2005), *Literature, Religion, and the Evolution of Culture 1660–1780* (2013), and the edited *Samuel Johnson: New Contexts for a New Century* (2014).

Preface

From the moment he stepped into the spotlight with the publication of his novel *Pamela; or, Virtue Rewarded* in 1740, Samuel Richardson's place in the English literary tradition has been secure. What exactly that place is, however, has been variously understood. Moral crusader, advocate for women, inventor of a new species of writing, pioneer of the realist novel, spokesman for bourgeois ideology, exposer of its underbelly, pre-Freudian high-priest of unconscious desire, innovator of the print medium – as well as the easy target of critical jibes for his prolixity and thin skin – Richardson has, over the almost three centuries since embarking on his printing career, meant many things. Yet for all the illuminating critical analyses that Richardson's novels have received, their readers have worked in the absence of some of the fundamental tools of scholarship. We are well served by the bibliographical work of William Merritt Sale, Jr and Keith Maslen, and by the magisterial scholarship in the biography by T. C. Duncan Eaves and Ben D. Kimpel, but it is only now that a complete critical edition of the works and correspondence of this prolific writer is under way. Similarly, aside from the rich body of analyses linking Richardson's fiction to the familiar letter genre or the eighteenth-century novel tradition, there are few resources assisting those new to Richardson, and perhaps even to the eighteenth century, with the task of situating his work in its social, intellectual, and material context.

It is this latter gap that *Samuel Richardson in Context* seeks to fill. With contributions from leading scholars worldwide, it is designed to be at once accessible to the advanced undergraduate student and informative for the more experienced researcher seeking an orientation to unfamiliar facets of the author and the period. Its thirty-seven concise chapters provide an overview of the 'Life and Works' and of Richardson's 'Critical Fortunes', followed by clusters on 'The Print Trade', 'The Book and Its Readers', 'Literary Genres and the Arts', and 'Social Structures and Social Life'. For such areas as the publication and reception histories of Richardson's works, this volume is designed to serve as a useful compendium of the scholarly tradition. Even here, however, a consideration of the biography through portraiture and a discussion of the full range of Richardson's correspondence reflect the new lights of recent scholarship, and hitherto scattered accounts of the author's complex and often rebarbative dealings with Irish and continental members of the trade are gathered together.

Pamela and its sequel, *Pamela in Her Exalted Condition* (1741), figure prominently in the volume, which also pays sustained attention to Richardson's masterpiece, *Clarissa* (1747–8) – arguably the greatest (and certainly the longest) tragic novel in English – and to his final novel, *Sir Charles Grandison* (1753–4), which has attracted increasing critical interest in recent years. Richardson was determined not to repeat himself, and just as *Clarissa* worked in an entirely different way from its predecessors, the two parts of *Pamela*, so did *Sir Charles Grandison* take a very different direction from that of his previous novels.

A number of chapters in *Samuel Richardson in Context* pay careful attention to the author's professional functions as entrepreneur, printer, and editor, placing these on a spectrum with his creative writing in a reflection of the period's own models of authorship. Other chapters push the boundaries of traditional Richardson scholarship, suggestively situating the author's work in relation to a common international discourse of sentiment, for example, or to a persistent strain of libertine humour, the emerging genre of the legal case, eighteenth-century practices around death and mourning, and the nascent discourse of English nationalism. In the sum of these respects Richardson emerges as a Janus-faced transitional figure, adhering to traditional high Anglicanism and valuing the good death on the one hand, while on the other challenging the elite posing of an author such as Alexander Pope; critiquing libertine licence and anti-Catholic xenophobia; supporting Hanoverian contractual political theory; and pointing the way to the future in areas as diverse as English language usage, generic innovations, gender identities, and the social practices of middle-class domesticity.

Other material in this volume includes a chronology, providing a detailed summary of Richardson's life and authorial career; some twenty illustrations, chosen to illuminate the visual culture of Richardson's age; and an extensive list of further reading. *Samuel Richardson in Context* will have fulfilled its purpose if it serves as a crossroads, gathering the fruits of decades, even centuries, of engagement by readers amateur and expert, and signalling new scholarly trajectories in contextualising this foundational, yet protean, English author. Indeed, if this volume generates further dialogue and debate, whether conversational or written, we can safely assume that our author himself, always eager to elicit and challenge the views of others, would have been delighted.

Acknowledgments

We give grateful thanks to the contributors to *Samuel Richardson in Context*; it has been a pleasure to collaborate with such a learned and congenial group. Heather Meek and Kate Oliver in particular went above and beyond the call of duty. We received much valuable aid from three research assistants at the Burney Centre, McGill University – Catherine Nygren, who prepared the index, Laura Cameron, and Caroline Boreham – as well as from Meghan Brennan, Holly Vestad, and David Weston at Simon Fraser University. Linda Bree at Cambridge University Press helped us to plan the volume, Tim Mason helped to bring it to completion, and the Press's anonymous readers improved it with their astute suggestions. Robert Whitelock was a superbly vigilant copy-editor. Jack Lynch's exemplary *Samuel Johnson in Context* provided us with a model for our work. For research funding, Peter Sabor thanks the Social Sciences and Humanities Research Council of Canada, the Canada Research Chairs programme and Le Fonds québécois de la recherche sur la société et la culture; Betty Schellenberg thanks the SFU Publications Fund. Merci, chère Marie et cher Christian, pour tout.

Chronology

1682

2 June — Marriage in London of SR's parents, Samuel Richardson, Sr (d. 1727), a master joiner, and Elizabeth Hall (d. 1736).

1687 — Family leaves London for Derbyshire at about this time, perhaps for political reasons.

1689

July–August — Born and baptised in Mackworth, near Derby, the fourth of nine children from the marriage.

1695–9 — Family returns to London during this period, settling in the Tower Hill district.

1701–2 — Probably educated at the Merchant Taylors' School, where his schoolfellows know him as '*Serious* and *Gravity*'.

1706

1 July — Apprenticed to John Wilde, a printer of Aldersgate.

1713

2 July — Completes apprenticeship with Wilde, where SR has become 'the Pillar of his House'.

1715

13 June — Made freeman of the Stationers' Company and a citizen of London.

1715–20 — Works as a compositor and corrector in Wilde's business.

1720 — Manages the printing business of the Leake family on the corner of Blue Ball and Salisbury Courts; begins printing private bills for James Blew, a lawyer and parliamentary agent.

1721 — Buys 'Printing Presses and Letter Utensils of trade' from the Leakes and sets up as master printer on their former premises, where he resides until 1736; remains in the Salisbury Court district for his entire career.

23 November	Marries Martha, daughter of John Wilde; five sons and a daughter from the marriage die in infancy.

1722

5 March	Granted the livery of the Stationers' Company.
6 August	Three Leake apprentices turned over to SR, the first of twenty-four apprentices bound to him during his career.
1722–4	Denounced to the ministry by Samuel Negus, a printer, as one of the 'disaffected printers … Said to be High-Flyers'; continues printing Tory-Jacobite material, including the duke of Wharton's periodical *The True Briton* (1723–4).

1725

December	Begins printing the *Daily Journal* (to 1737), one of several newspapers and periodicals printed by SR until the mid-1740s.

1727

11 April	Elected to junior office as Renter Warden in the Stationers' Company.
1728	Rents a second Salisbury Court house, opposite the first, for *Daily Journal* operations (to 1736).
September	Identified to the ministry by Edmund Curll as printer of a seditious number of *Mist's Weekly Journal*.

1730

December	*The Infidel Convicted*, possibly by SR.

1731

23 January	Death of Martha (Wilde) Richardson.
February	Becomes a junior shareholder in the Stationers' Company, purchasing progressively more senior levels of stock in 1736, 1746, and 1751.
October	Incurs financial losses on the collapse of the Charitable Corporation; embroiled until mid-1733 in related legal proceedings.

1733

3 February	Marries Elizabeth Leake (d. 1773), sister of the Bath bookseller James Leake.
February	Appointed first official printer to the House of Commons (to 1761), responsible for public bills and committee reports; SR thereby becomes 'more independent of Booksellers (tho' I did much Business for them) than any other Printer'.

December	*The Apprentice's Vade Mecum.*
23 December	Baptism of daughter Elizabeth, d. 1734.
1734	Expands business premises into a third house, in Blue Ball Court (to 1740).
1735	
2 January	Baptism of daughter Mary (Polly), m. 1757 (to Philip Ditcher), d. 1783.
April	*A Seasonable Examination of the Pleas and Pretensions of the Proprietors of, and Subscribers to, Play-Houses.*
June	Probably begins printing the pro-ministerial *Daily Gazetteer* (to 1746).
1736	Moves to 'House of a very grand outward Appearance' on Salisbury Square, which he occupies until 1756; also rents Corney House, a tenement of Sutton Court, Chiswick, as a weekend/summer retreat (to 1738).
January	*Gentleman's Magazine* publishes a light verse epistle by SR, noting that 'the Publick is often agreeably entertain'd with his Elegant Disquisitions in Prose'.
16 July	Baptism of daughter Martha (Patty), m. 1762 (to Edward Bridgen), d. 1785.
1737	
16 August	Baptism of daughter Anne (Nancy), d. 1803.
1738	
Summer	Rents large, semi-rural retreat at North End, Fulham (to 1754).
October	Edits and prints updated second edition of Defoe's *Tour*, also subsequent editions of 1742, 1748, 1753, and 1761–2.
1739	
26 April	Baptism of son Samuel, d. 1740.
10 November	Starts writing *Pamela*.
20 November	*Aesop's Fables.*
1740	
January	Completes draft of *Pamela*, revising the text over the ensuing months.
29 March	*The Negotiations of Sir Thomas Roe in His Embassy to the Ottoman Porte*, edited and printed by SR for the Society for the Encouragement of Learning.

17 July	Baptism of twelfth and last child, Sarah (Sally), m. 1763 (to Richard Crowther), d. 1773.
6 November	*Pamela; or, Virtue Rewarded.*
1741	Expands his printing premises behind Salisbury Court.
23 January	Letters Written to and for Particular Friends.
28 May	Opening volume of John Kelly's *Pamela's Conduct in High Life*, a spurious continuation, published; SR starts planning his own authorised continuation.
1 December	Elected to the Court of Assistants, ruling body of the Stationers' Company.
7 December	*Pamela in Her Exalted Condition*, SR's continuation.
1742	
8 May	Sixth edition of *Pamela*, in octavo format and with twenty-nine engravings by Hubert Gravelot and Francis Hayman: the first simultaneous publication of both parts.
May	Wins large contract to print the *Journals* of the House of Commons (to 1761).
1744	Begins printing the *Philosophical Transactions of the Royal Society* (to 1761), one of several major projects for learned societies.
June–July	Earliest references in SR's correspondence to *Clarissa*, which already exists in some form of draft.
December	Sends part of the novel in manuscript to Aaron Hill; manuscript copies in various states of revision circulate among SR's friends until 1747.
1746	
Summer	Assists the ministry in finding shorthand experts to help prosecute Jacobite rebels.
December	Hill sends SR his 'Specimen of New Clarissa', a test abridgment of the novel's opening.
1747	
1 December	*Clarissa*, Vols. I and II.
1748	
28 April	*Clarissa*, Vols. III and IV.
5 July	William Richardson, nephew, apprenticed to SR.

2 August	Advertises in the *Whitehall Evening-Post* for contact with Lady Bradshaigh, who has been sending pseudonymous letters about *Clarissa*.
6 December	*Clarissa*, Vols. v–vii.

1749

June	Prints *Answer to the Letter of a Very Reverend and Worthy Gentleman*, a defence of Clarissa's fire scene, for private distribution.
August	Publishes notes responding to Albrecht von Haller's critique of *Clarissa* in the *Gentleman's Magazine*.
December	Prints *Meditations Collected from the Sacred Books* for private distribution.

1750

6 March	First face-to-face meeting with Lady Bradshaigh, thereafter his closest literary adviser.
August	Death of SR's brother Benjamin; household joined by Benjamin's fourteen-year-old daughter Susanna (Sukey), 'whom my Wife has in a manner adopted'.

1751

January	Sections of *Sir Charles Grandison* start to circulate in manuscript among SR's friends.
19 February	Publishes an essay (no. 97) on courtship and marriage in Samuel Johnson's periodical *The Rambler*, based on SR's letter of 8 September 1750 to Frances Grainger.
20 April	Expanded third edition of Clarissa; new material separately published as *Letters and Passages Restored from the Original Manuscripts of the History of Clarissa*.

1752

28 September	Fire at SR's printing-house causes extensive damage and loss of stock; takes on additional Salisbury Court premises at about this time, probably as a warehouse and workmen's residence.

1753

May	Begins distributing printed sheets of *Sir Charles Grandison* among friends.
2 June	Writes autobiographical letter to Johannes Stinstra, his Dutch translator.

30 June	Attains rank of Upper Warden in the Stationers' Company.
August	Learns that four Dublin booksellers have stolen most of *Sir Charles Grandison* in printed sheets and plan to publish an unauthorised edition; halts printing and dismisses suspected employees.
14 September	*The Case of Samuel Richardson, of London, Printer … with Regard to the Invasion of His Property* printed for free distribution.
13 November	*Sir Charles Grandison*, Vols. I–IV, simultaneously published in duodecimo ('first') and octavo ('second') editions; Vols. I–VI of the piracy appear in Dublin the same month, before SR can bring out his authorised Vols. V and VI.
11 December	*Sir Charles Grandison*, Vols. V and VI (duodecimo) and Vol. V (octavo).
1754	
1 February	Prints *An Address to the Public*, a further attack on the Dublin pirates and on George Faulkner, an Irish bookseller, with whom he had failed to negotiate a solution.
14 March	*Sir Charles Grandison*, Vol. VII (duodecimo) and Vol. VI (octavo).
19 March	Revised third edition of *Sir Charles Grandison* (duodecimo).
April	Prints two commentaries on *Sir Charles Grandison*, *Answer to a Letter from a Friend*, and *Copy of a Letter to a Lady*, for private distribution; the latter explains that there will be no further volumes.
6 July	Becomes Master of the Stationers' Company for a one-year term.
July–October	Rents and renovates new weekend house at Parson's Green, which his wife and daughters make their main home.
1755	
February	Begins writing a fragmentary 'History of Mrs Beaumont' (partly published in 1804), possibly as the basis for a new novel.
6 March	*A Collection of the Moral and Instructive Sentiments, Maxims, Cautions, and Reflexions, Contained in the Histories of Pamela, Clarissa, and Sir Charles Grandison.*
5 August	William Richardson completes apprenticeship and becomes SR's overseer.

July–December	Builds expensive new business premises in Salisbury Court, renovating the adjoining house as a residence, which he occupies the following spring.
1757 June	Approached by Erasmus Reich, a Leipzig bookseller, with proposals to bring out a German edition of his selected correspondence, which he starts to prepare.
1758 May	Abandons the Reich project, but continues preparing letters for possible posthumous publication.
August–September	Revises and corrects Urania Hill Johnson's novel *Almira*, which she publishes six months after SR's death, rejecting most of the revisions.
1759 May	Prints Edward Young's *Conjectures on Original Composition*, composed by Young with SR's collaborative involvement.
Summer	William Richardson leaves SR's employment to start his own printing business.
1760 28 April	Revises and contributes to a translation of Marguerite de Lussan's *The Life and Heroic Actions of Balbe Berton*, printed by William Richardson.
24 June	Enters partnership with Catherine Lintot, heir to the printer Henry Lintot, in a law patent with monopoly rights to print books on common law.
1761 March	Borrows Lady Bradshaigh's annotated copies of *Pamela* and *Clarissa* to make further revisions.
28 June	Suffers stroke during a visit from the portraitist Joseph Highmore.
4 July	Dies, leaving an estate of £14,000 and bequeathing manuscripts to his daughters; buried in St Bride's, Fleet Street, beside his first wife and infant children.
September	William Richardson returns to Salisbury Court, taking over SR's business with a partner, Samuel Clarke.
1762	Posthumous revised editions of *Pamela* and *Sir Charles Grandison*.
1765 March	'Six Original Letters upon Duelling' published in the *Candid Review and Literary Repository*.

1771

25 January   Publication of Anna Meades's *The History of Sir William Harrington, Written Some Years Since, and Revised and Corrected by the Late Mr. Richardson*; SR's daughters contest the claim, but he had indeed advised Meades in 1757–8.

1780   William Richardson issues proposals for a uniform edition of the novels, 'with corrections', but the edition does not materialise.

1784   Anne Richardson and Martha Bridgen plan a new edition of *Pamela*, based on unpublished final revisions by SR, to be 're-revised' by themselves.

1786
January–
February   Authorised 'Memoirs of Richardson', perhaps by Edward Bridgen, published in the *Universal Magazine*.

1792   'New edition' of *Clarissa*, 'with the last corrections by the author', prepared with the involvement of Anne Richardson and SR's granddaughter Sarah Crowther Moodie.

1801   Fourteenth edition of *Pamela*, prepared from Anne Richardson's copy, 'with numerous alterations … by the Author'.

1803   Death of Anne, SR's last surviving child.

1804
July   *The Correspondence of Samuel Richardson*, edited, with a substantial biographical memoir, by Anna Laetitia Barbauld.

1810   'New edition' of *Sir Charles Grandison*, probably from Anne Richardson's copy, 'with the last corrections by the author'; fifteenth edition of *Pamela*, with further 'numerous corrections and alterations', apparently from Anne's annotated copy of the fourteenth edition.

Abbreviations

All quotations of Richardson's correspondence are taken from *The Cambridge Edition of the Correspondence of Samuel Richardson*.

Works by Richardson

Barbauld *Correspondence*	Anna Laetitia Barbauld, *The Correspondence of Samuel Richardson*, 6 vols. (London: Richard Phillips, 1804)
C	*Clarissa; or, The History of a Young Lady*, 1st edn, 7 vols. (London, 1748)
Case	*The Case of Samuel Richardson … with Regard to the Invasion of His Property* (London, 14 September 1753)
CECSR	*The Cambridge Edition of the Correspondence of Samuel Richardson*, gen. eds. Thomas Keymer and Peter Sabor (Cambridge: Cambridge University Press, 2013–)
EW	*Early Works: 'Aesop's Fables', 'Letters Written to and for Particular Friends' and Other Works*, ed. Alexander Pettit (Cambridge: Cambridge University Press, 2012)
P	*Pamela; or, Virtue Rewarded*, ed. Albert J. Rivero (Cambridge: Cambridge University Press, 2011)
PE	*Pamela in Her Exalted Condition*, ed. Albert J. Rivero (Cambridge: Cambridge University Press, 2012)
SCG	*The History of Sir Charles Grandison*, 1st edn, 7 vols. (London, 1754)

Other Works

Boswell, *Life of Johnson*	James Boswell, *Boswell's Life of Johnson*, eds. George Birkbeck Hill and L. F. Powell, 6 vols. (Oxford: Clarendon Press, 1934–50)
Bueler, *'Clarissa': The Eighteenth-Century Response*	Lois Bueler (ed.), *'Clarissa': The Eighteenth-Century Response, 1747–1804*, 2 vols. (New York: AMS Press, 2010)
Doody and Sabor, *Tercentenary Essays*	Margaret Anne Doody and Peter Sabor (eds.), *Samuel Richardson: Tercentenary Essays* (Cambridge: Cambridge University Press, 1989)
Eaves and Kimpel, *Biography*	T. C. Duncan Eaves and Ben D. Kimpel, *Samuel Richardson: A Biography* (Oxford: Clarendon Press, 1971)
Keymer, *Richardson's 'Clarissa'*	Tom Keymer, *Richardson's 'Clarissa' and the Eighteenth-Century Reader* (Cambridge: Cambridge University Press, 1992)
Keymer and Sabor, *'Pamela' in the Marketplace*	Thomas Keymer and Peter Sabor, *'Pamela' in the Marketplace: Literary Controversy and Print Culture in Eighteenth-Century Britain and Ireland* (Cambridge: Cambridge University Press, 2005)
Keymer and Sabor, *The 'Pamela' Controversy*	Thomas Keymer and Peter Sabor (eds.), *The 'Pamela' Controversy: Criticisms and Adaptations of Samuel Richardson's 'Pamela', 1740–1750*, 6 vols. (London: Pickering & Chatto, 2001)
Maslen, *Samuel Richardson*	Keith Maslen, *Samuel Richardson of London, Printer: A Study of His Printing Based on Ornament Use and Printers' Accounts* (Dunedin: University of Otago, 2001)
Sale, *Bibliographical Record*	William Merritt Sale, Jr, *Samuel Richardson: A Bibliographical Record of His Literary Career with Historical Notes* (New Haven: Yale University Press, 1936)
Sale, *Master Printer*	William Merritt Sale, Jr, *Samuel Richardson: Master Printer* (Ithaca, NY: Cornell University Press, 1950)

PART I

Life and Works

CHAPTER I

Portraying the Life

Thomas Keymer

Samuel Richardson did not come from the portrait-commissioning classes, and we have no likeness of him from the first fifty years of his life. In this respect he resembles Daniel Defoe – whose portrait was painted, but whose appearance we know most vividly from a newspaper description calling for his arrest – more closely than he resembles celebrity authors of the era like Alexander Pope or Laurence Sterne. For Pope in association with several artists, or Sterne with Joshua Reynolds in particular, portraiture was a way to shape or promote reputation in a process of strategic self-definition, one that could be further advanced by means of public exhibition or dissemination of engraved copies. Approached in this way, an authorial portrait did more than simply record physical appearance, display social standing and suggest personal character; it contributed to a larger project of creative self-fashioning or identity-projection of the kind also at work in the *Imitations of Horace* and Pope's emblematic Twickenham garden, or in *Tristram Shandy* and Sterne's role-playing as Parson Yorick. For the most theoretically self-conscious of Pope's portraitists, Jonathan Richardson (no relation), portraiture could even approach the condition of a narrative genre. 'A Portrait is a Sort of General History of the Life of the Person it represents', this artist wrote in a treatise of 1719. He developed the point six years later: 'upon the sight of a Portrait the Character, and Master-strokes of the History of the Person it represents are apt to flow in upon the Mind ... So that to sit for one's Picture, is to have an Abstract of one's Life written, and published, and ourselves thus consign'd over to Honour, or Infamy.'[1]

Richardson was famous for no quality so much as personal diffidence, and seems to have disdained direct self-promotion (as opposed to promotion of his books), portraiture especially. 'I am not fond of being hanged up in Effigy', he wrote with macabre innuendo to Samuel Lobb, distancing himself from a mezzotint portrait by the young engraver James Macardell 'that was done by Command of a great Man; and which I have never permitted

Figure 1.1 James Macardell, *Samuel Richardson* (1753), after Joseph Highmore, mezzotint, 353 × 252 mm (paper size), National Portrait Gallery, London, and elsewhere.

to be sold' (1 July 1754; Figure 1.1). As with Defoe, one effect of this attitude is to give special value to surviving pen-portraits from Richardson's lifetime: even the briefest, like the report of his 'large, blue, fiery, roguish, witty eyes' made to the poet Klopstock in 1756.[2] That said, it is clear that his reservations about portraiture went only so far. Between 1740 and 1754 – exactly the span of his career as a novelist – Richardson personally commissioned or otherwise sat for at least five formal portraits of himself. As for the mezzotint desired by the 'great Man' – probably the politician Arthur Onslow, long-serving Speaker of the House of Commons – it was Richardson who ordered and paid for the engraving, and he privately distributed copies on some scale, including to friends of friends. The oil portraits – by Francis Hayman (*c.* 1740–1), Joseph Highmore (1747, *c.* 1747–50, 1750), and Mason Chamberlin (*c.* 1754) – are all accomplished pieces in their own right, and in the first four cases are connected with illustrations discussed below by Lynn Shepherd (pp. 197–202). They project Richardson's authorial identity with intriguing differences of emphasis, and open up valuable insights not only into the shape of his personal and literary life but also into the meanings he sought to attach to it.

Conspicuously absent from, or at best deeply buried within, these meanings is Richardson's profession as master printer, though it was from this
profession that his career as novelist arose, and it makes him an important
figure in book history independently of his standing as an author. He was
born in middling-sort provincial obscurity in 1689, in a Derbyshire vil-
lage to which the family had withdrawn after his father, a London master
joiner, became entangled in some way in the conspiratorial Whig politics
of the Exclusion Crisis, perhaps even in the Monmouth rising of 1685, in
which the duke of Monmouth attempted to overthrow James II (a glamor-
ous reminiscence on Richardson's part; there may have been more hum-
drum business reasons). By the mid-1690s the Williamite revolution had
made it safe to return to London, and Richardson may have been educated
at the Merchant Taylors' School there, but if so only to a certain level,
and he always thought of himself as an autodidact. He never attained the
classical learning flaunted in the work of his great rival Henry Fielding,
and when creating the voice of Elias Brand, a pedantic cleric, for the third
edition of *Clarissa*, he seems to have had to rely for help on an erudite
book-trade colleague.[3]

Richardson once apologised to Aaron Hill that he 'seldom read but as
a Printer, having so much of that' (2 April 1743), a comment sometimes
used to support a view of him as, like Ben Jonson's Shakespeare, a 'natural' genius. Potentially, however, reading as a printer meant reading on a
prodigious scale across multiple fields. In the mid-twentieth century, the
bio-bibliographical researches of William Sale made clear that Richardson's
printing business was among the most important of the day, but we now
know that its output was up to five times larger than Sale recognised, on
a scale comparable to the great printing-houses of the Bowyer family or
William Strahan. By 1734 Richardson was employing twenty compositors
and pressmen as well as four apprentices bound to him and doubtless other
hands (warehousemen, devils, a corrector of the press); in 1753 he had forty
workmen on the payroll, and in 1759 he was still expanding capacity, to a
total of nine presses.[4] In this context, it hardly needs saying that we must
not think of Richardson as personally reading the huge and diverse range
of material he printed. On the other hand, delegation was not his forte,
and we know that he won commissions from booksellers precisely because
of his ability, unusual in a printer, to give qualitative advice about copy
and supply paratextual additions from his own pen.[5] Some booksellers (in
effect, publishers) 'thought fit to seek me, rather than I them, because of the
Readiness I shewed, to oblige them, with writing Indexes, Prefaces, and …
Dedication[s]; abstracting, abridging, compiling, and giving my Opinion

of Pieces offered them', he recalled in the best single source we have for his early career: an autobiographical letter of 2 June 1753 to Johannes Stinstra, his Dutch translator.

After apprenticeship and years of fairly menial employment (as compositor, corrector, and eventually overseer of his former master's printing-house), Richardson set up in business for himself on the corner of Salisbury Court, off Fleet Street, in late 1720. He was to live and work in this neighbourhood for the rest of his life, though from 1738 he also maintained semi-rural retreats (at North End, Hammersmith, then Parson's Green, Fulham) where much of his writing was done. He took over a going concern (from the Leake family, with whom he maintained close lifelong ties), but even so, getting securely established cannot have been easy. Richardson's biographers T. C. Duncan Eaves and Ben D. Kimpel use this fact to explain the dissident cast of his early output as a printer, or at least of a conspicuous part of it. 'There is no evidence that Richardson was ever opposed to the House of Hanover', they maintain, and where his printing activities indicate otherwise, they suggest that he was glad of whatever work he could get, that he may not have fully understood what he was printing, or that he was simply helping out a book-trade colleague.[6] Yet it is hard to think of Richardson as stupid or rash, and his creative output gives no grounds at all for thinking him deaf to nuance or subtextual meaning. He ran obvious risks by printing dissident material, and persisted in these risks through a politically fraught decade. Prominent among the authors whose works he handled in the 1720s were Bishop Francis Atterbury, recently banished for his role in the abortive Jacobite plot of 1722; George Kelly, a participant in the Jacobite rebellions of both 1715 and 1745, whose defence speech in the 1723 treason trials was printed by Richardson in five editions; and Philip, duke of Wharton, whose cover as an 'Old Whig' critic of ministerial encroachment on the 1688 settlement was blown when he later defected to the Jacobite court in exile. None of this work escaped official attention. In 1722 Richardson appeared on a blacklist of 'disaffected printers' (specifically those 'Said to be High Flyers', i.e. Tory ultras, sympathetic to the Jacobite cause) supplied to the ministry by a book-trade insider; in 1723 he escaped prosecution for seditious libel only when the publisher of the *True Briton* (Wharton's journal, printed by Richardson) falsely confessed to doing the printing himself; in 1728 he was implicated in the production of another crypto-Jacobite organ, *Mist's Weekly Journal*.[7] Like his father in the 1680s, though from another position, Richardson was keeping dangerous political company – the common element in both cases being a doomed, charismatic nobleman (Monmouth, Wharton) whose type he was to anatomise in *Clarissa*.

It was only after 1730 that Richardson was able to transform his political reputation into that of a trusted insider to the Hanover Whig establishment, and quite how he managed to do it is still unclear. In 1733 he became the first official printer to the House of Commons, responsible for printing sessional papers for the use of MPs only, and in 1742 he expanded this role further by winning an enormous contract, extended in 1756, to print the Commons *Journals* all the way back to 1547 and forward in the ongoing present. No longer the printer of opposition polemic, Richardson became, for the rest of his life, as much a presence in the seat of government as any minister or official. The costs were high: 'Half a Day every Day obliged to be thrown away on a personal outdoors Attendance at Westminster', he wrote with frustration while trying to revise *Clarissa* (to Aaron Hill, 10 May 1749). But the rewards were immense. Parliamentary printing is clearly the activity that Richardson had in mind when he told Stinstra of developing a branch of business that made him 'more independent of Booksellers (tho' I did much Business for them) than any other Printer' (2 June 1753). This activity, moreover, reaches back to the very start of his career. Perhaps building on relationships established by the Leakes, Richardson carried out extensive work over four decades as a printer of private parliamentary bills concerning estates, trusts, wills, marriages, and the like; there were also local bills (roads, canals). This printing was commissioned not by booksellers but by lawyers and lobbyists acting on behalf of real-world Harlowes and Solmeses who wished, as Keith Maslen drily puts it, 'to alter the condition of their lives by securing an act of Parliament in their favour'.[8] No doubt Richardson's dominant position in the private bills market helped him to secure the official Commons contract in 1733, but that may not be the whole story. William Bowyer, who competed unsuccessfully for the contract, sourly attributed Richardson's victory to 'his superior knowledge of mankind': an innuendo not hard to unpack in the Walpole era.[9]

Secure in these lucrative official contracts, Richardson become one of the most prosperous printers of his day, and rose to be elected, in 1754, as Master of the Stationers' Company, the ancient book-trade livery guild. This is the Richardson depicted in the three-quarter-length portrait now hanging in Stationers' Hall, originally with a companion portrait of Richardson's second wife, Elizabeth Leake, destroyed in the Blitz (Figure 1.2); it may always have been intended for that destination, though it stayed in family hands until 1811. The paradox is that

Figure 1.2 Joseph Highmore, *Samuel Richardson* (1747), oil on canvas, 1245 × 996 mm,
Stationers' Hall, London.

this representation, by Richardson's friend and favourite portraitist Joseph
Highmore, largely erases his professional identity. Even the bookselling
magnate Jacob Tonson, who liked to pose as landed gentry, holds one of
his own publications – *Paradise Lost*, gilt title displayed to the viewer –
when sitting for Sir Godfrey Kneller in 1717. Richardson too is shown
holding a book, but not in a posture of display, and with no indication
of the contents. The volume points to his contemplative character, not
his frenetic day job, and is closed around his index finger as though to
show him pausing as he reads and strolls at leisure – a condition he rarely
if ever knew – in a landscaped garden with statuary and mature trees.
The landscape is clearly a studio backdrop, not a *plein-air* setting, but it
serves important functions nonetheless. At one level it bespeaks a natur-
alness intensified by its unkempt, 'wilderness' state and its chipped, overgrown stonework, while Richardson is shown with matching gestures of
warts-and-all authenticity. He is jowly, thick-browed, with a prominent
mole on the cheek facing the spectator. Like Sir Peter Lely's celebrated
Cromwell portrait, the painting gives out a message of frankness and
honesty above all, and this was the meaning picked up by the novelist
Mme de Genlis on seeing it in 1785: a 'portrait de grandeur naturelle' that
expressed Richardson's truest self, 'sa physionomie et ses yeux … remplis
de douceur'.[10] Yet at the same time the landscape also makes an implicit claim about social standing, placing Richardson in an elite milieu to

Figure 1.3 Francis Hayman (1708–76), *Samuel Richardson, the Novelist (1684–1761), Seated, Surrounded by His Second Family* (c. 1740–1), oil on canvas, 995 × 1252 mm, Tate Britain, London.

which he certainly aspired, but to which he had yet to secure full access. In this respect, nothing here is natural at all. With his rich, plum-coloured coat, laced cuffs, and (Lynn Shepherd notes) 'the fashionable "hand-in-waistcoat" pose recommended in François Nivelon's *Rudiments of Genteel Behavior* (1737) … which became the staple pose of much mid-century society portraiture', he is depicted not as the tradesman he was but as the gentleman he aspired to be.[11]

Richardson holds the same pose in two slightly later Highmore portraits, which makes it possible that he sat only once, leaving Highmore to fulfil further commissions by reworking the first composition. He appears somewhat differently, however, in the earliest portrait we have, done in the popular 'conversation piece' idiom of the era by Francis Hayman, who made his name in the theatre as a scene painter but was developing a new line in portraiture by 1740–1, the date usually assumed for this canvas (Figure 1.3). It is a characteristic Hayman piece, marked by his sensitivity to domestic relationships, though also by a

style 'easily distinguishable', Horace Walpole noted, 'by the large noses
and shambling legs'.[12] Richardson comes across as a benign, burgh-
erly patriarch, surrounded by his family in the extended eighteenth-
century sense: not only his second wife Elizabeth Leake and four young
daughters but also – stealing the show in a bravura rendering of blue
silk – Elizabeth Midwinter, an orphan who lived with the Richardsons
until her marriage of 1742 to Francis Gosling, Richardson's banker.
In its decorous way, it is a joyful image, transcending the pain that
Richardson still felt from the loss of his first wife, Martha Wilde
(daughter of the printer whose apprentice he had been), who died in
1731, as did six children from this first marriage and two from the second, all in infancy. Some lived long enough 'to be delightful Pratlers'
(Richardson to Lady Bradshaigh, 15 December 1748); four, with dreadful poignancy, were named Samuel.

Other elements of the painting look forward to Highmore: a fanciful
rural setting with distant mountains (though the nearest thing to a moun-
tain that Richardson ever saw was a rocky outcrop in Kent);[13] the dignified
hand-in-waistcoat pose (but no sign of the mole); again the finger marking
the page of a book, as though looking up from reading (despite the prox-
imity of four children aged under eight – but perhaps he has been reading
to them). Janet Aikins conjectures that the unlabelled book, at the geo-
metric centre of the canvas, is a volume of *Pamela*, published to overnight
success in November 1740 and still intensely in vogue when Richardson
brought out his handsome octavo edition (May 1742) with illustrations
by Hayman and a collaborator. In this view, the painting not only catches
the glow of the moment but also registers the stages of ideal femininity
promoted in the novel and its sequel, while also alluding to the domestic circumstances of composition, when Richardson read passages to his
wife and Miss Midwinter as he drafted them.[14] More pragmatically, the
painting may have been designed to enhance Miss Midwinter's prospects
in the marriage market (a big nose, but gorgeous silks), in which, if so, it
succeeded.

Shepherd notes the relative privacy of the conversation-piece genre, and
if this painting was intended to represent a domestic ideal, to celebrate
Pamela's success, or to link these things, it did so within a restricted audience of family and visiting friends.[15] Richardson's growing fame as *Pamela*'s
author (the mask of anonymity lasted only so long, and he craved recognition) is better reflected by a second Highmore of *c.* 1747–50, again in three-
quarter profile but this time at bust length, to which a gold inscription was

Figure 1.4 Joseph Highmore, *Samuel Richardson* (*c.* 1747–50), oil on canvas, 764 × 635 mm, National Portrait Gallery, London.

at some point added reading '*S. Richardson/Author of Clarissa*' (Figure 1.4). Within the standard rectangular canvas, painted spandrels indicate the frame-within-a-frame format known as the 'feigned oval', a descendant of the Roman *imago clipeata* tradition: a heroic, emphatically public style of portraiture originating in the use of sculpted or painted shields to frame bust-length images of victorious generals. The form thus implied a claim to public standing, and became the eighteenth-century norm for authorial frontispiece portraits. 'The typical sitter in an *imago* portrait was not the aristocrat, who owed his public position primarily to his lineage, but the private man brought into public view by his works, his talents, and his moral qualities', Shepherd writes; this example may even have been intended for a private collector's gallery of worthies, possibly with a companion piece showing Pope.[16]

Publication of *Clarissa* in 1747–8 took Richardson's reputation to fresh heights, not only in the literary world and with the broader public, but also in elite circles whose way of life he was able to represent with new confidence in *Sir Charles Grandison* (1753–4). For its literary consequences, his most important social conquest was Lady Bradshaigh of Haigh Hall, Lancashire, who engineered a lengthy, playful correspondence with Richardson before finally meeting him in 1750, by which

Figure 1.5 Joseph Highmore, *Samuel Richardson* (1750), oil on canvas, 527 × 368 mm, National Portrait Gallery, London.

time she had already seen his portrait exhibited in Highmore's studio. Eventually, Richardson thought the letters between them 'the best Commentary that could be written on the History of Clarissa' (to Lady Bradshaigh, 19 November 1757), and these exchanges were consolidated at an early stage by a remarkable exchange of portraits. The resulting painting of Richardson, again by Highmore and now in the National Portrait Gallery (Figure 1.5), is a conscious exercise in relationship-building. Richardson is shown at full length and, as Lady Bradshaigh requested, 'in your study, a table or desk by you, with pen, ink, and paper; one letter just sealed, which I shall fancy is to me' (3 June 1750). Behind him hangs his portrait of Sir Roger and Lady Bradshaigh at Haigh Hall (copied from the original in their London house), and it was at Haigh, *mise-en-abyme* style, that she kept the portrait. The intimacy thereby expressed was very real, and the air of genial reciprocity was noted by Lady Echlin, Lady Bradshaigh's sister, who thought Richardson's image 'looks pleased with notice from a friendly eye, and seems to return a sensible obliging smile' (13 December 1759). But this was no less a matter of social display, enshrining a connection that gave different kinds of cachet to both parties, and projecting the ideal of candour and benevolence that Richardson was to make central to his last novel. Guests picked up the message, Lady Bradshaigh reported: 'The first time my friend saw your picture, he asked, "What honest face have you got there?" And, without staying for an answer, "Do you know, I durst trust that man with my life, without farther knowledge of him"' (*c.* 26 December 1750).

Similar comments were elicited within Richardson's wider circle as he distributed Macardell's mezzotint adaptation of the Stationers' Hall portrait, which, in another gesture of intimacy to recipients, replaces the book in Richardson's hand with a manuscript letter. Like a letter, this engraving made absence presence ('I sometimes almost fancy myself actually with you', said Thomas Edwards); it caught the truth of inward character ('Such a sweet Benevolence in the Countenance', said Sarah Chapone), indeed of deepest identity ('yes sure it was your very self', said Sarah Wescomb).[17] As Shepherd emphasises throughout her fine analysis, all the portraits suggest privacy in terms of their visual cues or their practical contexts, and Richardson never used portraiture with the campaigning, self-advertising directness of Pope or Sterne. At the same time, the wide distribution of the Macardell mezzotint should not be discounted, nor the pride its owners must have taken in showing an image that was not for sale and could be had only as a gift from the author himself, albeit sometimes to recipients Richardson did not know (Edwards received four copies to present to neighbours). By the time of *Sir Charles Grandison*, few literate people in England can have been at many degrees of separation from a Richardson portrait.

The most genuinely private image in Richardson's lifetime, not reproduced until Anna Laetitia Barbauld's 1804 edition of the *Correspondence* and now in the Pierpont Morgan Library, is a pencil drawing by Highmore's daughter Susanna. Dating from *c.* 1751, it shows Richardson reading his in-progress *Sir Charles Grandison* manuscript to a group of admirers, including the brilliant Bluestocking feminist Hester Mulso, in his fashionable grotto at North End (Figure 1.6). As such, it catches an important and still under-recognised feature of Richardson's novels, which we tend to think of as expressions above all of print culture, but which were shaped at first by practices associated with pre-existing, ongoing traditions of manuscript circulation and coterie production. *Pamela* was drafted quickly and published without great delay, but *Clarissa* circulated privately for years before eventually going into print, latterly in bound manuscript volumes interleaved with blank pages for readers' comments. Consultative composition was even more systematic

Figure 1.6 Susanna Highmore, *Mr Richardson Reading the MS History of Sir Cha. Grandison at North End* (*c.* 1751), pencil drawing with grey wash, 6 × 7 5/8 in, Pierpont Morgan Library, New York.

in the case of *Sir Charles Grandison*, and reached its extreme point with Richardson's plan to have readers adopt his characters' voices and compose an additional volume themselves (the plan went unfulfilled, but an unpublished contribution survives from Lady Bradshaigh as Charlotte).[18] Even the 'great Man' Speaker Onslow had some involvement in these processes, and was said to have thought Richardson 'hard pressed' in one of the epistolary debates that proliferated around *Clarissa* and circulated, as the text had done, in manuscript form: pressing him in this case was Hester Mulso, who drew on political theory and natural law to question the novel's thematics of authority and power.[19]

It was for Onslow that Mason Chamberlin painted what is probably the latest of the portraits, undated, but newly displayed at Onslow's much-visited country seat by the autumn of 1754, when Thomas Edwards had 'the pleasure of seeing that speaking likeness of You in your picture' (7

Figure 1.7 Mason Chamberlin, *Samuel Richardson* (*c*. 1754), oil on copper, 249 × 197 mm, National Portrait Gallery, London.

October). Executed in oil on copper, and now in the National Portrait Gallery, it shows Richardson quite emphatically as an author in solitude, formally dressed but without his wig, writing on a hand-held board with no audience except – in an audacious but by now defensible visual claim – a bust of Milton in the background (Figure 1.7). Physically, Chamberlin makes no effort to flatter the corpulent Richardson (but gives him better legs than Hayman, muscled at the calf); the dignity flows from the sitter's obvious prosperity and repose, a slightly suburbanised version of the *beatus ille* ideal, with an elegant summerhouse outside the window, and behind it soaring trees.

Richardson died on 4 July 1761, following a stroke – the worst of his long-standing 'Paralytic Fits' (to Lady Bradshaigh, 15 October 1759) – suffered a few days earlier. As it happens, he was taking tea with Joseph Highmore, who reports that on being offered a second dish 'he would not or could not drink it, and immediately faltered in his speech, and from that time spoke no more articulately'. The portraits of course continue to speak, but the illuminating stories they tell – about authorship, character, social milieu – are also incomplete, and leave Richardson's trade vocation out of account. In the year of his death, Richardson was developing an ambitious new line of work as partner, with a member of the Lintot dynasty, of the patent conferring exclusive rights to print books about common law. 'My Business, Sir, has ever been my chief Concern', he told Stinstra in the autobiographical letter: 'My Writing-time has been at such times of Leisure as have not interfered with that.' He was buried in St Bride's, Fleet Street: the printers' church.

Notes

1 Jonathan Richardson, *Two Discourses* (1719), p. 45, and *An Essay on the Theory of Painting* (1725), pp. 13–14; quoted by Joe Bray, *The Portrait in Fiction of the Romantic Period* (Routledge, 2016), p. 14.

2 Eaves and Kimpel, *Biography*, p. 524, quoting and translating Bernhard von Hohorst to Friedrich Gottlieb Klopstock, 29 October 1756.

3 Eaves and Kimpel, *Biography*, pp. 218–19; see also Darryl P. Domingo, '"Well observed by the poet": Elias Brand and Richardson's British Ancients', *Eighteenth-Century Fiction*, 24.4 (2012), 597–622.

4 Maslen, *Samuel Richardson*, pp. 2, vii, 11–12, 10, 44; see also Sale, *Master Printer*.

5 Several essays by John A. Dussinger attempt to trace this material: see, for example, his 'Fabrications from Samuel Richardson's Press', *Papers of the Bibliographical Society of America*, 100.2 (2006), 259–79; also Alexander Pettit's overview of the attribution issue in *EW*, pp. xxxii–xxxiv.

6 Eaves and Kimpel, *Biography*, pp. 35, 30, 32.

7 *Ibid.*, pp. 21, 22–8, 32.

8 Maslen, *Samuel Richardson*, p. 18; Maslen is the best source for this crucial aspect of Richardson's career, discovered by Sheila Lambert in the late 1960s and unknown to Eaves and Kimpel or Sale.

9 John Nichols, *Literary Anecdotes of the Eighteenth Century*, 9 vols. (London, 1812–16), Vol. II, p. 354.

10 Stéphanie-Félicité du Crest Genlis, *Mémoires inédits de Mme la comtesse de Genlis*, 10 vols. (Paris, 1825), Vol. III, p. 360, quoted by Eaves and Kimpel, *Biography*, p. 525.

11 Lynn Shepherd, 'Samuel Richardson and Eighteenth-Century Portraiture' (dissertation, University of Oxford, 2006), p. 73.

12 Horace Walpole, *Anecdotes of Painting in England*, ed. R. Wornum, new edn, 3 vols. (1849), Vol. II, p. 325, quoted by Hugh Belsey, 'Hayman, Francis (1707/8–1776)', *Oxford Dictionary of National Biography*, online edn, May 2009.

13 Eaves and Kimpel, *Biography*, p. 73.

14 Janet E. Aikins, 'Picturing "Samuel Richardson": Francis Hayman and the Intersections of Word and Image', *Eighteenth-Century Fiction*, 14.3–4 (2002), 465–505.

15 Lynn Shepherd, *Clarissa's Painter: Portraiture, Illustration, and Representation in the Novels of Samuel Richardson* (Oxford University Press, 2009), pp. 50–7.

16 Shepherd, 'Samuel Richardson and Eighteenth-Century Portraiture', p. 50; for further detail see pp. 47–57 and Shepherd's summary in *'Clarissa's Painter*, pp. 50–1.

17 Edwards to Richardson, 8 February 1751; Chapone to Richardson, 20 March 1751; Wescomb to Richardson, 19 December 1751.

18 Eaves and Kimpel, *Biography*, pp. 205–13, 365–86, 412–13.

19 *Ibid.*, p. 344, quoting John Mulso to Gilbert White, 5 December 1750. See also Curran, below, p. 28; and Keymer, *Richardson's 'Clarissa'*.

CHAPTER 2

Publication History

Peter Sabor

In a letter to Lady Bradshaigh of 9 October 1756, Richardson looks back with alarm, real or feigned, at the extent of his literary production: 'Nineteen or Twenty Vols. closely printed! A Man of Business too! – Monstrous!' As a man of business, he might be expected to have made an exact count. His novels had indeed appeared in nineteen duodecimo volumes – two each for *Pamela* and its continuation, eight for the much expanded third edition of *Clarissa*, and seven for *Sir Charles Grandison* – and it is with the publication history of these novels that this chapter is primarily concerned. Richardson also, however, published a considerable number of minor and occasional works, of which the most substantial is a volume of instructive letters, *Letters Written to and for Particular Friends*, published just two months after *Pamela* in January 1741. In acknowledging to Lady Bradshaigh that, by one count, he had produced twenty volumes in all, Richardson was probably alluding to this 'little Volume of Letters' (letter to Johannes Stinstra, 2 June 1753), while ignoring previous publications that he evidently thought too insignificant to be counted as part of his collected works. (These publications include the many works edited by Richardson, both before and after *Pamela*, discussed by Pat Rogers, below (pp. 131–4).) As he wrote to Stinstra in the same letter, 'a few other little things of the Pamphlet kind I have written; all with a good Intention; But neither are they worthy of your Notice'.

Pamphlets and Occasional Prose

Because Richardson published his early writings, including these pamphlets, anonymously and never acknowledged them to his family or friends, it is difficult to make secure attributions. In 1736, Edward Cave, the publisher of the *Gentleman's Magazine*, noted that 'the Publick is often agreeably entertain'd with his Elegant Disquisitions in Prose', suggesting that Richardson had had some success as an occasional writer.[1] John

Dussinger contends that Richardson's first appearances in print date from 1723, when five letters signed by 'A. B.' appeared in the *True Briton* (1723–4) – one of seven journals that Richardson printed in the 1720s and 1730s. In his *Biographical and Historical Anecdotes of William Bowyer* (1782), published only twenty years after Richardson's death, John Nichols identified the first of these letters as Richardson's; Dussinger supports the attribution and extends it to the other 'A. B.' letters of 1723.[2] Four years later, in 1727, Richardson printed a two-volume abridgment of *Gulliver's Travels* (1726). As the earliest abridged *Gulliver* published in book form, this edition is of considerable interest. There is an intriguing possibility that Richardson was not only the anonymous abridger but also the author of a brief prefatory letter.[3] It is possible too, as Dussinger suggests, that in 1733 Richardson contributed a series of letters to another of the journals that he printed, the *Weekly Miscellany*, as well as a subsequent letter to the same journal in 1739.[4]

The earliest of Richardson's pamphlets to be identified is *The Infidel Convicted* (1731).[5] Richardson drew on this treatise at length in *The Apprentice's Vade Mecum; or, Young Man's Pocket Companion* (1734), which also amplified a letter of advice that he had written in 1732 to his fifteen-year-old nephew and apprentice, Thomas Verren Richardson. In addition, *Vade Mecum* contains material taken from several other authors, most of them unacknowledged. The pamphlet, with its stern warnings about the apprentice's obligation to be industrious, sober, and dutiful at all times, gives little indication of the imaginative powers that Richardson would later display in his fiction. Neither does his third known pamphlet, *A Seasonable Examination of the Pleas and Pretensions of the Proprietors of, and Subscribers to, Play-Houses* (1735), with its clunking alliterative title and its anti-theatrical prejudices. Richardson had an extensive knowledge of English drama and had seen many plays performed, but he believed that apprentices, tradesmen, and other workers were in danger of being corrupted by the excesses of the contemporary stage.

A less sentential side of Richardson is seen in two other occasional publications of the 1730s. The first, published in the *Gentleman's Magazine* for January 1736 and signed 'S. R.', is a reply in rhyming couplets, humorously declining an invitation to a 'Society Feast' for London printers. Surprisingly, as Alexander Pettit observes, it was 'the first publication that Richardson acknowledged'.[6] The second, persuasively attributed to Richardson by Wolfgang Zach, is a theoretically interesting anonymous preface to Penelope Aubin's three-volume *Collection of Entertaining Histories and Novels* (1739).[7] Here Richardson, for the first time, gives his views on the nature of prose fiction, which should display the rewards of virtue 'either *here* or *hereafter*' (*EW*, p. 94). Shortly afterwards, in November 1739, he would begin writing a novel of his own, published a year later in two duodecimo volumes as *Pamela; or, Virtue Rewarded*.

Novels and Their Supplements

The astonishing popularity of *Pamela* took everyone by surprise, including Richardson himself. Despite Cave's polite words in 1736 about his 'Elegant Disquisitions in Prose', it was as a master printer that Richardson had made his substantial reputation, not as a creative writer. Although after 1740 he would continue to be one of London's foremost printers, it was now as a best-selling novelist that Richardson was primarily known. As one of the many contemporary commentators on the vogue for *Pamela* wryly observed:

> Since Printers with such pleasing Nature write,
> And since so aukwardly your Scribes indite,
> Be wise in Time, and take a Friendly Hint;
> Let Printers write, and let your Writers print.[8]

The verse epigram indicates that although he had published *Pamela* anonymously, Richardson's authorship of the novel was an open secret. He was in an enviable position: not only had his first attempt at novel-writing been a spectacular success but also, as his own printer, he could determine precisely when it would appear in new editions and what form those editions would take.

Although the number of copies printed of the early editions of *Pamela* is unknown, Richardson claimed that the first edition of November 1740 appeared in a 'large Impression'. It was, however, rapidly exhausted, and followed by a second edition three months later, in February 1741. With the popularity of *Pamela* then at its height, a third edition followed within four weeks, in March; a fourth less than two months after that, in May; and a fifth in September. Richardson made extensive textual alterations in each of these new printings, and made still more drastic stylistic revisions in later editions of the novel. These revisions were intended primarily to raise the tone of the novel and make its heroine a more worthy counterpart to her successors, Clarissa Harlowe and Harriet Byron. Richardson also added some fifty pages of introductory material to the second edition, supplementing the novel's original preface. Most of this new material was taken from a series of egregiously flattering letters to Richardson by the poet, playwright, and critic Aaron Hill, together with an introduction by Richardson himself and a concluding commendatory poem by Hill. Despite the widespread ridicule that Hill's encomia attracted in Henry Fielding's parodic *Shamela* (1741) and elsewhere, Richardson retained the introductory material in all of the succeeding duodecimo editions while deleting or revising some of Hill's most extravagant passages.

In one edition of *Pamela*, however, Richardson dropped both the original preface and the additional introduction. This was the sixth edition of May 1742, published in a deluxe octavo format and bringing together, for the first time, the original novel and its sequel, the unfortunately titled *Pamela in Her Exalted Condition*, which Richardson had published in December 1741. 'Beautifully printed', according to an advertisement for the new edition, 'on a Writing-Paper',[9] the octavo edition was also lavishly illustrated with twenty-nine engravings by two fashionable artists, Hubert Gravelot and Francis Hayman. In a prefatory note, Richardson remarked that 'the kind Reception which these Volumes have met with, renders the *Recommendatory Letters* unnecessary' (1, viii): a specious claim, since he would restore them in subsequent duodecimo editions. Replacing them in the octavo edition was an 'Epitome of the Work': a thirty-six page table of contents which, like the illustrations by Gravelot and Hayman, was designed to dignify the novel, presenting it as a 'Work' worthy of such an apparatus, rather than as merely prose fiction. Dignity was also conferred on the novel by the acquisition of a Royal Licence, granted to Richardson and his co-proprietors, the booksellers Charles Rivington and John Osborn, in January 1742, giving them exclusive rights to the sale and distribution of *Pamela* for fourteen years. Despite its attractive appearance, however, the octavo edition of *Pamela* sold poorly. Priced at 6s per volume, it was twice as expensive as any of the lifetime duodecimo editions. As late as 1772, over ten years after Richardson's death, remaining sheets of the edition were issued with new title pages but without the illustrations.[10] And although Richardson would later publish octavo editions of both *Clarissa* and *Sir Charles Grandison*, neither was illustrated.

Pamela in Her Exalted Condition was designed to supplant three spurious continuations of the novel by other hands. In a prefatory note, Richardson boasts that the original novel has 'met with a Success greatly exceeding the most sanguine Expectations'. While admitting that he had originally intended to complete the work in its first two volumes, he hopes that the additional volumes will have 'the good Fortune, which few Continuations have met with, to be judg'd not unworthy' of their predecessors (p. [3]). This wish was not fulfilled. After the commercial failure of the octavo

edition of both parts of *Pamela*, Richardson published only one other edition of *Pamela in Her Exalted Condition* in his lifetime: a second duodecimo
in January 1743. Copies of this edition remained available for almost twenty
years: the next edition of *Pamela in Her Exalted Condition* would not appear
until October 1761, published together with the original *Pamela* as a four-
volume set and labelled as the eighth edition of both parts. Richardson, as
always, made textual revisions for this edition, but he did not live to see it
in print. In addition, he rewrote both parts of the novel entirely, leaving
scarcely a sentence unchanged, for an edition that would not be published
until 1801, under the supervision of his daughter Anne Richardson and
labelled as the fourteenth.

While *Pamela in Her Exalted Condition* is widely regarded as the least
successful of Richardson's novels, *Clarissa* has long been acknowledged as
his masterpiece. Its initial sales, however, were disappointing. Richardson
published it in instalments, with the first two of seven volumes appearing
in December 1747, Volumes III and IV in April 1748, and the last three
volumes in December 1748. A second edition followed in June 1749, con-
sisting of the first four volumes in substantially revised form, together with
unsold copies of the final three. The traditional explanation for this hybrid
form of publication is that put forward by Richardson himself in a manuscript note: 'The vth, vith and viith, were not required, a larger Number
having been printed of them.'[11] Tom Keymer, however, argues persuasively
that there is a more probable rationale: rather than printing additional
copies of Volumes v to vii of the first edition in anticipation of demand for
a second edition of the whole, Richardson printed the second edition of
Volumes i to iv in order to 'mop up surplus copies' of the final volumes –
'copies he had expected but failed to sell'. Keymer also notes that the print
run for the second edition was relatively small, enabling Richardson to
dispose of it in less than three years and publish a fully revised edition of
the entire novel in April 1751.[12]

Richardson's textual revisions for *Clarissa* were on the same massive scale
as those he undertook for both parts of *Pamela*. In the second edition,
he added a forty-three-page table of contents, providing a tendentious
abstract of each of the novel's letters, as well as thoroughly revising the
text and inserting interpretative footnotes throughout. He also made substantial changes to the editorial commentary: his preface to the first two
volumes was replaced by a brief 'Advertisement', while the list of characters
was shortened; William Warburton's preface to Volumes III and IV, which
Richardson had always disliked, was removed; and an endnote to Volume
IV was also dropped. In the same month, June 1749, Richardson printed

the first of what would become a series of supplements to *Clarissa*: a pamphlet entitled *Answer to the Letter of a Very Reverend and Worthy Gentleman, Objecting to the Warmth of a Particular Scene in the History of Clarissa*. Richardson printed this response to an unnamed critic of the novel, probably the Irish curate Philip Skelton, for distribution to a few of his friends. A more substantial supplement followed six months later, in late December 1749. Entitled *Meditations Collected from the Sacred Books*, it too was printed by Richardson for private distribution. While the first edition of *Clarissa* contains five spiritual meditations, presented as compilations by the heroine of verses from a variety of biblical sources, *Meditations* contains thirty-six.

Surprisingly, none of these supplements was included in the third edition of *Clarissa*, published simultaneously in eight duodecimo and seven octavo volumes, although it does contain much other new material. The paratextual apparatus includes a new preface and postscript, a substantial collection of 'Moral and Instructive Sentiments' culled from the novel, and verse commendations by two friends of Richardson, Thomas Edwards and John Duncombe. In addition, some 200 pages are added to the text itself – 'restored', according to Richardson, from the original manuscript of the novel. Richardson gathered up most of this newly printed material, together with passages first appearing in the second edition, and published it as another supplement to the novel, entitled *Letters and Passages Restored from the Original Manuscripts of the History of Clarissa*. There is little evidence either to support or to contradict Richardson's claim that these passages were taken from the 'original manuscripts' of his novel; more probably, they represent a mixture of restored, revised, and newly written material. In the third edition of *Clarissa*, Richardson drew attention to the presence of the additional passages by marking them with marginal bullets.

Although the third edition of *Clarissa* is often thought to represent Richardson's final intentions for the novel, this is far from being the case: in preparing new editions of his work he could never leave the text unchanged. A fourth duodecimo edition of *Clarissa* of 1759 contains relatively few textual alterations, but Richardson was working on further revisions in the last months of his life – and the title page of a new edition of *Clarissa* published in 1792 claimed that it contained 'the Last Corrections of the Author'.[13] As Keymer remarks, 'on the day of [Richardson's] death in 1761, the texts of *Pamela* and *Clarissa* were left in a state that was no more definitive or final than on the day of their first publication'.[14]

Like *Clarissa*, Richardson's final novel, *Sir Charles Grandison*, was published in three instalments, with duodecimo and octavo editions appearing simultaneously: Volumes I to IV of both editions in November 1753; Volumes V and VI (duodecimo) and V (octavo) a month later; and Volumes VII (duodecimo) and VI (octavo) in March 1754. The final volume in each edition included several ancillary items, such as a 100-page 'Historical and Characteristical Index' and a list of similes and allusions. The texts of the two editions were similar (though not identical), but the larger format of the octavo edition allowed Richardson to print it in six volumes. An extensively revised edition of the seven duodecimo volumes followed almost immediately in March 1754, just five days after publication of the final volume. Richardson made further revisions for a posthumously published edition of 1762, and yet more followed long after, in an 1810 edition containing, according to its title page, 'last corrections by the author'. There were also the inevitable supplements, of which the first two are discussed by Norbert Schürer, below (pp. 92–4): *The Case of Samuel Richardson*, a pamphlet issued in September 1753 deploring Richardson's treatment by Dublin booksellers who had published *Sir Charles Grandison* without his permission; *An Address to the Public*, a second pamphlet attack on Dublin printers and booksellers of February 1754; and finally two commentaries on the novel, distributed privately in April 1754, *Answer to a Letter from a Friend* and *Copy of a Letter to a Lady*.

In the *Letter to a Lady*, Richardson declared that he had 'no intention of pursuing further the History of *Sir Charles Grandison*' (p. 1), and indeed no other fiction followed. He did, however, publish a final supplementary volume to all three of his novels in March 1755: *A Collection of the Moral and Instructive Sentiments, Maxims, Cautions, and Reflexions, Contained in the Histories of Pamela, Clarissa, and Sir Charles Grandison*. Equipped with a preface by Richardson's friend Benjamin Kennicott, this compilation contains revised versions of the 'sentiments' appended to the final volume of the third edition of *Clarissa* and the final volume of *Sir Charles Grandison*, together with a newly created set of similarly didactic material for *Pamela*. 'I could not', Richardson wrote to Lady Echlin, 'expect a great Sale of it, tho' it is the Pith and Marrow of Nineteen Volumes, not unkindly received' (letter of 17 July 1755). Sales of the *Collection*, which never went into a second edition, were as sluggish as Richardson predicted. His novels, however, have appeared in scores of editions and translations and have never lacked readers, from Richardson's lifetime to the present day.

Notes

1 Edward Cave, *Gentleman's Magazine*, 6 (January 1736), 51. The occasion is a humorous poem signed 'S. R.', described below.

2 John A. Dussinger, 'Samuel Richardson's "Elegant Disquisitions": Anonymous Writing in the *True Briton* and Other Journals?', *Studies in Bibliography*, 53 (2000), 195–226.

3 See Peter Sabor, '"A large portion of our etherial fire": Swift and Samuel Richardson', in Hermann J. Real and Helgard Stöver-Leidig (eds.), *Reading Swift: Papers from the Fourth Münster Symposium on Jonathan Swift* (Fink, 2003), pp. 387–401 (pp. 388–9); and John A. Dussinger, '"Stealing in the great doctrines of Christianity": Samuel Richardson as Journalist', *Eighteenth-Century Fiction*, 15.3–4 (2003), 451–506 (p. 460 n. 19).

4 Dussinger, 'Samuel Richardson as Journalist'.

5 John A. Dussinger, 'Fabrications from Samuel Richardson's Press', *Papers of the Bibliographical Society of America*, 100.2 (2006), 259–79.

6 Alexander Pettit, 'General Introduction', in *EW*, pp. xxxi–xciv (p. lv).

7 Wolfgang Zach, 'Mrs Aubin and Richardson's Earliest Literary Manifesto (1739)', *English Studies*, 62.3 (1981), 271–85.

8 *Daily Advertiser* (7 April 1741).

9 *London-Evening Post* (8–10 June 1742).

10 Sale, *Bibliographical Record*, p. 22.

11 Tom Keymer, 'Clarissa's Death, *Clarissa's* Sale, and the Text of the Second Edition', *Review of English Studies*, n.s. 45.179 (1994), 389–96 (p. 390).

12 *Ibid.*, pp. 390, 393.

13 O. M. Brack, Jr, '*Clarissa's* Bibliography: Problems and Challenges', in Florian Stuber and Margaret Anne Doody (eds.), *Samuel Richardson's Published Commentary on 'Clarissa'*, 3 vols. (Pickering & Chatto, 1998), Vol. II, pp. 305–24 (p. 314).

14 Tom Keymer, 'Assorted Versions of Assaulted Virgins; or, Textual Instability and Teaching', in Lisa Zunshine and Jocelyn Harris (eds.), *Approaches to Teaching the Novels of Samuel Richardson* (Modern Language Association of America, 2006), pp. 24–31 (p. 26).

CHAPTER 3

Correspondence

Louise Curran

Lovelace famously eulogises familiar letter-writing in *Clarissa* as 'writing from the heart' because of the etymology of the word '*Cor-respondence*' (the Latin for 'heart' being *cor*).[1] His assertion is, like much else in Lovelace's character, persuasive yet erroneous, based as it is on a false derivation. Richardson added these words to later editions of the novel and they serve to emphasise the duplicitousness of this 'notoriously brilliant epistolary deceiver'.[2] Richardson was always on guard against those he termed 'designing' letter-writers, yet Lovelace's opinion that letters record 'friendship given under hand and seal' echoes Richardson's description of the art of correspondence in idealised terms as 'friendship avowed under hand and seal ... more pure, yet more ardent, and less broken in upon, than personal conversation' (Richardson to Sarah Wescomb, 27 August 1746).

Samuel Richardson was, even by the standards of a period known as a golden age for letter-writing, an indefatigable correspondent. Today, Richardson's extant correspondence archive consists of some 1,700 letters, of which 600 or so are by the author.[3] Though he professed there to be a powerful connection between epistolary writing and true character – he writes that 'styles differ ... as much as faces, and are indicative, generally beyond the power of disguise, of the mind of the writer!' (Richardson to Sarah Wescomb, 27 August 1746) – throughout his letters, Richardson and his correspondents debate the limits of sympathetic response and testify to the way that epistolary writing explores and shapes personal and social identity.

Writing and Receiving Letters

Richardson's correspondence has long been viewed as narrow in scope compared with that of other letter-writing contemporaries, such as Horace Walpole or Lady Mary Wortley Montagu. Recently, however, critics have become increasingly interested both in the particular kind of correspondence that Richardson's literary celebrity invited and in the way letters supported his role as an important book-trade professional. Some of Richardson's earliest correspondences were with the renowned physician George Cheyne and the playwright, poet, and critic Aaron Hill (as well as Hill's family more generally, particularly his daughter, the writer Urania Johnson); other letters were exchanged with significant people in the literary and artistic milieu of his day, including Thomas Birch, Colley Cibber, Patrick and Mary Delany, Henry and Sarah Fielding, Samuel Johnson, Charlotte Lennox, Thomas and Frances Sheridan, and William Warburton. Richardson's longest correspondence was with Dorothy, Lady Bradshaigh (of Haigh Hall in Wigan), an enthusiastic reader of his novels, as well as a spirited writer, who became a close confidante and adviser. Lady Bradshaigh's sister, Lady Echlin, also became an intimate correspondent of the author's and sent him an alternative ending to *Clarissa* in which the rape does not take place and Lovelace is converted before his death. As well as these correspondences with individuals and groups of friends, he also wrote and received letters on his novels, *Pamela* and *Clarissa* (mostly during the period 1732–49), and *Sir Charles Grandison* (particularly during the years 1750–4).

Like many writers of his time, Richardson generally differentiated between the letters he wrote to women and those he wrote to men. In letters to young women, such as Hester Mulso (later Chapone) and Susanna Highmore (daughter of the painter Joseph), he is their 'Papa'. Whereas the tone of these letters is often an uneasy mixture of encouragement against diffidence and straightforward patronisation, in other letters, as in those to the respected authors Sarah Chapone and Elizabeth Carter, Richardson's esteem of female learning is more apparent. His letters to men, such as the poet Edward Young and the writer and lawyer Thomas Edwards, tend to focus on the question of what constitutes a moral man and artist, and frequently involve debates about authors such as John Milton and Alexander Pope. Rehearsing the merits of a 'good' man, Richardson and Edwards and Young test ideas surrounding writing and ethical practice as well as literary posterity.

Inevitably, letters appear to have been lost along the way, including many from the 1730s, the period before Richardson became famous as an author and began to preserve his correspondence more methodically. Evidence that Richardson sought widely for additional correspondents and was not always gratified with responses gives an indication of his epistolary aspiration. He attempted a correspondence with Louise D'Epinay, the writer and friend of Voltaire and Diderot, though no letters survive between them. He also lamented that his request for correspondence with the Revd Mark Hildesley was not answered, at least initially: 'A Slight from a good Man', he wrote sadly, 'must be a little (*not* a little) mortifying' (Richardson to Lady Echlin, 17 May 1754). Equally, though he listed a 'D. of P.' in a list he made of thirty-six cherished female correspondents, the duchess of Portland, Lady Margaret Cavendish Bentinck, was never an enthusiastic fan of the writer.[4] The list seems to have been more an ideal representation of Richardson's networks than a strictly representative one, as the controversial memoirist Laetitia Pilkington was omitted completely, despite their notable exchange of letters.

Richardson's correspondence was the site for much discussion of the composition, development, distribution, and influence of his novels. Though there is much truth in the portrait of Richardson as a correspondent who presided over his networks attempting to control and enforce a correct reading of his novels, his correspondence attests, also, to his enjoyment of conflicting interpretations. When he received two letters objecting to Clarissa's primness on the one hand and coquetry on the other, he dealt with the situation by sending each correspondent the other's letter (Richardson to Lady Bradshaigh, February 1751). Just as Richardson's novels are concerned with the power of letters both to transform and to deceive, his own personal letters demonstrate a deep and abiding interest in the nature of private and public character, as well as the relationship between actual and future readers.

Richardson thought there was 'no amusement equal to an improving and an agreeable correspondence' (Lady Bradshaigh to Richardson, 28 January 1750). Though he enjoyed raillery and in-jokes with his correspondents he could also be combative and relished debate. He admitted as much to one young friend, Frances Grainger, when he promised her that he would 'never flatter' his correspondents but instead would 'always tell them freely of their Faults' and hoped that they would do likewise with him (Richardson to Frances Grainger, 5 December 1749). His correspondence with Hester Mulso about the limits of parental authority in the first instalment of *Clarissa* is a well-known case in point. It was widely circulated at the time of writing (1750–1) and later printed posthumously as *Letters on Filial Obedience and a Matrimonial Creed* (1807); Richardson referred to it uncertainly as both a 'Controversy' and a 'Debate' (to Sarah Wescomb, 1 February 1751). In the absence of much of Richardson's side of the argument (unfortunately lost), we might wonder if the correspondence was much more of a deeply involved dialogic exchange than the printed version suggests.

Richardson proselytised continually about the ethical power of correspondence. When he was a young boy he wrote in the disguise of an older man to a woman known for 'continually fomenting Quarrels and Disturbances', quoting 'Scripture Texts that made against her' (Richardson to Johannes Stinstra, 2 June 1753) in order to reform her character. He depicts Clarissa as doing likewise when she impersonates 'an anonymous elderly lady' in a letter urging Lady Drayton, the mother of a friend, to be less severe with her children (*C*, II.xiii.74). When Frances Grainger commented approvingly about this moment in *Clarissa* to its author, he encouraged her to take 'the Hint ... and write to such Mothers' for 'You cannot know, till you try, whether your Arguments will *harden*, or *convince* them' (Richardson to Frances Grainger, 28 February 1750).

Harriet Guest has written that letters are used in *Sir Charles Grandison* as 'social currency'.[5] In a similar way, Richardson's real-life correspondence often mentions the value of the letters in such a manner as to imply a correlation between the length of a letter and its worth. Sarah Wescomb wished that every one of Richardson's letters would 'exceed the other in length' and thus 'make them more & more Valuable', a thought that Richardson as recipient of this letter made literal when he annotated it with the note that it contained '775 words/62 lines' (Sarah Wescomb to Richardson, 5 March 1757). In order to deal with the overwhelming length of some of the letters between Lady Bradshaigh and himself, Richardson even suggested they number their paragraphs 'that we may the better refer to them, and the easier see what each omits answering to' (to Lady Bradshaigh, 9 July 1754). Lady Bradshaigh refused this invitation, writing that it had 'the resemblance of slavery' (to Richardson, 20 July–6 August 1754). Such material obsessiveness reflects the all-consuming nature of the act of writing letters for Richardson, whereby 'the pen is jealous of company', engrosses 'the writer's whole self', 'disdains company; and will have the entire attention' (Richardson to Sarah Wescomb, 27 August 1746).

Editing and Organising Letters

The life of letters went far beyond their ephemeral moment of composition. As well as sharing some of his exchanges with Hester Mulso, Richardson also showed his correspondence with Lady Bradshaigh (the early portion of it in which she hid her identity) to several of his 'select friends' (Richardson to Lady Bradshaigh, 20 November 1752). He also frequently recycled parts of his correspondence for authorial purposes.

Richardson's letter of 8 September 1750 to Frances Grainger exists in two manuscript versions today. One is an autograph retained copy and one a heavily edited draft that, as John Dussinger discovered, is the basis for Richardson's only contribution to Samuel Johnson's *Rambler*.[6] On occasion, the way in which Richardson mined his letters for fictional purposes alarmed those involved. Lady Bradshaigh was mortified when she read aloud a section of *Sir Charles Grandison* to two elderly auditors only to discover that Richardson had taken details from her own letters about one of these women to furnish his novel (Richardson to Lady Bradshaigh, 4 January 1754). Additionally, the pamphlets he later produced in response to critiques of his novels, such as his *Answer to the Letter of a Very Reverend Worthy Gentleman, Objecting to the Warmth of a Particular Scene in … 'Clarissa'* (1749) or his *Copy of a Letter to a Lady, who Was Solicitous for an Additional Volume to … 'Sir Charles Grandison'* (1754), reprinted actual responses to letters he had received.

The archive of Richardson's correspondence, mostly contained in the Forster Collection of the Victoria and Albert Museum, but also scattered in libraries across the UK and North America and elsewhere, attests to an abiding interest in organising his letter collections in such a way as both to memorialise friendship and to fashion the self for posterity. Letters were carefully preserved, copied by several different amanuenses, annotated and edited, and arranged in various collections of letter-books. All of Richardson's main characters cautiously contain, shape, and control their epistolary archives, and their author was no different. Richardson thought that his own letters were 'worthy of the public Eye', yet preparing his correspondence for possible public readership raised difficult questions about the uncontrollable nature of such publicity.

Richardson mentioned his intention to revise his letter collections in 1755 by 'looking over, & sorting, & classing … Correspondencies and other Papers' (to Thomas Edwards, 27 January 1755). It was probably somewhere around this time that he made an index to his correspondence with Edwards, as well as to those collections relating to each of his three novels. There is evidence, too, that Richardson considered publishing his correspondence with Elizabeth Carter in some form: in the letters that were in his possession he changed her name throughout to 'Carteret', and also replaced other names with initials and made some stylistic changes (see, for example, Richardson to Elizabeth Carter, 12 June 1753). When a correspondence with an attorney of Warwick called Eusebius Silvester (who contacted the author after reading *Sir Charles Grandison*) ended in animosity, Richardson set about editing it to such an extent that Tom Keymer has described it as having 'some claims to be considered as Richardson's last significant literary work'.[7]

In 1757 Richardson was contacted by an acquaintance, Philipp Erasmus Reich, a bookseller in Leipzig, who suggested that the novelist publish a selection of his letters in Germany (Richardson to Lady Bradshaigh, 2 January 1758). Richardson discussed the proposal with Lady Bradshaigh and they subsequently set about editing their letters. Copies of letters that had been arranged into 'bound Books' were submitted to Lady Bradshaigh's 'revising Eye' in the hope that a 'Critique' of *Clarissa* and *Sir Charles Grandison* would be 'extracted *anonymously*' (Richardson to Lady Bradshaigh, 19 November 1757). All along Richardson was vexed about epistolary propriety on the one hand (Reich was understandably confused that Richardson would agree to publish from his collections only if his correspondents formally requested of him that their letters appear in print) and, on the other hand, frustrated by his correspondents' double standards: the same people who displayed 'prudishness' at Reich's suggestion 'wou'd be glad to see a Volume or two of any Body's Letters but their own' (Richardson to Lady Bradshaigh, 11 February 1758).

Richardson divided up his correspondence in such a way as to suggest that he had a spectrum of publicity in mind, both at the time of writing his letters and afterwards as he organised them, as he refers to unbound 'private Correspondence', bound correspondence of a 'more Private and intimate Nature', and letters that were more obviously suitable for 'the public Eye' (Richardson to Lady Bradshaigh, 28 February 1758). Not all those informed of Reich's proposal greeted it with Lady Bradshaigh's enthusiasm. Sarah Scudamore (formerly Wescomb) was more circumspect, writing to the author, in words that must have alarmed his sense of decorum, that she declined 'the least desire of having them made known, as it might be mistaken for vanity' (to Richardson, 15 April 1758). In the end, the plan for publication during Richardson's lifetime did not come to fruition.

Publishing Letters: Reception and Legacy

When Richardson's correspondence finally came to be published in any kind of comprehensive form for the first time in Anna Laetitia Barbauld's six-volume *The Correspondence of Samuel Richardson* (1804), its reception was lacklustre. Not all commentators were as forceful in their assessments as Francis Jeffrey in the *Edinburgh Review*, yet his final judgment was influential: 'they consist almost entirely of compliments and minute criticisms on his novels ... and some tedious prattling disputations with his female correspondents'.[8] The next edition of the correspondence fared little better. John Carroll's 1964 selection contains only 128 letters and solely ones that Richardson wrote, none that he received. Under such circumstances it was little wonder that Robert Halsband opined that they offered primarily a 'critical commentary' or 'an authorial gloss' with little 'personal history' and even less 'social, political, or literary history'.[9]

Not all critics read Richardson's letters in this limited way. Rachel Trickett thought Carroll's edition undersold the letters' significance, for they revealed, in her opinion, 'the intense conviction, the deep absorption in his own imaginings' that produced 'the finest tragic novel in English'.[10] In the same year as Carroll's edition was published, Claude Rawson suggested a more complex legacy for Richardson's correspondence when he compared the verbal play on the word 'sentimental' in Austen's *Northanger Abbey* with a letter from Lady Bradshaigh to Richardson about the fashionable use of the term.[11]

Recent academic studies on eighteenth-century epistolary culture in general and Richardson's letter-writing practice in particular afford a new opportunity to reassess the links between Richardson's letters and his fiction, as well as understand the author more fully as a major networker in the print marketplace of his day.[12] Richardson's arrangement of his letters by correspondents and novels, and the indexes that survive, suggest that he envisaged that the letters would be read thematically rather than chronologically, just as Alexander Pope had arranged his *Letters* (1737) by correspondent in order to reflect the importance of classical ideas of friendship. In following Richardson's original organisation by particular persons and works, the editors of *The Cambridge Edition of the Correspondence of Samuel Richardson* (2013–) accentuate the way in which the writer's archive is not just a repository of biographical facts but also a record of his own acts of self-fashioning.

To date, much writing about Richardson's correspondence has tended to extrapolate broad interpretations from Barbauld's highly edited, if not always bowdlerised, corpus. Critics are now beginning to appreciate hitherto neglected areas of the author's epistolary collections: the varied tone of Richardson's letter-writing style both within the same letter and in letters to different friends, as well as the importance of the material aspect of his correspondence. So, for example, a facet of these letters rarely explored is the way in which they often function as part of wider manuscript exchange. Carefully preserved among Richardson's papers in the Forster Collection is a bound volume of manuscript poems, with signs of detailed arrangement and pagination, most of which were originally sent enclosed in letters. The Richardson–Edwards letters gave rise to an extensive exchange of poems, often experiments in sonnet form, by poets such as Martha Ferrar, Hester Mulso, and Susanna Highmore.

Lady Bradshaigh gave Martha Richardson her letters from Martha's recently deceased father in 1762 because the family had 'a right to them' and because she was assured that they would be used only 'for private amusement according to his order'. The manuscript of this note was later endorsed (in an unknown hand) with the words: 'This is a Letter of great consequence' (Lady Bradshaigh to Martha Richardson, 29 April 1762). Now that Richardson's correspondence is finally being systematically edited, scholars are beginning to work out the implication of these words for his entire epistolary archive.

Notes

1 Samuel Richardson, *Clarissa*, 3rd edn, 8 vols. (London, 1751), IV.xi.77.
2 Elizabeth Heckendorn Cook, *Epistolary Bodies: Gender and Genre in the Eighteenth-Century Republic of Letters* (Stanford University Press, 1996), p. 87.
3 A much larger number of letters must have been lost, including all of the correspondence from Richardson's earlier years; the first extant letter is from 1732.
4 Eaves and Kimpel, *Biography*, p. 186.
5 Harriet Guest, *Small Change: Women, Learning, Patriotism, 1750–1810* (University of Chicago Press, 2000), p. 109.
6 John A. Dussinger, 'Samuel Richardson's Manuscript Draft of *The Rambler* No. 97 (19 February 1751)', *Notes and Queries*, 57.1 (2010), 93–9.
7 Keymer, *Richardson's 'Clarissa'*, p. 34.
8 Francis Jeffrey, *Edinburgh Review*, 5 (October 1804), 23–44 (pp. 33–4).
9 Robert Halsband, 'A World of His Own', *New York Times Book Review* (4 April 1965), 18.
10 Rachel Trickett, 'Review of Selected Letters of Samuel Richardson', *Review of English Studies*, 17 (1966), 323–6 (p. 326).
11 Claude Rawson, ' "Nice" and "Sentimental": A Parallel between *Northanger Abbey* and Richardson's *Correspondence*', *Notes and Queries*, 209 (1964), 108.
12 See for example Clare Brant, *Eighteenth-Century Letters and British Culture* (Palgrave Macmillan, 2006); Betty A. Schellenberg, 'Introduction', in Betty A. Schellenberg (ed.), *Correspondence Primarily on 'Sir Charles Grandison'*, in *CECSR*, Vol. x, pp. xxxv–xlvii; and Louise Curran, *Samuel Richardson and the Art of Letter-Writing* (Cambridge University Press, 2016).

PART II

Critical Fortunes

CHAPTER 4

Editions

Hilary Havens

Samuel Richardson, a notorious reviser, poses a challenge to editors: he polished the rustic Pamela and blackened the seductive Lovelace in later editions of *Pamela* and *Clarissa*. In a letter of February 1758, Richardson even admitted to altering some of his letters, not knowing 'into whosoever Hands our Letters might fall' (Richardson to Lady Bradshaigh, 11 February 1758). Besides these questions of textual authority, editions of Richardson's novels and letters have been shaped by changing editorial practices that, until recently, neither respected textual fidelity nor included explanatory notes. Thus, early collected editions tended to fall far short of current editorial standards.

Barbauld and Early Editions of the Correspondence

Anna Laetitia Barbauld's *The Correspondence of Samuel Richardson* (1804) is the first edition of Richardson's correspondence and, until the completion of the Cambridge edition, remains the most important.[1] After Richardson's daughter Anne died in 1804, his grandchildren sold his correspondence to the publisher Richard Phillips, who tasked Barbauld with selecting, editing, and arranging the letters. Barbauld's edition appeared in six volumes containing letters between Richardson and forty-three other individuals, organised by recipient and presented chronologically when possible. There are occasional footnotes providing glosses on texts and situations, as well as Richardson's own notes. The final volume contains an index that lists people, places, texts, and various didactic themes. The edition also has thirteen plates, some in colour, which include portraits of people and important locations. Eight of the plates are facsimiles of Richardson's correspondence.

One of the most significant contributions made by this edition is Barbauld's more-than-200-page biography, *Life of Samuel Richardson with Remarks on His Writings*, which appears in the first volume. It begins as a thoughtful description of the history of fiction and then presents a biography of Richardson that combines narrative with extracts from his letters. Barbauld also includes plot summaries, reception accounts, and analysis of Richardson's novels and minor works. Towards the end of her introduction, Barbauld gives an overview of the correspondence, which contains biographies of some of Richardson's correspondents. She also amusingly assesses the writing style of each contributor; for example, she describes Aaron Hill's prose as 'turgid and cloudy, but every now and then illuminated with a ray of genius'.[2] Her edition, however, is weakened by the many editorial interventions that occurred between the manuscripts and published text. As is usual with nineteenth-century editions, the work ignores the manuscripts' capitalisation, spelling, and punctuation, substituting house style. More significant is the invisible editorial work undertaken by Barbauld: she acknowledges that she selected the letters to be included, but she does not give a clear justification for these decisions, instead simply noting that 'No two persons probably would fix precisely upon the same standard of choice.'[3] Her edition abridges letters, omits dates, and contains erroneous transcriptions and additions, although her biographer William McCarthy argues that many errors were probably introduced by the printers and that Barbauld succeeded in her 'aim ... to illustrate the general tenor of the Richardson correspondence'.[4]

Barbauld's selection provided the impetus for a number of shorter editions of Richardson's correspondence that were published in periodicals in the first two decades of the nineteenth century. The best example of these is the correspondence between Richardson and Edward Young that appeared in the *Monthly Magazine* between 1813 and 1819. In his introductory notice, Richard Phillips draws attention to the 'necessary ... curtailment' that Barbauld's selection of letters had entailed and prints the presumably complete 148-letter correspondence. A comparison between Barbauld's and Phillips's printings of Richardson's correspondence with Young confirms the unreliability of Barbauld's edition: 'many passages which appear in one letter in Mrs. Barbauld are scattered through several letters in the later printing, and the dates often vary widely'.[5] Other printings of Richardson's correspondence include his letters to Sarah Wescomb in the *European Magazine and London Review* for 1808–9; his correspondence with Elizabeth Carter in the *Monthly Magazine* for 1813; and his correspondence with Tobias Smollett in the *Monthly Magazine* for 1819. More letters, not all of them from Phillips's holdings, appeared in the *Gentleman's Magazine* for 1816–17, Rebecca Warner's miscellany *Original Letters* (1817), and other posthumous collections. After Phillips sold his manuscript collection of Richardson's correspondence in 1828, most of it was purchased by William Upcott; after Upcott's death in 1845, the letters were scattered among numerous archives, though the chief portion of them was purchased by John Forster and later formed the bulk of the Forster Collection held at the National Art Library in London. Until the mid-twentieth century, no further editions of Richardson's correspondence appeared.

Nineteenth- and Early-Twentieth-Century Collected Works

Around the same time that Barbauld's and other selected editions of Richardson's correspondence were published, collected editions of his works began appearing in print. The earliest of these, introduced by the Revd Edward Mangin, was published in nineteen volumes in octavo in 1811.[6] It was advertised as a complete edition of Richardson's works and included a translation of Denis Diderot's 'Eloge de Richardson'. The first volume begins with 'A Sketch of the Life and Writings of Samuel Richardson', which Mangin acknowledges is little more than an abridgment of Barbauld's biography. He gives a very brief sketch of Richardson's life, followed by a summary of anecdotes gleaned from Barbauld's text. Mangin summarises Richardson's novels as well as Barbauld's assessment of them, but emphasises the importance of Richardson's precepts 'in *our* day of *politics* and *pamphlets*'.[7] As with the other early collected editions, there is no indication of which copy-texts were used, though the novels retain their original volume divisions. Another collected edition of Richardson's works was published for the Ballantyne's Novelists series in 1824, which prints Richardson's complete novels in octavo, but places the text in two columns and uses about one volume per novel, though *Clarissa* occupies 221 pages of the first volume and all of the second.[8] The only noteworthy aspect of this edition is that Sir Walter Scott provided the 'Prefatory Memoir', an important critical essay on Richardson. While Scott, like Mangin, borrows much biographical information from Barbauld, his analysis of Richardson's novels is incisive and foreshadows *Clarissa*'s preeminence during the nineteenth century: he calls Clarissa 'a character as nearly approaching to perfection as the pencil of the author could draw'.[9] His analysis of the novels is heightened by his accounts of their separate receptions and the responses of Richardson's friends.

The next significant nineteenth-century edition of Richardson's works is Leslie Stephen's, published in 1883 in twelve volumes octavo, a handsome edition intended for library use.[10] Yet his version does not keep Richardson's original volume divisions or reveal which editions were used as copy-texts. The lack of divisions, especially between *Pamela* and *Pamela in Her Exalted Condition*, where the textual break is indicated only by the restarting of the letter numberings, indicates Stephen's ambivalent attitude towards the texts, especially Richardson's first novel. Indeed, *Pamela* is wholly neglected; other than mentioning it briefly in the biographical component, Stephen does not discuss it in his 'prefatory chapter of biographical criticism'. Stephen's assessment of Richardson and his works is opinionated and insulting: Richardson is 'a man … whose special characteristic it was to be a milksop', and his characters are 'queer and old-fashioned'.[11] Yet he acknowledges Richardson's attention to detail and knowledge of human emotions, and reserves high praise for *Sir Charles Grandison* and *Clarissa*, calling the latter Richardson's masterpiece and Lovelace Richardson's most ambitious character. Stephen's preface was largely reprinted from his contribution to *Hours in a Library* (1874), which in turn was reprinted from his contribution to the *Cornhill Magazine* (1868). Despite its sweeping generalisations, it was considered 'valuable' by contemporary critics.[12]

Two further collected editions of Richardson's works appeared in the early years of the twentieth century. The first and best of these is William Lyon Phelps's *The Novels of Samuel Richardson* (1901–2), which is the most scholarly of the early collected editions and returns to the standard nineteen-volume division.[13] Phelps's edition contains a general introduction accompanied by passages from Richardson's correspondence and is informed by Clara Thomson's *Samuel Richardson: A Biographical and Critical Study* (1900). Each novel has a separate introduction, which supplies its composition history and reception, as well as critical analyses. Phelps's introduction to *Clarissa* is preceded by an account of Richardson's influence on other novelists in other countries, and his introduction to *Grandison* follows his essay on Richardson's place in the English novel as the successor to Defoe and as one of the first literary realists. Each volume also contains several engravings, and the introduction has a facsimile of a letter to Richardson from Samuel Johnson. In addition to the expanded introductory material, adapted from essays previously published in the *Independent* and *Essays on Books*, Phelps provides a substantial bibliography. The first part of the bibliography, taken from Thomson's *Samuel Richardson*, gives information on the manuscripts in the Forster Collection. The rest is an expanded version of Thomson's: it cites the previous published collected editions by Mangin, Scott, and Stephen, as well as individual editions and translations dating from the eighteenth century. It also mentions publications of Richardson's other writings, including *Aesop's Fables* and the correspondence, as well as critical approaches to Richardson and his works. While this edition does not explicitly reveal which copy-texts were used, facsimiles of the first-edition title pages are given before each text. A. M. Logan's review of the edition in *The Nation* praises Phelps's paratextual material. The other early-twentieth-century edition, Ethel M. M. McKenna's of 1902, adds very little to Phelps's. By stretching *Clarissa* into nine volumes, it fills twenty in total.[14] As with Phelps's edition, there are some illustrations and no textual annotations, so there is little to distinguish it besides McKenna's introduction, which emphasises Richardson's knowledge of and sympathy for women.

The Shakespeare Head Edition to the Present

The collected editions of Richardson's works from the nineteenth century through the early decades of the twentieth culminated in the publication of the Shakespeare Head edition (1929–31), which has been seen as the standard edition of Richardson's works since its publication.[15] Its anonymous editors based the text on the octavo editions of Richardson's novels, replicating the typography of the eighteenth-century editions and providing no notes other than Richardson's own markings. The use of the octavo editions bespeaks luxury: the Shakespeare Head edition was printed in only 500 copies, 100 of them on large, gold-gilded pages of pure rag that cost the then-staggering price of £7 17s 6d per volume. However, the use of the octavo editions was not a wise editorial decision because they reflected neither Richardson's initial nor his final intentions.

Richardson's three novels, including the *Pamela* continuation, are printed in eighteen volumes in the Shakespeare Head edition, and each novel is preceded by a bibliographical note. In the case of *Pamela*, this note is only two paragraphs long, identifying the edition used and the inclusion of the introductory matter from the third edition. It says nothing, however, about the Shakespeare Head editorial decisions and provides no background information about Richardson's revisions and continuation to the novel. The note to *Sir Charles Grandison* is longer: it reprints the title page; it explains that other than the long 's', the punctuation and spelling have been retained; and it clarifies that there are six instead of seven volumes, in imitation of the octavo edition of 1753–4. The note for *Clarissa* is the longest and best; it gives an account of the composition of the novel and Richardson's anxieties about its initial reception. It describes both the second and third editions and justifies its use of the third as the copy-text, correcting only obvious misprints and doubtful passages, and retaining inconsistencies of spelling and punctuation.

Although the Shakespeare Head remains the standard collected edition by default, significant annotated editions of individual works and Richardson's correspondence have emerged since the middle of the twentieth century. Annotated editions of Richardson's novels have been published since the 1970s, especially in the Oxford English Novels, Oxford World's Classics, and Penguin Classics series, which contain important paratextual material, including introductions and clear notes on the texts that indicate which editions are used. These textbook or trade editions targeted only Richardson's canonical works, so his minor works and sequel to *Pamela* were not reprinted. Modern editions of Richardson's correspondence, beginning with Charles F. Mullett's edition of George Cheyne's correspondence with Richardson (1943), have used annotations to clarify eighteenth-century contexts, such as people and texts, mentioned in the letters. William C. Slattery's edition of *The Richardson–Stinstra Correspondence, and Stinstra's Prefaces to 'Clarissa'* (1969) and John Carroll's *Selected Letters of Samuel Richardson* (1964) are sensitive examples of editorial work that preserve punctuation, spelling, and capitalisation from the manuscripts. Slattery's notes in particular display a keen knowledge of textual parallels, editions, and archives. And Carroll's edition, with Barbauld's, was the most cited collection of Richardson's correspondence until recently. Some of Richardson's letters have also appeared in modern editions of correspondence of other eighteenth-century figures, such as Samuel Johnson, Tobias Smollett, Edward Young, Sarah and Henry Fielding, Edward Moore, and Charlotte Lennox. While the standard of editing displayed in these editions shows a distinct improvement over that of Barbauld, their focused and selective nature is a limitation.

The Cambridge Edition of the Works and Correspondence of Samuel Richardson, of which ten out of twenty-four volumes are currently complete, promises to compensate for the shortcomings of Richardson's previous editors. The Cambridge edition of the correspondence aims to publish the 1,700 known letters between Richardson and his correspondents. Approximately half of these have never appeared in print, and half of the material that has been previously printed is represented only in Barbauld's flawed edition, which is the sole source for 324 letters. The Cambridge editors argue for the importance of including letters from Richardson's recipients to provide a fuller picture of his correspondence. Correspondences are organised by individuals rather than chronology to create uninterrupted relational arcs. There are also two volumes, published or forthcoming, on correspondence related to Richardson's novels, and additional appendices and a general index are the anticipated contents of the twelfth and final volume. Using various methods of textual recovery, the editors present the letters in their initial sent or drafted state. The editions provide a clear description of editorial practices and textual symbols used, as well as a useful chronology and volume-specific indexes. The seven volumes of the correspondence that have now been published speak to the edition's scholarly importance: they are generously annotated, contain accurate textual transcriptions, and provide clear accounts of locations of original manuscripts and source material.

The Cambridge edition of Richardson's works shows similar potential to be the authoritative version of Richardson's writings. It was launched with the publication of *Pamela* in 2011, and its *Early Works* and *Pamela in Her Exalted Condition* in 2012 confirm its aims to become the first collected edition of Richardson's works with a scholarly apparatus. Each volume contains detailed introductions, substantial annotations, and bibliographical appendices that provide the composition, publication, and subsequent textual history. For the first time in any of the collected editions, the Cambridge edition includes Richardson's early and later works, such as his *Familiar Letters* and 'The History of Mrs Beaumont'. As with the correspondence, each volume contains a chronology, as well as informative and intelligent introductions to the novels. There are useful, though not plentiful, endnotes, and the bibliographical descriptions and supplementary material are valuable. While the typography follows the uniformity prescribed by the Cambridge edition, the spelling, capitalisation, and punctuation of the original texts are preserved. The editors acknowledge their difficulty in selecting a copy-text for Richardson's works and settle on the earliest version of each text to be authorised and published, which is the logical choice given the nature of many of Richardson's revisions, his correspondents' use of the first-edition texts, and the electronic availability of later editions, even though post-publication revision was an integral part of Richardson's process of composition. Once all twenty-four volumes of the works and correspondence are published, the Cambridge edition will supplant the Shakespeare Head edition to become the unrivalled, comprehensive version of Richardson's correspondence and works.

Notes

1 Samuel Richardson, *The Cambridge Edition of the Works and Correspondence of Samuel Richardson*, gen. eds. Thomas Keymer and Peter Sabor (Cambridge University Press, 2011–).
2 Barbauld, *Correspondence*, Vol. 1, pp. cxciii–cxciv.
3 *Ibid.*, p. vi.

4 William McCarthy, 'What Did Anna Barbauld Do to Samuel Richardson's Correspondence? A Study of Her Editing', *Studies in Bibliography*, 54 (2001), 191–223 (p. 206).

5 Eaves and Kimpel, *Biography*, p. 183.

6 Samuel Richardson, *The Works of Samuel Richardson*, ed. Edward Mangin, 19 vols. (London, 1811).

7 Edward Mangin, 'A Sketch of the Life and Writings of Samuel Richardson', in Richardson, *Works*, ed. Mangin, Vol. 1, p. xxv.

8 Samuel Richardson, *The Novels of Samuel Richardson, Esq. viz. 'Pamela', 'Clarissa Harlowe', and 'Sir Charles Grandison'*, 3 vols. (London, 1824).

9 Sir Walter Scott, 'Prefatory Memoir to Richardson', in Richardson, *Novels*, Vol. 1, p. xxiv.

10 Samuel Richardson, *The Works of Samuel Richardson*, ed. Leslie Stephen, 12 vols. (London, 1883).

11 Leslie Stephen, 'Richardson's Novels', in *Works*, ed. Stephen, Vol. 1, pp. x, xii.

12 H. D. Traill, 'Samuel Richardson', *Contemporary Review*, 44.4 (1883), 529–45 (p. 531).

13 Samuel Richardson, *The Novels of Samuel Richardson*, ed. William Lyon Phelps, 19 vols. (Croscup & Sterling, 1901–2).

14 Samuel Richardson, *The Novels of Samuel Richardson*, ed. Ethel M. M. McKenna, 20 vols. (Chapman & Hall, 1902).

15 Samuel Richardson, *The Shakespeare Head Edition of the Novels of Samuel Richardson*, 18 vols. (Shakespeare Head, 1929–31).

CHAPTER 5

Contemporary Transnational Reception

Mary Helen McMurran

In their day, Samuel Richardson's novels were among the most talked about fictional works in England. They were also topics of heated literary conversations abroad. Continental readers consumed the novels with fervour, and expressed their diverse opinions in letters to friends, critical reviews, fictional dialogues, and more. All this literary chat was bolstered by adaptations of his narratives in multiple languages. In the case of *Pamela*, the reception echoed and extended the controversy over the novel's portrayal of morals and manners. *Clarissa* and *Sir Charles Grandison* were widely read, admired, and avidly discussed on the Continent as in England. Adaptations of these last two novels, unlike those of *Pamela*, were not merely parodic auxiliaries to the original, but agents in the evolution of the era's sentimental literature. Thus, modern critics have consistently discussed the author's reception along with the 'Richardsonian' legacy in the eighteenth century. Should this ripple effect be surprising? The answer to this question gauges the peculiar and pivotal role of Richardson's works as they emigrated from England to the Continent. In an already enriching traffic of fictions across national borders, these novels were crucial for the formation of cosmopolitan standards of literary taste.

Pamela: Situation Critical

Beginning with *Pamela*, Richardson's novels left England by the rutted pathways of the print trade: from London to Dublin and to continental European publishing centres. Yet, compared to other English novels before it, the number of translations, reviews, and adaptations of *Pamela* in Europe was large and the pace frenetic. The French translation came out within a year of the original, published first in London under the imprint of John Osborn, and then exported to francophone territories. Unlike many literary translations into French at this time, the French *Pamela* was complete and faithful, probably because of the author's involvement with the project. Within the first five years, there were also Dutch, Danish, German, and Italian translations, and the French translation became available in Sweden and Switzerland. In 1742–3, Benjamin Franklin printed *Pamela*, based on Richardson's fifth edition, in colonial Philadelphia. Franklin must have wagered that what was popular in England ought to attract colonial readers. It was the first novel published in an American colony and it was known well enough that Robert Feke of Rhode Island painted a portrait of the character, but *Pamela* did not cause a stir among American readers of the proportions seen on the other side of the Atlantic. All three of Richardson's novels were, however, relatively popular in post-Revolutionary America. By then, they were in abridged versions only, which allowed them to be assimilated to the growing American market for short, sentimental fictions.

Richardson's business acumen helped quicken the distribution and promotion of the novel outside England, but credit also goes to such entrepreneurs in the vernacular literary marketplace as the abbé Desfontaines, a Parisian translator of English works who wrote a lengthy and later contested review, and Jean Baptiste de Freval, a French translator living in London and the author of an introductory letter to the first English edition of *Pamela*, which was, in part, directly addressed to his former countrymen. In addition to early translations and reviews of *Pamela*, there were abridgments of the novel in French and Dutch, and translations of the English parodies and imitations.[1] Eliza Haywood's satirical *Anti-Pamela* (1741), translated into French, Dutch, German, and Danish, was the most successful of these, perhaps because of Haywood's own reputation abroad as a novelist and translator of several French narratives.

If the labourers in the book trade had primed a continental readership, readers' curiosity soon transformed the book into a *cause célèbre*. Foreign readers frequently commented upon the book's notoriety before making their judgments. Echoing the divisive reactions in England, *Pamela* was simultaneously the object of admiration by flatterers, who tended to mimic the author's own claims about moral instruction, and the target of sharp criticism. The Vatican placed the original novel, as well as *Anti-Pamela*, and their French translations, on the Index of Prohibited Books by 1745. Yet the overriding reaction on the Continent was distinctly quizzical. Could a young woman be so entirely lacking in the wiles and arts of her sex? And so unsuspecting of others' indecency? Could a lowborn servant marry so far above her station? Could her sentimental outbursts be affecting when her every swoon was such a convenient release from imminent danger? The anti-Pamela character, as in Haywood's novel, is a sly and duplicitous working girl, detached from sentiment in her quest to survive financially by relying on the men she encounters in the city. This parody of the heroine was often held up as more realistic than Richardson's character.

'Pamelas' on the Continent also included dramatic adaptations – four in French alone within a decade. If parodies relied on comic exaggeration, many of these imitators attempted to repair the novel's improbable outcome. Louis de Boissy's *Paméla en France* introduces a cross-dressing marquis to lure Pamela across the Channel, but the attempted seduction ends with a metamorphosis of the characters into the allegorical figures of Decency and Pleasure instead of a marriage that defies the class structure. The most favoured drama, Carlo Goldoni's *Pamela nubile* (1750), also avoids the misalliance since Pamela is revealed to be of noble birth; some tonal shifts also aim at greater *politesse*. Goldoni's play, widely performed in Italian, was also translated and became the first version of Richardson's story to entertain Spanish audiences (1761–2), since the Spanish translation of the novel would not appear until 1794. *Pamela nubile* had a second life with Goldoni's own sequel; some operatic adaptations; and another version of the sequel, *Pamela mariata*, by Pietro Chiari (1753). Many of these were also performed and translated in various European locales. Voltaire's *Nanine* (1749), a more distant relative of the novel, maintains the class difference, but moderates the rakishness of the Mr B character, and diminishes the egalitarian implications of the novel.

In a literary culture enlivened by business and personal connections that criss-crossed Europe, the moral and aesthetic debates over *Pamela* and its rewritings amounted to an international forum on literary taste. Rather than a few esteemed arbiters in each country separately pronouncing the novel's merits or faults for their readerships, the critical and creative adjudicators of *Pamela* were a self-appointed group. As a collective, they took the measure of Richardson's depiction of characters and manners. *Pamela* became a crucible for what David Hume and Immanuel Kant would identify later as new terms for judgments of taste. In place of applying ideal standards inherited from tradition by an elite, taste would now be conceived as a relation between one's individual feeling about a work and the impersonal standards of an educated vox populi.

Clarissa and *Sir Charles Grandison* in the European Community

The reception of *Clarissa* and *Sir Charles Grandison* in Europe was comparable to that of *Pamela* in magnitude, but more hospitably inclined.

Both novels benefited from Richardson's cultivation of continental contacts within and beyond the book trade: their personalised attention led to the efficient publication of translations. Both novels appeared in German, Dutch, and French with little delay, despite the taxing labour of rendering such lengthy works. Translations into other European languages occurred after Richardson's death. The German translation of *Clarissa* by Johann Michaelis, an academic specialising in Near Eastern studies, began to appear even before the final volumes of the English edition were published (1748–53). Christian Gellert, chosen with the help of bookseller Philipp Erasmus Reich to be the German translator of *Sir Charles Grandison* (1755), was also an academic as well as a poet, and, most importantly for the job, an admirer of Richardson. The Dutch translation of *Clarissa* (1752–5) was undertaken by Johannes Stinstra, a Mennonite clergyman temporarily suspended from his pastoral duties. He read the novel in English, fell in love with it, and applied directly to Richardson to translate it. Stinstra contributed a substantial preface, which summarises the plot and praises the author, to each of the two-volume instalments of the novel. He could not find time for the Dutch translation of *Sir Charles Grandison*, but helped shepherd the project into print by arranging for a group of trusted translators to do the work (1756–7).

Abbé Prévost authored the first French translations of *Clarissa* (1751) and of *Sir Charles Grandison* (1755). A journalist, editor, and major French novelist, Prévost was also an enthusiast for English literature, who promoted its exchange for the benefit of both nations. Unlike Michaelis and Stinstra, who attempted full equivalence, Prévost followed the practices of many literary translators by putting his own imprint on the text. To Richardson's chagrin, he shortened *Clarissa*, and, taking the editorial reins, he added footnotes to indicate the omitted passages. Prévost excised nearly a third of the novel, including many of the letters following Clarissa's rape. Many of those letters were restored after first being published in the *Journal étranger* in 1762. Subsequently, Pierre Le Tourneur wrote a complete French translation, *Clarisse Harlowe* (1785–6). Despite Richardson's efforts to have his friend Alexis Clairaut intervene in the translation process for *Sir Charles Grandison*, Prévost went ahead with a translation and entitled it *Nouvelles lettres anglaises, ou histoire du chevalier Grandisson*. He counted on the appeal of its Englishness, but also shrewdly signalled its link with his previous translation, *Lettres anglaises, ou histoire de Miss Clarissa Harlove*. Like his *Clarissa*, Prévost's *Sir Charles Grandison* was reduced in size and the content altered. Although Prévost's introduction to *Clarissa* is terse, with *Grandison* he justifies his changes in general, and specifically the ending, which he judges 'very insipid' in the original. The Italian Clementina, whom Grandison has loved and finally breaks with, has an uncertain fate in the English novel, but Prévost lends her more dignity by clarifying that she is cured of any madness. In the literary journal *Correspondance littéraire*, Denis Diderot and Friedrich Melchior Grimm, the journal's editor, upbraid the translator for his carelessness and his mutilations of the original. Demonstrating the inconsistency with which translations were judged in the eighteenth century, however, the same authors, in a review of the anonymously translated *Memoirs of Miss Sidney Bidulph* by Frances Sheridan, describe Prévost as a practised, fluent, and correct translator. They consequently rule him out as the responsible party for this poorer translation, though in fact Prévost was the translator of the version they reviewed.[2]

Another less liberal French translation of *Sir Charles Grandison* done by Gaspard Joël Monod appeared in Leyden and Göttingen concurrently with Prévost's (1755–6) with the help of German bookseller Reich and Dutch bookseller Elie Luzac. They attempted to ensure a translation that suited the author, but Richardson let Reich know he heard it was poorly done compared with Gellert's German translation (Richardson to Erasmus Reich, 2 April 1757). Prévost's translation was protected, however, from competition in its biggest market when a Lyon bookseller applied for permission to publish Monod's translation of *Sir Charles Grandison*. The French censors would consider the request only on the condition that copies not enter Paris. The Lyon bookseller subsequently abandoned his effort to bring the alternative translation into France and published an edition of Alexander Pope instead.[3]

Clarissa, which replaces the comedy of 'virtue rewarded' with tragic pathos, seemed to unblock the sympathetic response of readers that was withheld from *Pamela*. The range of reactions to the genteel heroine went from appreciation to fawning, and from identifying with her humanity to awe of her super-humanity. Even Voltaire, whose appraisal begins cynically and concludes negatively, admits that he was 'moved … greatly' by Richardson's ending.[4] Others expressed an unmediated sympathy with the central character. Friedrich Gottlieb Klopstock, for example, wrote a panegyric, 'Ode on the Death of Clarissa', in which the poet not only mourns the character's death, but imagines sharing his grief with a companion 'in many tears of admiration'. Reactions to *Sir Charles Grandison* were less voluminous and more moderate. Perhaps there was less to strain readers one way or another in this story of an impeccable man of feeling; or perhaps audiences on the Continent gravitated less to its nationalising typology of

English Protestants versus Italian Catholics. Nonetheless, Diderot's 'Eloge de Richardson' (1762), written on the occasion of Richardson's death, is the work of a consummate devotee of the whole corpus. Diderot's brilliant eulogy champions the English novelist in a personal testament to Richardson's powers to penetrate readers' souls and induct them in the cause of virtue. Diderot turns the role of an intensely private reader into a realisation of a sentimental community that knows no boundaries short of universal humanity.

Clarissa may be a paradigmatic sentimental novel because it both depicts and enables the communicability of sympathetic feeling. Yet responses to the novel were not purely affective. Most readers entangled their emotive response with views regarding Richardson's command of narrative realism. The novel engaged the heart, but this effect did not impede judgments about how the characters are drawn, how probable the events are, and how well it might inspire good morals. One model of critical reflection was comparison. Continental readers, like their English counterparts, compared *Clarissa* to *Pamela*, and compared Richardson's novels with other fictions: in particular, Marivaux's *Marianne* (1731–45) and *Le paysan parvenu* (1734–5), which were familiar to European readers in the original and in translation. In his review of *Clarissa*, Albrecht Haller, a Swiss polymath, remarks that the heroine of *Marianne* prefers honour like Richardson's female characters, but characterises it as a general virtue in contrast to Richardson's effectively particularised circumstances of virtuousness. Another inevitable comparison to *Clarissa* was Jean-Jacques Rousseau's *Julie, ou la nouvelle Héloïse* (1761), which seemed to owe the character of its heroine to Richardson. Joseph de La Porte's review of the French translation of *Clarissa* takes up another mode of reflective judgment in his summary-heavy review: he appeals directly to a critical concept – verisimilitude – as a universal barometer for good fiction. For La Porte, *Clarissa* does not entirely offend the literary value of realism, but the portrayal of a demonic Lovelace against the angelic Clarissa is exaggerated, and the fact that feminine virtue fails to reform the rake in order to resolve the story in a proper marriage is 'extraordinary'.[5] Other devices of critical reflection on the novel included the imagined dialogue in which readers explored their agreements and disagreements on certain aspects of the novel's success. Another model was borrowed from the scholastic practice of presenting a thesis, objections, and replies to the objections. Thus, mulling over what worked, what did not, and why resulted in an array of individual responses. Rather than reflecting an established regional or national standard, such expressions were individual inflections of discourses elaborated in Europe's critical commons.

Enlightenment theories of taste, such as Hume's nuanced 'Of the Standard of Taste' (1757), recognised the new sovereignty of individual experience in judging a work of art and its potential for disrupting classical universalism. Hume's premise that 'all sentiment is right' leads him to argue that although one may often reach consensus about whether a literary work is admirable or not, any truly objective standard of taste is elusive. It is nonetheless worth the effort to seek such a standard, not least by diminishing natural biases. In *Critique of Judgment* (1790), Kant also posits that judgments of taste are grounded in a subjectively determined feeling about the work of art. Kant, however, does not invoke an objective standard. Instead, he argues that any such judgments are articulated with an implicit demand for assent. When a reader says 'this novel is good', she is also saying that insofar as it is good to her, it ought to please everyone. Kant assumes two things. First, he supposes that aesthetic judgments derive from feeling rather than rational cognition. The feeling, however, is not a capricious reaction based on sensation of self-satisfaction, but rather a disinterested judgment. Second, Kant assumes that a feeling about a work of art is universally communicable. When readers of *Clarissa* declared the novel to be beautiful, this feeling may have been subjectively determined, but because it was also necessarily disinterested, it was a judgment the reader made by putting herself 'into the position of everyone else'.[6] For Kant, aesthetic judgments about novels, like other works of art, present us with the possibility of a *sensus communis* that shuttles between subjectivity and universality with no other stops in between. We can see Kant's idea of the universal communicability of judgments of taste prefigured in the opinions and creative adaptations of Richardson's works. Starting with readers' identification or lack thereof with the characters and incidents in the sentimental novel, individual reactions to the novel's success were calibrated to and mirrored by an unbounded community of readers who were trusted to feel as the individual felt. The subsequent judgment with respect to verisimilitude, probability, or moral instruction might easily demand the assent of any potential reader.

By the time of his death, Richardson had earned a distinguished reputation outside England. His importance from a transnational eighteenth-century perspective was, in the first instance, that the novels' immediate fame managed to scale up the response rate of readers all over Europe. Then, rather than bearing nationalist stamps, the feedback, whether critical or creative, publicly disseminated or privately shared, reverberated across Western Europe in a common idiom.

Notes

1 *Les mémoires de Pamela* (1743), by an anonymous author, reduces four volumes to two. The Dutch *Pamela Bespiegeld*, or 'Pamela Exposed' (Amsterdam, 1741), according to Alan Dugald McKillop, *Samuel Richardson: Printer and Novelist* (University of North Carolina Press, 1936), p. 100, is made up of a summary with occasional passages directly translated; there was also *De hollandsche Pamela*, an imitation (1754).

2 Denis Diderot and Friedrich Melchior Grimm, in Bueler, *'Clarissa': The Eighteenth-Century Response*, Vol. 1, pp. 378–9.

3 Edward P. Shaw, 'Malesherbes, the Abbé Prévost and the First French Translation of *Sir Charles Grandison*', *Modern Language Notes*, 69.2 (1954), 105–09.

4 Voltaire, in Bueler, *'Clarissa': The Eighteenth-Century Response*, Vol. 1, p. 265.

5 Albrecht Haller and Joseph de La Porte, in Bueler, *'Clarissa': The Eighteenth-Century Response*, Vol. 1, pp. 19–20, 68–79.

6 Immanuel Kant, *Critique of the Power of Judgment*, ed. Paul Guyer (Cambridge University Press, 2000), p. 174.

CHAPTER 6

Reputation

Sören Hammerschmidt

Concern with Samuel Richardson's reputation is at least as old as the day he commenced as master printer in late 1720 and as fresh as a recent piece in the *New Yorker* that praised the psychological realism of his characters but deplored the 'self-satisfied bourgeois, with a scold's horror of impropriety' who created them.[1] Between those two moments lie not only the histories of the writing, publication, and reception of Richardson's novels but also, and just as importantly, his readers' changing perceptions of Richardson himself.

Richardson's entrance into the public light actually began with a set of intensely self-effacing moves, born precisely from a concern for his reputation. In the first half of the eighteenth century, novels were still being regarded with suspicion because of the morally corrupting influence ascribed to them. For a printer whose continued business depended to a large degree on his reputation, to write and publish in such a problematic genre constituted a significant risk. Richardson was therefore intensely concerned not only with the ways in which readers interpreted his novels and their characters but also with how his readers perceived and interpreted him. As author, printer, and publisher in one, he was simultaneously in an ideal situation to influence those interpretations and especially vulnerable to criticism and detractions. Responsible for the composition, production, and dissemination of his fictions, Richardson was directly involved in shaping his reputation in all three arenas, and his success or failure in one always also reflected on the other two.

On first publishing *Pamela* in November 1740, Richardson accordingly disguised not only his authorship (passing himself off as the editor of a collection of real letters instead) but also his responsibility for printing and disseminating the novel; the title page mentions only the London booksellers in whose shops readers could purchase the book (Figure 6.1). By the time the first volumes of *Clarissa* appeared, he had given up on anonymity in at least one of those arenas: the title page now announces that the novel is 'Printed for S. Richardson' and '*Published by the* EDITOR *of* PAMELA' (Figure 6.2). The phrase 'Printed for' tells readers that Richardson is the publisher of *Clarissa* and hints that, as a well-known printer, he might also be responsible for the book's production; and the remark that Richardson is also the 'Editor' of *Pamela* casts him in a role that years before had been revealed to have been a mere disguise for the book's author. Curiously enough, by the time Richardson was publishing *Sir Charles Grandison*, his authorship of all three novels was widely known, and yet he kept up the persona of 'Editor of PAMELA and CLARISSA' on the title page (Figure 6.3). That Richardson persisted in playing coy about the extent of his responsibility for his novels speaks to his continued concern for his reputation, at a time when the novel was still considered a morally suspicious genre, as much as to the air of veracity that such posturing as the editor of authentic manuscripts might lend his fiction.

Pamela was an immediate commercial and critical success, so much so that it established Richardson's reputation as a serious literary writer and a reformer of the novel for the rest of the century. It is difficult now to conceive of the novelty and full impact of the '*Pamela* craze' that swept Britain and parts of the European continent when spin-offs, prequels and sequels, tie-ins, and augmented-reality and social media campaigns are becoming standard items in the public relations arsenals of popular franchises. Not only did five editions in London and two in Dublin bring the novel to more readers within the first year of its publication than most literary works – let alone any novels – had reached before, but that first year also saw a host of unauthorised reprints, spin-offs, and continuations of Richardson's text before he brought out his own continuation and a sixth, richly illustrated edition in early 1742. In addition, the novel was within five years of its first publication versified, turned into a waxworks, and adapted into two plays and an opera; in addition, its main characters and key scenes were painted on canvas, exhibited as pleasure garden murals, and used as fan designs, and at least one race horse was named after the novel's heroine. The cultural penetration of *Pamela*, and therefore of its (as yet anonymous) author, was unprecedented, a status confirmed by the slew of critiques and satires that inevitably followed. The best known of the more critical literary responses are those by Henry Fielding: first his short, quick cuts at Pamela's supposed innocence and Richardson's posing as an editor of actual letters in *Shamela* (1741), and then *Joseph Andrews* (1742), Fielding's own extended revision of the novel genre in conversation with Richardson's aesthetic and moral principles. Though Fielding's fictions did not sell quite as well as Richardson's in those years, they did attract

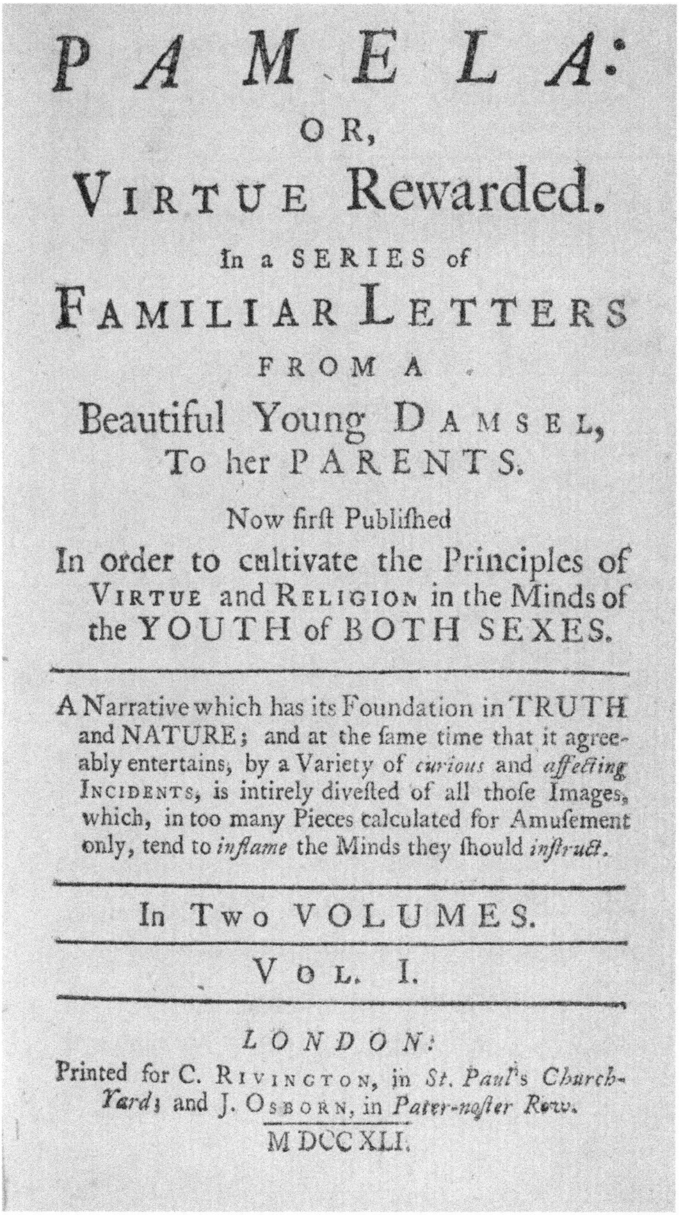

P A M E L A:

O R,

V I R T U E Rewarded.

In a SERIES of

F A M I L I A R L E T T E R S

F R O M A .

Beautiful Young D A M S E L, To her P A R E N T S.

Now firſt Publiſhed
In order to cultivate the Principles of
V I R T U E and R E L I G I O N in the Minds of
the Y O U T H of B O T H S E X E S.

A Narrative which has its Foundation in T R U T H
and N A T U R E; and at the ſame time that it agreeably entertains, by a Variety of *curious* and *affecting*
I N C I D E N T S, is intirely diveſted of all thoſe Images,
which, in too many Pieces calculated for Amuſement
only, tend to *inflame* the Minds they ſhould *inſtruct.*

In Two V O L U M E S.

V O L. I.

L O N D O N:

Printed for C. R I V I N G T O N, in *St. Paul's Church-
Yard;* and J. O S B O R N, in *Pater-noſter Row.*

M DCC XLI.

Figure 6.1 Samuel Richardson, *Pamela; or, Virtue Rewarded* (1740), title page.

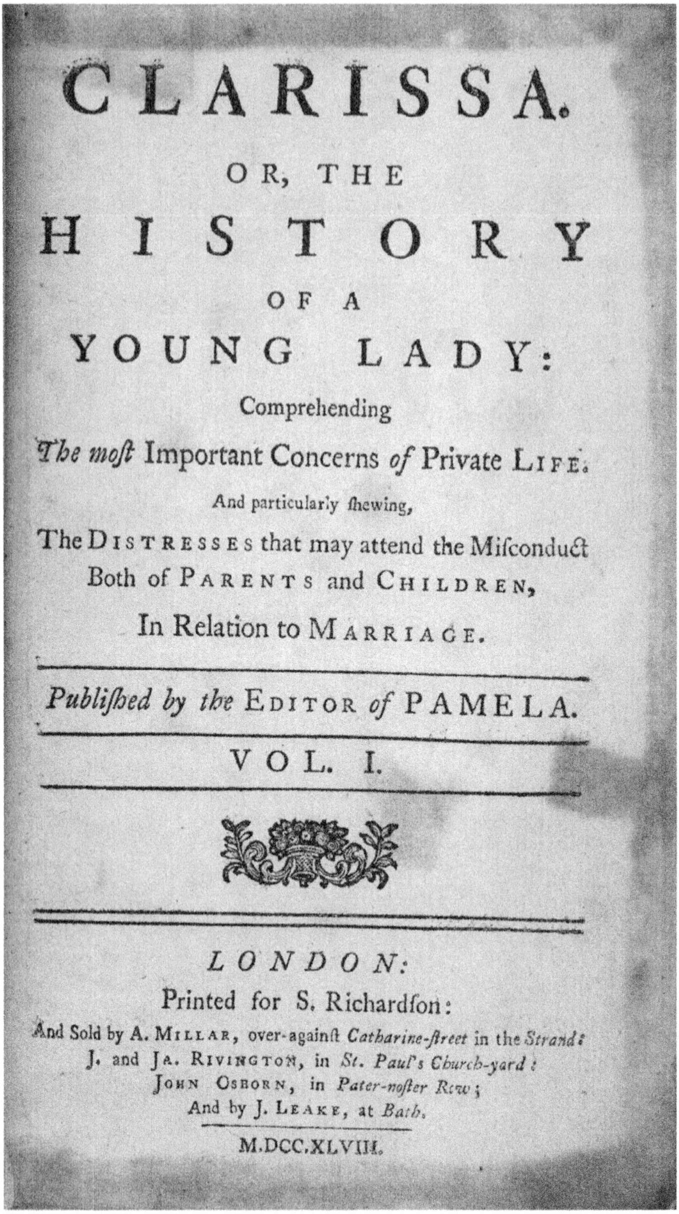

CLARISSA.

OR, THE

HISTORY

OF A

YOUNG LADY:

Comprehending

The most Important Concerns *of* Private LIFE.

And particularly shewing,

The DISTRESSES that may attend the Misconduct
Both of PARENTS and CHILDREN,

In Relation to MARRIAGE.

Published by the EDITOR *of* PAMELA.

VOL. I.

LONDON:

Printed for S. Richardson:

And Sold by A. MILLAR, over-against *Catharine-street* in the *Strand*:
J. and JA. RIVINGTON, in *St. Paul's Church-yard*:
JOHN OSBORN, in *Pater-noster Row*;
And by J. LEAKE, at *Bath*.

M.DCC.XLVIII.

Figure 6.2 Samuel Richardson, *Clarissa; or, The History of a Young Lady* (1747–8),
title page.

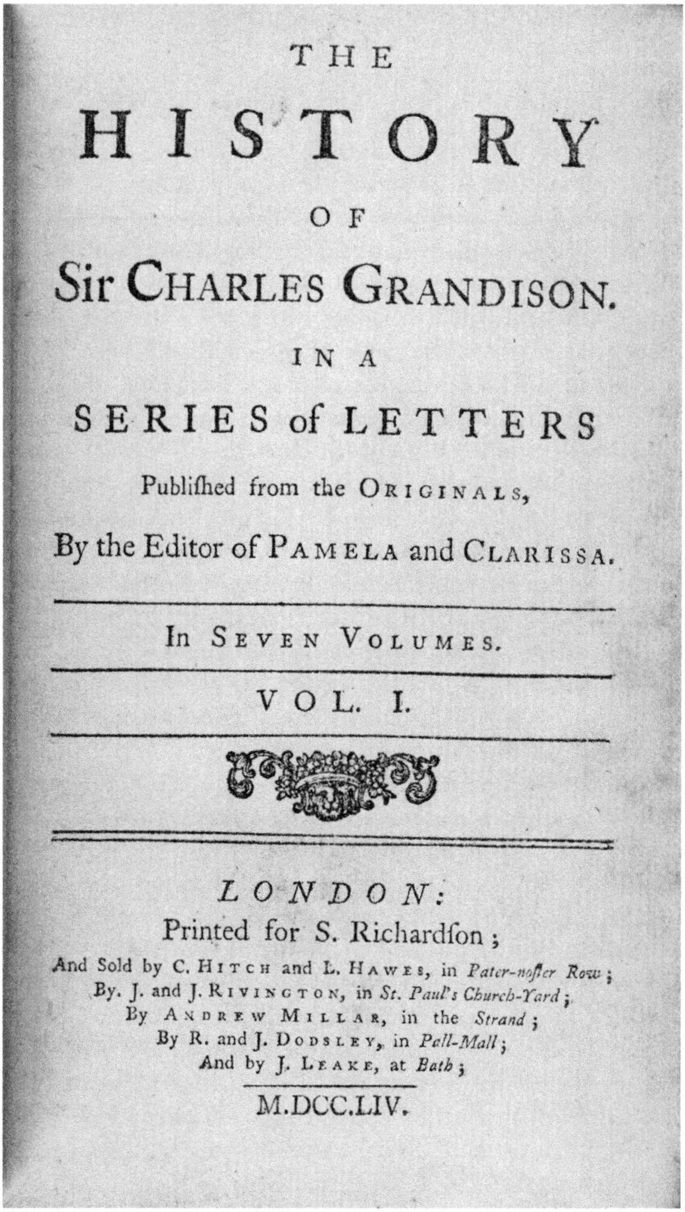

THE

HISTORY

OF

Sir CHARLES GRANDISON.

IN A

SERIES of LETTERS

Publiſhed from the ORIGINALS,

By the Editor of PAMELA and CLARISSA.

In SEVEN VOLUMES.

VOL. I.

LONDON:

Printed for S. Richardſon ;

And Sold by C. HITCH and L. HAWES, in *Pater-noſter Row* ;
By. J. and J. RIVINGTON, in *St. Paul's Church-Yard* ;
By ANDREW MILLAR, in the *Strand* ;
By R. and J. DODSLEY, in *Pall-Mall* ;
And by J. LEAKE, at *Bath* ;

M.DCC.LIV.

Figure 6.3 Samuel Richardson, *The History of Sir Charles Grandison* (1753–4), title page.

considerable audiences in their own right (two issues of *Shamela* and four editions of *Joseph Andrews* within the first year of publication), and significantly influenced perceptions of Richardson, his texts, and his project to reform the novel.

In the midst of the intense debate that followed over the merits of *Pamela* and the book's didactic and aesthetic programmes, the field of readers quickly split into Pamelists and Anti-Pamelists and eventually, more broadly, into Richardsonians and Fieldingites. There was also another, even broader division between those who managed to read Richardson's novels and those who could or would not make it through a volume or two, try as they might.[2] This rivalry between Richardson and Fielding came to structure much of the reception and reputation of both writers, and few critics (or indeed any other readers) did as much to help institute the dichotomy as Samuel Johnson. In his *Life of Johnson*, James Boswell records Samuel Johnson repeatedly comparing the two writers and finding in favour of Richardson: 'Sir, there is more knowledge of the heart in one letter of Richardson's, than in all "Tom Jones".'[3] This 'knowledge of the heart' became one of Richardson's perceived strengths, his 'characters of nature' the proof of Richardson's proficiency in 'div[ing] into the recesses of the human heart'.[4] And many readers agreed with Johnson that Richardson's particular abilities lay in the analysis and representation of human emotions, which in turn evoked emotional responses in his readers, with a view to reforming and improving them.

Richardson's novels came to be understood as 'paint[ing] nature ... as *it ought to be*', a concrete incarnation of Johnson's call for prose fiction 'to distinguish those parts of nature, which are most proper for imitation' in order to 'convey the knowledge of vice and virtue' and of his judgment that Richardson had 'enlarged the knowledge of human nature, and taught the passions to move at the command of virtue'.[5] As a corollary, Richardson's novels were said to require a different approach to reading and to understanding their narrative structure than was the case with other prose fiction. Johnson thus cautioned that 'if you were to read Richardson for the story, your impatience would be so much fretted that you would hang yourself. But you must read him for the sentiment, and consider the story as only giving occasion to the sentiment', an assessment with which Clara Reeve agreed:

> If you have a mind to see an Epitomé of Richardson's works, there is such a publication, wherein the *narrative* is preserved; but you must no longer expect the graces of *Richardson*, nor his pathetic addresses to the heart, they are all evaporated and only the dry *Story* remains.[6]

The value of Richardson's long, didactic novels was thus seen to lie not in his plots (which were fragmented, perpetually delayed, and 'dry') but in his idealised portraits of human emotions and the lessons to be drawn from them.

There were, however, also readers who disagreed with these characterisations of Richardson's fictions. James Boswell, for example, in responding to one of Johnson's most enduring metaphors, which likened Richardson to a watchmaker who understood the intricate workings of each clockwork mechanism, objected that 'the neat watches of Fielding [were] as well constructed as the large clocks of Richardson' and therefore made their points more clearly and more economically.[7] His fellow Scot, James Beattie, went one step further and complained that Richardson, 'with all his powers of invention, is apt to be tedious, and to fall into a minuteness of detail, which is often unnecessary'.[8] Moreover, Beattie was also concerned that 'His pathetic scenes [were] overcharged, and so long continued, as to wear out the spirits of the reader', and that they might thus become dangerous for the reader, 'whose imagination is apt to dwell upon melancholy ideas'.[9] Where Reeve (and Johnson implicitly, too) rejected abridgment as cutting away that which was most valuable in Richardson's novels, readers like Beattie tended to find those same qualities in Richardson tiresome and even dangerous for certain groups of readers. In fact, while many critics lauded Richardson's ability to craft incisive portraits of human emotion and motivation, and continued to assert his centrality to the English-language literary canon, a significant number of readers seem to have preferred abridgments or other writers' fictions altogether. In the later eighteenth and the early nineteenth centuries, Richardson became known to many as the purveyor of morally wholesome though somewhat boring fiction.

Some of the changes in the perception of Richardson and the reading of his novels may have had to do with his choice of letters as a narrative vehicle. Whether epistolary fiction lost its popular appeal in the late eighteenth and the early nineteenth centuries because of increasing associations of correspondence with insurgent, revolutionary politics, or whether it was because the subgenre fell prey to a growing predilection for omniscient, heterodiegetic forms of narration, Richardson's novels became gradually outmoded in form while retaining, maybe even cementing, their literary-historical significance. In print, letters came above all to document their own historicity, tied to past events and bygone cultures at the same time that they evidenced the historical significance of the messages they communicated.

Walter Scott's treatment of Richardson's novels in compiling Ballantyne's
Novelist's Library (1821–4) encapsulates some of Richardson's ambiguous
status in this posthumous literary landscape. While Scott was conducting
the project, he wrote to Hurst, Robinson and Co., the publishers eventually responsible for the Novelist's Library, that Richardson's 'works are
so insufferably long, that they will take a great deal of room in the proposed edition – while, on the other hand, a collection of novels without Richardson would be very incomplete'.[10] Richardson's eventual place
within the Novelist's Library, and thus within the novelistic canon as construed by Scott, reflects this attitude quite well. Not only do Fielding and
Tobias Smollett take precedence over 'the Author of Clarissa', but so do
a host of other writers, some of them with a considerably lower reputation today than Richardson's, such as Laurence Sterne, Henry Mackenzie,
Clara Reeve, and the French novelist Alain-René Lesage. Richardson's novels appear only in Volumes VI through VIII out of a total of ten. In Scott's
view, Richardson was historically important but did not score highly in
terms of readers' entertainment. Editors and publishers of late-eighteenth-
and early-nineteenth-century reprint series generally felt the same, either
relegating Richardson to a late slot in the series – e.g. *Harrison's Novelist's
Magazine* (1780–8), where Richardson's novels appeared in Volumes X–
XI (*Grandison*), XIV–XV (*Clarissa*), and XX (*Pamela*) – or dropping him
entirely. Reprints and abridgments of all of Richardson's novels, on the
other hand, fared relatively well throughout the nineteenth century.[11]

But while Scott clearly belonged to the Fieldingites, there were also
many Richardsonians who continued to assert Richardson's importance
to more than just the literary-historical archive. Anna Laetitia Barbauld
had installed him as the father of the modern novel from the moment
she edited his *Correspondence* (1804), and she did so again in *The British
Novelists* (1810; 2nd edn 1820). In the process, and while trying to explain
Richardson's predilection for letters as narrative vehicles, she also partially
salvaged epistolary fiction by declaring it to be the form best suited to
the discovery of characters' emotional and psychological interiorities: 'it
enables an author to assume, in a lively manner, the hopes and fears, and
passions, and to intimate the peculiar way of thinking of his characters'.[12] A
contemporary review of the *Correspondence* in the *Imperial Review* agreed
and asserted that 'we still love to weep over the woes of Clarissa'. His characters, not the writer himself, were the focus of Richardson's readers.

Indeed, over the century that followed, Richardson's characters became
models and touchstones for new fictional creations. The main character in
Walter Scott's *Redgauntlet* (1824), Darsie Latimer, is as much a Pamela or a

Clarissa for being imprisoned and abducted in other characters' attempts to impose their will on him as he is a Tom Jones who is banished from home and unwittingly gets embroiled in a Jacobite rebellion. Darsie's abduction even disrupts his correspondence and forces him to write a journal that he hides on his person, though in the end Fieldingesque third-person omniscient modes of narration and characterisation win out: from experiencing Darsie's world 'from the inside' we move to hearing about it from the outside. In *The Newcomes* (1855), William Makepeace Thackeray seems to invert this renewed contention between Richardson and Fielding in one of the central characters, the honest and somewhat naïve Colonel Newcome. Newcome, who used to read Fielding's novels when he was an unruly youth, turns in maturity to Richardson's Sir Charles Grandison as a model and a guide, and even gets compared to Richardson's eponymous hero by some of the other characters. Theodore Roosevelt in turn used Colonel Newcome to characterise his uncle, James Dunwoodie Bulloch, 'an Admiral in the Confederate navy' initially exempted from amnesty following the Civil War: 'utterly unable to "get on" in the worldly sense of that phrase, as valiant and simple and upright a soul as ever lived, a veritable Colonel Newcome'.[13] From a model of masculine virtue, Richardson's image of honesty, decency, and respectability had modulated into an embodiment of naïveté.

As his characters became a byword for psychological realism (and his novels for excessive length), Richardson himself lost stature and retreated behind the fictions and the characters that readers enjoyed, even during his own lifetime. In 1755, Lady Mary Wortley Montagu wrote to her daughter that 'This Richardson is a strange fellow. I heartily despise him, and eagerly read him, nay, sob over his works in a most scandalous manner.'[14] The incongruity between emotionally gripping fictions and characters on the one hand and the author's off-putting personality on the other that makes Richardson such 'a strange fellow' for Lady Mary continues to bedevil evaluations of the author and of his writing today. The recent *New Yorker* essay thus praises 'Richardson's talent for morally and emotionally sophisticated psychological realism' while decrying him personally as a 'touchy, straitlaced, and rather narrow man' – his abilities are expansive but his mind is not. According to such a view, Richardson 'succeeded despite himself. It was when his instructional aims were crowded out by the tortuous inner lives of his characters that he achieved greatness.'[15] In readings like these, Richardson turns into an unlikeable appendage to the genius that is his insight into human psychology and emotion. His reputation, in the positive sense of a justification for his inclusion in the novelistic canon and for our continued reading of his fiction, comes to rest entirely on the persistent qualities we identify in his novels because we recognise ourselves in them.

Such an understanding of the relationship between writer and writing would have been unfamiliar to Richardson and his contemporaries, for whom the virtues or flaws of an author and of her or his text were inextricably intertwined. No wonder, then, that Richardson was so concerned to disguise the writing, printing, and publication of his first novel until he could be sure of its favourable reception, and that so much of his non-fiction writing sought to modify and contain critical interpretations of his fiction. While we continue to value Richardson's novels despite the foibles of the author, eighteenth-century readers evaluated one via the other and judged the merits of each accordingly. For a craftsman whose livelihood depended to a significant degree on his standing within the community, the authoring and publishing of his own novels represented a significant risk.

Notes

1 Adelle Waldman, 'The Man who Made the Novel: Loving and Loathing Samuel Richardson', *New Yorker* (16 May 2016), 84–9 (p. 86).
2 For examples, see Eaves and Kimpel, *Biography*, pp. 287–8.
3 Boswell, *Life of Johnson*, Vol. II, p. 174 (6 April 1772).
4 *Ibid.*, Vol. II, pp. 48–9 (Spring 1768).
5 Clara Reeve, *The Progress of Romance, through Times, Countries, and Manners; With Remarks on the Good and Bad Effects of It, on Them Respectively; In a Course of Evening Conversations*, 2 vols. (Colchester, 1785), Vol. I, p. 141; Samuel Johnson, *Rambler*, 4 (31 March 1750), in W. J. Bate and Albrecht B. Strauss (eds.), *The Rambler, in The Yale Edition of the Works of Samuel Johnson*, 23 vols. (Yale University Press, 1969), Vol. III, p. 22; *Rambler*, 97 (19 February 1751), in Bate and Strauss, *The Rambler*, in *The Yale Edition of the Works of Samuel Johnson*, Vol. IV, p. 153.
6 Boswell, *Life of Johnson*, Vol. II, p. 175 (6 April 1772); Reeve, *Progress of Romance*, I, p. 137.
7 Boswell, *Life of Johnson*, Vol. II, p. 49 (Spring 1768).
8 James Beattie, *Dissertations Moral and Critical* (London, 1783), pp. 567–8.
9 *Ibid.*, pp. 568, 202.
10 Thomas Constable, *Archibald Constable and His Literary Correspondents*, 3 vols. (Edinburgh, 1873), Vol. III, p. 199; see also Scott's letter of 30 September 1821 to his own publisher, Archibald Constable, in which he calls Richardson 'a heavy dog but I fear we cannot do without him' (Walter Scott, *The Letters of Sir Walter Scott*, ed. H. J. C. Grierson, 12 vols. (Constable, 1934), Vol. VII, p. 15.
11 See Michael Gamer, 'A Select Collection: Barbauld, Scott, and the Rise of the (Reprinted) Novel', in Jillian Heydt-Stevenson and Charlotte Sussman

(eds.), *Recognizing the Romantic Novel: New Histories of British Fiction, 1780–1830* (Liverpool University Press, 2010), pp. 155–91; Michael Sadleir, xix *Century Fiction, A Bibliographical Record Based on His Own Collection*, 2 vols. (Constable, 1951), Vol. ii, pp. 86–176; Keymer and Sabor, *'Pamela' in the Marketplace*, pp. 206–15; and Leah Price, *The Anthology and the Rise of the Novel: From Richardson to George Eliot* (Cambridge University Press, 2000), pp. 50–2, 58–61.

12 Barbauld, *Correspondence*, Vol. i, p. xxvii.
13 Theodore Roosevelt, *Theodore Roosevelt: An Autobiography*, intro. Elting Morison (Da Capo Press, 1985), p. 12.
14 Lady Mary Wortley Montagu to the countess of Bute, 22 September 1755, in *The Complete Letters of Lady Mary Wortley Montagu*, ed. Robert Halsband, 3 vols. (Clarendon Press, 1965–7), Vol. iii, p. 90.
15 Waldman, 'The Man who Made the Novel', p. 89.

CHAPTER 7

Critical Reception to 1900

Brian Corman

Since the publication of *Pamela*, Richardson has polarised his critics. His novels were bestsellers; he had a huge number of admirers that included some of Britain's and Europe's most sophisticated readers, and he had many antagonists. The opposition between Richardson and one antagonist, Henry Fielding, provided a dialectic that continued to pervade the criticism of the later eighteenth and nineteenth centuries, as did issues of class, gender, and morality that excited readers and divided opinions during Richardson's lifetime. The Richardson–Fielding opposition was often used to define these issues: middle-class Richardson versus well-born Fielding, feminine Richardson versus masculine Fielding, priggish Richardson versus licentious Fielding; and they continued to influence Richardson's reception as well as that of the novel more generally, joined over time by questions about Richardson's epistolary form and the challenges posed by fiction from an increasingly distant historical past.

A rare point of agreement between Richardson and Fielding was that they had created a 'new species of writing' (Richardson to Aaron Hill, 1741), one that did not recognise kinship with most earlier prose fiction, especially earlier British prose fiction. Their campaign to dissociate themselves from their predecessors was so successful that they were widely recognised as the fathers of the novel and its greatest practitioners until the early nineteenth century. Their high reputation was bolstered by a widely held belief that after the death of Smollett in 1771, the novel went into a serious if not fatal decline.

Eighteenth-century critics who placed a premium on the moral function of literature valued Richardson. His friend Samuel Johnson's praise of him for having 'taught the passions to move at the command of virtue' succinctly captures their position.[1] And Johnson was not alone in preferring Richardson to the morally suspect Fielding. In *The Progress of Romance*, Clara Reeve presents both sides in the form of a dialogue between two women, Euphrasia (Reeve's alter ego) and Sophronia (a less learned novel reader), and one man, Hortensius (a sceptic about the value of novels). Reeve, through Euphrasia, clearly thinks Richardson is the greatest English novelist to date. She acknowledges Fielding's superiority in wit and learning, but considers Richardson's strengths – morality and exemplary characters – far more important. Hortensius dismisses Richardson as 'a writer all your own; your sex are more obliged to him and *Addison*, than to all other men-authors'. Euphrasia counters that Richardson provides a far better model for young women than Aphra Behn, Delarivier Manley, or Eliza Haywood had done. She adds that Fielding 'certainly painted human nature as it is, rather than as *it ought to be*'.[2]

The opposite assessment was made by Richard Cumberland, who acknowledges that Richardson's epistolary style 'perhaps' gives 'a natural scope to pathetic descriptions', but argues that 'fables replete with humourous situations, characteristic dialogue, and busy plot, are better suited' to the novel, which is why *Tom Jones* is 'universally allowed the most perfect work of its sort in ours, or probably any other language'.[3] Cumberland's essay fuelled Anna Seward's defence of Richardson as Fielding's moral superior. While *Clarissa* had often been recommended from the pulpit and was described by no less an authority than Johnson as 'not only the first *novel*, but perhaps the first *work* in our language, splendid in point and genius, and calculated to promote the dearest interests of religion and virtue', *Tom Jones*, for all its engaging qualities, remained 'inimical to good sense, discretion, and morality'.[4]

James Boswell, in turn, took issue with Johnson's judgment 'that the virtues of Fielding's heroes were the vices of a truly good man', arguing that Fielding was 'ever favourable to honour and honesty, and cherishes the benevolent and generous affections'. Boswell also recorded a discussion of Richardson and Fielding that he had instigated with high praise for Fielding. Johnson responded with an endorsement of Richardson's pronouncement that 'had he not known who Fielding was, he should have believed he was an ostler. Sir, there is more knowledge of the heart in one letter of Richardson's, than in all of "Tom Jones".' Johnson even defended Richardson from claims that the length of his novels made him 'tedious': 'Why, Sir, if you were to read Richardson for the story, your impatience would be so much fretted that you would hang yourself. But you must read him for the sentiment.'[5]

Cumberland also raised concerns about Richardson's influence on the moral values of his readers, especially in *Clarissa*. He was not alone. Vicesimus Knox, the influential master of Tonbridge School, was suspicious of all modern novels, though he was prepared to tolerate Richardson and a few others as the best of a dangerous lot. He acknowledged that Richardson wrote with 'the purest of intentions of promoting virtue', but still thought that it 'would be safer to conceal' scenes and sentiments 'which would be more advantageous to early virtue not to admit'.[6] But these remained minority views. Germaine de Staël expressed the majority view in her 'Essay on Fictions' (1795), a defence of novels on moral grounds, that Richardson was able to capture real life in such a way that 'the results of experience come down to the morality of actions and the advantages of virtue'.[7]

Systematic critical attention to the novel began in the early nineteenth century. The history of the British novel was a Regency invention, and the reputations and canons of novelists were first determined by the tastes and values of Regency critics. The three most important novel critics of the period were Anna Laetitia Barbauld, John Colin Dunlop, and Sir Walter Scott, respectively the producers of the first critical anthology, the first history, and the first biographical-critical study of the novel. Their placement of Richardson determined the course of discussions about him for the remainder of the century.

Barbauld had already edited Richardson's letters before producing her anthology. Her edition of the letters includes a biography with critical reflections. She divided the novels into three groups based on their mode of narration: third-person (her favourite because of its flexibility), epistolary (good at capturing the moment but lacking in probability), and first-person (her least favourite because of the limitations of a single voice and perspective). Barbauld considered Richardson 'the first author who has given celebrity to the modern novel';[8] she included *Clarissa* and *Sir Charles Grandison* in her anthology of twenty-eight novels. Dunlop's history is an encyclopedic account from earliest times; British fiction is given but a single chapter in his three-volume study. He divided British fiction into three groups: serious, comic, and romantic. His preference was for the latter, and Ann Radcliffe was his favourite novelist. Comic novels were not to his taste. Of serious novels, Richardson was 'at the head of the ... class'.[9]

Scott's contribution began as prefaces for another anthology, Ballantyne's Novelist's Library (1821–4), a project that was neither successful nor completed. The model for Scott's 'Biographical and Critical Sketches' was Samuel Johnson's *Lives of the Poets* (1779–81). Like Johnson's *Lives*, Scott's 'Sketches' were collected and published as *Lives of the Novelists*, and they proved to be one of the most influential works on the novel throughout the nineteenth century. Scott saw Richardson as having rescued the novel from the romance tradition, with its 'huge folios of inanity', through the presentation of realistic characters who were 'placed before us bare-faced, in all the actual changes of feature and complexion, and all the light and shade of human passion'. Scott saw Fielding's ridicule of *Pamela* as unfortunate because of its importance as 'a tale so true to nature'. But it is *Clarissa* 'on which Richardson's fame as a classic of England will rest for ever', since 'no work has appeared before, perhaps none has appeared since, containing so many direct appeals to the passions, stated too in a manner so irresistible'.[10] *Sir Charles Grandison* was the least successful of Richardson's novels for Scott; his assessments hold for the majority of readers to this day.

Barbauld, Dunlop, and Scott brought a new level of balanced, thoughtful criticism to their evaluations of British novelists. But Richardson's reputation was also influenced by their less thorough contemporaries in less comprehensive formats and venues. William Hazlitt admired Fielding and Smollett as observers of human life but found capturing Richardson more challenging since he 'seemed to spin his materials entirely out of his own brain, as if there had been nothing existing in the world beyond the little room in which he sat writing'. Hazlitt acknowledges that Richardson's attention to minute detail helps overcome his artificiality, but finds that 'his infinite circumspection, his exact process of ratiocination and calculation, which gives such an appearance of coldness and formality to most of his characters … makes prudes of his women and coxcombs of his men'. Nevertheless, in the end, 'we feel the same interest in the story as if it were our own'.[11]

Debates about Richardson's morality intensified in the nineteenth century, often linked to comparisons that increasingly favoured Fielding. The opinions of such influential critics as Coleridge and Leigh Hunt did Richardson's reputation no good. Coleridge declared that 'I do loath the cant which can recommend Pamela and Clarissa Harlowe as strictly moral, though they poison the imagination of the young with continued doses of *tinct. lyttae*, while Tom Jones is prohibited as loose.'[12] Hunt echoed: 'How charming, how wholesome, Fielding is! To take him up after Richardson, is like emerging from a sick room heated by stoves, into an open lawn, on a breezy day in May.'[13] But Richardson continued to have his defenders. Jane Porter asserted: 'I have ever believed the novels of Richardson to be unequalled. Their pure morality, and their unity of design' earned them the honorific of 'epic poems in prose'.[14] And Frances Burney wrote to her son in 1822: 'Had the last volume of Clarissa failed to move you, you might certainly have set yourself down as invulnerable; for it has the deepest tragic powers that the pen can address to the heart.'[15]

By the 1820s, the eighteenth-century novel had been historicised, and the predominant mode was a Whiggish view of its development. Unlike poetry (Homer) or drama (Shakespeare), the novel had yet to have its golden age. It was a young and ever-improving form, and its critics judged the past by what it contributed to the present. Richardson and Fielding remained the most admired early novelists, but while Fielding's popularity was constant or on the rise, Richardson's began to decline. Growing nationalism accompanied by a devaluing of sensibility and an intensification of the gendering of the novel all worked in Fielding's favour and against Richardson. These tendencies continued to increase over the remainder of the century.

With the unprecedented success of Scott's Waverley novels, followed soon after by the similar success of Dickens, the novel finally attained respectability as a literary form. Earlier novelists were not granted the new respectability retroactively. By the 1840s, the recognition of Austen as the master at representing women and their concerns – replacing Richardson, who had hitherto held that position – removed one need for Richardson in the canon. Richardson remained feminised for many critics, but this was less than ever an honorific. Thackeray's famous vignette exemplifies the mix of class and gender stereotypes that damaged Richardson's reputation

> Fielding ... couldn't do otherwise than laugh at the puny, cockney bookseller, pouring out endless volumes of sentimental twaddle, and hold him up to scorn as a moll-coddle and a milksop. *His* genius had been nursed on sack-posset, and not on dishes of tea. *His* muse had sung loudest in tavern choruses ... Richardson's goddess was attended by old maids and dowagers, and fed on muffins and bohea.[16]

Such views as Thackeray's helped further devalue Richardson's reputation. Demand for his novels was so weak that major Victorian reprint series such as Bentley's, Roscoe's, Routledge's, Bohn's, and Tauchnitz's did not include his novels. In terms of popular readership, he was all but forgotten, but he remained an important and foundational figure for critics and literary historians throughout this period of ever-increasing critical interest in the novel and its history. Most critical works continued to present the history of the novel as progressive, so interest in the eighteenth-century novel remained largely historical. Discussions continued to be structured around comparisons of Richardson and Fielding with preferences consistently, but not exclusively, going to Fielding. But neither eighteenth-century master met the standards of critics who considered Victorian realism the full realisation of the potential of the novel.

Hippolyte Taine argued that English morality vacillates within a set of dualities: conscience versus instinct, grace versus nature, rule versus liberty. For Taine, Richardson represents the triumph of rule and Fielding that of nature. Taine sees Richardson as 'delicate … gentle, nervous, often ill, with a taste for the society of women … whose only fault was a timid vanity'. Conscience and Christian casuistry dominate Richardson's writing; the results are novels unequalled in their age in the exploration of subtle moral dilemmas. The explorations are, however, flawed by their representation: a writer should 'insinuate morality', not 'inflict it'.[17] Nevertheless, Taine considers Richardson the best eighteenth-century novelist, since he finds Fielding's faults greater.

Taine's balanced analysis was shared by the majority of serious Victorian critics – though his preference was not. For Anthony Trollope, the divide is defined as Richardson the 'saint' and Fielding the 'sinner'. Richardson represents 'high-toned feminine virtue', and Trollope prefers Fielding's more masculine perspective on reality.[18] His conclusion, however, is that neither will pass the test of time since better novels continue to appear in his more enlightened age. George Eliot echoed Trollope's assessment of the eighteenth-century novel, judging that even 'Richardson's pictures of life' are 'revolting to our more fastidious tastes'.[19]

For David Masson, Richardson was 'the nervous, tea-drinking, pompous little printer, coddled … by a bevy of admiring women, who nursed his vanity'. Richardson's novels were rarely read, 'and it cannot be helped', since 'there are the novels of a hundred years between us and him' and 'time is short'; Masson believed that Richardson deserved a fuller analysis than offered by attackers such as Coleridge or defenders such as Macaulay (who considered Richardson a 'prose Shakespeare'), and he provides that analysis. He respected Richardson as a moralist and as a producer of 'pathetic and tragic' effect. But the novelist's field of understanding was too limited; there is more to life than 'romances of love and its consequences'.[20] Masson preferred Fielding.

Leslie Stephen also comments on Richardson's 'celebrity', unaccompanied by 'popularity'. He was no longer read. 'His second-rate, eighteenth-century priggishness and his two-penny tract morality' would seem to be the most obvious cause. Yet Stephen notes the ongoing continental admiration from Diderot to George Sand to Alfred de Musset. Richardson's femininity makes him the rare male novelist who writes about women well; his major flaw is that same femininity. He was 'a man of true genius', but he was oblivious to 'the influence of nature'.[21] Stephen much prefers Austen. Later in the century, Edmund Gosse repeated the now familiar line. Richardson was 'a man of unquestionable genius' with 'extraordinary insight into female character'. Fielding, however, 'is the greatest of English novelists' because 'he knew men ten times better'.[22] The last quarter of the nineteenth century brought the beginning of academic criticism. Classroom lectures by Sidney Lanier and William Minto helped usher in this addition to the literature on the novel; their assessments emphasise Richardson's historical importance.[23] But both also consider him far too long-winded and too feminine. Both prefer Fielding. Walter Raleigh echoes most of their views, though he resists their gendering of Richardson.[24] Finally, 1900 saw Clara Thomson's book-length study of Richardson, the first since Barbauld's – an early sign of the reassessment to take place in the twentieth century.[25]

Notes

1 Samuel Johnson, *Rambler*, 97 (19 February 1751), in W. J. Bate and Albrecht B. Strauss (eds.), *The Rambler*, in *The Yale Edition of the Works of Samuel Johnson*, 23 vols. (Yale University Press, 1969), Vol. IV, pp. 153–9 (p. 153).

2 Clara Reeve, *The Progress of Romance*, 2 vols. (Colchester, 1785), Vol. I, p. 135.

3 Richard Cumberland, 'Letter', *Observer*, 27 (1785), repr. in Ioan Williams (ed.), *Novel and Romance 1700–1800: A Documentary Record* (London: Routledge and Kegan Paul, 1970), pp. 332–5 (p. 333).

4 Samuel Johnson quoted in Anna Seward, *Variety*, 25 (1787), repr. in Williams, *Novel and Romance*, pp. 357–66 (p. 358).

5 Boswell, *Life of Johnson*, Vol. II, pp. 49, 174, 175.

6 Vicesimus Knox, 'On Novel Reading', repr. in Williams, *Novel and Romance*, p. 304.

7 Germaine de Staël, 'Essay on Fictions' (1795), in *Major Writings of Germaine de Staël*, ed. and trans. Vivian Folkenflik (Columbia University Press, 1987), pp. 60–78 (p. 71).

8 Anna Laetitia Barbauld, *The British Novelists*, 50 vols. (London, 1810), Vol. I, p. 63.

9 John Colin Dunlop, *The History of Fiction* (1814), 3rd edn, 3 vols. (London, 1856), Vol. II, p. 410.

10 Sir Walter Scott, 'Samuel Richardson', in *Lives of the Novelists*, in *Sir Walter Scott on Novelists and Fiction, ed. Ioan Williams* (Routledge and Kegan Paul, 1968), pp. 14–32 (pp. 22, 25, 31).

11 William Hazlitt, *Lectures on the Comic Writers*, ed. Arthur Johnston (Dent, 1963), p. 117.

12 Samuel Taylor Coleridge in *Marginalia ii*, ed. George Whalley, in *The Collected Works of Samuel Taylor Coleridge*, 23 vols. (Princeton University Press, 1984), Vol. XII, p. 693.

13 Leigh Hunt, *Periodical Essays, 1822–38*, in *The Selected Writings of Leigh Hunt*, ed. Robert Morrison, 6 vols. (Pickering & Chatto, 2003), Vol. III, p. 309.

14 Jane Porter, 'Preface', in *Thaddeus of Warsaw* (Boston, 1809), p. 7.

15 Frances Burney, *Mayfair 1818–24*, in *The Journals and Letters of Fanny Burney (Madame D'Arblay)*, ed. Joyce Hemlow, 12 vols. (Clarendon Press, 1984), Vol. XI, p. 376.

16 William Makepeace Thackeray, *The English Humourists of the Eighteenth Century* (1853), ed. Edgar F. Harden (University of Michigan Press, 2007), p. 84.

17 Hippolyte Taine, *History of English Literature* (1872), trans. Henri Van Laun, 3 vols. (Chatto & Windus, 1890), Vol. III, p. 270.

18 Anthony Trollope, 'On English Prose Fiction as a Rational Amusement' (1870), in *Four Lectures*, ed. Morris L. Parrish (Constable, 1938), pp. 94–124 (p. 101).

19 George Eliot, 'The Novels of Richardson, Fielding, and Smollett', in John Charles Olmsted (ed.), *A Victorian Art of Fiction: Essays on the Novel in British Periodicals*, 3 vols. (Garland, 1979), Vol. II, p. 86.

20 David Masson, *British Novelists and Their Styles* (Cambridge, 1859), pp. 103, 107, 108, 118, 119.

21 Leslie Stephen, 'Richardson's Novels', in Olmsted, *Victorian Art of Fiction*, Vol. II, pp. 599, 600, 619.

22 Edmund Gosse, *A History of English Literature (1660–1780)* (Macmillan, 1889), pp. 250, 261, 258.

23 Sidney Lanier, *The English Novel: A Study in the Development of Personality* (Scribner's, 1897); William Minto, *The Literature of the Georgian Era* (Harper, 1895).

24 Walter Raleigh, *The English Novel* (London, 1895).

25 Clara L. Thomson, *Samuel Richardson: A Critical and Biographical Study* (Horace Marshall, 1900).

CHAPTER 8

Critical Reception since 1900

Albert J. Rivero

Looking back to Anna Laetitia Barbauld's edition of Richardson's correspondence (1804) in 1900, Clara Linklater Thomson declares that Barbauld's biographical sketch preceding the letters 'still forms the chief source of information concerning a writer whose importance in the development of English fiction would seem to render necessary a cheaper and more accessible biography'. Thomson draws from Barbauld's memoir, as well as unpublished letters and other contemporary sources, for the biographical information in her book; 'the critical chapters', she explains, 'are intended chiefly as a guide to those readers who are quite unacquainted with Richardson's novels'.[1] Thomson sounds a note heard throughout the nineteenth century, that, while Richardson is an important author, his novels are no longer read. In *Samuel Richardson* (1902), Austin Dobson identifies 'a feminine streak' in the author and finds the novels neglected because long-winded, not likely to appeal 'to-day, when with the headlong hurry of life, the language of literature seems to tend ... towards ... the short-cut and the snap-shot'.[2] Thomson and Dobson thus inaugurate a century of scholarship that would reassert Richardson's importance by correcting and enriching the biographical and bibliographical record and giving his works the close critical attention they demand, eventually moving beyond the generally reductive nineteenth-century view of Richardson as dull printer and untutored genius; effeminate in sensibility (as opposed to the manly Fielding); and humourless, pompous, religious prig.

Important articles about or referencing Richardson appeared in the opening decades of the twentieth century: on his influence and his relations to French fiction, on English epistolary fiction before *Pamela*, and on the middle-class reader and the English novel.[3] Brian W. Downs's *Richardson* (1928) and Paul Dottin's *Samuel Richardson, 1689–1761, imprimeur de Londres, auteur de 'Pamela', 'Clarissa', et 'Grandison'* (1931), coupled with the publication of the Shakespeare Head edition of the novels (1929), attested to Richardson's growing critical reputation. In the 1930s, Alan

Dugald McKillop and William Merritt Sale, Jr, the two most influential Richardson critics of the first half of the twentieth century, began to publish their indispensable essays and books. In correcting factual errors and providing new information, McKillop's *Samuel Richardson: Printer and Novelist* (1936) became the first authoritative biographical and critical study. Supporting bibliographical descriptions of lifetime editions of Richardson's novels and other works with facsimiles of their title pages, Sale's *Samuel Richardson: A Bibliographical Record of His Literary Career with Historical Notes* (1936) set a high standard for bibliographers of eighteenth-century texts, as well as providing bibliographical information for future editors of the novels.

In the 1940s, T. C. Duncan Eaves, the future co-biographer of Richardson, completed his Harvard doctoral dissertation, 'Graphic Illustrations of the Principal English Novelists of the Eighteenth Century' (1944), ushering in the close critical scrutiny of such seemingly peripheral extra-textual features; his influential 'Graphic Illustration of the Novels of Samuel Richardson, 1740–1810' would appear in 1951. In 1943 McKillop attributed *The Apprentice's Vade Mecum* to Richardson; found real-life precedents for the mock marriage in *Pamela* (1947); and gave scholarly support to the old anecdote that villagers in Slough celebrated Pamela's wedding by ringing church bells (1949). In a major and influential study of 1948, F. R. Leavis excluded both Fielding and Richardson from the great tradition of English novelists, partially salvaging the latter 'as a major fact in the background of Jane Austen', echoing the well-worn cliché that Richardson, while strong in his 'analysis of emotional and moral states', is limited in his range and makes undue demands on the reader's time and attention.[4]

In 1950, Sale published *Samuel Richardson: Master Printer*, a descriptive study of books printed by Richardson, along with reproductions of his printer's ornaments, which would remain the authority on this topic until superseded by Keith Maslen's *Samuel Richardson of London, Printer* (2001). Several important essays appeared during the first half of the decade: Frank Kermode's 'Richardson and Fielding' (1950); McKillop's 'Epistolary Technique in Richardson's Novels' (1951); Ian Watt's 'Defoe and Richardson on Homer' (1952); Dorothy Van Ghent's 'On *Clarissa Harlowe*' (1953); and Christopher Hill's 'Clarissa Harlowe and her Times' (1955). In a typical all-male grouping of the period, Richardson appeared alongside Defoe, Fielding, Smollett, and Sterne in McKillop's *The Early Masters of English Fiction* (1956). Reducing the number of foundational eighteenth-century novelists to Defoe, Fielding, and Richardson, Watt's *The Rise of the Novel* (1957) offered what remains, arguably, the most compelling account of Richardson's role in defining the protocols of realism for English prose fiction in the 1740s and 1750s. If McKillop and Sale shaped Richardson scholarship in the first half of the twentieth century, Watt, blending histori-cal sociology with literary analysis, founded a new species of Richardsonian criticism, whose emphasis on class and gender informs our readings of the novels to this day.

In the 1960s, T. C. Duncan Eaves and Ben D. Kimpel published a series of articles on topics ranging from Richardson's dealings with the publisher of *Pamela* (1960) and his London houses (1962) to the compo-sition and revisions of *Clarissa* (1968), all leading up to the appearance of their still definitive *Samuel Richardson: A Biography* (1971). Leslie Fiedler (1960) claimed Richardson (with Goethe and Rousseau) as one of the sentimental 'founding fathers' of the novel, asserting that 'a continuing tradition of prose fiction did not begin until the love affair of Lovelace and Clarissa (a demythicized Don Juan and a secularized goddess of Christian love) had been imagined'.[5] Fiedler has had an enormous influence, sometimes unacknowledged, on Richardson scholars who approach the novels from psychological or mythical contexts, such as Morris Golden in *Richardson's Characters* (1963) and Cynthia Griffin Wolff in *Samuel Richardson and the Eighteenth-Century Puritan Character* (1972). Though informed by a dismissive attitude towards Richardson and his novel, Bernard Kreissman's *Pamela-Shamela: A Study of Burlesques, Parodies, and Adaptations of Richardson's 'Pamela'* (1960) surveyed works appear-ing during the so-called *Pamela* craze. Martin C. Battestin's introduc-tion to his Riverside edition of *Shamela* and *Joseph Andrews* (1961) gave eloquent re-enunciation to the old opposition between manly Fielding and feminine Richardson, much to the latter's detriment, while William Park's 'Fielding *and* Richardson' (1966) emphasised the considerable common ground between the two authors. Robert Adams Day's *Told in Letters* (1966) and John Richetti's *Popular Fiction before Richardson* (1969) described the fictional milieu from which Richardson's novels emerged, thus providing a much needed corrective to Watt's male-centred 'rise' narrative. Ira Konigsberg's *Samuel Richardson and the Dramatic Novel* (1968) illustrated the novelist's use of theatre and dramatic techniques. Reaffirming Richardson's credentials as a canonical author, two critical anthologies were published in 1969. *Richardson: A Collection of Critical Essays*, edited by John Carroll, reprinted, among others, excerpts from works by Golden, Hill, McKillop, Van Ghent, and Watt, mentioned above. *Twentieth-Century Interpretations of 'Pamela'*, edited by Rosemary Cowler, included material from McKillop and Watt as well as from pieces cited earlier in this paragraph, by Day, Fiedler, Golden, Kreissman, and Park.

In the 1970s, though interest in *Pamela* remained strong and *Sir Charles Grandison* (after the publication of Jocelyn Harris's Oxford edition in 1972) began to gain more ground, *Clarissa* emerged as the main focus of critical attention, beginning with Irwin Gopnik's linguistic approach in *A Theory of Style and Richardson's 'Clarissa'* (1970) and ending with the deconstructive demolition of the heroine in William Warner's *Reading 'Clarissa': The Struggles of Interpretation* (1979). John Preston's two incisive chapters on the novel in *The Created Self: The Reader's Role in Eighteenth-Century Fiction* (1970) gave early evidence that reader-response criticism was particularly well-suited to Richardson's works, and especially *Clarissa*. Important essays on the novel appeared throughout the decade, ranging from John Carroll's 'Lovelace as Tragic Hero' (1972) and Sheldon Sacks's '*Clarissa* and the Tragic Traditions' (1972), to Leo Braudy's 'Penetration and Impenetrability in *Clarissa*' (1974) and a chapter establishing *Clarissa*'s central place in the history of the sentimental novel in R. F. Brissenden's *Virtue in Distress: Studies in the Novel of Sentiment from Richardson to Sade* (1974), to Judith Wilt's provocative but ultimately unconvincing 'He Could Go No Farther: A Modest Proposal about Lovelace and Clarissa' (1977), suggesting that Clarissa was raped not by Lovelace but by the prostitutes in Mrs Sinclair's brothel. Several books, focusing on various aspects of Richardson's novels, also appeared during this decade: Donald L. Ball's *Samuel Richardson's Theory of Fiction* (1971), Mark Kinkead-Weekes's *Samuel Richardson: Dramatic Novelist* (1973), Elizabeth Bergen Brophy's *Samuel Richardson: The Triumph of Craft* (1974), and Gerald Levin's *Richardson the Novelist* (1978). Margaret Anne Doody's wide-ranging *A Natural Passion: A Study of the Novels of Samuel Richardson* (1974), its close readings informed by literary and theological contexts, introduced a powerful voice in Richardson studies.

Clarissa's rape became the focal point of three major books published in the early 1980s. Feminist in emphasis but deploying different critical methodologies, Terry Castle's *Clarissa's Cyphers* (1982), Terry Eagleton's *The Rape of Clarissa* (1982), and Rita Goldberg's *Sex and Enlightenment: Women in Richardson and Diderot* (1984) agreed on the misogyny of the critical tradition on this topic. One of the consequences of feminist critical interest in Richardson in the 1970s and 1980s was the move away from emphasising his 'feminine' sensibilities to gauging the extent of his 'feminism' – that is, whether Richardson was advocating for women's liberation from patriarchal constraints or simply reasserting the status quo, especially in light of what some critics have construed as his rigid (if not downright bigoted) religious views. During these years a convincing counter-narrative began to emerge – for example, in Jocelyn Harris's *Samuel Richardson* (1987) – in the portrayal of a more nuanced Richardson, whose religious views, rather than being retrograde and 'Puritan' (an erroneous label, given that he was an Anglican), were in tune with those of the early English feminist Mary Astell, whose arguments for women's equality were informed by her profound Christian faith.[6] James Louis Fortuna's *'The Unsearchable Wisdom of God': A Study of Providence in Richardson's 'Pamela'* (1980) explored a prominent theme in *Pamela*, of importance to all of Richardson's novels. In the wake of such comprehensive accounts as Doody's and Kinkead-Weekes's, Carol Houlihan Flynn's *Samuel Richardson: A Man of Letters* (1982) offered a generous overview of Richardson's career. Gerard A. Barker's *Grandison's Heirs: The Paragon's Progress in the Late Eighteenth-Century Novel* (1985) and Sylvia Kasey Marks's *'Sir Charles Grandison': The Compleat Conduct Book* showed growing appreciation of Richardson's last novel. Michael McKeon's *The Origins of the English Novel, 1600–1740* (1987), while recalibrating Watt's Marxist 'rise' narrative, yielded disappointing results in its superficial reading of *Pamela*, the only Richardson novel closely analysed. Richard Gordon Hannaford's *Samuel Richardson: An Annotated Bibliography of Critical Studies* (1980) and Sarah W. R. Smith's *Samuel Richardson: A Reference Guide* (1984) surveyed assessments of Richardson's work from the eighteenth century to the 1970s. Siobhán Kilfeather's 'The Rise of Richardson Criticism' expertly surveyed critical trends into the 1980s. Kilfeather's piece appeared in *Samuel Richardson: Tercentenary Essays* (1989), edited by Margaret Anne Doody and Peter Sabor – one of two indispensable collections of original Richardson scholarship appearing in the 1980s, the other being *Samuel Richardson: Passion and Prudence* (1986), edited by Valerie Grosvenor Myer. Harold Bloom's *Modern Critical Views: Samuel Richardson* (1987) reprinted ten essays or book excerpts, including ones from books noted above by Goldberg, Kinkead-Weekes, and Watt.

Usually regarded as a failure by critics from Barbauld to Doody, *Pamela in Her Exalted Condition*, Richardson's sequel to his spectacularly successful first novel, began to receive less dismissive notice in the 1980s – for example, in Terry Castle's 'The Recarnivalization of Pamela: Richardson's "Pamela," Part 2', in *Masquerade and Civilization* (1986) and Lois Chaber's 'From Moral Man to Godly Man: "Mr Locke" and Mr B in Part 2 of *Pamela*' (1988). Interest in the sequel continued into the 1990s, in influential essays by Ruth Perry, 'Colonizing the Breast: Sexuality and Maternity in Eighteenth-Century England' (1992); Toni Bowers, '"A Point of Conscience": Breastfeeding and Maternal Authority in *Pamela 2*' (1995); and Janet Aikins, 'Pamela's Use of Locke's Words' (1996).

Clarissa, however, remained at the centre of critical attention, beginning with the publication by AMS Press, in 1990, of an eight-volume reprint of the third edition of the novel (1753), introduced by Florian Stuber, thus launching the ambitious but ill-fated *Clarissa* Project. After a long hiatus, one of several volumes of contextual and critical materials planned for the series finally appeared: *Clarissa and Her Readers: New Essays for The Clarissa Project* (1999), edited by Carol Houlihan Flynn and Edward Copeland. Critical books on the novel continued to be published throughout the decade: Thomas O. Beebee, *'Clarissa' on the Continent: Translation and Seduction* (1990); Lois E. Bueler, *'Clarissa's' Plots* (1994); Donnalee Frega, *Speaking in Hunger: Gender, Discourse, and Consumption in 'Clarissa'* (1998); and Gordon D. Fulton, *Styles of Meaning and Meanings of Style in Richardson's 'Clarissa'* (1999). *The Annotations in Lady Bradshaigh's Copy of 'Clarissa'* (1998), edited by Janine Barchas (with the collaboration of Gordon D. Fulton), gave wider circulation to the critical responses of one of Richardson's most astute contemporary readers. Tom Keymer's *Richardson's 'Clarissa' and the Eighteenth-Century Reader* (1992) marked a significant turn in our understanding of Richardson as epistolary novelist. Questioning the traditional assumption that 'Richardson turned to letters simply as a convention for achieving dramatic immediacy', Keymer examined 'the experience of *writing*' in order to argue that the novels 'are preoccupied ... by the deformations that arise from the rhetorical or performative tendencies of first-person discourse'.[7]

Among studies spanning all the novels, two deserve special mention: Tassie Gwilliam's *Samuel Richardson's Fictions of Gender* (1993), a close interrogation of ideological contradictions inherent in Richardson's representations of male and female characters, and Stephanie Fysh's *The Work(s) of Samuel Richardson* (1997), a brief but useful review of Richardson's career as author and printer. Allen Michie's *Richardson and Fielding: The Dynamics of a Critical Rivalry* (1999) charted the reception history of both novelists from the eighteenth century to Ian Watt. *New Essays on Samuel Richardson* (1996), edited by Albert J. Rivero, featured thirteen essays analysing in depth issues regarding Richardson's biography and literary achievement. Though appearing in 2001, *Passion and Virtue: Essays on the Novels of Samuel Richardson*, edited by David Blewett, collected fourteen of thirty essays on Richardson's novels originally published in *Eighteenth-Century Fiction* from 1988 to 1999.

Critical trends from the twentieth century continue to be evident in the first decade-and-a-half of the twenty-first. Gender is still of paramount concern, as in Kathleen M. Oliver's *Samuel Richardson, Dress, and Discourse* (2008) and Bonnie Latimer's *Making Gender, Culture, and the Self in the Fiction of Samuel Richardson* (2013). The move away from regarding Richardson and Fielding as the 'founding fathers' of the English novel and seeing them instead as heirs to a rich tradition of women-centred fiction, exemplified by Aphra Behn, Delarivier Manley, Eliza Haywood, and Penelope Aubin, has by now become canonical.[8] Theology remains an important context as well. In *Reason and Religion in 'Clarissa': Samuel Richardson and 'The Famous Mr Norris, of Bemerton'* (2009), for example, E. Derek Taylor has identified a crucial influence on Richardson's most doctrinally complex novel. *Approaches to Teaching the Novels of Samuel Richardson* (2006), edited by Jocelyn Harris and Lisa Zunshine, offers a good pedagogical guide; its editors' optimistic assertions notwithstanding, it is not clear that, beyond *Pamela*, Richardson's novels are much taught these days, certainly not to undergraduates. Nor is there any evidence that Richardson, whatever his rise in stock in the academy in the twentieth century, has fared well with common readers since the nineteenth. Richardson's prolixity continues to present difficulties, as evinced by the publication in 2010 of an abridgment of *Clarissa* (edited by Toni Bowers and John Richetti) by Broadview Press. With the publication of *The 'Pamela' Controversy: Criticisms and Adaptations of Samuel Richardson's 'Pamela'* (2001), edited by Thomas Keymer and Peter Sabor, and their co-authored monograph, *'Pamela' in the Marketplace: Literary Controversy and Print Culture in Eighteenth-Century Britain and Ireland* (2005), Richardson's first novel has moved once again to the centre of critical attention. The recent publication of scholarly editions of both *Pamela* and its sequel (2011, 2012), along with a volume comprising the early works (2012), will no doubt influence and shape future Richardson criticism, as will the appearance of new editions of *Clarissa* and *Sir Charles Grandison*, as well as of his letters, over the next decade, in the Cambridge Edition of the Works and Correspondence of Samuel Richardson. A forthcoming wide-market edition of *Pamela in Her Exalted Condition*, in preparation by Broadview Press, might spur critical interest in Richardson's least known novel.

Because of the multiplicity and complexity of his texts, his formal innovations, his focus on rank, and his obsession with human sexuality, Richardson was perfectly positioned to attract attention from practitioners of the major critical trends of the twentieth century, from new critics to deconstructionists, from reader-response critics to book historians, from Marxists to feminists, from old to new historians, from Freudians to Jungians, from historians of pornography to historians of religion. Yet other, less text-centred critical movements have left Richardson largely untouched. There is no colonial or postcolonial Richardson, no ecological Richardson, very little on Richardson and race or empire or slavery. As his first readers recognised, Richardson derives his peculiar strength as a novelist from his unswerving gaze on the secrets of the human heart.

Notes

1 Clara Linklater Thomson, *Samuel Richardson: A Biographical and Critical Study* (Horace Marshall; M. F. Mansfield, 1900), p. v.
2 Austin Dobson, *Samuel Richardson* (Macmillan, 1902), pp. 196–7.
3 See, for example, Frederick S. Boas, 'Richardson's Novels and Their Influence', *Essays and Studies by Members of the English Association*, 2 (1911), 37–70; R. S. Crane, 'Richardson, Warburton, and French Fiction', *Modern Language Review*, 17 (1922), 17–23; Helen Sard Hughes, 'English Epistolary Fiction before *Pamela*', in *Manly Anniversary Studies in Language and Literature* (University of Chicago Press, 1923), pp. 156–69; and Helen Sard Hughes, 'The Middle-Class Reader and the English Novel', *Journal of English and Germanic Philology*, 25 (1926), 362–78.
4 F. R. Leavis, *The Great Tradition* (London: Chatto & Windus, 1948), p. 4.
5 Leslie Fiedler, *Love and Death in the American Novel* (New York: Criterion, 1960), p. xx ('founding fathers' appears on p. 23).
6 Richardson printed the fourth edition of Astell's *Some Reflections upon Marriage* in 1730.
7 Keymer, *Richardson's 'Clarissa'*, p. xvi.
8 See, for example, Ros Ballaster, *Seductive Forms: Women's Amatory Fiction 1684–1740* (Clarendon Press, 1992); and William Beatty Warner, *Licensing Entertainment: The Elevation of Novel Reading in Britain, 1684–1750* (University of California Press, 1998).

PART III

The Print Trade

CHAPTER 9

The Stationers' Company

Ian Gadd

Samuel Richardson was a Stationer. For forty-six years, he was a member of the Stationers' Company, the trade and craft body that regulated London's book trade. At his admission in 1715, its members numbered perhaps around 800, including a handful of women.[1] By his death in 1761, he was one of its most senior members, having sat on its governing body (the Court of Assistants) for two decades, and serving as Master for 1754–5. He attended his last Court meeting less than two months before he died.[2] Three of his executors were Stationers, and two were Assistants: Francis Gosling had served as Master for 1756–7 and Allington Wilde was elected Master on the day of Richardson's death.[3] Richardson's portrait hangs to this day in the Court Room of Stationers' Hall, barely a third of a mile away from where he spent most of his printing career. The Stationers' Company, then, played an enduring role in Richardson's life, but in order to appreciate its significance, we need to understand exactly what it was.

The origins of the Stationers' Company lie in the early fifteenth century with the city's recognition of a body overseeing the trades of Textwriters (non-legal scribes), Limners (who illustrated and illuminated manuscripts), and those who 'use to bind and sell books'. By 1417, 'Stationers' appears as part of the organisation's title, and from 1441 onwards it was known solely as the company of Stationers.[4] 'Stationer' did not have a particular association with paper-selling: rather it was a generic term that accommodated the entirety of the book trade. In the mid-seventeenth century, Thomas Blount complained the term was 'often confounded with Book-seller, and sometimes with Book-binder', and by the eighteenth century, its modern meaning was dominant.[5] The Company's name, however, remained unchanged, and while Richardson described himself as 'printer' in his will, he would have freely acknowledged himself as a 'Stationer' in relation to the Company itself.[6]

The organisation of trades and crafts into distinct bodies was standard urban practice across medieval and early modern Europe. Such bodies oversaw training, wages, and prices; they provided welfare and sociability; and they often ensured quality standards. They enabled city authorities to reach a large proportion of the citizenry: they were used to circulate proclamations, raise money, even recruit soldiers. They were frequently integral to urban governance, with city officers drawn directly from their ranks.

By the seventeenth century, London had several dozen companies. The Stationers' Company was a relatively minor one, ranked about forty-seventh in civic processions. Important crafts and trades, such as those relating to cloth and leather, were represented by several companies. Others were grouped together into more heterogeneous bodies – as was the case with the Stationers' Company, which included booksellers, bookbinders, printers, and paper-sellers. City custom forbade individuals to retail in the city without being a member of a Company, so being a 'freeman' brought commercial privileges. Membership gave access to loans, protected one's family in the case of sickness or death, enabled the binding and freeing of apprentices within the city, and provided a court of arbitration. It also supplied a hierarchy that, with sufficient personal wealth, connections, and ambition, could see an individual rise from freeman, to the privileged rank of 'liveryman' (which came with the right to wear the company's colours at corporate and civic events and to vote in city and parliamentary elections) to more senior positions in the company's governing body.

The usual method of becoming a freeman was by apprenticeship. In London it was also possible if one's father was a freeman at one's birth, which meant one could become a freeman three years earlier than by apprenticeship (at the age of twenty-one rather than twenty-four). In addition, it allowed an individual to join his (or occasionally her) father's company regardless of the craft or trade being practised. (Richardson, the son of a member of the Joiners' Company, could have exercised this right.) Given the disparity in wealth between the companies, their differing practices regarding the number of apprentices that could be assigned to a master, and the various commercial opportunities available within each company, being able to choose one's father's company over a company more directly related to one's trade could bring distinct advantages. Thus, the Stationers' Company never comprised the entirety of the London book trade (there were, for example, many booksellers who were freemen of other companies), nor were all its members active in the book trade (as in the case of an important dynasty of scientific instrument makers who were all Stationers), but nonetheless it was the largest single grouping of book producers and booksellers in the city.[7]

As Richardson himself would have been well aware, the most important event in the history of the Stationers' Company came during the reign of Mary Tudor. From at least the fifteenth century London companies had been seeking incorporation from the Crown in order to establish themselves as legal entities that could enter into contracts, protect their rights at law, and own property. Crucially, incorporation also provided an opportunity to seek powers that extended beyond the city's boundaries and to define the crafts and trades over which a company had jurisdiction: in cases such as the Goldsmiths' and Pewterers' companies, incorporation granted them national rights of search and confiscation for substandard wares.[8] For the Stationers' Company, while its incorporation in 1557 meant that it could now own a hall in its own name, the Act brought with it new rights regarding printing and publishing. No one could print anywhere in England unless he either was a member of the Company or held a royal privilege – a near-monopolisation that in effect restricted printing to London for almost 140 years. Furthermore, incorporation enabled the Company to establish its own system for managing publishing rights.

Prior to 1557, the only way for English printers or publishers to protect their publications from others reprinting them without permission and selling them more cheaply was to seek a privilege, nearly always from the Crown. It was a complex and costly process, and there was no simple way to resolve disputes. For major works, such as Bibles or law books, privileges were a worthwhile investment, but for less important or more topical works, a more straightforward and flexible process was needed. Given that incorporation had, in effect, made the Company the primary printing and publishing authority in the country, it was well placed to develop a system for its members that was reliable, easy, and relatively cheap to use, and that provided a straightforward means for handling disagreements. Any member wishing to publish a work visited Stationers' Hall to seek the permission of the Company's senior officers, who would assess whether the work was likely to affect adversely any other member's existing publication. This was purely a commercial decision; the officers had no power to judge a work's contents. This permission granted the publisher the Company's protection over his work; should any other member publish the same work without permission or publish something that threatened his publication rights, the original publisher could appeal to the Company's Court. The process of approval required only a signature from an officer on the manuscript and the payment of a fee; the formal written 'entrance' of that permission in the 'Register' was not obligatory. By the early seventeenth century, such rights were considered to be perpetual and could be bequeathed or transferred to any other member without limitation.[9]

The Stationers' Register did not stop all 'piracy' but it did provide a ready mechanism for restitution should the 'pirate' in question be a member of the Company, and for over a century it was the London book trade's primary way of protecting individual publishing rights. It also created a new abstract entity, the 'copy', which had commercial value (and would later become the basis for the legal notion of copyright). 'Copies' could be leased, mortgaged, subdivided, bought, sold, and bequeathed, and it became possible to develop one's career primarily through the acquisition and management of 'copies'. Some of these transactions are noted in the Register itself and others are recorded in the minutes of the Company's Court, but much, if not most, of the activity relating to copies took place outside the Company's records.

The early seventeenth century saw the establishment of a 'joint-stock' company within the Stationers' Company. It consisted of two royal privileges granted in 1603 and 1616 for the sole right to print 'psalters[,] psalms[,] prymers, Almanack[es] & other book[es]' in perpetuity.[10] Members – who had to be Stationers – could purchase shares according to their seniority in the Company, and in return received generous annual dividends. The English Stock, as it was known, transformed the Company: it substantially improved its finances and provided work for printers as well as an important source of welfare. The limited number of shares, however, increased social inequality within the Company itself, and the Company's own strategic priorities shifted as the protection of the English Stock became a primary concern for the officers.

The preceding paragraphs have all focused on the period well before Richardson joined the Stationers' Company. In part, this is because the sixteenth and seventeenth centuries represent the high-water mark for London's companies in terms of their power and efficacy. Historians have seen the eighteenth century as a period of decline – with some exceptions – for companies and similar bodies both in London and elsewhere in Europe. In London's case, a rapidly expanding city that had long outgrown the traditional limits of the city government created commercial opportunities for non-freemen; moreover, as companies struggled to impose their regulatory authority across the capital as a whole, there were fewer advantages to becoming a member of any company. For the Stationers' Company, the lapse of the so-called Printing Act in 1695 overturned its near-monopoly over printing, enabling the establishment of provincial presses. It also, in effect, did away with the system of pre-publication licensing that had been the state's standard model for print regulation for almost two centuries; the government sought other ways (including taxation) to regulate the output of the press, further marginalising the role of the Company.

The authority of the Register, too, was challenged, particularly as Parliament looked at new ways of managing the 'ownership' of printed works. The number of entries being made in the Register dropped precipitously after 1695, and publishers began to explore different ways of protecting their rights. Some returned to the practice of seeking royal grants for specific titles, while others established copy-owning 'congers' or partnerships of booksellers, 'who put in Joynt Stocks for the Buying and Printing of Copies, and Trading for their common Advantage'.[11] When a system of statutory protection was proposed in 1710 the Company responded with petitions that stressed the importance of preserving the rights to 'copies', that copy-ownership be underwritten by common law, and that 'copies' be perpetual. The bill was duly revised to downplay the rights of authors and to give greater legal weight to the trade's ownership of copies. The Register was added as the primary mechanism for recording ownership, and the English Stock privileges were left untouched.[12] The resulting statute – the so-called 'Copyright Act' of 1710 – placed the Company, its procedures, and above all its Register at the centre of a 'new' system of 'literary property' that, in effect, was a continuation of its existing practices.[13] The statute stipulated that existing 'copies' could last only for a further twenty-one years and that the Register should be accessible to outsiders, but neither was honoured in practice. Publishers continued to enter titles in much the same way that they had done in previous years. However, although the 'copy' remained fundamental to the economy of the book trade, the practices that developed outside the Company following the lapse of the 1695 Act endured. The frequency of entrances in the Register dropped away markedly from 1715, and instead 'copies' were increasingly established, managed, and sold outside the Register.

Its regulatory powers had been curtailed, but in other ways, the Company that Richardson joined was one that his predecessors 100 years earlier would have easily recognised. Stationers' Hall had been rebuilt after the Great Fire but stood in the same spot just off Ludgate Hill. Apprentices were bound and freed, membership fees were collected every quarter-day, the clerk maintained the Register, and the Court met regularly. Richardson's stellar career in the Company also followed a trajectory familiar to any Stationer of a century earlier: freeman in 1715, liveryman in 1722, Renter Warden in 1727–8 (responsible for collecting all fees and rents), and Assistant in 1741. He declined the position of Under Warden in 1750, but served as Upper Warden in 1753–4, and as Master the next year.[14] Richardson too benefited from the English Stock: he purchased a half-yeomanry share (£40) in 1731, and two decades later had progressed to an Assistant's share (£320), receiving a 12.5 per cent dividend every year.[15]

The Company's character, though, had changed. A smaller proportion of the London book trade were members and it was increasingly possible to become a successful member of the trade without being a Stationer. Apprenticeship practices were less effectively applied – in Richardson's own case, for example, he seems to have worked for two years after his apprenticeship was completed before becoming a freeman. Apprentices were increasingly drawn from much closer to London and more came from professional backgrounds.[16] The Company was more homogeneous and more unequal. Richardson's appointment to the Court was part of an attempt to head off a legal challenge from junior members unhappy with election procedures and the allocation of English Stock shares. The Court, presumably looking to limit access to the English Stock shares, was also becoming increasingly hostile to applications for membership from individuals who had not served a full apprenticeship to a Stationer or who did not have a Stationer as a father.[17]

In the year of Richardson's Mastership, a fellow Assistant and former Master, Stephen Theodore Janssen, was elected Lord Mayor of London.[18] Janssen was the third Stationer to hold this office but the first not to have to 'translate' to a more senior company – a sign of the Stationers' Company's rising status. A generation later, its prominence in the city was so great that, for the next five decades, a Stationer would serve as Lord Mayor on average every five years.[19] The Company's ascendancy contrasted with the decline of many London companies, and the reasons lay primarily with the lucrative opportunities afforded by the English Stock. While the number of freemen admitted each year increased only during the second half of the century, the proportion of apprentices completing their terms was rising from the 1720s, indicating that membership itself was becoming more desirable. During Richardson's career, the livery grew only slightly, numbering 241 by 1761, but forty years later it was approaching 500.[20] The demography, too, changed. More printers were now binding apprentices but fewer booksellers were joining the Company, for reasons that are not entirely clear.[21] A new elite, though, was emerging from an unexpected direction. The first Stationer to be elected as Lord Mayor, Thomas Davies in 1684, had been a bookseller; John Barber, Lord Mayor in 1732, was a printer. Lord Mayor Janssen, however, was a paper-dealer. Samuel Richardson's career as a Stationer, then, coincided with both a major change in the Company's fortunes thanks to the English Stock, and a decisive shift in the overall balance of power in the senior ranks – from those who held the 'copies' to those who provided the paper.

Notes

1 Cyprian Blagden, 'The Stationers' Company in the Eighteenth Century', *Guildhall Miscellany*, 1.10 (1959), 36–53 (p. 41).

2 Michael Treadwell and Michael Turner, 'The Stationers' Company: Members of the Court, 1600–1830' (unpublished paper, 1998), 56.

3 The National Archives, PROB 11/867, fos. 215r–219v; Treadwell and Turner, 'Members', pp. 28, 45, 75.

4 Peter W. M. Blayney, *The Stationers' Company and the Printers of London, 1501–1557*, 2 vols. (Cambridge University Press, 2013), Vol. I, pp. 4–19.

5 Thomas Blount, *Glossographia; or, A Dictionary* (London, 1656), sig. 2O5v; *Oxford English Dictionary*, s.v. stationer (n. (1)).

6 The National Archives, PROB 11/867, fo. 215r.

7 Ian Anders Gadd, ' "Being like a Field": Corporate Identity in the Stationers' Company 1557–1684' (dissertation, University of Oxford, 1999).

8 Ian Anders Gadd and Patrick Wallis, 'Reaching beyond the City Wall: London Guilds and National Regulation, 1500–1700', in S. R. Epstein and M. Prak (eds.), *Guilds, Innovation and the European Economy, 1400–1800* (Cambridge University Press, 2008), pp. 288–315; John Forbes, 'Search, Immigration and the Goldsmiths' Company: A Study in the Decline of Its Power', in Ian Anders Gadd and Patrick Wallis (eds.), *Guilds, Society and Economy in London, 1450–1800* (Centre for Metropolitan History, 2002), pp. 115–25.

9 Peter W. M. Blayney, 'The Publication of Playbooks', in John D. Cox and David Scott Kastan (eds.), *A New History of Early English Drama* (Columbia University Press, 1997), pp. 383–422; Gadd, 'Being like a Field', 180–1; remarks made by Blayney at 'Mapping the British Book Trades' workshop, Oxford, May 2014.

10 Edward Arber (ed.), *A Transcript of the Registers of the Company of Stationers 1554–1640 AD*, 5 vols. (London and Birmingham, 1875–94), Vol. III, pp. 42–4, 679–82.

11 Shef Rogers, 'The Uses of Royal Licences for Printing in England, 1695–1760: A Bibliography', *The Library*, 7th series, 1 (2000), 133–92; Thomas Bennet and Henry Clements, *The Notebook of Thomas Bennet and Henry Clements (1686–1719)*, eds. Norma Hodgson and Cyprian Blagden (Oxford Bibliographical Society, 1956), pp. 85–6.

12 John Feather, 'The Book Trade in Politics: The Making of the Copyright Act of 1710', *Publishing History*, 8 (1980), 19–44.

13 Act for the Encouragement of Learning 1710 (8 Anne, *c.* 19).

14 Treadwell and Turner, 'Members', pp. 56, 75; D. F. McKenzie (ed.), *Stationers' Company Apprentices, 1701–1800* (Oxford Bibliographical Society, 1978), no. 8791; Blagden, 'The Stationers' Company', p. 43.

15 Maslen, *Samuel Richardson*, p. 7; Cyprian Blagden, *The Stationers' Company: A History 1403–1959* (George Allen and Unwin, 1960), p. 244.
16 Blagden, 'The Stationers' Company', pp. 37–9.
17 *Ibid.*, pp. 43–8.
18 Treadwell and Turner, 'Members', p. 37.
19 Blagden, *The Stationers' Company*, pp. 251–2.
20 Michael L. Turner, 'Personnel within the London Book Trades: Evidence from the Stationers' Company', in Michael F. Suarez, S. J., and Michael L. Turner (eds.), *The Cambridge History of the Book in Britain, Vol. v: 1695–1830* (Cambridge University Press, 2009), pp. 309–34 (pp. 320–1).
21 *Ibid.*, pp. 326–7; Blagden, 'The Stationers' Company', 48; Blagden, *The Stationers' Company*, pp. 245–8.

CHAPTER 10

Transnational Print Trade Relations

Norbert Schürer

Richardson's career as a successful printer and novelist was characterised in part by his desire to maintain control of his creations. The intense reactions to *Pamela* seem to have caught him by surprise, and in various revisions, as well as *Pamela in Her Exalted Condition*, he sought to circumscribe the possibilities for interpretations. In the cases of *Clarissa* and *Sir Charles Grandison*, his extensive pre-publication correspondence with readers, consulting them on ideas for and developments in the plot, attempted to anticipate any challenges to his literary intentions. While it is obviously necessary to examine how Richardson contained the proliferation of opinions about the content of his novels, it is equally important to consider how he tried to exert authority over his creations in the material sense as a printer and member of the book trade. In this respect, a distinction can be drawn between Richardson's relations with printers and booksellers in the British nations outside England on the one hand – where his concern seems to have been mostly about financial profit – and his relations with these parties on the European continent on the other – where his concern was more about how his works were presented.

Most significant in the former respect are Richardson's relations with various booksellers in Ireland. Throughout the eighteenth century, Ireland was not covered by English copyright, as rudimentary as that was before 1774. Irish readers often had two options for purchasing books: they could acquire works imported from London by local booksellers, or they could buy cheaper reprints of the London originals produced by Irish printers. These reprints were known as 'piracies', though actually they were not violating any laws – unless they were produced from sheets that had been stolen in London. From the perspective of London publishers, however, all 'piracies' were considered unacceptable since neither they nor the authors could make any profit from them.

As a printer, Richardson would certainly have been aware of this situation, but he does not seem to have prepared for the Irish distribution of *Pamela*.[1] The novel was published in London on 6 November 1740; by 27 January 1741 the booksellers George Faulkner and George Ewing were advertising both the London edition and a cheaper Dublin reprint. The reprint succeeded so well that a second edition was available by mid-March. Richardson did not respond to Faulkner and Ewing's reprint, but when he was preparing *Pamela in Her Exalted Condition* he contracted with another Dublin bookseller, Thomas Bacon, to print a Dublin edition. Thus, he hoped to pre-empt a 'piracy' and guarantee himself some part of the profits while also ensuring that a local Irish member of the book trade was benefitting. Faulkner and Ewing, however, joined by the bookseller William Smith, were faster than Bacon: *Pamela in Her Exalted Condition* was published in London on 7 December 1741; on 22 December 1741 Faulkner, Ewing, and Smith advertised their 'pirated' edition. When he learned of the reprint, Richardson apparently immediately sent 250 copies of his London edition to Bacon, but the damage was done. Subsequently, Richardson was granted a Royal Licence for *Pamela* in April 1742 that superseded copyright and gave him the exclusive right to print the entire novel (original and continuation) in all of the king's domains – and indeed put an end to 'piracies' of his first novel in Ireland.

For his next novel, *Clarissa*, Richardson, once again trying to find an arrangement with the book trade in Ireland, sold the sheets of the novel directly to Faulkner for 70 guineas.[2] Thus, he could determine what text was published and also make a profit. According to Richardson's recollections, Faulkner tried to renege and pay only 40 guineas, but eventually Richardson received the full amount. Consequently, the first two volumes of *Clarissa* were published in London on 1 December 1747 and in Dublin on 19 December 1747.

Any control that Richardson had established over the Irish reprints of his novels was lost, however, in the altercation around *Sir Charles Grandison*.[3] Once again, Richardson signed an agreement with Faulkner that the latter would publish a Dublin edition and pay Richardson 70 guineas. Yet before the arrangement could be executed, three other Dublin booksellers – Peter Wilson, John Exshaw, and Henry Saunders – announced that they were publishing their own 'pirated' reprint. Apparently, they had managed to bribe somebody in Richardson's printing-house to send unpublished sheets of the first six of seven volumes to Dublin.

In this situation, Faulkner decided to withdraw from the arrangement, which brought the full wrath of Richardson down on him, rather than on the other three booksellers. Richardson vented his anger in two publications: *The Case of Samuel Richardson, of London, Printer; with Regard to the*

Invasion of his Property (14 September 1753) and *An Address to the Public, on the Treatment which the Editor of the History of Sir Charles Grandison Has Met with from Certain Booksellers and Printers in Dublin* (1 February 1754 and appended to the London edition of the last volume of *Grandison*). As Stephanie Fysh observes, Richardson offered three main arguments to explain his objections to Faulkner's behaviour: 'the first dealing with the workshop economy and the Stationers' Company, the second with the nature of authorship, and the third with religion and morality'.[4] Thus, he was once again trying to assert his authority while also invoking the financial ramifications of 'piracy'.

As Richardson probably knew, he had no legal case, so at the same time he tried to buy off Wilson, Exshaw, and Saunders and agreed to sell his London edition at a cheaper price through the Dublin bookseller Robert Main. Richardson characterised Main as one 'Who has kindly undertaken to do the Proprietor that Justice, which almost all the Booksellers and Printers of Dublin have refused him, against a Confederacy of Pyrates in that City.'[5] Richardson also made arrangements for the sale of *Sir Charles Grandison* in Scotland – which was also not covered by English copyright – through the Edinburgh booksellers Alexander Kincaid, Alexander Donaldson, Gavin Hamilton, and John Balfour. His relations with the Scottish book trade were perhaps more cooperative, since many of his printer colleagues in London were originally from Scotland and had connections there. In the event, the first four volumes of *Sir Charles Grandison* were released almost simultaneously in London and in Dublin, but the fifth and sixth volumes were published in Dublin (13 November) by the 'pirate' consortium four weeks before they appeared in London (11 December 1753). The sheets of the seventh and final volume, however, had not been stolen, so Richardson was able to publish the conclusion to his last novel before it was 'pirated' in Dublin.

This episode, then, illustrates the tensions in the book trade even within the British nations. Richardson tried to assert his authority over his novels in order to reap financial benefits, but he was stymied in this effort by the legal situation in which Irish printers and booksellers could legitimately reprint his works. He attempted to cooperate with members of the book trade in Dublin, but when those cooperations did not work to his satisfaction he took to the press with *ad hominem* attacks and moral arguments – to no avail. While most biographers of Richardson have taken his side in this episode, critics more recently have explored different interpretations. Examining several instances of kidnapping in *Grandison*, Kathryn Temple interprets the novel as inadvertently exposing colonial violence, and the episode as Irish booksellers developing colonial solidarity,[6] while Fysh reads the story of the novel and the Dublin publication as part of larger moral and legal debates about property.

If this situation was vexing, matters became even more complicated when literature migrated to the Continent in translation. As in Ireland, Richardson had no copyright protection on the Continent, so he had to work collaboratively with booksellers, publishers, and translators to remain involved in the dissemination and presentation of his work. He did this to an extent unusual among professional authors of his period, who generally lacked international connections. In the process, Richardson had some contact with members of the book trade in the Netherlands and in francophone areas, and interacted extensively with one of his publishers in Germany, Philipp Erasmus Reich.[7] Beyond the curious similarity of names (*reich* means 'rich'), Reich and Richardson shared a common interest in improving the quality of books as material objects and in establishing uniform copyright laws across their countries. Reich came from a modest background, but rose to take over the Weidmann publishing house in Leipzig and make it one of the most important booksellers of the German Enlightenment.

Reich was also Germany's greatest importer of English and Italian books, so it was no surprise that he promoted Richardson. Reich's connection to Richardson must have gone back to the early 1750s, but their surviving correspondence is from the years 1754–8. Reich probably wrote in French, which was translated into English for Richardson; Richardson responded in English, which was translated for Reich into German. Their first piece of surviving correspondence (if only the English translation) is from 10 May 1754. In this letter, Reich claims that the presentation copy of *Sir Charles Grandison* he has received from Richardson is 'the first Copy of it, that went out of England'. Reich entrusted the translation to Christian Fürchtegott Gellert, an author who, inspired by *Pamela*, had published the sentimental novel *Das Leben der schwedischen Gräfin von G**** (*The History of the Swedish Countess of G**) in 1747–8. Now, Reich sent Richardson the first two volumes of Gellert's translation and commented that '[t]he new present you have Lately made to the Public, the History of Sir Charles Grandison, has been received by my Countrymen with as much admiration, and thankfulness, as it was by yours'. Richardson's response of 5 August unfortunately exists only in a manuscript translation partially burnt during the Second World War, but it seems the London author and printer thanks Reich, worries over whether Reich will make a profit, and discusses possible continuations of the novel's plot. The final volumes of the translation were published in 1755 with a high print run of 2,500.

In August 1756, Reich visited England, apparently for the express purpose of meeting Richardson. Reich's account of 'that divine man' and their 'mutual tenderness depriv[ing] us of speech' reads like a scene from a sentimental novel.[8] Subsequently, Reich approaches Richardson about more material, asking 'Would there not be a way, Sir, to see something from your pen once again? Your letters, for example, with those of your selected friends, would do much good for the world!' (quoted in Richardson to Lady Bradshaigh, 2 January 1758). Richardson grants that an edition would be interesting, but he suggests that the correspondents should write to him to ask permission for Reich to publish the letters. Under those conditions, he concedes, 'there might appear, anonymously, & under proper Restrictions, in the Language of *your* Country, & in *that only*, a Volume or two' (quoted in Richardson to Lady Bradshaigh, 2 January 1758).

This edition came to naught when (Saxon) Leipzig was occupied by the Prussians during the Seven Years' War. Richardson comments on Reich's situation: 'The dreadful way they have been in at Leipsick, ever since last Octr. has hinder'd my Correspondent there from writing to me. God preserve us here from being the Seat of War!' (Richardson to Lady Bradshaigh, 2 January 1758). Nevertheless, Reich did find 'something from [Richardson's] pen once again', and in 1757 he published translations of two works by his English friend: *Sittenlehre für die Jugend* (*Æsop's Fables*), translated by none less than Gotthold Ephraim Lessing, and *Gemeinnützige Lehren der Tugend* (*Collection of the Moral and Instructive Sentiments*, though without the page references to Richardson's novels). With his last known letter to Richardson of 12 June 1758, Reich most likely presented a copy of one of these works. For his part, Richardson was probably not making a profit but rather interested in promoting his moral agenda.

In the same letter, Reich refers to 'the new edition of Grandison in German', which was published in 1759. This edition is remarkable for twenty-one images, designed by the French artist Charles Eisen and the German illustrator Gottfried Eichler the Younger and engraved by Johann Martin Bernigeroth, which could be purchased separately from the novel (Figure 10.1).[9] Even more remarkably, the subjects for the images had apparently been suggested by Richardson himself when Reich visited him in London back in 1756, and Richardson mentions them in a letter to Reich of 2 April 1757. This serves as an excellent example of Richardson's cooperation with foreign booksellers to influence the interpretation of his novel, here through a choice of subjects for illustrations.

Figure 10.1 Samuel Richardson, *Geschichte Herrn Carl Grandison: In Briefen entworfen* (1759), engraving by J. M. Bernigeroth after Charles Eisen and Gottfried Eichler the Younger. Houghton Library, Harvard University, *EC7.R3961.En754gbv, Vol. VII.

Reich's commitment to Richardson in turn was demonstrated by Reich's involvement in a French translation of *Sir Charles Grandison* with the Dutch bookseller Elie Luzac in Leyden.[10] (Luzac, a philosopher in his own right, also had a shop in Göttingen.) Since the book market in France was subject to strict censorship, many books in French were released in the surrounding countries. The first French translations of *Pamela*, for instance, were published in London (1741) and Amsterdam (1742). No correspondence between Richardson and the French translators of *Pamela* and *Clarissa* is known, but it is probable that he communicated with John Osborn or John Nourse – the publishers, respectively, of two London French translations. From Richardson's correspondence with Johannes Stinstra, we know that he was writing back and forth with Luzac: 'His Letter is dated 17 ultimo. My Answer bears Date the 9th of the present Month' (Richardson to Stinstra, 24 July 1755). Richardson was aware of the collaboration between Reich and Luzac and hoped that their French translation of *Sir Charles Grandison* by Gaspard Joël Monod would be better than Prévost's truncated version of *Clarissa*. Richardson also writes that he has 'mentioned to [Luzac] a <more than> sufficient Number of Subjects' for illustrations of *Grandison* – presumably the same subjects that ended up illustrated in Reich's 1759 German edition of the novel. The 1756 French translation was eventually published with two different imprints, one giving 'A Leipsic, Chez les Herit de G. M. Weidmann', and the other 'Göttingue & Leide, de l'Imp. d'Elie Luzac, Fils.'

Finally, both Reich and Luzac are referenced in Richardson's correspondence with Stinstra, who translated *Clarissa* into Dutch and helped arrange the Dutch translation of *Sir Charles Grandison*. Through this correspondence, Richardson also communicated with Folkert van der Plaats, the Dutch bookseller who published his works in the city of Harlingen. In a series of letters, Stinstra organised the exchange of unbound sheets as well as books between Richardson and Van der Plaats as payment for various services – Richardson was anxious to settle financial matters precisely. In an echo of Richardson's concern for Reich, Van der Plaats was apparently worried that he might lose money with *Clarissa*, but Stinstra assures Richardson that Van der Plaats 'will not suffer any loss from it' (Stinstra to Richardson, 2 April 1753). When Stinstra, in his preface to the third and fourth volumes, specifically declares that five bishops have praised *Clarissa* and that one of them has read the novel eleven times, Richardson asks him to have Van der Plaats remove that sheet from circulation, which turned out to be impossible. Perhaps since he was not dealing directly with the bookseller, but through the translator as intermediary, Richardson was not able to collaborate in the production of the material book to the extent he desired.

Through Stinstra, Richardson learned of the competition that arose when Isaac Tirion, another Dutch bookseller from Amsterdam, announced a Dutch translation of *Sir Charles Grandison* before *Clarissa* was completed. The personal enmity between Tirion and Van der Plaats, who acquired a collaborator in Amsterdam to 'be more secure from the opposition of Mr Tirion' (Stinstra to Richardson, 24 December 1753), might have reminded Richardson of his concurrent dealings with Ireland. In a letter of 24 July 1755, Richardson praises the German and French translations of *Sir Charles Grandison* and brings up the fact that Luzac planned to provide three illustrations per volume. According to Stinstra, however, Van der Plaats decided that including images 'would to [*sic*] much heighten the price of their book, and diminish the number of buyers' (Stinstra to Richardson, 17 September 1755).

Thus, Richardson had to contend with different challenges within the British archipelago and on the European continent. In his dealings with Ireland, he mixed negotiation with the assertion of moral, legal, and financial rights – successfully with *Pamela* and *Clarissa* and with more acrimonious results in the altercation around *Sir Charles Grandison*. He was able to provide input into the Dutch production of his novels through a long correspondence with Stinstra in the Netherlands, though the two never met in person. On the Continent, Richardson collaborated closely with Reich in Leipzig, which gave him some influence over the novels' presentation in German (such as the quality of the translation and the subjects for illustrations) and brought him in touch with one French translation. Still, the further away from London they travelled, the more difficult it became for Richardson to have any influence on the presentation of his novels.

Notes

1 Keymer and Sabor, *'Pamela' in the Marketplace*, pp. 177–80.
2 Eaves and Kimpel, *Biography*, p. 378.
3 William Merritt Sale, Jr, 'Sir Charles Grandison and the Dublin Pirates', *Yale University Library Gazette*, 7.4 (April 1933), 80–6.
4 Stephanie Fysh, *The Work(s) of Samuel Richardson* (University of Delaware Press, 1997), p. 108. See also Stern's discussion, below, of the forensic mentality displayed in Richardson's *Address to the Public*.
5 Richardson, *Public Advertiser*, 5940 (8 November 1753), p. 4.
6 Kathryn Temple, 'Printing like a Post-Colonialist: The Irish Piracy of *Sir Charles Grandison*', *Novel: A Forum on Fiction*, 33.2 (2000), 157–74.

7 Hazel Rosenstrauch, *Buchhandelsmanufaktur und Aufklärung: Die Reformen des Buchhändlers und Verlegers Ph. E. Reich (1717–1787)* (Buchhändler-Vereinigung, 1986).

8 Erasmus Reich quoted in Barbauld, *Correspondence*, Vol. 1, pp. clxv–clxx.

9 Mark Lehmstedt, *'Ich bin nicht gewohnt, mit Künstlern zu dingen …': Philipp Erasmus Reich und die Buchillustration im 18. Jahrhundert* (Deutsche Bücherei, 1989), pp. 18–22.

10 Rietje van Vliet, *Elie Luzac (1721–1796): Bookseller of the Enlightenment* (AFdH Uitgevers Publishers, 2014).

CHAPTER II

Authorship

Betty A. Schellenberg

It is widely acknowledged that Richardson's road to authorial fame lay through the printer's shop. Sometime in the late 1730s, market demand for instruction in letter-writing motivated him to begin composing a volume of familiar epistles, from which a short exchange between a servant girl and her father regarding the unwelcome attentions of her master drew him into the creation of *Pamela*. It is almost as widely acknowledged that Richardson's creative impulses expressed themselves much earlier, leading him as a young adolescent to write epistles intended to correct social faults and to further courtships (Richardson to Johannes Stinstra, 2 June 1753). These ostensibly contradictory stories of origin in fact illustrate Richardson's position at a writerly crossroads in mid-eighteenth-century Britain. His brand of authorship – at once entrepreneurial, combinatory, proprietary, sociable, and creative – was both reflective of understandings of the author in the generation after the great poet Alexander Pope, and influential upon the generation that succeeded his own decades of prominence on the literary scene.

The Model of Pope

Pope's shadow looms large over the period's articulation of literary authorship under the regime of print. Whether denouncing the denizens of commercial print as venal hacks or, paradoxically, successfully manipulating booksellers, the law, and 'the great' to fashion a print-based authorial identity as the English Homer, Pope rendered a virtuoso performance of the poet's life. His published poems and letters won him fame, fortune, and prestige through print remediations of both classical literary models and the ideals of a sociable, manuscript-exchanging literary culture. As Raymond Stephanson has summarised it, 'Pope's impact was enormous ... He was in many ways symbolic of the poetical character itself, a public icon exemplifying male genius, literary fame and wealth, and the cultural status of the new professional author'. Both Stephanson and Linda Zionkowski have highlighted the increasingly insistent gendering of this authorial identity.[1] Specifically, for Richardson and his male peers Pope raised the question of the relation between the man and his authorial practice. Although the oppositional pairing of Richardson and Henry Fielding has served as a long-lived framework for critical commentary, as detailed by Sören Hammerschmidt and Brian Corman above, in the 1740s and early 1750s Pope and his career were the operative points of reference for a male writer with aspirations to a position of cultural significance. Born just one year after the poet, but beginning his authorial career as Pope's drew to a close, Richardson appears to have responded to this unavoidable model through the articulation of difference within similarity. Colley Cibber, formerly a target of Pope's satire and a friend of Richardson, illustrates this device of comparison and contrast when he writes to the novelist, in his enthusiasm over *Sir Charles Grandison*, 'Can any man be a good moral writer that does not take up his pen in the cause of virtue? I had rather have the fame that your amiable zeal for it deserves, than be preferred as a poet to a *Pope*, or his *Homer*' (Colley Cibber to Richardson, 19 November 1753).

Both Pope and Richardson represented independence from patrons as fundamental to the manly virtue embodied in their writing. To the French translator Jean Baptiste de Freval, Richardson complains in 1751 of the demands of business that delay his writing, but the complaint quickly transitions to a manifesto about the grounds of his literary authority:

> You know how my business engages me. You know by what snatches of time I write, that I may not neglect that, and that I may preserve that independency which is the comfort of my life. I never sought out of myself for patrons. My own industry, and God's providence, have been my whole reliance. The great are not great to me, unless they are good. (Richardson to de Freval, 21 January 1751)

In this hymn to independence Richardson echoes Pope's insistence that even though he may 'live among the Great', he is 'To VIRTUE ONLY and HER FRIENDS, A FRIEND', and that 'if he please[s], he please[s] by manly ways'.[2]

Like Pope, Richardson expresses a sense of writerly vocation in calling the world to virtue. But he and his correspondents repudiate Pope's coupling of independent virtue with a stance of satiric potency and moral superiority. Beginning with the publication of the 1743 *Dunciad in Four Books*, Aaron Hill takes the lead in articulating an alternative position for the author. Hill's biographer Christine Gerrard has noted that the two men shared an ' "anti-Scriblerian" literary sensibility', including a belief that 'all writing is in essence autobiographical'.[3] Upon news of Pope's death in 1744, Hill declares that 'the heart of [any writing man] still shews, and needs must shew itself, beyond all power of concealment', invoking Richardson as the axiom's proof: 'How many have I heard declare (and people, too, who loved truth dearly, and believed they spoke it), that they charmed themselves in reading Pamela; when, all the while, it was Mr Richardson they had been reading.' Pope is then cited as the cautionary example: '[Pope's] own sentiments were low and narrow, because always interested ... and sour and acrid, because writ in envy ... He stuck himself into his subjects, and his muse partook his maladies' (Hill to Richardson, 10 September 1744). For Hill, Pope's vaunted good nature and benevolence were a mere pose; his 'narrow conduct' was in fact characterised by the stereotypical tradesman's 'mercenary malignity' (Hill to Richardson, February 1744). Although Pope's writing 'bewitch[es]' and 'out-charms even a poet' (February 1744), 'his memory ... will very rarely be disturbed by that time he himself is ashes' (10 September 1744).

The Printer as Author

From these ashes rises an authorial identity much more attractive to Richardson than it could have been to Pope in the preceding decades: that of the successful middle-class professional. This model of authorship, bringing with it a social status founded upon expertise and achievement in a specialised trade, was adopted by Richardson with conscious pride. In his assertion to de Freval of his earned independence and freedom from the patronage of the 'great', Richardson tellingly continues: 'And it is a glorious privilege, that a middling man enjoys who has preserved his independency, and can occasionally ... tell the world, what he thinks of that world, in hopes to contribute, though but by his mite, to mend it' (Richardson to de Freval, 21 January 1751). For Richardson, this authority was earned through his achievements as a printer who rose from apprenticeship to election as Master of the Stationers' Company in 1754, and whose expertise and friendship were sought out and respected by booksellers, authors, and other professionals alike. As Christopher Flint's chapter on the material book demonstrates in detail, within this milieu it was not unheard of for a printer or bookseller to undertake 'authorship' as an extension of other elements of book-making such as formatting, editing, and compiling. Thus Richardson in the course of his profession created new material for publications such as Daniel Defoe's *Tour thro' the Whole Island of Great Britain*, of which he shared copyright ownership; composed a letter manual; and produced a volume of Aesop's fables, all before attracting notice for the original and extended work of epistolary fiction titled *Pamela; or, Virtue Rewarded*.

Richardson explicitly juxtaposes this earned professional status to the traditional cultural authority of the educated and socially privileged male. He expresses to his friend Benjamin Kennicott, Oxford fellow and Hebrew scholar, his disdain of men such as the new Vice-Chancellor of Oxford, Sir George Huddesford, and the Jacobite Dr William King, Principal of St Mary Hall, for their antics at the notorious 1754 Oxford Commemoration of Benefactors. According to Richardson, such gentlemen have forfeited their claim to respect by abusing privilege and encouraging blasphemous and seditious views in the young:

> when your Capital Men make such poor Figures, with their short written-down Speeches;[4] and the Men who have been in the World, so much out-do them, at their own Weapons; why blamed you a Friend of yours, for not using his little Powers in favour of the Universities in this Kingdom? ... It will be no Credit to your University-Admirers of such Old Boy Harangues, were they to be told, that, Party out of the Question, there are Men, among us, in the great Town, of whose Judgment in other Matters, you all at Oxford would be proud, and Learning revere, who will not allow your Orator to be either a Gentleman or a Scholar; and think meanly of his *Admirers* for being *so* – But all this between ourselves. (Richardson to Kennicott, 15 July 1754)

Though he may hesitate to say so more publicly, Richardson here proclaims a cultural shift, led by people of 'Judgment' and 'Learning', away from the elite model of the educated gentleman in favour of a new urban ideal of the professional man of letters.

Two other features of Richardson's identity as print-author can be linked to this 'manly' professionalism: his relations with professional women writers and his adherence to the emerging proprietorial model of authorship. In the first instance, his unique position within the London trade enabled Richardson to express his generosity through energetic advocacy of many women's publishing careers. Especially notable is his instrumental support of Charlotte Lennox in the completion and publication of her commercially successful novel *The Female Quixote*, a project in which he served as the more influential partner to Samuel Johnson. But similar sorts of tangible assistance – mediation with powerful figures such as Andrew Millar and David Garrick, editorial advice (as detailed by Rogers, pp. 130–2, below), gifts of money, and promotion of publications – were extended

to Mary Leapor (posthumously), Sarah Fielding, Jane Collier, Frances
Sheridan, Anna Meades, and Hill's daughter Urania Johnson.

Secondly, Richardson was deeply committed to the view that his writings were his property. While this position was indisputable because of his role in their print production – a role that for most authors would have been ceded to a bookseller – its legal basis was in the copyright provisions for authors first enacted in the 1710 Statute of Anne and articulated ever more clearly through court rulings as the century progressed. When the London papers announced continuations of *Pamela* by several other writers, Richardson's protests invoke the patriarch whose daughter has been kidnapped or even raped: his 'Plan' risks being 'basely Ravished out of [his] hands, and, probably, my Characters depreciated and debased' (Richardson to James Leake, August 1741).

But the fullest expression of this proprietorial conviction was roused in 1753 when three Dublin booksellers advertised an unauthorised edition of *Sir Charles Grandison*, to be produced from unpublished sheets stolen from the novelist's own printing-house in London, as described by Schürer in the previous chapter. In his public and vociferous assertions of grievance against these 'Invaders of his property', Richardson insists that his cause is nothing less than 'the cause of Literature, and of Authors in general' against the '*established, invariable, constant* custom among the Booksellers of Dublin' of publishing any copy they can procure. Richardson, stoutly supported by author friends such as Samuel Johnson and Elizabeth Carter, thereby links the principle of an author's proprietary right with the health and viability of literary production – indeed, with the good of '*the whole Republic of Letters*'.[5] This was a link not universally acknowledged in the mid-eighteenth century, as signalled by the enterprising booksellers of Dublin, but it is the one later elaborated by Edward Young in his 1759 manifesto *Conjectures on Original Composition*, addressed 'to the Author of *Sir Charles Grandison*', wherein Richardson is held up as, unlike Pope, a writer of original genius who has 'the sole Property of [his works]; which Property alone can confer the noble title of an *Author*'.[6]

Richardson as Scribal Author

Richardson's achievements as author of epistolary fiction cannot be separated from his lifelong commitment to the art of letter-writing, a scribal form that gained new centrality in the eighteenth century, alongside print, with the development of the postal service and the improvement of road travel throughout Britain. While the media of script and print intersected with and fed one another – in Richardson's case, through his *Familiar Letters*, the premises of the novels themselves, and their stimulation in turn of reader correspondence – it is important to consider the degree to which Richardson sought out and fostered epistolary exchange as a sociable form of authorship in its own right. In the case of Carter, for example, although she was already a published author and Richardson was in the throes of *Sir Charles Grandison*'s early printing, the letters explore childhood memories and spin out imaginative depictions of local events and mutual friends. In fact, Carter joins others of Richardson's correspondents of the early 1750s (Susanna Highmore, Hester Mulso (later Chapone), Thomas Edwards, John Duncombe, and others) in forming a scribal literary coterie.

In addition to the exchange of lively letters, original poetry is circulated among the coterie's members and copies are found in the manuscript collections of individuals tangentially linked to the circle (for example, Thomas Birch and Elizabeth Montagu); Hester Mulso's fame as a polemicist also stemmed from manuscripts circulated within this group. Despite John Duncombe's 1754 *The Feminead*, which celebrates female members of the coterie and expresses the hope that they will agree to print publication, a prime motive of the group's existence seems to have been appreciation for the exclusivity of scribal authorship. Edwards's comment to Richardson, in reference to this corresponding circle – 'There is, and I doubt not but that you have felt it, there is something more deliciously charming in the approbation of the Ladies than in that of a whole University of He-Critics' – is about more than a taste for female adulation. It recognises the unique pleasures of coterie authorship, with its context of mutual support and collaborative criticism, in distinction to the verbal combat fostered by printed critical discourse (Edwards to Richardson, 30 March 1751).

In another sign of the literary stature of the familiar letter form, Richardson carefully preserves the whole of his correspondences with Edwards and Carter, marking the former collection with a select list of seven eligible readers, and revising the latter with an eye apparently to eventual publication as a literary work in its own right. Indeed, Louise Curran has suggested that his success as a writer of epistolary fiction motivated Richardson 'more insistently to fashion himself as a letter writer' in the last years of his life, whether through the origin story of the ghost-writing boy cited at the start of this chapter or through the cataloguing and editing of a number of his correspondences.[7] In one notable example detailed by Tom Keymer, Richardson's 1756–9 exchanges with the Warwickshire attorney Eusebius Silvester are retrospectively given shape as a 'Warning Piece to Posterity', a narrative of deceit and betrayal, through Richardson's editorial commentary.[8]

The principal writers depicted in Richardson's fictions – Pamela Andrews, Clarissa Harlowe, Robert Lovelace, Anna Howe, Jack Belford, Harriet Byron, and Sir Charles Grandison – are all devoted practitioners of scribal authorship. They use the medium of script not only to recount events, but to explore states of mind and heart, compose poems and prayers, set minutely detailed scenes and record the dramas played out in them, and create fictional pasts and imaginary futures. Richardson's endorsement of a culture characterised by the active exchange of manuscript literary materials encouraged its survival and cultivation beyond the circles of the social elites, extending, as research by Susan Whyman has shown, to the provinces and the lower middle classes.[9] Through his own adoption of the role of professional print-based author addressing a wide, anonymous audience, Richardson as 'editor' enabled the extensive circulation, and contributed to the persistence of a model of authorship that was its opposite: amateur, selective in its choice of audience, and based in the medium of script.

When Young, the highly successful author of *Night Thoughts*, constructed his image of authorship in the *Conjectures on Original Composition*, he demoted the neoclassical and tuneful Alexander Pope to the second rank of imitators in favour of Richardson as the epitome of authorial originality and virtue. In 1781, an elderly Samuel Johnson faulted Pope, in his biographical prefaces on the 'Lives of the Poets', for narrow-mindedness, parsimony, and a contrived disdain for the general audience from which he gained his fortune. A reading of this assessment in light of Richardson's expressions of authorial identity suggests that a younger Johnson, too, might have fashioned his ideal of the commercially successful, proudly independent, and authentically benevolent and moral author, the ideal against which he measured Pope's conduct, with reference to his old friend and supporter. In a century that saw the emergence and consolidation of notions of the author as proprietor and original genius, Richardson stood at the crossroads as a writer who, in the generation after Pope, embraced print publication and its developing infrastructure of law, advertising, and wide distribution as the means to a successful middle-class professional career – all the while endorsing and practising scribal authorship and limited circulation in the genre of the familiar letter.

Notes

1 Raymond Stephanson, *The Yard of Wit: Male Creativity and Sexuality, 1650–1750* (University of Pennsylvania Press, 2004), pp. 18–19; Linda Zionkowski, in *Men's Work: Gender, Class, and the Professionalization of Poetry, 1660–1784* (Palgrave Macmillan, 2001), pp. 98–128.

2 Alexander Pope, *Imitation of Horace*, ii.i, line 121; *Epistle to Dr Arbuthnot*, lines 341, 347.

3 Christine Gerrard, *Aaron Hill: The Muses' Projector, 1685–1750* (Oxford University Press, 2003), pp. 203, 234.

4 I.e. the Vice Chancellor, Dr George Huddesford, who according to Kennicott had read, badly, a speech a quarter-page long.

5 Samuel Richardson, 'Address to the Public', in *Correspondence Primarily on 'Sir Charles Grandison' (1750–1754)*, ed. Betty A. Schellenberg, *CECSR*, Vol. x, pp. 103, 114, 108, 119; see also Johnson to Richardson, 26 September 1753; Carter to Richardson, 6 October 1753.

6 Edward Young, *Conjectures on Original Composition: In a Letter to the Author of 'Sir Charles Grandison'* (London, 1759), p. 54. Simon Stern further analyses the nature of Richardson's defence of his proprietary right to *Sir Charles Grandison* in his chapter below (pp. 236–7).

7 Louise Curran, *Samuel Richardson and the Art of Letter-Writing* (Cambridge University Press, 2016), pp. 11–12.

8 Keymer, *Richardson's 'Clarissa'*, pp. 34–44.

9 Susan E. Whyman, *The Pen and the People: English Letter Writers 1660–1800* (Oxford University Press, 2009), Chapter 5.

CHAPTER 12

The Literary Marketplace

Catherine Ingrassia

Reflecting on the popularity of his fiction in a letter to Lady Bradshaigh of 25 February 1754, Samuel Richardson observes, 'It is not an unartful Management to interest the Readers so much in the Story, as to make them differ in Opinion as to the Capital Articles, and by Leading one, to espouse one, another, another Opinion, make them all, if not Authors, Carvers.' That 'not ... unartful Management', or shrewd manipulation, calculated to generate a dynamic discussion of differing opinions ('one, to espouse one, another, another'), served Richardson well in the literary marketplace during his career as printer and author. Richardson's strategy for launching a book into a competitive commercial space, most fully realised during the '*Pamela* craze', ensured increased sales, popularity, and cultural notoriety. By making readers 'Authors' or even 'Carvers' who interpret the novel independently, Richardson sought to increase readers' emotional (and consequently financial) investment in the text, securing a more favourable reception. As this chapter reveals, Richardson's knowledge of the relationship between printer and bookseller, his nuanced approach to advertising and publicity, and his ability to capitalise on his relatively privileged position within print culture made him one of the more commanding authors within the literary marketplace in the first half of the eighteenth century. His skilful mastery reconfigured the capacity of commercial authorship.

Relationship with the Marketplace and the Print Trade

Samuel Richardson possessed a keen awareness of the possibilities of the literary marketplace, a competitive commercial site offering literary commodities created by a diverse group of professional writers. A master printer, and therefore proprietor of his own business, from 1721, Richardson recognised the need to diversify both his products and his clients. He printed materials that appealed to the varied interests of a new class of often first-generation readers. Newspapers and periodicals (more than 7,500 issues by one count), parliamentary proceedings, novels, travel narratives, sermons, periodicals, self-help books, poetry, and private bills were among the many products of his shop.[1] He printed twenty-three subscription editions and, as Keith Maslen observes, '[a]n obliging printer knew better than any author' how to facilitate the sale of a book by subscription, 'by placing advertisements in newspapers, collecting subscriptions at his shop, and seeing to binding, storage, and distribution'.[2] He printed elite, high cultural productions such as *The Works of Pope* (1735); popular prose fiction such as the third edition of Eliza Haywood's *Secret Histories, Novels, and Poems* (1732) and a reissue of Delarivier Manley's *History of Rivella* (1725); subscription volumes by labouring-class poets such as Stephen Duck (1730) and Mary Barber (1735); and any number of pamphlets and books capturing cultural preoccupations, ranging from *A Present State of the British Sugar Colonies Consider'd* (1731) to *The Histories of Some of the Penitents in the Magdalen House* (1760). While Richardson claimed, in a letter to Aaron Hill of 2 April 1743, 'I seldom read but as a Printer', the range of texts he published (and thus read) necessarily gave him considerable insight into eighteenth-century cultural preoccupations, and a clear sense of the variety of texts that could be marketed and sold effectively.

Richardson recognised that, as with types of materials printed, diversity in clients was also financially advantageous. He printed for booksellers – that is, owners of bookshops who also held the copyright of the book being printed – and for publishers: individuals who sold books for an author but did not hold the copyright.[3] Perhaps most lucratively, Richardson also printed the proceedings of the House of Commons, as well as private bills for individual MPs, a profitable enterprise allowing him to remain, as he described to Johannes Stinstra in a letter of 2 June 1753, 'more independent of Booksellers (tho' I did much Business for them) than any other Printer'. While he may have shared George Cheyne's opinion that 'All Booksellers … are Curls by Profession' (Cheyne to Richardson, 27 March 1739) – a reference to the notorious Edmund Curll (d. 1747) – he recognised the essential role within the marketplace played by booksellers, 'whose business is to watch the taste and foibles of the public' (Richardson to Aaron Hill, 27 October 1748).

Richardson knew that the savvy choice of a bookseller could determine a book's success. To his good friend Aaron Hill (1685–1750) Richardson recommended Andrew Millar as a bookseller who 'has great Business, and is in a Way of promoting the Taste of what he engages in' (Richardson to Hill, 12 January 1749). Millar's sensitivity to timing when advertising a volume, waiting until 'after the Holidays [when] The Town is yet Full', satisfied Richardson's concern 'As to the Time for publishing' (Richardson to Hill, 10 May 1749, Hill to Richardson, 15 September 1746). Attentive to the distractions presented by seasonal events, well-publicised trials, or popular theatrical productions, Richardson timed publication to avoid diverting attention from a new book.

Like other colleagues in the trade, Richardson used increasingly sophisticated techniques to ensure the most favourable reception of a book: post-dating texts published at the end of the year so they would appear 'new' longer (*Pamela* was published in November 1740, although the date on the title page was 1741), or inserting 'puffs' or written praise in the prefatory material to cultivate credibility and interest. Richardson also recognised the need to create a demand within the marketplace to heighten anticipation for a forthcoming book. For example, to build interest in a 1746 publication of Hill's, the men agreed that a 'pre-cursor Piece ... must greatly tend to further the Demand for the Prose Tract'; that piece 'might prove of Use toward making the long Work expected, and when publish'd sell it off the faster' (Hill to Richardson, 21 July 1746). The strategic use of advertisements could generate similar anticipation.

Richardson's attention to detail extends to subtleties of a publication's physical appearance. He was careful visually to distinguish authorised from pirated editions. Corresponding with Millar on 31 July 1750 about the proofs for a new edition of Edward Young's *The Complaint*, Richardson focuses on very detailed elements of the book (title page, running titles, the trim for binding) so 'it will look still better, and be a more sizeable Volume than the pirated one'. Similarly, he regards title pages as a kind of 'invitation to the purchaser', counselling Hill to choose wisely for 'hundreds ... will see the title', which 'alone must strike ... the public Attention' (Richardson to Hill, 27 October 1748, 25 June 1746).

This attention to the nuances of the marketplace – appearance, timing, and placement of a publication – stemmed, in part, from Richardson's belief that in this new commercial space readers actually constituted what Hill characterises as the 'new Rank of Purchasers' (Hill to Richardson, 10 July 1746). Although Richardson benefited tremendously from the dynamic quality of the marketplace, he observes to Hill in a letter of 27 October 1748 that readers 'want you to descend to their level'; 'the world has no thought to bestow. Simplicity is all their cry.' However, readers or 'purchasers' secure books for many reasons. Discussing the popularity of Alexander Pope with Richardson in a letter of 10 July 1746, Hill attributes the 'constant Clan of Buyers' for Pope's work in part to 'Men who bought his Pieces rather to oblige his Patrons, than from any Motive of their Judgement'. '*Curiosity* induc['d]' them to 'examine into the true Merit of so nois'd a Writer … as serv'd well enough the present Prospect of a Bookseller', continues Hill. Curiosity, celebrity (being a 'nois'd' writer), and personal connections advance a text and an author in the marketplace – all elements important to the popularity of Richardson's most successful novel, *Pamela*.

Pamela in the Marketplace

Richardson drew on his knowledge and experience in the marketplace when publishing *Pamela*. Understanding the risks involved in any publication, and considering texts a kind of investment property, Richardson retained only one third of the copyright of *Pamela*, minimising his own financial liability. (He subsequently kept the entire copyright for *Clarissa* and *Sir Charles Grandison*.) That minimised risk did not diminish his intensity in marketing the novel, however. Emerging out of Richardson's composition of *Familiar Letters on All Occasions*, *Pamela* responds to Richardson's desire to 'introduce a new species of writing, that might possibly turn young people into a course of reading different from the pomp and parade of romance-writing, and dismissing the improbable and marvellous, with which novels generally abound, might tend to promote the cause of religion and virtue' (Richardson to Aaron Hill, *c.* 1 February 1741).

This 'species', 'written in an easy and natural manner', to some degree answered the desire for simplicity Richardson perceived among readers. His epistolary novel, with its aspirational tale of social ascent interwoven with moral instruction and titillating episodes, sought to improve, educate, and entertain. 'I am of the opinion', writes Richardson, 'that it is necessary for a genius to accommodate itself to the mode and taste of the world it is cast into' (Richardson to Aaron Hill, 27 October 1748). Thus the novel's straightforward narrative, accessibility, and colloquial language, all mercilessly parodied by Richardson's contemporaries ranging from Henry Fielding to Eliza Haywood, strive to accommodate the 'taste of the world'. Richardson's connections in the trade gave *Pamela* unusual advantages that also contributed to the book's overwhelming popularity. He had 'to his credit a large stock of goodwill in the commercial sense … [and] … the book was published under conditions much more favourable than those usually enjoyed by works of fiction',[4] observes Alan McKillop.

Within weeks of its November 1740 publication, *Pamela* ignited a discussion that generated what Thomas Keymer and Peter Sabor term a 'Riot of print'.[5] *Pamela* saturated the marketplace. By January of 1741, advertisements for a second edition of *Pamela* appeared; a third edition followed quickly in March, with a sixth edition, illustrated with twenty-nine engravings, released at the end of 1742. *Pamela* was praised or partially reprinted in some of the leading periodicals of the time: *Weekly Miscellany, History of the Works of the Learned*, and *Gentleman's Magazine*. As the *Gentleman's Magazine* observes in January 1741, in London it was judged 'as great a Sign of want of Curiosity not to have read *Pamela*, as not to have seen the French and Italian dancers'. In little more than a year after the initial publication of *Pamela*, more than two dozen pamphlets, sequels, translations, and parodies appeared, along with consumer goods including a *Pamela* fan, waxworks, and engravings. Publications that had nothing at all to do with *Pamela* appended that name to their title page in hopes of attracting purchasers. 'Virtually anything with the name "Pamela" attached to it could make a profit', notes Albert Rivero.[6] This practice was not unique to Richardson's rivals; Richardson's 11 December 1742 advertisement in the *Daily Gazetteer* for an edition of *Aesop's Fables* reads 'N.B. This is the ÆSOP quoted in PAMELA'.

These often tangentially connected publications, regardless of their origin, maintained a focus on *Pamela*, arguably benefitting Richardson initially. The businessman in Richardson recognised the value of what he described in an August 1741 letter to James Leake as 'Remarks, Imitations, Retailings of the Story, Pyracies, &c' that kept the narrative visible in the marketplace (some of his critics even suggested that Richardson himself was responsible for some of those publications). Yet over time, such publications, proliferating so quickly that Richardson could not keep track of them, threatened to erode the power of Richardson's originating text. Many were, in Hill's words, merely a 'Bookseller's Contrivance' designed to appeal to the 'Light & Loose Readers' (Aaron Hill to Richardson, 25 May 1741). But they forced Richardson to be reactive. Threatened by a sequel planned by 'those who knew nothing of the Story, nor the Delicacy required in the Continuation of the Piece', Richardson composed *Pamela in her Exalted Condition* (Richardson to James Leake, August 1741).

The sequel captures the contradictory dilemma that defined much of Richardson's career – how to maintain marketability while preserving his (self-appointed) didactic mission. In early January 1742, Richardson expresses to George Cheyne his concern about the critical response to this sequel. Responding to the charge that the text was 'Defective in Incidents', Richardson asserts his aim, 'as far as my poor Talents would permit, to instruct, rather than to Surprize ... For I always had it in View ... to make the Story rather *useful*, than *diverting*.' Richardson remains steadfast in his commitment morally to educate his readers; nevertheless, a concern about sales immediately follows such high-minded claims: 'I printed a very large Number, and the Bookseller advises me to proceed with another Impression.' He asks for 'hints' from Cheyne about its reception only to learn from him in a 10 January 1742 letter that 'The Booksellers here says [*sic*] it sells very well, but not so quick as the first.' Richardson never strayed far from an abiding concern with the marketability of a text or from the preservation of his own hard-won cultural capital.

Post-*Pamela*

With his subsequent two novels, Richardson tried to duplicate the commercial success of *Pamela* and generate a comparable level of cultural engagement. He discusses with Hill strategies for the length, timing, and publication sequence of *Clarissa*: 'I find my principal Design and End so liable to be misapprehended', he laments in a 26 January 1747 letter, 'and the story so likely to be thought *Inferior*, which I thought *Superior*'. He fears that he 'cannot recommend it as to Sale'. Marketing the novel, Richardson exploited the potential commercial value of *Pamela*. The title page to *Clarissa* advertises that text as 'Published by the Editor of *Pamela*'; the title page to *Sir Charles Grandison* then adds *Clarissa* to the list of the 'Editor's' publications. However, Richardson also confronts '[t]he present low taste' in 'that indolent (that lazy, I should rather call it) world', which might resist the novel's length (Richardson to Aaron Hill, 27 October 1748). Hill urges Richardson to consider the 'Publication of one Volume, as it stands', as a kind of 'Trial'. 'After the Experiment', depending on the 'Reception', Richardson can either 'publish all the written' letters, 'without contracting them' or 'reduc[ing] their Number' (Aaron Hill to Richardson, 23 January 1747).

After the novel's length proved too formidable for some, Richardson constructed a table of contents so detailed that it essentially eliminated the need to read the novel itself. Hill scolds Richardson for catering to 'mean Book poachers' who could, as a result, 'overcheaply' satisfy their 'superficial Curiosity, which, but for That, the Fame of your Clarissa had compell'd to buy' (Aaron Hill to Richardson, 10 July 1749). Richardson simultaneously invites the superficially curious to engage the text ('overcheaply') either by purchasing and reading only the table of contents, or by not purchasing but reading the table of contents at a bookseller's. Either gesture, however, contributed to the 'fame' of *Clarissa*.

With *Sir Charles Grandison*, Richardson sought to engender the same kind of cultural conversation *Pamela* inspired. To Lady Echlin, he expresses his hope that the title character will be like 'a Gauntlet thrown out … on purpose to provoke friendly debate' (10 October 1754). Again, he seems willing to extend the debate to those who will not read the entire text. He laboured over an index to that novel (comparable to the detailed table of contents to *Clarissa*) that he imagined would generate discussion even among non-readers. As he details to Susanna Highmore in a letter of 10 January 1754, 'it will be a great Help to such as will like to join in Talk on the Story, without giving themselves the Trouble of reading the Book'. Richardson tacitly acknowledges the diverse paths to his fame or notoriety: some buy but don't read (at least not beyond the 'superficial curiosity' satisfied by an index or table of contents); others read, but don't buy. All, he hopes, will discuss or even learn from his texts. All, he knows, will help maintain his reputation.

In a book published six years before his death, Richardson yoked morality with marketability by publishing extracts from his three novels as *A Collection of the Moral and Instructive Sentiments, Maxims, Cautions, and Reflexions, contained in the Histories of Pamela, Clarissa, and Sir Charles Grandison*. He designed it as a 'Pocket Volume, to serve as a kind of Vade Mecum to such as either have read, o<r>, having not read, can dispense with the Stories, for the Sake of the Instruction aimed <to b>e given in them' (Richardson to Johannes Stinstra, 28 June 1754). While Richardson admits to Benjamin Kennicott in a 26 November 1754 letter that 'I cannot expect much' from such a volume, its design and intended use reflect – and attempt to resolve – the central tensions defining Richardson's career. The text's detailed citation system, complemented by the index or 'Table of Sentiments', directs readers to the location of the original (albeit revised) passages whether in the octavo or '3rd and subsequent Editions of the Twelves' (or duodecimo). The text appeals equally to those who have or have not read the book, those who seek the story or the instruction, those who own all or no previous editions of the novels. Using both product differentiation and diversification, niche and mass marketing, this publication is the apotheosis of Richardson's 'not … unartful management' of the literary marketplace.

Notes

1 William Merritt Sale, Jr's important early work, *Samuel Richardson: Master Printer*, has been complemented by Keith Maslen's *Samuel Richardson of London, Printer: A Study of His Printing Based on Ornament Use and Business Accounts*. The count of newspaper and periodical issues is Maslen's (p. 2).
2 Maslen, *Samuel Richardson*, p. 38.

3 For a discussion of the differences between printer, publisher, and book-seller, see Sale, *Master Printer*, Chapter 5; and James Raven, *The Business of Books: Booksellers and the English Book Trade, 1450–1850* (Yale University Press, 2007).

4 Alan Dugald McKillop, *Samuel Richardson, Printer and Novelist* (Chapel Hill: University of North Carolina Press, 1936), p. 14.

5 Thomas Keymer and Peter Sabor, 'Introduction', in Keymer and Sabor, *The 'Pamela' Controversy*, Vol. 11, pp. xiii–xxix (p. xiv). See also Keymer and Sabor, *'Pamela' in the Marketplace*.

6 Albert J. Rivero, 'General Introduction', in *PE*, pp. xxxi–lxxxi (p. xxxiv).

PART IV

The Book and Its Readers

CHAPTER 13

The Material Book

Christopher Flint

When Samuel Richardson began apprenticing at a printing-house in 1706, commercial books, even of a single edition, were more variable and self-evidently products of manual labour than they appear now. Although the European hand press had been transforming textual economies since the mid-fifteenth century, gradually diminishing manuscript sales, books were still expensive items fashioned for a small, literate segment of the populace. Most were made in London for various 'booksellers' (publishers in today's terms) by a limited number of affiliated printers. A member of the book industry coming of age in this context, Richardson would have been attuned to literature's material dimensions, inclined to regard his novels as a set of physical objects assembled for publication. While such material concerns cannot adequately explain what made the fiction groundbreaking, they certainly contributed to Richardson's perception of its cultural value.

Assembling the Book

Richardson's novels appeared in the 1740s and 1750s, when he was not only a seasoned printer who knew every detail about bookmaking but also Master of the Stationers' Company, the guild originally established by royal charter to regulate and organise English printing. Having achieved a social position higher than his modest origins augured, he undoubtedly valued all elements of the material book and the means of its production and distribution, many of which depended on arranging material that first existed in parts. The act of collecting thus became a governing concept for a figure now regarded as a pioneer of the modern novel and psychological realism.

It helps, then, to imagine Richardson in his printing-house overseeing the making of books, pamphlets, public and private bills, parliamentary papers, newspapers, short jobbing work, and proceedings from learned

Figure 13.1 The interior of an eighteenth-century printing-house. J. G. Ernesti, *Die Wol-eingerichtete Büchdrückerey* (Nuremberg, 1733).

societies (Figure 13.1). For him, books were part of a nexus of printed materials and business relations that shaped Enlightenment culture, and his work as a printer encompassed religious, moral, social, professional, legal, political, scientific, and literary discourses. Most involved contributions by others that Richardson assembled for publication: the *Philosophical Transactions of the Royal Society*; any of several newspapers he printed; or his revised version of Roger L'Estrange's *Aesop's Fables*, a compilation whose authorship, despite the name Aesop, was the work of many hands, including Richardson's, as discussed by Pat Rogers in the following chapter (pp. 132–3). Conversely, he presented each of his novels as a 'series of letters' collected by an unidentified editor, Richardson's name visible only at the bottom of the title page with the phrase 'printed for', which identifies the publisher. While assemblage applies to many commodities, Richardson's profession would have encouraged him to observe the relation of part to whole in the production of books, arguably shaping how he viewed language, a literary work's unity or meaning, and a publication's relation to the public sphere.

Rising from apprentice to a master printer operating several presses, Richardson gained first-hand experience with the diverse aspects of book-making and marketing. He acquired a substantial collection of moveable type – the letters, numbers, punctuation, blanks, florets, figures, lines, rules, and ornaments that constitute the sign system upon which the book depends. He probably observed, if he did not participate in, the making of printing ink, which was still produced on site by late-seventeenth-century printers according to carefully guarded recipes that guaranteed suitable viscosity for presswork. For print runs Richardson needed to calculate the appropriate size and amount of printer's paper, stored in stacks on his premises. Even distinctive hand-cut headpieces topping prominent pages in the books he printed reflect Richardson's rising stature, since the uniqueness of such ornaments authenticated a given work – and remains today a means to identify Richardson's output.

Early in his career Richardson also probably corrected copy and composed 'galleys': wooden or metal trays containing lineated and spaced typeface (positioned in reverse) for a given page. He undoubtedly knew how to assemble the page galleys into the 'forme' (the layout of pages on the large sheet of paper according to the prescribed imposition scheme so that when folded correct pagination and orientation resulted). He likewise understood the mechanical operation of the press: inking the formes; feeding the paper; applying correct hand pressure on the lever; extracting, hanging, and piling the printed sheets. Periodically, he would order further proof-reading and correcting. He would, finally, attend to folding the sheets into quires, gathering these in the right order according to their signatures (the combination of letters and numbers on select galleys that distinguish the particular forme they belong to), sewing them into the stitched text that comprises individual books, and then arranging for the volumes to be bound or packaged unbound for sale. Throughout, Richardson would perform the main activities defining print culture: writing, assembling, distributing, and reading published matter. Even his management of workmen – senior employees acting as the 'master's deputy', correctors, journeymen responsible for main tasks such as composing and presswork, apprentices, and printer's devils (boys who remove printed sheets from the tympan) – involved orchestrating various 'hands' who functioned as a collective (a 'chapel' in the parlance of the print industry).

As his career progressed, Richardson changed residence several times, but until his final relocation in 1752 the buildings his family occupied also housed his operations (the custom of most master printers). The personal and professional would thus have been deeply affected by the material book. Although Richardson regarded writing fiction as 'leisure', the printing business always accompanied that activity. Unlike many other authors he could not ignore the pragmatic elements of book-making; writing novels underlined powerful links between leisure and work, writing and printing, family life and business.

Marketing the Book

Though addressing a rapidly expanding readership, eighteenth-century novels remained expensive. Richardson's officially sold from 2s 6d per volume, as sheets in paper wrappers for custom binding, to 6s per bound volume (e.g. the de luxe illustrated edition of *Pamela*), but the most commonly advertised price was 3s per bound volume. Such prices would consume a considerable part of an average labourer's yearly earnings, so owning a book signalled economic privilege (though books often circulated in ways that did not necessitate personal purchase). Paper absorbed most production costs (upwards of 50 per cent according to book historians), and authors customarily received payment by the sheet – an arrangement Richardson presumably waived when publishing his own fiction.

Richardson occasionally complained in letters about the quality of the paper he obtained, whether purchased directly or as commissioned by the bookseller or author of a particular work he was hired to print. Mindful of print economy, he also vacillated over such matters as whether a 'crowded' number of words per page offset the cost of lengthy novels or subjected readers to illegible and aesthetically unappealing text. He likewise puzzled over the appropriation of literary works in the print marketplace. Many popular books, such as *Robinson Crusoe*, circulated in abbreviated and poorly printed volumes distributed on the streets by peddlers and chapmen; *Pamela* similarly prompted numerous spurious sequels, adaptations, and abridgments that both vexed Richardson for their frequent 'baseness' (Richardson to James Leake, August 1741) and benefited him by prompting continued interest in the novel. That is, tensions in the book trade repeatedly arose over class-based marketing, economic conditions, the alternative means by which texts reached wider audiences, and professed Enlightenment claims of egalitarianism.

While such material considerations affected other authors, they concerned Richardson especially. He published his novels as multi-volume works, in different configurations over several editions, each title representing a *set* of material books (though in eighteenth-century usage the word 'book' could denote both a unified collection of volumes and an individual volume). The four-, seven-, and eight-volume forms of his fiction distinguished it from the popular amorous fiction that often appeared initially in single volumes, which Richardson both exploited and disparaged: self-avowed 'novels' by writers such as Aphra Behn, Delarivier Manley, and Eliza Haywood. The differing editions of Richardson's fiction functioned as a collection of renewable parts that could offset what he perceived as the corrupting influence of such 'novels'. And while the multi-volume nature of his fiction aligned it with another precursor, the romance, his focus on a contiguous set of characters modelling 'the Conduct of common Life' (*PE*, p. 454) belied the connection. He scrutinised, in other words, how book production affected the dignity of his chosen genre.

In Richardson's lifetime, the way in which book formats functioned in the literary marketplace changed significantly. Until mid-century most books appeared in folio, the largest format, based on a single folding of the sizeable sheets of paper used to produce a single signed gathering of four paginated leaves. After mid-century, folios were generally reserved for extensive reference works such as Johnson's *Dictionary* or lavish volumes containing full-scale engravings. Smaller formats became much more prevalent, from quartos (based on two folds or a quarter of a sheet) to octavos (an eighth of a sheet) and duodecimos (a twelfth). The two smallest formats became standard for novels and other serious literature from just before the middle until the end of the century. As with *Pamela* in 1742 and *Clarissa* in 1751, Richardson published *Sir Charles Grandison* in a special octavo version for high-end purchasers in 1754; this parallel appearance of editions in different formats produced indexical problems that made citation difficult when he sought to regularise the means of identifying passages for 'a *comparing* Reader' judging the accumulating versions of his texts (Richardson to Thomas Edwards, 4 August 1755). The disposition of the literary work in diverse forms both amplified and encumbered his instructional, aesthetic, and commercial aims.

The variant forms of paratext, corrections, and added or subtracted letters from edition to edition similarly reveal Richardson's focus on a pliable physical design. *Clarissa* alone, the novel Richardson reconfigured most, appears substantially different from version to version. The third edition, for instance, not only retained numerous changes introduced in the second edition, but also added enough fresh material to necessitate an eighth volume, including testimonials from readers in poetry and prose, editorial footnotes that clarify and sometimes defend narrative choices, new explanatory paragraphs, expanded scenes of as many as ten pages, and various 'restored' letters omitted in prior editions. It featured a larger type to accommodate audience needs, 'Fault having been found, particularly by elderly Readers, and by some who have weak Eyes, with the smallness of the Type, on which some Parts of the Three last Volumes were printed'.[1] But perhaps most visually arresting were the marginal 'Dots or inverted Full-points' distinguishing each line of 'restored' text, creating a reading experience that highlights the text's material evolution. All of these changes modulate the visual appearance of the text, and Richardson ensured that his readers would recognise the difference by emphasising on the title page that 'Many Passages and some Letters are restored from the Original Manuscripts', as well as adding an augmented preface that describes the edition's new print features.

From these permutations, which appeared as well in the concurrent octavo fourth edition, Richardson selected the material for *Letters and Passages Restored from the Original Manuscripts of the History of Clarissa*, marketed to those owning prior editions of *Clarissa*. Such myriad alterations seem to confirm the power of print to guarantee, over time, a standardised form, yet they highlight the inconsistencies that make that intention elusive. Without access to the original manuscripts of the novels (none of which have survived), we can never really be sure of whether any such additions were created after the fact and introduced as if they were restored elements, or whether they were indeed reinstated from what was left behind in earlier editions. But whether a marketing ploy or not, the text's mutability mattered to Richardson as a way of shaping reader response, enhancing aesthetic pleasure, and promoting sales.

By the time Richardson had edited all three of his novels towards the end of his career they effectively constituted a body of work united by the nimble hand of the editor – Richardson's preferred designation for the compiler of the text he authored. It is the term he used when defending his last novel from pirating by Irish booksellers in 1753. On the title page to *The Case of Samuel Richardson, of London, Printer; with Regard to the Invasion of His Property in the History of Sir Charles Grandison*, he first calls himself 'printer' and then subsequently 'editor' but never author, ultimately referring to the text as physical pieces of property, 'sheets' that he alone is permitted to gather and sell. He describes the work not in the terms of post-Romantic notions of authorship (that is, based on genius and a protected right to the words, thoughts, and ideas themselves apart from their material form) but in specific empirical terms – though he does emphasise the work's 'originality'. As he puts it, 'Never was work more the property of any man than this is his. The copy never was in any other hand. He borrows not from any author. The paper, the printing, entirely at his own expense, to a very large amount, returns of which he cannot see in several months' (*Case*, p. 2).

Even the length of Richardson's novels suggests a fixation on accumulation. Responding to demands for more after the completion of *Sir Charles Grandison*, he exclaims, perhaps disingenuously, '19 Volumes in Twelves, close Printed – In Three Stories – Monstrous – Who, that sees them ranged on one Shelf, will forgive me?' (Richardson to Lady Echlin, 17 May 1754). Here the size, format, and number of volumes unite in one 'monstrous' body of work. Given this, it is all the more surprising that at the very moment he was castigating himself for voluminousness Richardson was mining the already published work, including the collection he had already gleaned from *Clarissa*, to produce auxiliary forms of the originals, *Meditations Collected from the Sacred Books* (a volume supposedly written by Clarissa) and *A Collection of the Moral and Instructive Sentiments, Maxims, Cautions, and Reflexions, Contained in the Histories of Pamela, Clarissa, and Sir Charles Grandison*. These and other works reveal an author constantly supplementing the fiction with advice works that gathered parts of the novels into wholly new books that retained mysterious connections to the source texts. Richardson called this form of collecting 'sentimentalizing' (coalescing the double meaning of sentiment as 'idea' and 'feeling'), and its structure reflects the lexicographic bias of one of the people who requested the work, Samuel Johnson. Interestingly, Richardson did not merely cull sentiments from the already published fiction; he also revised and added sentiments that never appeared in the published works from which they derived.

In repurposing the novels, Richardson's practice reflected the pervasive eighteenth-century remediation of printed works in pirated volumes, redactions, dramatisations, commonplace books, magazine reprints, and even illustrations, paintings, tapestries, and china. This was a period that famously struggled over definitions of copyright; insofar as Richardson's fiction (often pirated) features characters concerned with copying, extracting, sharing, annotating, revising, possessing, and losing letters, it reflects the real-world cultural appropriation of texts. Richardson's efforts at retaining proprietary control of his works, from publishing the *Case of Samuel Richardson* to supplementing the novels, reinforce the notion that pre-existing quasi-autonomous documents authorise the fictive enterprise. The novels could always, in a sense, be disassembled, downsized, and reassembled.

Reading the Material Book

Richardson's occupation as a printer relates to his fiction on many levels: the representation of particular books within the fiction; the differences between editions of the novels and the corresponding obsessive rewriting by the protagonists; the function of libraries or book collections in both the real and fictive worlds; and the characters' claims of ownership over their writing as reflections of Richardson's concerns over copy as property, and so on. But perhaps the most striking textual self-consciousness occurs when Richardson highlights paper and ink, arguably the most crucial elements constituting a book. These moments include internal line breaks filled with distinctive florets, the particular signalling of enclosed documents, left-justified columns of quotation marks that signify one transcribed letter within another, offset justified lists, italicised poetry and narrative intrusions, indices, a variety of printer's ornaments, constant letter-numbering and running titles, and the compulsion in so many characters to stockpile or proscribe paper and ink, as well as references to tear-stained ink, shaky handwriting, and scratched-out or torn pages. Frequently, these textual features blur the lines between a printer's and a character's contribution to the book's composition.

Because of their size, Richardson's works scatter textual innovations: *Clarissa* alone contains paper fragments printed diagonally and upside down to express mental and physical disorder, a fold-out sheet of music attributed to the heroine but based on a poem by Elizabeth Carter and used initially without the author's permission, cursive print that mimics penmanship, pages of aggressive indices (or 'printer's fists') marking Lovelace's angry responses to an intercepted letter, copious cross-referencing footnotes, bullet points designating restored passages, asterisks and bracketed inserts, a will reproduced in a smaller font, strategic italicisation and capitalisation, and various concluding appendices that stress how much *Clarissa* is a book in the reader's hands. Cumulatively, these details accentuate how material forms of public discourse frame the lives of the characters writing private letters. They also signal the care with which Richardson managed the visual aspects of the printed page in his fictional work; very little of the material text escaped his inspection, from typography and formatting to bibliographical matters and paper quality. This attention to detail was, in turn, calculated to promote a more knowing consumer.

A busy professional reader of both correspondence and public discourse, Richardson weighed how material books mediated producer and consumer.

The distributing, redistributing, and collecting of letters in the novels parallel the flow of handwritten and printed documents that defined his business life and fuelled the copious remediation of the fictional works that made him famous. By foregrounding the vagaries of discursive networks and the unpredictable ways in which pages of writing take on an existence of their own, Richardson accentuates the physical processes by which his printed volumes move through the public sphere. The sharing of Pamela, Clarissa, and Harriet's collected texts by disparate readers within the story world prefigures their fictional and real circulation as published books. The visual traces of this activity, in turn, offered one of the many ways in which Richardson sought to cultivate a more alert readership of what he called on many occasions 'a new species of writing'.

Note

1 *Clarissa*, 3rd edn, 8 vols. (London, 1751), 1.ix.x.

CHAPTER 14

Editing

Pat Rogers

Suppose that we were able to ask Richardson what kind of editing he was involved in during his career. To start with, he would have wanted to have the term clarified, since the notions covered today by the term 'to edit' were not all present in eighteenth-century idiom. Until very recently the *OED* had no place for senses connected with the physical treatment of films or aural tapes, and it was silent on newly extended usages such as 'edit in' or 'edit out', quite apart from the meaning of 'self-editing' used in psychology for the process of analysing and attempting to alter the self. What then would Richardson have been able to point to? Certainly he would have identified the extensive process of revision that he carried out in his own novels, discussed by Peter Sabor above (pp. 20–4). But he might have thought too of the routine work he performed on manuscripts that came to him as a printer or more rarely as a publisher. Third, the term might extend to the collaborative assistance he gave to fellow authors such as Sarah Fielding and Edward Young. Last, and most significantly for this chapter, he could instance a few books in which he acted as what today is generally called the editor. The first three activities can be described here in a summary fashion; the fourth will be explored in a little more detail.

Self-editing

Students of Richardson learn almost from their first acquaintance with the three novels that Richardson never liked to leave his texts alone. Each went through repeated editions in different formats, each was modified by means of cancelled pages, and each gained by some mode of what Derrida calls *supplémentarité*. We have a battery of paratextual items such as prefaces, notes, postscripts, indexes, contents pages (typically, in what has become the French manner, at the end), cast-lists, collections of choice sentiments from the text, verses addressed to the author – and more. These make up a veritable editorial apparatus, in the style of traditional editions of classical authors. This is apart from the afterlife of each novel in the form of sequels, pamphlets, rejoinders, and *disjecta membra*, such as the *Meditations* from (chiefly) the Old Testament prophets that Richardson brought out in a limited edition (1750) to boost the scriptural authority of *Clarissa*.[1] Some of these belong to the world of advertising and promotion rather than what we normally regard as editing, but they all had to do with interpreting the text in some way, and constitute a sort of hermeneutic gloss on the narrative. The author made sure that readers were aware of even small alterations, bringing out, for example, *Letters and Passages Restored from the Original Manuscripts of the History of Clarissa* in 1750. Much as we have today online continuations of favourite books by readers driven to emulation, contemporary readers offered up alternative openings and closures to the novels, and Richardson took note of their suggestions, even if he did not generally adopt them.

In-House Editing

Richardson printed at least 500 items, ranging from single-sheet announcements and pamphlets to multi-volume blockbusters. In the latter case, as was normal, the work was most often shared out among a number of printers, seen in a publication such as Nathaniel Salmon's *New Survey of Great Britain* (1718–30, 1731). Some of the commissions that he undertook might be regarded as jobbing work, but this term would be misleading as it implies occasional items such as playbills or tradesmen's ledgers. Richardson's day-to-day labours in his shop included printing the official records of Parliament, which covered bills, votes, committee reports, and later the issue of the historic *Journals* of the House of Commons from the time of Edward VI. This was a mammoth task, highly important in archiving the course of British politics over the centuries, and its significance for Richardson's own career has seldom been properly appreciated. The series ran to twenty-seven volumes, each amounting to more than 600 pages. The last of these came out in March 1762, a few months after Richardson's death; the entire venture contained thousands of pages and tens of millions of words. Not only was a large amount of capital tied up (and payment from the contractor Nicholas Hardinge often in arrears), a huge amount of time must have gone into overseeing this project. The parliamentary authorities might have expected a simple verbatim reprint of the manuscript journals, but decisions about presentation would have been made in the printing-house, with Richardson himself likely to have taken the main responsibility.

Another quasi-official role came when he purchased a half-share of the exclusive patent to print law books from Catherine Lintot in 1759. This allowed him to bring out remunerative items such as Richard Burn's *Justice of the Peace and Parish Officer*, a best-seller since its appearance in 1755, and already into six editions. Unfortunately Richardson died too soon to collect full returns on this investment, but the few items that he had time to produce, such as Burn's *Digest of the Militia Laws* printed for Andrew Millar in 1760, would have needed basic editing – if anyone carried this out, it would have been Richardson himself, as Millar was seldom given to extensive interference with the text.

In addition a number of periodicals emerged from the shop in Salisbury Court. These included the political and cultural biweekly the *Plain Dealer* (1724–5) run by his friend Aaron Hill, and the mainly theatrical journal *The Prompter* (1734–6) in which Hill again took a leading share. It is possible that Richardson had some responsibility for the editorial contents in the latter, but in any case he would certainly have had to attend to the nuts and bolts of production. The same applies, with qualifications, to the newspapers in which he had some financial interest: that is the *Daily Journal* (from around 1725 to 1737) and the *Daily Gazetteer* (from about 1735 to 1746). In the newspaper press it was then customary for printers to serve both as proprietors of a given organ and also as what we should call today the editor. You could be simultaneously William Randolph Hearst and Katharine Graham, or, should you wish, Rupert Murdoch and Piers Morgan. But at the very same moment you would be the person standing alongside the press supervising production and circulation as the physical copies were delivered. It has not been shown that Richardson took an important part in determining what went into the columns of these papers, but neither can it be convincingly disproved. His opinions changed over time and his willingness to offend those in power certainly diminished over the decades. It seems unlikely that he ever harboured Jacobite sentiments, though when he printed the duke of Wharton's *True Briton* in 1723–4 he did skirt some controversial issues.

Collaborations

Abundant evidence exists to show that Richardson enjoyed sharing literary undertakings with others. He operated in some sense as a mentor to friends such as Aaron Hill and Sarah Fielding, but it is hard to be sure just how active a part he took in planning or revising their works. On one occasion we do get a clue in a remark by Fielding, who engaged in a friendly exchange of letters with Richardson over several years. On 14 December 1758 she wrote to him about her novel *The History of the Countess of Dellwyn*, which Millar would publish in the following March. She asks her friend, 'I beg that you will be so very kind to cast an Eye on the printing of it if your Health will permit without injury and pray be not scrupulous to alter any Expressions you dislike.'[2] If he was too busy, she intended to leave the matter to his nephew and successor in the business, William Richardson. Perhaps Fielding was simply paying due deference to the great master of the novel, and did not expect her request to be taken literally. However, it is possible that Richardson had made suggestions to improve the text of other works she wrote, such as *The Governess* (1749) and *The Lives of Cleopatra and Octavia* (1757).

Another writer whom Richardson helped was Charlotte Lennox, who in 1751 was trying to persuade Millar to accept her novel *The Female Quixote*, then at an advanced stage of composition. Richardson gave Millar a glowing endorsement of the manuscript and made detailed comments on the story, as well as suggesting paragraph breaks. Lennox did not take all his advice: where she refers to an exemplary triumvirate of wits, 'a *Young*, a *Richardson*, or a *Johnson*', he had urged her with real or affected modesty to omit his name as 'utterly unworthy' of mention in this company. The passage remained unchanged when the book appeared in March 1752.[3]

We are on slightly stronger ground in the case of another literary ally, the poet Edward Young. In May 1759 Millar and the Dodsley brothers published Young's influential critical salvo, *Conjectures on Original Composition, in a Letter to the Author of 'Sir Charles Grandison'*. It was not such an original composition after all, as Richardson may have planted the first seed in Young's mind for such a work, and the two corresponded about its material for a long period before publication. Richardson urged in strong terms that Young's praise of Pope should be toned down, explicitly because the poet lacked 'originality' and 'creative power' (14 January 1757). Here we have perhaps moved beyond the normal function of an editor, in terms of suggesting changes in matters such as phrasing, expression, argumentative coherence, and the like. Richardson is asking Young to change his mind, or at least to suppress his inconvenient opinions.

Fully Edited Books

Finally we come to books by others in which Richardson played an active and substantial part. He had considerable help with *The Negotiations of Sir Thomas Roe, in His Embassy to the Ottoman Porte, from the Year 1621 to 1628 Inclusive*, drawing on the services of the historian Thomas Carte. The manuscript letters were in his possession, though they have been split up and in some cases lost since then. According to his bibliographer, William M. Sale, Jr, 'In preparing the material for the press, [he] made the index and tables; and, with some assistance from John Ward, Professor of Rhetoric, Gresham College, London, he wrote the dedication and preface.'[4] This probably indicates the sort of contribution Richardson would have made to a number of other works that passed through his printing-house. Nothing very distinctive emerges in the dedication to the king, which he signed, though it is less cloying and sycophantic than some of its kind. Part of the preface, relating to conclusive publishing negotiations with the Society for the Encouragement of Learning, can only have been written by Richardson himself. In this portion he explains that a life of Roe was originally intended, but this was dropped when it was decided to bring out only the first section of the manuscript. Instead he provides an excerpt from the entry for Roe (*c.* 1581–1644), a career diplomat, that was found in Anthony Wood's *Athenæ oxonienses*. In the event the promised continuation never appeared.

Some years after Richardson died, a work in four volumes by Anna Meades (*c.* 1734–79) was published under the title *The History of Sir William Harrington* (1771). Meades was an unabashed admirer of the novels – especially, we might suppose, *Sir Charles Grandison*. She had contacted Richardson in 1757 and asked for his advice on her attempt to follow in his steps as a chronicler of modern domestic life. As was his wont, he gave the manuscript careful attention, and his detailed suggestions for revisions survive. He also made 'a list of pointed revision recommendations' to Urania Johnson, eldest daughter of his friend Aaron Hill, when she gave him a draft of her novel *Almira* (1762). His criticisms were severe enough to cause her to break off correspondence with him.[5]

A more extensive act of retrieval is found in the collection of *Aesop's Fables*, which came at the start of Richardson's career as a writer – the first edition ('1740' for 1739) makes up no. 1 in Sale's bibliography. Richardson told Johannes Stinstra that he had been commissioned 'to revise the numerous editions of Æsop's Fables in English, and to give the Public one I would commend for Children' (letter of 2 June 1753). In the event, he considered only two of the numerous previous efforts to render Aesop to be 'worthy of Notice', namely the versions by Roger L'Estrange (1692) and Samuel Croxall (1722). In his preface he quotes both of these authors at length, agreeing with Croxall that the high Tory principles inculcated by L'Estrange are unsuitable for modern British youth, who now need lessons on 'that Spirit of Truth and Liberty' brought about by the Glorious Revolution and Hanoverian accession. However, he criticises Croxall for pedantry and strained political interpretations (this time in a Whiggish direction), and bases his own version on L'Estrange, seeking to preserve the 'principal Graces and Beauties' of the earlier text, while scaling down the style to make it more appropriate to a readership of children.[6] Despite these laudable aims, it was Croxall who ultimately won the battle of the editors: his version reached sixteen editions in the remainder of the century, and lived on long enough to become the favourite of the infant Robert Browning when his mother read it in the nursery.

Even before this item, Richardson had begun a long-term project, a series of publications bringing up to date Daniel Defoe's *Tour thro' the Whole of Great Britain* (1724–6). It is now known that he must have overseen as well as printed the second edition of 1738, in three volumes; and he carried out further recensions with the third (1742), fourth (1748), fifth (1753), and sixth (1761), all in four volumes. The most interesting is 1738, where Richardson sets out his aims and lays down the template for revisions in future years. He claims that 'We have taken very great Liberties with our Author in the first two Volumes' (1, ix) – less so in the third, dealing with the north of England and Scotland, where the editor was much less well informed. In the first volume only, he marked his interpolations by placing them in square brackets. Actually the substantial changes are fewer than we might expect. Richardson did omit some out-of-date material, supplemented a few sections (for example on Oxford and Cambridge), and beefed up the account of Bath, where he was able to insert a cumbrous puff on behalf of his brother-in-law, the bookseller James Leake; as detailed by Linda Bree below (pp. 283–4), the important London section also features notable updating. He naturally suppressed an element oddly included by Defoe: an account of the siege of Colchester in the English Civil War. However, long sections are left almost intact: to give one example among many, the description of Hampton Court in the first volume. In a well-intentioned but rather clumsy device, the editor attempted to incorporate into the seventh letter passages from Defoe's famous appendix on English roads, originally concluding the second volume.

Richardson kept the overall scheme of thirteen letters, sticking closely to the precise itinerary as it shaped the ongoing narrative, and retained the pose of a first-person traveller as author. He quoted at length Defoe's own statement of intent in his preface, and though he could not match the detailed understanding of economic issues found in the original he did attempt to incorporate 'very great Additions, Improvements, and

Corrections' (as the title page had it) in all the areas of life that Defoe had described. Of course, Richardson being Richardson, he could not always leave well alone. As Godfrey Davies pointed out, 'From the second to the eighth editions [the later ones were supervised by others], the editors of Defoe were responsible for the sort of emendation that editors seem impelled to make and authors are inclined to resent.'[7] This refers in particular to small changes in phrasing that sometimes have the good effect of pruning Defoe's redundant clauses, but often appear to be tinkering for the sake of tinkering.

Most of the alterations made in the second edition persisted in the third and its successors; some did not. The section on Bath was further augmented in 1742 and 1748, with Leake still running 'one of the finest Booksellers Shops in *Europe*' (II, 288). One of the editor's informants in this part of the country was the physician George Cheyne, who wrote to Richardson on 7 November 1740 that Leake had told him 'in his dark confused Manner' that more material on Cheltenham waters was needed for the new *Tour*, and he duly supplied this. The switch to four volumes in 1742 enabled Richardson to reorganise and amplify the Scottish sections that conclude the work.

All in all, the revisions of this text, which he made between 1738 and 1761, constitute Richardson's most sustained attempt to operate in the modern sense as the 'editor' of books by others. The activity resembled what he had done with Aesop, and in some ways his procedures when he revised his own novels. His work on the *Tour* was a legitimate exercise in refurbishment of a text that was becoming dated, even if most of the truly vivid passages in the work came from the hand of the original author.

Notes

1 For the significance of this item, see Tom Keymer, 'Richardson's *Meditations*: Clarissa's *Clarissa*', in Doody and Sabor, *Tercentenary Essays*, pp. 89–109.

2 *The Correspondence of Henry and Sarah Fielding*, eds. Martin C. Battestin and Clive T. Probyn (Clarendon Press, 1993), p. 149.

3 Richardson's role in the proceedings was first explored in detail by Duncan Isles in an appendix to Charlotte Lennox, *The Female Quixote*, ed. Margaret Dalziel (Oxford University Press, 1970), pp. 419–28, with citations from his letters of December 1751 and January 1752.

4 Sale, *Bibliographical Record*, p. 7.

5 Nicholas D. Nace, 'The Publication of Urania Johnson's "Unpublishable" *Almira*', *Papers of the Bibliographical Society of America*, 103.1 (2009), 5–18 (p. 5).

6 [Samuel Richardson], *Aesop's Fables: With Instructive Morals and Reflections, Abstracted from All Party Considerations, Adapted to All Capacities; and Design'd to Promote Religion, Morality, and Universal Benevolence* (London, 1740), pp. i–x.

7 Godfrey Davies, 'Defoe's "A Tour thro' the Whole Island of Great Britain"', *Modern Philology*, 48.1 (1950), 21–36 (p. 22). This remains the only thorough examination of the issues.

CHAPTER 15

Reading and Readers

Eve Tavor Bannet

One way of understanding the wide range of responses among contemporary British readers of Richardson's novels, and the controversies they sparked, is through some of the conflicting reading protocols that the novels invited and that Richardson cleverly solicited and provoked. Richardson generated more varied and violent reactions in private letters and journals, in manuscript rewritings, and in the press, than any other contemporary British novelist. Translations of his novels also produced reader responses all over Europe, but on the basis of divergent protocols.

Curious or Improving Reading

Curiosity was considered the great driver of reading. The seventeenth-century philosophers Thomas Hobbes and John Locke had described curiosity as our primary motive for learning – a point reiterated by the academic critics of the Scottish Enlightenment. An unending source of scholarly pleasure and delight, curiosity was an 'Appetite after Knowledge', a 'Lust of the Mind', and 'Desire to know why and how' that was aroused by things new, strange, surprising, rare, or uncommon (thus as yet unknown or imperfectly known). Eighteenth-century writers for the popular market rapidly discovered that what held for scholars also held for the 'unlearned', and that arousing and 'gratify[ing] this Curiosity which is so natural to a Reader' sold periodicals and books. What Addison called 'yearning curiosity' impelled 'the generality of readers' to read newspapers, periodicals, tales of wonder, histories, and adventures for the pleasure of encountering new, strange, surprising, or uncommon people and things.[1] The same held for those 'secret [amatory] histories' or 'histories of private life' that Eliza Haywood called 'novels' (the primary meaning of 'private' was still 'secret'). Novels pandered to readers' curiosity about the gentry's 'most hidden' – because most scandalous and surprising – 'Secrets'. As Haywood explained: 'I found that Curiosity had, more or less, a Share in every Deed;

and my business was to hit upon this reigning Humour in such a Manner, as That the Gratification it should receive from being made acquainted with other Peoples' Affairs, should at the same time teach everyone to regulate their own.'[2] Haywood, whose popularity and sales rivalled those of Defoe and Fielding (despite perennial difficulties in determining print runs), gratified the public's curiosity by 'plucking off the mask of hypocrisy' from the Town, as she and other women writers had from the Court, to reveal the vicious intrigues and scandalous sexual conduct that the gentry concealed behind outward proprieties and polite forms.

Richardson appealed to curiosity by the same means. In *Pamela* and *Clarissa*, he offered the public 'familiar letters' not intended for public view. While it was considered a servant's primary duty to keep his or her family's secrets, Pamela's letters and journal promised to 'tell all'. She would 'acquaint you with' the sexual depredations and abuses of physical and social power to which a maidservant was subject in a genteel household, and show how she nevertheless rose from low life to become mistress of a splendid house and fortune. Even more pointedly in response to Anna Howe's request that she inform 'all [her] friends without doors' about what was hidden from them within the Harlowe household, Clarissa's letters regaled their readers with her family's scandalous secrets: Machiavellian schemes to gain unrivalled power, property, or position; sensational excesses of sadistic cruelty; libertine intercourse between illicit lovers; irregular sex in the form of rape and prostitution. Publishing in instalments, as Richardson invariably did, heightened readers' curiosity about what shocking things they would learn next – and their desire to acquire further volumes to find out.

At the same time, people were thought to become what they read. There were longstanding learned precedents for this too – for instance, Thomas Aquinas argued in his *Commentary on Aristotle's 'De anima'* (c. 1269) that in learning, knower, knowledge, and knowing become one. This was traditionally figured in an image of consumption that portrayed readers as 'eating' books. Most famously, Bacon warned that 'Some books are to be tasted, others to be swallowed, and some few are to be chewed and digested',[3] while Henry Fielding offered readers of *Tom Jones* (1749) a menu and a feast. Books that were consumed – ingested by the body and absorbed into the fabric of the mind and heart – were said to shape what readers thought, felt, and desired, and consequently how they acted. Reading therefore had real, beneficial or detrimental, effects on people's character and conduct; novels had the power to affect the manners and morals of the nation. By mid-century, concern that the market for novels had expanded well beyond the masculine elite to merchants, tradesmen, artisans, farmers, servants, labourers, and above all women at all ranks, led clergy, moralists, critics, and educationists to attack novel-reading as virulently as they had attacked the popular theatre before the 1737 Theatre Licensing Act. After the Jacobite rising of 1745 – which topped a series of insurrections and food- and work-related riots – there was a growing sense that, rather than feeding the public a diet of shocking vice and immorality, and inviting the populace to emulate the profligacy, luxury, and infidelity of their betters, novels should be 'improving': they should nourish readers with moral philosophy and religious precepts entertainingly exemplified in fictional genteel characters and plots. As Samuel Johnson argued in *Rambler*, no. 4, while novels served the young and the ignorant as 'lectures of conduct and instructions into life', their chief protagonists should demonstrate 'the most perfect idea of virtue', and their villains 'should always disgust'. Richardson sought to embody the most perfect ideas of masculine and feminine virtue in *Sir Charles Grandison*. But he published *Pamela* in its initial form and *Clarissa* on the cusp of this turn to moral didacticism; and though interpellating readers with moral-political concerns on his title pages or in his prefaces by promising to 'inculcate Religion and Morality', he seems to have underestimated the magnitude and severity of the turn. Adding a conduct book for wives to *Pamela*, highlighting *Clarissa*'s moral and religious lessons more urgently from preface to preface and edition to revised edition, and publishing moral and religious *sententiae* extracted from the novels can be seen as efforts to reassure an increasingly vocal body of readers with moral-political concerns.

Didactic scandal fiction (or 'moral Romance') was intrinsically unstable – as Henry Fielding noted, there was incongruity in trying to 'reform a whole nation, by making use of a vehicular story, to wheel in among them worse manners than their own'.[4] So readers split. There were curious readers, who marvelled at their inability to put *Pamela* or *Clarissa* down – the novel had kept them up half the night; they threw it aside but felt impelled to pick it up again, or to go on reading though it was miserable stuff. And there were readers who debated whether the novels would have a beneficial or harmful effect on society, often by guessing what lessons others would take from them. Some readers did both at different moments. But satires and criticism in the press highlighted the incongruity between scandalous or prurient matter that gratified public curiosity and Richardson's improving moral and religious goals; and this led almost immediately to the production of cheaper, bowdlerised abridgments, which many buyers read instead of Richardson's originals. Interestingly, readers did not record the same compulsive consumption of bowdlerised, simplified, third-person abridgments – or indeed of *Sir Charles Grandison*; but then, in these texts, the role of curiosity in driving reading was diminished, redirected, or contained.

Reading with Head or Heart

Writers and educationists complained that readers of all ranks had lamentably short attention spans; their curiosity was soon sated. 'Lust of the Mind' had to be stoked by other passions to make readers read long narratives. Women novelists from Delarivier Manley on argued that to 'inspire the Reader with Curiosity, and a certain impatient Desire to see the end of Accidents', it was necessary to create characters in whom readers could see something of themselves, and move them to 'enter into all the Motions and Disquiets of the Actor'.[5] Or as John Hawkesworth put it in *Adventurer*, no. 4: to hold readers' attention, novels had to both 'gratify Curiosity and move the passions' by exciting our 'solicitude' for the hero to the point where 'we tremble when he is in danger … weep when he suffers, and … burn when he is wronged'. The woman-centred fictions of popular women novelists such as Aphra Behn, Manley, and Haywood were (in)famous for representing the passions as the 'secret springs' of human conduct, and for engaging readers by exciting their emotions.[6] And thanks to a literary convention going back to *The Portuguese Letters* (1678) and Behn's *Love Letters between a Nobleman and His Sister* (1684), fictional letters could display even forbidden feelings and acts with an honesty and openness that people rarely permitted themselves in real correspondences. By offering his readers letters written 'to the moment' that vividly portray their writers' shifting passions and invite solicitude for the heroine's interminable sufferings, Richardson co-opted the market for passionate, woman-centred fictions for *Pamela* and *Clarissa*. Readers responded accordingly, especially to *Clarissa*: some ladies declared that they saw something of themselves, their family, or their friends in the heroine or the Harlowes; many described themselves as overcome by Clarissa's distresses, or as experiencing tormenting passions as they read (Figure 15.1); some fell a little in love with Lovelace; men found the 'warm' scenes with Clarissa *en déshabillé* arousing; almost everyone confessed that they had cried.[7]

But reading was also a 'rational pleasure' – an occasion for reflection and conversation about issues that books raised, and for judgment of their execution and style. As Tom Keymer has shown, Richardson's novels 'stimulated and provoked' reflection and conversation in two

Figure 15.1 G. Scorodomow, *Reflections on Clarissa Harlowe*, engraving after the portrait by Joshua Reynolds of his niece Theophila Palmer reading *Clarissa*. Royal Collection Trust.

principal ways. First, he centred his novels on controversial contemporary 'cruxes' – the relative duties of masters and servants, and of husbands and wives in *Pamela*; relations between Protestants and Catholics in *Sir Charles Grandison*; conflicts between paternal authority and filial independence, and between libertinism and morality, infidelity, and piety, in

Clarissa. Second, he left readers to decide altercations and differences of worldview among characters for themselves: *Clarissa*'s plurivocal epistolary form presented duelling arguments and competing versions of experience, while in *Pamela*, the 'anti-Pamelist' position was inscribed in Pamela's citations of Mr B's criticisms and complaints.[8] Printers had found that sparking controversies around pamphlets or books (for instance by paying hacks to attack them) got them talked about, and thus promoted sales – people would acquire and read the book or pamphlet to be able to converse about it with their friends. Richardson's controversial cruxes certainly got his novels talked about, orally and in writing, but not always as we might expect.

The rules of polite oral and epistolary conversation often made disagreement difficult, especially when addressing Richardson himself. Politeness demanded complaisance, and deference to one's superiors, elders, and the opposite sex – never mind to an interlocutor like Richardson, who assumed paternal authority and got testy if crossed. Younger men writing to Richardson and wary of giving offence often fell back on flattery and hyperbole, while younger women wrapped their disagreements in copious expressions of tentativeness, uncertainty, self-deprecation, submission, and respect. Harsh critics sometimes chose anonymity. Women readers often preferred to convey their opinions on controversial topics indirectly, either through their judgments of Richardson's execution and style, or through rewritings that altered the course of the plot. In novels, judging execution meant judging not only the writer's management of characters, plot, and diction, but also whether these were true to nature; whether they accurately represented the manners of people of their age, gender, and rank; and whether they reflected the probable course of events. To mention to a friend that Lovelace was unnatural, or failed to show how wickedness really manifests itself in men's characters, was to repudiate two-thirds of the novel, and all that Richardson used his villain for. To pronounce Harriet Byron's excellencies unnatural and unattainable indicated that one rejected Richardson's idea of female virtue. To declare that the novels did not accurately reflect manners in 'high life' questioned their relevance to the genteel. Similarly, producing a rewriting in which Clarissa was not raped and was restored to respectability after her elopement by marrying a reformed Lovelace countered Richardson with a view of society in which social pressures, customary practices, and reawakened consciences combined to rein in black sheep, rectify human errors, and avert the worst excesses of passion and power.

Conversing with Books

To converse with a book meant that, in reading, one was conversing with its author through the medium of his or her text. Isaac Disraeli compared this to 'shuttlecock, where, if the reader does not quickly rebound the feathered cork to the author, the game is destroyed'.[9] Authors invited readers to participate in the making of their text, for instance by leaving them things to guess at, puzzle out, question, or debate as they read. And in playing their part, readers learned what they could expect from an author and came to know that author's 'Character'. Readers who had never met Richardson gave him a Character on the basis of his novels. They said that he had an excellent heart and skill in painting and moving the passions; or that he was like Shakespeare, not 'correct', but pre-eminently the poet of nature and of the human heart; or that he was low and mean, never having set foot in polite circles. The Characters readers gave him were so contradictory that John Hawkins observed in 1787 that 'the Character of Richardson as an Author is to this day undecided, otherwise than by the avidity with which his publications are by some readers perused, and the sale of numerous editions'.[10]

To converse with books also meant making books party to oral conversations. Novels (also sermons, poetry, sometimes plays) were read aloud serially or in extracts in a variety of urban and rural settings, both as entertainment and to give people who saw each other too often something novel to talk about. Someone was delegated to read novels aloud to accompany artisans' and labourers' repetitive work and women's spinning and sewing, as, earlier, singing or chanting had done. Novels were also read aloud serially in families (including Richardson's) at fixed times daily; at other times, wives read to husbands, husbands to wives, and daughters to the sick or elderly. In great country houses and tradesmen's rooms above the shop, reading favourite extracts to one's guests, and discussing them afterwards, provided the evening's entertainment. Authors (including Richardson) read their latest work to company to drum up interest among potential patrons. Sociable conversations about novels and plays were both modelled and satirised in print, from Sarah Fielding's *Remarks on 'Clarissa'* (1749) and the Puppet Show chapters in Henry Fielding's *Tom Jones* (1749) to the anonymous *Female Mentor* (1793). Such conversations often showed participants judging works by their own experience, disposition, knowledge, or prejudices, and being corrected, *ancien régime*-style, 'by authority'.

Finally, to converse with books meant making talk of books part of written (epistolary) conversations. Friends corresponded with one another about what they were reading; recommended and sent each other books; transmitted information about what people in their localities were saying about them; and discussed their opinions of the same book. Because people frequently read novels at the recommendation of others, or after having heard that 'everyone' was talking about them, Richardson did all he could to get people talking about his novels under pretence of asking their advice (which he generally ignored). He circulated instalments in manuscript prior to printing, and sent free volumes to potentially useful acquaintances. He embarked upon correspondences about his novels with readers all over the country, sometimes even resorting to sending one correspondent's letters around to others to promote further discussion. All this gave Richardson's correspondents ever new matter for conversation in their local social circles or letters to friends, spreading grateful talk about this kindly author's letters and novels far beyond the people to whom he actually wrote.

Different reading protocols thus entailed different perspectives, each with a different range of possible interpretations and judgments. Invoking a wide range of reading protocols helped Richardson to reach and engage a wide range of readers. But Richardson also made it clear that he wanted to make all these readers judge his characters and interpret their words and acts as he did; and he found, to his consternation, that what he had unleashed, he could not control.

Notes

1 Thomas Hobbes, *The Moral and Political Writings of Thomas Hobbes* (London, 1750), pp. 21–2; Joseph Addison, *The Spectator*, 8 vols. (London, 1711–13), 1.452.
2 Eliza Haywood, *The Female Spectator*, 4 vols. (London, 1745–6), Vol. 1, p. 4.
3 Francis Bacon, *The Essays or Counsels, Civil and Moral, of Sir Francis Bacon* (London, 1701), p. 135.
4 Quoted in Peter Sabor, 'Richardson, Henry Fielding, and Sarah Fielding', in Thomas Keymer and John Mee (eds.), *The Cambridge Companion to English Literature 1740–1830* (Cambridge University Press, 2004), pp. 139–56 (p. 141).
5 Delarivier Manley, 'Preface', in *The Secret History of Queen Zarah* (London, 1702), n.p. This preface is said to borrow heavily from the French critic l'abbé Morvan de Bellegarde.
6 Rebecca Tierney-Hynes, 'Fictional Mechanics: Haywood, Reading and the Passions', *The Eighteenth Century*, 51.1–2 (2010), 153–72.

7 Elspeth Knights, '"Daring but to touch the hem of her garment": Women Reading *Clarissa*', *Women's Writing*, 7.2 (2000), 221–45. See also Katherine Binhammer's discussion of sentimental reading, below (pp. 289–94).

8 Keymer, *Richardson's 'Clarissa'*, pp. xx, 31, 95. See also April London, below (p. 148), on Richardson's use of internal reader figures in his novels as guides to interpretation.

9 Isaac Disraeli, *Miscellanies* (London, 1796), p. 199.

10 John Hawkins, *The Life of Samuel Johnson* (London, 1787), p. 216, quoted in Bueler, *'Clarissa': The Eighteenth-Century Response*, p. 218.

PART V

Literary Genres and the Arts

CHAPTER 16

The Novel

April London

Samuel Richardson's alertness to the state of contemporary fiction coupled with his wish to manage the reception of his own work proved critical to the development of the novel genre. The epistolary novels of Aphra Behn, Catherine Trotter, Mary Davys, and Elizabeth Rowe provided him with a formal model and a recurring subject: the individual power gained by resisting domestic and exotic hazards, whether autocratic parents, competitive siblings, libertines, kidnappers, or seraglio keepers. Rowe and Penelope Aubin, Richardson's favoured precursors, set religious piety and steadfast virtue against such threats and offered the rewards of an afterlife to their embattled heroines. But as Thomas Keymer and Peter Sabor note, '*Pamela*'s success lay as much in commercial strategy as in literary achievement.'[1] Key to that success was its assimilation of additional, often prurient, elements from the tales, romances, secret histories, and novellas of authors such as Behn, Delarivier Manley, Daniel Defoe, and Eliza Haywood. Even as Richardson proclaimed his objectives to be moral and pedagogical, his ambivalent and often voyeuristic representations of sexuality, particularly in *Pamela* and *Clarissa*, opened him to charges of inconsistency that both admirers and critics promptly exploited.

Important as the '*Pamela* controversy' was to his immediate fame, Richardson's lasting influence owes more to the complex cross-currents generated by the imitation, adaptation, and even rejection of his novels (often in a single career), and to his ongoing commitment to redressing the problems, both narrative and ethical, that his competitors identified in his work. The counter-fictions of Eliza Haywood and Henry Fielding suggest how quickly combative responses changed direction. Haywood initially capitalises on *Pamela*'s notoriety with her *Anti-Pamela; or, Feign'd Innocence Detected* (1741), but later develops Richardson's exploration of moral inequality in *Betsy Thoughtless* (1751), whose deferred marriage plot anticipates *Sir Charles Grandison*'s. Fielding, author of the cutting rejoinder *Shamela* (1741), assigns to the heroine of his final novel, *Amelia* (1751),

Clarissa's characteristic inwardness, repeats her troubled relationships with both siblings and real and surrogate parents, and modifies B's conversion from rakishness to suit Booth's family circumstances. Richardson, in turn, having multiplied the correspondents in *Clarissa* to offset the problem of Pamela's unmediated self-representation, laid bare in Haywood's and Fielding's parodies, incorporates into *Sir Charles Grandison* the social and political sweep of Fielding's middle novel, *Tom Jones*.

The tension between inheritance and innovation evident in these multiple adjustments is also felt in the mid-century novel's concern with interpretation, often explored internally through characters' reading and writing. In *Pamela* and *Clarissa*, the libertines' responses to the heroines' stolen letters allow devious sophistication to be contrasted with guileless innocence. *Sir Charles Grandison* muffles this epistolary individualism by casting the patriarchal hero as arbiter of value (to the point that he takes on many of the features of Fielding's omniscient narrator) and by including scenes in which characters collaboratively write and comment on each other's letters. While regulated reading in the Grandisonian mode continues to be an important motif in novels from Sarah Fielding's *Ophelia* (1760) to Eaton Stannard Barrett's *The Heroine* (1814) and Jane Austen's *Northanger Abbey* (1817), the connotations of women's writing change after *Pamela*. The latter novel connects the therapeutic effects of writing to both the heroine's eventual triumph and B's turn to virtue. After *Clarissa*, records of women's suffering provide spiritual or psychic comfort, but not the social remediation of *Pamela*, as Frances Sheridan's *Sidney Bidulph* (1761) and Mary Hays's *The Victim of Prejudice* (1799) suggest (a consensus emphasised by their political differences). Men's fluency, by contrast, retains the potential for powerful, if mostly negative, societal consequences. In Elizabeth Hamilton's *Memoirs of Modern Philosophers* (1800), Jane West's *A Tale of the Times* (1799), Thomas Holcroft's *Anna St Ives* (1792), and Austen's *Sense and Sensibility* (1811) – all deeply indebted to Richardson – Lovelace's pleasure in story-telling, his hyperbolic romance vocabulary, and his multiple identities become familiar signatures of the libertine, whose eloquence works by inversion (made more pointed in the successors to the plain-speaking Belford) to authenticate the solid virtues of the order threatened by rakish vice.

Many of these verbal skills are familiar from Pamela; Lovelace might even be seen as a masculinised near-parody of her. But his ubiquity in later fiction is not matched by hers: few novelists, outside pornography or satire, risk the dangers of self-congratulatory female narrators. *Clarissa* proves a richer source for formal innovation in its managing of stylistically distinct correspondents and its furthering of the material text motif adapted from Jane Barker's *A Patch-Work Screen for the Ladies* (1723) and *The Lining of the Patch-Work Screen* (1726) and touched on in Pamela's sewing of her correspondence into her clothes. The typographical oddities of Clarissa's shredded mad letters set the terms for later meditations on transience, both sentimental (as in the ostensible rescue of the manuscripts of Henry Mackenzie's *The Man of Feeling* (1771) from gun-wadding and of his *Julia de Roubigné* (1777) from food-wrapping) and satiric (as in the marbled, blank, and flourish-marked pages of Laurence Sterne's *Tristram Shandy* (1760–7)). Such fragments testify to the expressive limits of language by exacerbating the gap between lived and recorded experience that is central to the Richardsonian technique of 'writing to the moment'.

Formal documents, testamentary statements, and scenes of judgment add to these distancing effects, and here again later novelists draw on *Clarissa*: the device of the 'Will' recurs in Frances Burney's *Evelina* (1778), Elizabeth Inchbald's *Simple Story* (1791), Charlotte Smith's *Old Manor House* (1793), and Amelia Opie's *Adeline Mowbray* (1805); and that of Clarissa's trial scenes in William Godwin's *Caleb Williams* (1794), Inchbald's *Nature and Art* (1796), and Hays's *The Victim of Prejudice*. But late-century miscarriages of justice tend not to be subordinated, as in Richardson, to the standard of divine judgment. In radical novels, in particular, the refusal of Scripture as an absolute point of reference generates disconcertingly abrupt conclusions that triangulate a quasi-innocent protagonist, a corrupt judiciary, and a utopian future free from restrictive laws. Other adaptations of *Clarissa*'s legal discourse suggest the growing importance of authorial gender to the terms of novel endings. The unclaimed inheritance, for example – a key early source of Harlowe family dissent – has Clarissa-like tragic consequences for Sibella in Eliza Fenwick's *Secresy* (1795), but in Oliver Goldsmith's *Vicar of Wakefield* (1766) and Robert Bage's *Hermsprong* (1796), the heroes assert their entitlement to real property in order to restore traditional, albeit lightly modified, hierarchies.

The indebtedness to Richardson embodied in such works can be seen across the period. But the strains of reconciling sensibility with increasingly rigid constructions of gender quickly became apparent. For mid-century novelists championed by Richardson – Sarah Fielding, Charlotte Lennox, and Sheridan – the heroines' compliance with social norms is harder won, the rewards less celebrated, and the penalties for even minor infractions harsher than Pamela's. Their disempowerment goes hand in hand with the heightened importance of parents, who are provided with detailed anterior plots that bear directly on their children's. *Clarissa*'s and

Sir Charles Grandison's concluding representations of marriage as a social, even dynastic, compact (rather than a matter largely of individual choice as in *Pamela*) contribute to this emphasis on family structures. The latter also support another striking aspect of mid-century fiction: a focus on the maternal, exemplified in Sir Charles's tribute to his mother as his 'oracle' (*SCG*, II.iv.56). Casting female agency back a generation and imagining it in filial terms opens up the possibility of seeing women's influence as ameliorative, without sacrificing the primacy of male direction. Subsequent novels pursue this course in a variety of ways, not all of them reformist in intent.

Sentimental and picaresque fictions endorse 'good' mothers through contrast with 'bad' ones whose emotional profligacy is matched to their ideological typecasting, from the arch-reactionary Lady Bidulph to the parvenue Mrs Baynard of Tobias Smollett's *Humphry Clinker* (1771). This structure of paired opposites helps to set the narrative course towards a more temperate social vision reminiscent of *Sir Charles Grandison*'s patriarchal 'family of love' (I.xxvi.185). Sarah Scott's *Millenium Hall* (1762) and Ann Radcliffe's convent of Santa della Pieta in *The Italian* (1797) offer single-sex variations on this model, creating the illusion of a feminist alternative while still preserving class entitlements. Late-century novels committed to re-masculinising the genre in the service of loyalist doctrine retain an alignment with the Grandisonian standard. But radical fictions, attentive to the casualties of privilege, more often favour *Clarissa*. What emerges from their borrowings, however, is frequently at odds with the principles of the source text. The maternal generational plots of Inchbald's *Nature and Art*, Mary Wollstonecraft's *Wrongs of Woman* (1798), and Hays's *Victim of Prejudice*, for instance, chart the misogynistic perpetuation of undeserved misery from mother to daughter in order to argue for sexual equality. Others, including Opie's *Adeline Mowbray* and Smith's *Young Philosopher* (1798), begin by treating the mother/daughter plot as an occasion for vigorous feminist debate, only to reinstate the social hierarchies that their plots seemed initially set to confound. Conversely, Austen's meddling parents in *Sense and Sensibility*, *Pride and Prejudice* (1813), *Mansfield Park* (1814), and *Persuasion* (1817) limit the force of the generational imperative, releasing possibilities for the protagonists' self- and social awareness.

As such variations suggest, one mark of the less successful reworkings of Richardson is the tendency to extract a single element – Clarissa's victimhood, Grandison's family of love – from the reciprocally defining contexts of their source. Sibling and dynastic conflicts in novels such as *Sidney Bidulph* or M. G. Lewis's *The Monk* (1796) thus appear thin and untethered when compared to the interrelations of maternity and filial obedience in *Clarissa* (or religious integrity in *Sir Charles Grandison*). Austen, however, brings her own fully imagined narrative ends to bear on Richardson's motifs, marrying the generational plot to the maternal one in mutually illuminating ways. Characteristically, she invokes a familiar construct and then diminishes it in order to clear the way for an alternative perspective, often one more psychological than social. When, for instance, John Dashwood takes up James Harlowe's instrumental view of daughters as marriage pawns, Austen's ironic handling of his role as paterfamilias is completed by saddling him with a shrewish wife, who is also a bad mother tormented by questions of social precedence. The intervening *Betsy Thoughtless* had similarly used sibling rivalry to question the commodification of women, but *Sense and Sensibility* undercuts the narrative force of this trope by emphasising the heroines' sustaining inwardness. Stereotypically bad mothers – such as Mrs Thorpe, Mrs Ferrars, or Lady Catherine de Bourgh – with their equally limited, self-serving children, are in turn contrasted with good ones (even if, as with Mrs Tilney and Lady Elliot, they are dead) who have bequeathed to the heroines a legacy of independent thought and social responsibility that also discredits selfish and domineering male relatives.

As these examples suggest, Austen further enhances her characters' motivational complexity by adapting the Richardsonian device of doubles, itself an extension of the master/servant pairings in Defoe, where the lesser figure had served as confidant and occasionally provocateur – Roxana and Amy, Crusoe and Friday, Moll and the Governess. In developing Defoe's contractual dynamic and the scope for negotiation it makes central, Richardson differentiates *Pamela* from earlier amatory novels with their one-sided triumph of predator over victim, or, as in Aubin's pious fictions, the equally absolute triumph of spirit over body. Additional layers of complementary pairs, such as Mrs Jewkes and Mrs Jervis, reinforce the contest between B and Pamela and point to its political, social, and ethical implications. But it is the expansion of correspondents in *Clarissa* and *Sir Charles Grandison*, and with it the increasingly intricate configurations of paired friendships, that proves the most enduring of Richardson's techniques.

Clarissa sets the terms for the gender distinctions that continue to define these alliances well into the nineteenth century. As its plot unfolds, the foil characters temper the intensity of the principals in stylistically diverse ways. Anna Howe, whose avowed love for the heroine will prove without practical force, has a sprightly, often ironic mode of writing that resembles Lovelace's. His friend and fellow rake, Belford, is comparatively subdued, but unlike Anna, he ultimately helps the woman whose fall he initially conspired to effect. The ending allocates rewards in accordance with sex: for Belford, the active pursuit of Clarissa's dying wish for the restoration of order through compromise; for Anna, marriage to an intellectual inferior. The paired women of later novels maintain the configuration of thoughtful principal and effervescent friend tamed by an unequal marriage: Harriet Byron and Charlotte Grandison; *Sense and Sensibility*'s Elinor and Marianne Dashwood; and, semi-parodically, *Northanger Abbey*'s Catherine Morland and Isabella Thorpe (*Hermsprong*'s Caroline Campinet and Maria Fluart provide a deliberate variation). Male doubles, however, follow a different trajectory, a consequence in part of Richardson's discomfort with occasionally positive responses to Lovelace. Intent on forestalling renegade interpretations of his final novel, he flattens the libertine to the pasteboard Sir Hargrave Pollexfen, substitutes for the contemporary Belford the older priest Dr Bartlett, and adapts from Mary Davys what Jane Spencer calls the 'lover mentor' figure to serve as the ideal partner for the sensible Harriet Byron.[2]

Domestic heroism in the mode of Sir Charles Grandison provides a template for later protagonists whose feminised sensibility and judicious estate management are given political, national, and international colourations. In the period between Richardson's last novel and the revolutionary decades, the rakish foil to the lover mentor rarely achieves the power of a Lovelace, even when, as in Frances Brooke's *Emily Montague* (1769), he corresponds directly with the hero. More often, the libertine appears less as friend than acquaintance, and increasingly takes on the contours of romantic rival: *Evelina*, *Mansfield Park*, and *Emma* (1815) thus pair the morally questionable Willoughby, Crawford, and Churchill with the protagonists Orville, Edmund Bertram, and George Knightley. In an audacious late-Austen twist, *Persuasion*'s Anne Elliot assumes the role of the lover mentor, is pursued by the conventional contrasted suitors, William Elliot and Wentworth, and, despite her gentry roots, deviates from the norm once more by choosing maritime adventure over landed certainty. *Persuasion* is also notable for its sophisticated treatment of another inherited trope: the plot of second chances, introduced in *Pamela*, furthered in *Clarissa*'s Belford, and given religious and political definition in Grandison's turn to Harriet Byron after the failed courtship of Clementina della Porretta. Goldsmith's *The Vicar of Wakefield* (1766), a somewhat unstable compound of Richardsonian motifs, uses Primrose's concluding semi-conversion to question *Sir Charles Grandison*'s patriarchal view of marriage as social panacea. In Austen, second-chance plots similarly cast a sceptical light on received truths, while also marking positive changes in both male and female protagonists.

But it is novels of the 1790s that engage most intensely and combatively with Richardson, seizing on the political, religious, cultural, and sexual logic of his fiction to gain a purchase on their own divergent perspectives. The seduction plot he adapted from amatory tales in order to condemn libertine behaviour, for instance, is revived in radical fiction not to support gender hierarchies but to suggest contrarily that denying women independence licenses male rakishness. Clarissa-like oppression recurrently serves as a metaphor for wider social tyrannies, sometimes with ironic intent, as in *Caleb Williams*: despite the titular anti-hero's representation of himself as a latter-day Clarissa, his persecution of Falkland finally indicts predator and prey as interchangeably victims of what Godwin construes as an English *ancien régime*. 'Jacobin' writing in turn provoked conservative ripostes that retrospectively tainted novelistic interest in class mobility (*Pamela*); the imperatives of individual morality, even when rooted in scriptural principle (*Clarissa*); and the civil exploration of cultural and religious difference (*Sir Charles Grandison*). After 1795, epistolary narrative itself declines precipitously, largely because of associations with Pamela's self-making and Clarissa's heightened sensibility. Some male liberal and loyalist writers continue to evoke Grandsonian hierarchies in novel endings celebrating traditional marriages and retirement to landed estates. But women writers for whom, in Isobel Grundy's pithy phrase, Richardson had long been both 'trainer and sparring partner', faced greater representational challenges, since even committed loyalists were reluctant to follow the lead of male colleagues in refusing agency to the heroine.[3] West and Hamilton respond to the dilemma by making polemical use of Richardson's doubles motif. Both cast the Lovelacean libertine as a Jacobin opportunist who traps the credulous heroine by praising her political acumen. By this means, ostensibly independent, highly principled figures become tragic victims of doctrines that leave them susceptible to the exploitation of unscrupulous arrivistes. After the exposure of the libertine and penitent death of the heroine, their virtuous counterparts look forward to realising a Grandisonian order nourished by women's moral and domestic authority.

The manifold ways of charting the reflected presence of *Pamela*, *Clarissa*, and *Sir Charles Grandison* in eighteenth-century fiction underscore Richardson's transformation of received forms and the scope of his influence. To focus on just a single one of his motifs will illuminate, for instance, the hardening of attitudes to gender exceptionalism: the 'Man-Woman' status Defoe's Roxana sees as necessary to her celebrated financial success acquires in *Clarissa's* Mrs Sinclair a perverse sexuality that 1790s loyalists such as Hamilton politicise in such vilified figures as Emmeline, the mistress and destroyer of the Jacobin villain of *Memoirs of Modern Philosophers*. Alternatively, a wider view of the structures that organise his fiction reveals a virtual catalogue of period binaries that later writers root in Richardson through direct allusions, character types, and adapted plots: autonomy and conformity, patrician and plebeian cultures, given and chosen family, dynastic and companionate marriages, hierarchy and self-direction, good and bad deaths, individual sensibility, and domestic collectivities. But the 1790s saw a significant weakening of Richardson's currency, with the near-extinction of epistolary writing, the distrust of class mobility (*Pamela*) and sensibility (*Clarissa*), and growing resistance to overtly didactic fiction (satirised in the Gothic-lover Isabella Thorpe's dismissal of the unread *Sir Charles Grandison* as an 'amazing horrid book').[4] Austen's fiction does, of course, continue to develop Richardson's preoccupation with women as sisters, daughters, and wives. It is Walter Scott, however, who recapitulates for the nineteenth century Richardson's mid-eighteenth-century elevation of the novel. But in place of *Pamela's* authentication of female integrity, *Waverley* emphasises the masculine, the regional, and the historical.

Notes

1 Keymer and Sabor, *'Pamela' in the Marketplace*, pp. 21–2.
2 Jane Spencer, *The Rise of the Woman Novelist: From Aphra Behn to Jane Austen* (Oxford: Basil Blackwell, 1986), p. 145.
3 Isobel Grundy, '"A novel in a series of letters by a lady": Richardson and Some Richardsonian Novels', in Doody and Sabor, *Tercentenary Essays*, pp. 223–36 (p. 225).
4 Jane Austen, *Northanger Abbey* (1817), eds. Barbara M. Benedict and Deirdre Le Faye (Cambridge University Press, 2006), p. 35.

CHAPTER 17

Fables and Fairy-Tales

Margaret Anne Doody

Richardson's *Aesop's Fables, with Instructive Morals and Reflections, Abstracted from All Party Considerations* (1741) seems an important spark for his explosion into fiction writing. In Richardson's first novel the heroine has few works of literature to turn to in trying to understand her situation. (It is Mr B, not Pamela, who has read romances.) Richardson's fable collection shadows the novel. Special treatment is given to the story of 'An Ant and a Grass-Hopper' (Fable 164; *EW*, pp. 257–8). This story troubles Pamela, implying rebuke both to herself and to her elders. Her parents and now-deceased employer failed to ensure that she is equipped for a practical working life. Even to herself Pamela now seems almost wasteful and extravagant; she has learnt things of no moment, degenerating into the ornamental rather than useful. Pamela does not want to be seen as a grasshoppery sort of person. Richardson's reading in his own collection of fables mitigates the fault. If the Grasshopper erred in careless enjoyment, the Ants telling the Grasshopper to live with the consequences are too harsh: 'the Ants ought to have reliev'd the Grass-hopper in her Distress' (*EW*, p. 258).

Aesopic fables are well calibrated to the discussion of economic and social survival. They stare directly at bad outcomes. Their harshness is part of their charm. Fables may be technically 'Abstracted from All Party Considerations', but they cannot resist dealing with central political matters – power, oppression, property, and cruelty. Fables' rapid plots are swift and biting. The imaginary animals are slightly removed from us. Yet the kinship of animal and human is constant; a bond of both consciousness and mortality cannot be severed. Fables are good bearers of bad news. A structure of unhappy, cruel Fate is never to be overcome. We are pulled down by the gravity of a central old truth. Venturing away from the customary is usually foolish, even fatal. The view from the fable is a view from below.

As *Pamela* progresses, the number of fable references diminishes. The heroine develops in powers of observation and analysis, relying less on her simple reading matter than she did earlier. Yet the fables' handling of power is never too far from her mind. Mr B's marital lecture – 'this awful Lecture' (*P*, p. 412) – turns for its own support to the fable of 'An Oak and a Willow' (Fable 163; *EW*, p. 407). Pamela makes her own commentary: '*yet, sure, the Tempest will not lay me quite level with the Ground neither*' (*P*, p. 412). Power exhibits active force, but she won't let herself be blown down.

Towards the end of *Pamela in Her Exalted Condition*, Lady Towers cites a fable endorsing sticking to one's proper place. Overtly criticising silly young gentlemen rather than Pamela, she refers to 'the Ass in the Fable … emulating the Lap-dog' who 'merited a Cudgel rather than Encouragement' (*PE*, p. 580). Observing his master's 'Favourite Spaniel', the mistaken ass is harshly informed of his mistake (Fable 15; *EW*, pp. 143–4). We may suspect Lady Towers of some unacknowledged antipathy to Pamela, who has certainly changed her place. Earlier, Pamela alluded to a similar fable in assuring her sister-in-law that she does not intend to forget who she is: 'don't think me … too much like the Cat in the Fable, turn'd into a fine Lady' (*PE*, p. 83). This story, 'A Cat *and* Venus', tells us that no change can get rid of an underlying nature: 'A Young Fellow was so passionately in Love with a Cat, that he made it his humble suit to *Venus*, to turn her into a Woman'. The cat, though transformed by Venus into a most attractive lady, leaps out of bed to pounce upon a mouse. 'Puss, even when turn'd into a Madam, will be a Mouser still' (Fable 52; *EW*, pp. 172–3). Richardson's 'Reflection' on this fable is harsh; the beguiling cat-woman may be 'lewd or immoral', concealing vices native to her gender beneath her meretricious attractions. Oddly, in the illustration to this story Venus seems to beam approvingly upon the large and attractive cat in its master's lap (Figure 17.1).

Fables offer Richardson's characters something to grasp when at a loss or in difficulty. These compact stories, even if harsh, offer momentary assurances of the solid. They are promissory notes for reality. There are things one should not do, places where one should not venture, as the Country Mouse learned (Fable 139). Fables give rules and set boundaries; they pronounce social law. Fables are readily used to cast blame upon others – as Pamela effectively does, in her use of the fable of the sheep accused by the wolf. Mr B objects: 'So, *Mrs. Jewkes*, said he, you are the Wolf, I the Vultur, and this the poor innocent Lamb, on her Trial before us. – Oh! you don't know how well this Innocent is read in Reflection' (*P*, p. 170).[1] Pamela is

Figure 17.1 Samuel Richardson, *Aesop's Fables* (1740). University of Oxford, Bodleian Library, MS Douce A.421 (illustration opposite p. 41).

good at 'Reflection', a Lockean process productive of further ideas. Mr B rightly fears Pamela's talent for commentary.

Fables recur in Richardson's novels, though they are scarcely used in his last work. Charlotte Grandison parodically plays with the central situation of *Sir Charles Grandison*, Sir Charles's hesitation between Clementina and Harriet: 'Ass and two bundles of hay, Harriet', Charlotte comments, drily adding, 'But my brother is a nobler animal' (*SCG*, vi.xlv.284). Unlike the Aesopic ass, Sir Charles will not starve; he will never lack for feminine attention. Recourse to fables would be inappropriate to the privileged characters in *Sir Charles Grandison*. We are no longer supposed to be living constantly in an animalistic, greedy, and predatory world.

Arguably, Richardson's best use of fables is found in *Clarissa*, where the uneasy characters have reason to blame others and suspect themselves. Clarissa writes resentfully to Anna about her reaction to Lovelace's offer of clothes: 'Do you think me the jay in the fable? said I. – Would you have me visit the owners of the borrowed dresses in their own cloaths?' (*C*, iii.xxix.160). Richardson's major characters are all aware of the dangerous

nature of clothing – a sort of fable in itself. Pamela makes her new clothing – and the three bundles – into allegory bounded by fable. We want to
be pure self, but are encumbered by the social integuments, the 'lendings'
that trouble King Lear. 'Borrowing' is ever a problem, suggesting obscure
disgrace, too much neediness.

As well as 'A Daw and Borrowed Feathers', *Clarissa* includes 'The Sun
and the Wind', 'Mercury and a Statuary', and 'Death and an Old Man'. At
an important juncture Lovelace employs a very *Pamela*-like fable – while
denying its applicability: 'A little pretence, indeed, served the wolf, when
he had a mind to quarrel with the lamb; but this is not now my case'
(*C*, v.xxxviii.283; see Fable 3, *EW*, pp. 133–4). Wherever in *Clarissa* we
come upon a fable reference, we find stress. Usually we find cruelty lurking
there too, along with guilt and anxiety. Fables exhibit things at a tipping
point, falling towards a (probably fatal) moment of revelation. Anna Howe
makes her own fable of her game chickens: 'Peck and be hanged, said I …
for I see it is the *nature of the beast*' (*C*, iii.xlii.211).

At times the grudging conservative Aesopic fable appears to dominate.
Everything must inevitably turn out the same way. Richardson uses that
motif brilliantly in Paper iii of Clarissa's 'Mad Papers'. Months ago, Anna
Howe teased that Clarissa is 'the first of our Sex … who has been able to
turn that lion, Love, at her own pleasure, into a lap-dog' (*C*, i.xii.66). In
Paper iii of the 'Mad Papers', Clarissa acknowledges too late how greatly
she has been mistaken:

> A Lady took a great fancy to a young Lion, or a Bear, I forget which – But
> a Bear, or a Tyger, I believe, it was. It was made her a present of, when a
> whelp. She fed it with her own hand … And its tameness, as she used to
> boast, increased with its growth; so that, like a lap-dog, it would follow her
> all over the house … At last, some-how, neglecting to satisfy its hungry
> maw, or having other-wise disobliged it on some occasion, it resumed its
> nature; and on a sudden fell upon her, and tore her in pieces. – And who
> was most to blame, I pray? The brute, or the lady? The lady, surely! – For
> what *she* did, was *out* of nature, out of character, at least: What *it* did, was
> *in* its own nature. (*C*, v.xxx.234–5)

This bitter fable almost parodies the Aesopic tone in its certainty that all
must turn towards the norm – the dreadful norm. That's the way men
are. This is *the nature of the beast*. That is all Lovelace ever was or could
be. Fables assume the presence of a dreadful predetermined status quo.
Transformation is always reversal, a fall to a lower point that is the glum
bedrock of the real. Yet the estrangement and uncertainty within the fable,
as well as its context, also take us towards the borderland – towards the

unknowable, and unclassifiable, regions where other contemporary genres may better operate.

Such genres are invested in transformation. These sliding forms of fiction, harder to pin down generically, are important to Richardson's imaginative creation. The 'Oriental Tale' truly came into England with the publication of *The Arabian Nights' Entertainments* (1704–17), produced by an anonymous translator of Antoine Galland's *Mille et une nuits* and published in parts.[2] The frame story superintending the whole collection is a story of conversion. As Fatema Mernissi says, '*The Thousand and One Nights* begins as a tragedy of betrayal and revenge, and ends as a fairy tale, thanks entirely to Scheherazade's intellectual capacity to read her husband's mind … The heroine's second talent is of a psychological nature: the ability to change a criminal's mind by using words alone.'[3] A process of transformation takes place during a prolonged and multi-faceted narrative. Although Richardson officially writes no 'Oriental Tale', Pamela's instalments take the place of Scheherazade's stories, incrementally altering the hearer's (or reader's) outlook. Mr B's moral transformation should be seen against the background of the education of the sultan Schahriar. Fables endeavour to be absolute, but cannot succeed. Competing and opposing forms suggest change and development.

Among these new forms is the 'fairy-tale'. The fairy-tale is a true Enlightenment form, looking to a future different from the past. In the late seventeenth century Charles Perrault set up the fairy-tale as a national genre, product of (French) folk wisdom, and superior to the fantasy fiction of the Ancients.[4] Perrault, a leader of the 'Modern' pack in the 'Querelle des Anciens at des Modernes', is nationalistic – to that extent conservative. But Perrault the Modern actually prizes the fantastic 'conte' as not bound by the past. It is simultaneously both traditional and new; 'Sleeping Beauty,' Joan DeJean holds, is 'the ultimate Modern work'.[5]

Whereas the fable tells us that the future will inevitably always be like the past, the fairy-tale asserts that this is not true. Women writers in France were strong contributors to the invention of this new genre. Writers such as the baronne D'Aulnoy, the comtesse de Murat, and Charlotte-Rose de Caumont de la Force composed fairy-tales – and also historical fiction and 'Histoires secrètes' ('Secret Histories'). These writers' lives were not happy. Accused of libertinism and lesbianism, the comtesse de Murat was imprisoned in several strongholds including the chateau of Angers. Charlotte-Rose Caumont de la Force married the man whom she loved – but the marriage was annulled by relations and she was thrown into a convent.[6] Imprisonment for sexual reasons – variously the temporary fate of Pamela,

Clarissa, and Clementina – seems as normal in life as in literature. The treatment of Clementina in *Sir Charles Grandison* recalls the ordeal of the heroine of D'Aulnoy's 'The Blue Bird' and of Caumont de la Force's 'Perinette'. We may call Clementina's story a 'fairy-tale' – for fairy-tales offer ordeals and permit undesired outcomes. D'Aulnoy's 'The Yellow Dwarf' and 'The Ram', for example, offer impressively unhappy endings. The references to the 'Orange-grove' of the della Porrettas' garden, and Clementina's unhappy dream of the murdered Sir Charles lying beneath the orange tree, recall the malevolent Yellow Dwarf, whose haunt is the Orange-tree (*SCG*, iii.xxii.219, xxx.350).

The fairy-tale is hospitable to risk, change, and new experiences. Perrault introduces contemporary luxuries: the ogress in 'La belle au bois dormant' speaks tastefully of *sauce Robert* in ordering her cannibal meal. Above all there is the new luxury, the mirror, rendering 'self' fantastic and accessible. In Perrault's verse fairy-tale 'Peau d'âne' ('Donkey-Skin') and his short prose tale 'Cendrillon', a heroine suffers deprivation and then is transformed into beauty – fully knowable to herself because of the mirror. In 'Peau d'âne', the heroine is on the run from her incestuous father. Disguised in an ugly donkey-skin, she becomes a grimy menial in a farmer's kitchen. But when she is alone, on Sunday, she goes to her room, has a wash, and then wears one of the magnificent dresses her fairy godmother created for her:

> Devant son grand miroir, contente et satisfaite,
> De la lune tantôt la robe elle mettait,
> Tantôt celle où le feu de soleil éclatait.

> Before her great mirror, happy and satisfied,
> She put on sometimes the dress of the Moon,
> Sometimes the one where the fire of the sun shone.[7]

Richardson's *Pamela* adapts this situation. Pamela in her own room takes pleasure in looking at herself in the mirror, content and satisfied. Women with looking-glasses are traditionally vain hussies, or aggressive sexual sirens. This is not where the scene in *Pamela* takes us. Fable dislikes mirrors – they are ministers of vanity. Fairy-tales love them – they are transformers. So we see in Perrault's chaste princess fleeing patriarchal power, and in Pamela trying on her new clothes before a mirror. The ever-transforming self, momentarily crystallising, is held in regard.

The fairy-tale can set about transformation of the fable. In D'Aulnoy's 'La chatte blanche' ('The White Cat'), the Prince, lost in a forest in a storm, comes to 'the Gates of a stately Castle … The Walls were of fine China, whereon the Histories of all the Fairies since the Creation of the World were represented'.[8] The Prince finds shelter. After being given a bath and fresh clothes he is conducted 'into a stately Hall richly furnished, where he saw in fine Paintings, the Stories of the most famous Cats ... the Cat in Boots, the Marquis de Carabas, the writing Cat, the Cat turn'd Woman, Witches in the Shape of cats' (p. 256). There enters 'a little Figure about half a yard high' dressed in 'a veil of black Crape':

> The Prince was in the greatest Amazement ... when the little figure in black coming up to him, and lifting up its Veil, he saw the prettiest little White Cat he ever had set his Eyes on, which seem'd to be young, but withal very melancholy, and set up such an agreeable and charming Mewing, as went to the Prince's Heart. (p. 256)

His witty hostess makes her castle into a scene of enchanting entertainments – like the great Hunt of Rats and Mice, or the sea-fight between Cats and Rats. Madam *is* a mouser still – and also a poet. The White Cat writes 'such passionate Songs and Verses, that he beg[ins] to think ... she [can]not ... be insensible of the power of Love' (p. 259). We suspect the Cat has been subjected to metamorphosis – but that could go two ways: 'he regretted his not being a Cat, that he might pass his Life in such pleasant Company. "Alas! *said he to the White Cat,* how sorry am I to leave you, since I love you dearly: Either become a Woman, or change me into a Cat"' (p. 259). What the fable decries the fairy-tale celebrates. The White Cat is a mouser? So what? We can see D'Aulnoy rewriting that particular fable into fairy-tale. So Richardson really does with the cat fable in *Pamela*.

Self-consciousness is a peculiar province of the new fairy-tale, which encourages investigation of instability in consciousness and in self-representation. When Pamela as mother tells stories, however, she must tell the most cut-and-dried of moral tales. Pamela could not tell fairy-tales – as Pamela herself is in a fairy-tale. Or, rather, she *is* a fairy-tale. Miss Goodwin praises Pamela as her own virtuous character: 'PRUDENTIA is YOU!' (*PE*, p. 600). Had the child said 'YOU are PRUDENTIA!' then Pamela should have come clean and denied that identification. She *knows* she is not truly Prudentia. On the contrary, she is a gambler and a risk-taker. She lives on the borderlands of possibility.

Notes

1 See Albert J. Rivero, 'Explanatory Notes', in *P*, p. 557; and 'A Dog, a Sheep and a Wolf', Fable 29, in *EW*, pp. 153–4.
2 See the introduction by Robert L. Mack to his edition of the first English version of *Arabian Nights' Entertainments* (Oxford University Press, 1995). See also Robert Mack's introduction to *Oriental Tales* (Oxford University Press, 1992).

In Richardson's teens and twenties 'Oriental' stories and fairy-tales must have been noticeable on the book market.

3 Fatema Mernissi, *Scheherazade Goes West: Different Cultures, Different Harems* (Washington Square Press, 2001), pp. 44–7.

4 Charles Perrault, 'Préface' to the fourth edition of verse tales, 1695. See Charles Perrault, *Complete Fairy Tales in Verse and Prose; L'intégrale des contes en vers et en prose*, ed. and trans. Stanley Appelbaum (Dover Publications, 2002).

5 Joan DeJean, *Ancients against Moderns: Culture Wars and the Making of a Fin de Siècle* (University of Chicago Press, 1997), 118–19.

6 For further discussion of these authors see Jack Zipes, *The Irresistible Fairy Tale: The Cultural and Social History of a Genre* (Princeton University Press, 2012); and Marina Warner, *Once upon a Time: A Short History of the Fairy Tale* (Oxford University Press, 2014).

7 Charles Perrault, 'Peau d'âne', in *Complete Fairy Tales*, p. 84.

8 *A Collection of Novels and Tales of the Fairies, Written by that Celebrated Wit of France, the Countess D'Anois*, 3 vols. (London, 1728), Vol. 1, p. 324. Further references to this volume are cited parenthetically in the text.

CHAPTER 18

Letters

Joe Bray

The relationship between real and fictional letters in the late seventeenth and early eighteenth centuries has been the source of much critical debate. Disagreement particularly surrounds the extent to which the increasingly popular genre of the epistolary novel, which flourished following the publication of *Les lettres portugaises* in 1669, drew on the practices and techniques of actual correspondence. On the one hand are those who see epistolary fiction as developing out of real-life letters, with some literary-stylistic additions such as polyphonic point of view. The chief proponents of this argument are the authors of the two classic histories of the epistolary novel, Godfrey Frank Singer and Robert Adams Day; critics of French epistolary fiction and its emergence from letter-writing manuals, such as Bernard Bray and Laurent Versini; and, with some qualifications, writers on women's letters of the period, such as Shari Benstock and Linda Kauffman.[1] On the other hand are those who reject this teleological approach in favour of one that emphasises the functional versatility of the letter in the period, and the difficulty, if not impossibility, of drawing a distinction between its real and fictional incarnations. Adherents to this view include James How, whose discussion of how the establishment of the Post Office in the 1650s opened up new 'epistolary spaces', applies to letters of all kinds,[2] and Thomas O. Beebee, whose conception of the letter 'as a Protean form which crystallized social relationships in a variety of ways' leads him to claim that 'epistolary fiction is a function rather than a thing; it arises when an outside "real" reader takes up the position of the fictional addressee'. As Beebee acknowledges, 'this line of argument tends to blur the boundary between real correspondence and epistolary fiction'.[3]

This debate is brought into sharp relief by the case of Samuel Richardson. As many have observed, Richardson's first novel *Pamela* arose, at least in part, from a letter-writing manual he was commissioned to write, which was published in 1741 (after *Pamela*) as *Letters Written to and for Particular Friends, on the Most Important Occasions* (commonly known as *Familiar*

Letters). As is well known, Letters cxxxviii ('A Father to a Daughter in Service, on hearing of her Master's attempting her Virtue') and cxxxix ('The Daughter's Answer') are closely related to the opening of *Pamela*. Yet the exact nature of this relationship is the crux of the debate between the two positions outlined above. In one view the model letters designed for real-life occasions provided the raw material that Richardson then transformed in his fiction. Singer identifies 'the germ of *Pamela*' in *Familiar Letters*,[4] while Day uses evolutionary theory to chart the development of Richardson's epistolary method: 'In progressing from the *Familiar Letters* to *Clarissa* and to the less intense but even more complex structure of *Grandison*, he recapitulated in his own work all the evolutionary developments of his precursors and went beyond them.'[5] In contrast, for those who emphasise the discursive flexibility of the letter in the period, it is harder to draw a line between the letters in Richardson's manual and those in his novels. How, for example, argues that *Clarissa* is an 'absorption' of *Familiar Letters*,[6] while Beebee suggests that 'in offering their letters as models to be imitated, manuals and novels both functioned interactively', positing a 'larger feedback-loop between real, model, and fictional letters as they cross-pollinate and mutually condition each other through the centuries'.[7]

The specific stylistic aspects of this 'cross-pollination' have rarely been examined in detail, however. In the remainder of this chapter I will make a first step towards narrowing down just what Richardson's model and fictional letters have in common, and how they might 'mutually condition each other'. Without hazarding a line of direct influence, I argue that stylistic points of connection offer support for a flexible view of the letter in the period. Equally though, I will propose that the novel offered Richardson greater possibilities for the expansion of stylistic techniques that are present only in glimpses in his letter-writing manual. I thus hope to steer a middle ground between those who see fictional letters as a transformational advance on model or real-life examples, and those who see the two as interchangeable, arguing that a precise demonstration of the creative potential of both Richardson's fictional and his non-fictional letters must also allow for the fact that as a genre the novel allowed him a fuller range of expressive possibilities than the manual.

The style of *Familiar Letters* has tended to receive only passing attention. In her study of Richardson's work and Defoe's *The Complete English Tradesman* (1725), which together, she claims, 'laid the essential foundation for transforming collections of epistles into the epistolary novel', Victoria Myers concentrates on each writer's 'moral concerns', arguing that Richardson 'found the familiar letter an attractive locus for negotiating the reformation of the public sphere, and continued that task in the epistolary novel'. She does, however, pay welcome attention to the ways in which *Familiar Letters* differs from previous examples of the genre, such as John Hill's *The Young Secretary's Guide; or, A Speedy Help to Learning* (1687) and G. F. Gent's *The Secretary's Guide* (1705?), noting that 'the key to the difference between Richardson's manual and these others is their use of humour'. Pointing particularly to Letter xxxix, which provides a model for 'Ridiculing a romantick Rhapsody in Courtship', Myers suggests that 'Richardson's refinements signal what will also be remarkable in his epistolary novels, the deliberate integration of distinctive voices and situations with deep plumbing of character.'[8] More detailed analysis of stylistic features in the collection, especially those concerned with the representation of speech, will demonstrate just how these 'distinctive voices' and a sense of 'character' are created, and show that techniques for generating humour in the novels are also present, in different forms, in *Familiar Letters*.

There are several exchanges in *Familiar Letters* that move beyond the model of a standard letter outlining a problem or request and its reply. One such takes place between Letters clxi and clxv, headed 'Advice of an Aunt to a Niece, in relation to her Conduct in the Addresses made her by Two Gentlemen; one a gay, fluttering Military Coxcomb, the other a Man of Sense and Honour' (*EW*, p. 505). After an opening letter from the aunt desiring her niece Lydia's opinion of the two men, the latter gives an account of her 'sensible Lover', Mr Rushford, over two letters. In the first she admits that she finds him 'a very valuable Gentleman' but notes that he is 'over-nice Sometimes as to the Company I see' and that he 'gives himself wonderful *grave Airs* already' (*EW*, p. 507). The second letter elaborates on these airs, with a lively description of one of his visits:

> He comes last *Thursday* with great Formality, and calls himself *my humble Servant*; and I saw he was pleased to be displeased at something, and so look'd as grave as he, only bowing my Head, and following my Work; for I was hemming a Handkerchief. *You are very busy, Madam* – Yes, Sir – *Perhaps I break in upon you* – Not much, Sir – *I am sorry if I do at all, Madam* – You see I am pursuing my Work, as I was before you came. – *I do, Madam!* – very gravely, said he – *But I have known it otherwise, when Somebody else has been here* – Very likely, Sir! – But then I did as I pleased – so I do now – and who shall controul me? – *I beg pardon, Madam; but 'tis my Value for you* – That makes you troublesome, said I, interrupting him. – *I am sorry for it, Madam! – Your humble Servant.* – Yours, Sir. – So away he went. (*EW*, p. 508)

The way in which this conversation is represented, with Mr Rushford's direct speech in italics and Lydia's in roman font, and the dashes between them, gives a strong sense not only of the lover's grave awkwardness, but also of Lydia's spirited, quick-witted defiance. She even interrupts one of his ponderous utterances to turn his justification for his jealousy against him. The relative lack of speech tags creates a directness and spontaneity that also hints at the humour that Myers has observed in the collection as a whole, especially in the final truncated '*Your humble Servant.* – Yours, Sir. – So away he went'.

Lydia's attitude towards her gravely serious lover can be compared with that of Anna Howe towards Mr Hickman in *Clarissa*. In Letter xxvii of Volume II, Anna gives a report to Clarissa of one of her awkward suitor's visits, which begins with him stroking his ruffles:

> I could most freely have ruffled him for it. – As it was – Sir – saw you not some one of the servants? – Could not one of them have come in before you?
>
> He begg'd pardon: Looked as if he knew not whether he had best keep his ground, or withdraw. – Till, my mamma. Why, Nancy, we are not upon particulars. – Pray, Mr. Hickman, sit down.
>
> By your le-ave, good madam, to me. – You know his drawl, when his muscles give him the respectful hesitation –
>
> Ay, ay, pray sit down, honest man, if you are weary! – But by my *mamma*, if you please. I desire my hoop may have its full circumference. All they're good for, that I know, is to clean dirty shoes, and to keep ill-manner'd fellows at a distance.
>
> Strange girl! cry'd my mamma, displeased. (*C*, II.xxvii.159)

Again, the way in which Anna represents her own and her suitor's speech here captures her mocking attitude towards him, as well as her lively quick-wittedness. The integration of direct speech in her narrative, often without any attributing clause, creates humour, with the speed of her responses contrasting with the ponderous drawl of Hickman's speech, who seems as awkward in this exchange as Mr Rushford when visiting Lydia. In this case there is of course a third speaker, Anna's mother, who takes the suitor's side. As previous letters have established him as her favourite, the reader can judge that Anna's behaviour here and her satirical tone are aimed as much against her mother as the unfortunate Hickman (for whom she elsewhere grudgingly acknowledges her esteem).

The representation of speech is also central in creating an impression of character in Letter lxxxiii of *Familiar Letters*: 'A facetious young Lady to her Aunt, ridiculing her serious Lover'. Having thanked her aunt for 'recommending Mr. *Leadbeater* to me for a Husband', the niece adds, 'But

I must be so free as to tell you, he is a Man no way suited to my Inclination'
(*EW*, p. 415, italics in original). Her satirical account of the first visit of this
'*honest Man*' clarifies her feelings:

> After he had pretty well rubbed Heat into his Hands, he stood up with his
> Back to the Fire, and with his Hand behind him, held up his Coat, that he
> might be warm all over; and looking about him, asked with the Tranquillity
> of a Man a Twelve-month married, and just come off a Journey, How all
> Friends did in the Country? I said, I hoped, very well; but would be glad
> to warm my Fingers. Cry Mercy, Madam! – And then he shuffled a little
> further from the Fire, and after two or three Hems, and a long Pause –
>
> I have heard, said he, a most excellent Sermon just now: Dr. *Thomas* is
> a fine Man truly: Did you ever hear him, Madam? (EW, p. 415, italics in
> original)

Again, the awkwardness of the prospective lover is indicated by his hesitant
style of speech, and the gravity of his topic when he does embark upon it
is a further mark in his disfavour. The niece's satirical attitude towards Mr
Leadbeater is similar to that of Lydia towards Mr Rushford, and indeed of
Anna Howe towards Mr Hickman. In this case it is not just the way that
his direct speech is represented that conveys her mockery, however. Her
suitor's 'ask[ing] with the Tranquillity of a Man a Twelve-month married,
and just come off a Journey, How all Friends did in the Country?' starts as
indirect speech, from the reporting niece's perspective, before suggesting
with the capitalisation of 'How' and the question mark after 'Country' a
flavour of Mr Leadbeater's actual words and intonation. This is in other
words a snippet of free indirect speech, the style that is often said to reach
its apotheosis early in the nineteenth century in the novels of Jane Austen.
Its hallmark is the mixture of perspectives (reporter and speaker) which
allows for a variety of attitudes to be taken towards the spoken words and
the person speaking them. Later in the same letter the style appears briefly
again when Mr Leadbeater comes to take his leave:

> he press'd my Hand, look'd frightfully kind, and gave me to understand,
> as a Mark of his Favour, that if, upon further Conversation, and Inquiry
> into my Character, he should happen to like me as well as he did from my
> Behaviour and Person; why, truly, I need not fear, in time, being blessed
> with him for my Husband! (*EW*, p. 416)

Here again what starts as indirect speech, with the convoluted clauses
following 'gave me to understand' indicating the tedious pomposity
of the speaker, modulates after the semicolon into a more direct style,
with the expression 'why, truly' and the final exclamation mark allowing

more of a flavour of Mr Leadbeater's actual speech. Again this snippet of free indirect speech enables the reporting niece to mix her own perspective with the reported speaker's voice, and add a mocking slant to her suitor's words.

The dismissive attitudes of the female characters discussed so far towards their lovers are nothing, however, to that of Richardson's most 'facetious' letter-writer: Charlotte Grandison. As the newly married Lady G, Charlotte writes a succession of letters to Harriet Byron in Volume IV of *Sir Charles Grandison*, detailing with her characteristically lively wit the travails of married life with Lord G. In Letter xxxvii, for example, she reports that 'we live very whimsically, in the main: Not above four quarrels, however, and as many more chidings, in a day', before revealing that 'we have had a serious falling-out, and it still subsists' (*SCG*, IV.xxxvii.256, 257). The cause is a dispute over the fact that 'we have not made *our appearance at court*': she being 'fervent against it' partly because of her brother's absence abroad. Lord G's argument is given in a mixture of her and his words: 'I was the only woman of condition, in England, who would be against it' (IV.xxxvii.257). This looks like direct speech, especially with the presence of quotation marks, yet the person and tense have been shifted from what Lord G would actually have said: 'You are the only woman of condition.' This is in other words another example of free indirect speech, with the combination of reporter's and speaker's voices again allowing Lady G to add her own angle to her husband's words.

After the night has passed off 'with prayings, hopings, and a little *mutteration*' their dispute resumes:

> The entreaty was renewed in the morning; but no! – 'I was ashamed of him', he said. I asked him, If he really thought so? – 'He *should* think so, if I refused him.' Heaven forbid, my Lord, that I, who contend for the liberty of acting, should hinder you from the liberty of thinking! Only one piece of advice, honest friend, said I: Don't imagine the worst against yourself. (*SCG*, IV.xxxvii.258)

Here free indirect speech emerges more fully in Charlotte's representation of her husband's words, with 'I was ashamed of him' and 'He *should* think so if I refused him' each exhibiting the switches of person and tense noted above (compare 'You are ashamed of me' and 'I shall think so if you refuse me'). The style again captures Charlotte's satirical perspective, presenting Lord G as under the sway of his domineering wife, even in the way his speech is represented. Her words, in contrast, are predominantly given here in forceful direct speech.

In each of his novels, especially *Sir Charles Grandison*, Richardson develops stylistic techniques that demonstrate and expand the expressive possibilities of the letter and its capacity for creating voices, attitudes, and character. His skills as an epistolary stylist are perhaps sometimes lost in appreciation of other aspects of his handling of the letter form. One way of recuperating them would be to go back to the model letters that he was composing at the time of writing *Pamela*, which display glimpses, albeit sometimes brief and tantalising, of the innovative playfulness and experimentation with style that were to characterise his greatest achievements.

Notes

1 Godfrey F. Singer, *The Epistolary Novel: Its Origin, Development, Decline, and Residuary Influence* (University of Pennsylvania Press, 1933); Robert A. Day, *Told in Letters: Epistolary Fiction before Richardson* (University of Michigan Press, 1966); Bernard Bray, *L'art de la lettre amoureuse: des manuels aux romans (1550–1700)* (Mouton, 1967); Laurent Versini, *Laclos et la tradition: essai sur les sources et la technique des 'Liaisons dangereuses'* (Klincksieck, 1968); Shari Benstock, 'From Letters to Literature: *La carte postale* in the Epistolary Genre', *Genre*, 18.3 (1985), 257–95; Linda S. Kauffman, *Discourses of Desire: Gender, Genre, and Epistolary Fictions* (Cornell University Press, 1986).

2 James How, *Epistolary Spaces: English Letter Writing from the Foundation of the Post Office to Richardson's 'Clarissa'* (Ashgate, 2003).

3 Thomas O. Beebee, *Epistolary Fiction in Europe 1500–1850* (Cambridge University Press, 1999), pp. 3, 8, 9.

4 Singer, *The Epistolary Novel*, pp. 37–8.

5 Day, *Told in Letters*, p. 210.

6 How, *Epistolary Spaces*, p. 17.

7 Beebee, *Epistolary Fiction*, pp. 18, 21. See also Bonnie Latimer's argument, below (pp. 170–7), regarding the common pedagogical theory underlying '*The Apprentice's Vade Mecum*,' *Familiar Letters*, and Richardson's novels.

8 Victoria Myers, 'Model Letters, Moral Living: Letter-Writing Manuals by Daniel Defoe and Samuel Richardson', *Huntington Library Quarterly*, 66.3–4 (2003), 373–91 (pp. 373, 381, 382, 386).

CHAPTER 19

Educational Writing

Bonnie Latimer

Any attempt to separate out 'educational writing' as a subcategory of Richardson's work risks creating false divisions: in all his writing, delight mingles with instruction. Critically, there is a long tradition of reading his novels as conduct fiction; equally, non-fiction such as *The Apprentice's Vade Mecum* or the *Familiar Letters* contains satiric sparkles and embryonic plots, as demonstrated by Joe Bray in the preceding chapter (pp. 164–8). The earlier behavioural literature stems from a set of traditional and popular instructional genres with which Richardson was deeply familiar, including the conduct book, letter manual, and trade guide or *vade mecum*, but it also provides didactic imagery later reprised in the novels. An example is Richardson's characteristic pedagogic metaphor of the chalked-out path. An apprentice in the *Familiar Letters* humbly 'be[gs]' that a relative will 'chalk out for me the Paths in which you would have me tread', whilst similar ideas pepper *The Apprentice's Vade Mecum*, which promises to 'pave the Way' to 'Perfection', leading 'Youth' out of the 'high Road to Perdition', and avoiding 'Diversions' (*EW*, p. 387; *AVM*, *EW*, pp. 6, 17, 24). *Clarissa's* understanding of moral exemplarity is dominated by the metaphor: Anna Howe promises that Clarissa 'shall chalk out every path that I shall set my foot in', and the heroine is responsible for establishing a 'path for the sake of future passengers who travel the same way' (*C*, vi.lxxix.293, xxxiv.125). Clarissa's self-sufficiency leads her erroneously to assume her 'own knowledge of the right path' (iii.lxxix.365). In the *Moral and Instructive Sentiments*, Lovelace is glossed as wishing he had never quitted 'the fore-right path', and the *Passages Restored* sees him ruing the 'dull beaten path of virtue'.[1] Similarly, the errant Lord W wishes that Sir Charles Grandison would 'chalk me out my path' (*SCG*, ii.xlvii.336).

This recurrent image invokes a didacticism animated by a tension between prescription and free will – relating Richardson's thought to a fault line in eighteenth-century pedagogy. On the one hand is a strand of broadly latitudinarian devotional and conduct writings. Informed by an implicitly Lockean free will, this active, rational practice in the tradition of *imitatio Christi*, and moral exemplarity more generally, is recommended in the sermons of John Tillotson, Edward Fowler, Gilbert Burnet, Isaac Barrow, and others. On the other is the tradition of rote learning to be found in many didactic texts, especially those aimed at children; this often frames the acquisition of knowledge as an imprinting of lessons onto an impressionable mind, which cannot then choose but follow them. The difference is one of agency. Richardson's printing of conduct literature (as distinct from sermons and religious controversy) is not extensive, although it includes such important pieces as Jane Collier's anti-conduct book *An Essay on the Art of Ingeniously Tormenting* (1753). Even so, illustrative examples of both didactic approaches occur in his press's output. One of his first productions as a master printer, for example, was George Hickes's translation of Fénelon's *Instructions for the Education of a Daughter* (1721), which sees children's brains as 'soft' and needing 'Impression', but also holds up 'the best Patterns for Imitation', creating 'Inclination' to virtue, and assuming liberty of action.[2] Richardson's 'Preface' to his edition of Penelope Aubin takes a more restrictive view, describing her as 'imprin[ting] noble principles in the ductile Souls of our Youth' (*EW*, p. 96). By contrast, Defoe's *New Family Instructor*, which Richardson printed in 1727, 1732, and 1742, consists of a series of dialogues, which the reader must choose to imitate.

Richardson's own formulation of the chalked-out path tends to the more liberal method: it simultaneously provides a clear way forward, but inherently contains the idea of straying, since one false step sees one 'striking out a new path thro' overgrown underwood' (*C*, v.xi.105). Put another way, Richardson's account of his educative method opens up a gap between the proffered moral and its practical application; his metaphorics conjure up the free will and choice so crucial to all his fictions. Pamela requests 'a little Free-will, a very little' to pursue her own moral lights, whilst Clarissa follows 'self-set Lessons' from 'free will' (*PE*, p. 320; *C*, vii.cv.387–8). As *The Apprentice's Vade Mecum* phrases it, 'where there is no Choice, there can be no Merit' (*EW*, p. 50). Throughout his career, Richardson imagines a self *capable* of adhering to moral precept, a self first limned out in his earliest conduct writing.

This self is initially embodied in the apprentice, a figure that often represented bumptiousness or veniality, and that the period's many apprentice guides sought to stabilise. Caleb Trenchfield insists on the apprentice's lowliness – 'not any (that I know of) hath stoopt so low, to give advice to an Apprentice' – and his consequent complete obedience.[3] Richardson's private epistolary advice to his apprentice nephew is riddled with anxieties: Thomas Verren Richardson represents disruption, with his 'roughness of behaviour' and talkativeness (Richardson to Thomas Verren Richardson, *c.* 1 August 1732). Richardson generally, and *The Apprentice's Vade Mecum* particularly, share concerns with other apprentice-guides, as Alexander Pettit's edition has usefully traced.[4]

Where Richardson differs is in his didactic method. Some apprentice-guides, such as George Fisher's *The Instructor* (1735), are simply miscellanies of useful knowledge. Even discursive guides more akin to Richardson's contain little reflection on instructional method, and their pedagogic metaphors tend to the coercive: Nicholas Zinzano's *The Servants Calling* (1725) conceives of lessons being 'grafted' onto an implicitly vegetable young mind.[5] Equally, these writers address themselves to apprentices as servants, rather than future masters. Nathaniel Crouch considers apprenticeship as a 'Genteel Servitude', and his text uses such heads as 'Commands', 'Instructions', and 'Rebukes and Correction'.[6] Here, apprentices are indistinguishable from servants; this is true of Zinzano, who notes that 'what is said' about servants 'may be applied to both'.[7]

By contrast, for Richardson the apprentice is one who, 'when he comes to be Master, in his Turn, may contribute to amend the Age' (*EW*, p. 5). This formula is revealing: Richardson's apprentice is a moral subject in the process of becoming. Pragmatically, like Crouch, Richardson enjoins the apprentice's observance of his master's commands, but this is because 'when he comes to be a Master, [he] would not be willing to be thus [disobediently] used by his own Servants' (*EW*, 39). Richardson does not 'imprint' lessons, but chalks out for the apprentice a path to mastery, twinning business with moral advancement in a latitudinarian formulation: he wishes his nephew to become 'not only … a good printer, but a good man' (Richardson to Thomas Verren Richardson, *c.* 1 August 1732). Additionally, the apprentice assumes a figurative dimension. The notion of the apprentice as one who may 'amend the Age' suggests a scope not limited to teenaged would-be printers: indeed, Richardson hopes that 'a Person of riper Years and Judgment will find some things in the following pages' (*EW*, 8). For Richardson, then, writing for the apprentice is a bid to reform society, because the apprentice will eventually constitute a member of that society, but also because *all* men are apprentices in the school of virtue. One might draw attention to the hybridity implied in *The Apprentice's Vade Mecum*: the period produces multiple apprentice-guides, but no other titles itself a '*vade mecum*', which is usually applied to manuals addressed to those already adept in specific trades. *The Apprentice's Vade Mecum* addresses both a youthful and a 'ripe' audience, all of whom may benefit from moral instruction.

It is noteworthy that Richardson's first writing for an apprentice – his letter to Thomas Richardson – takes an epistolary form. The apprentice-guide as a pedagogic genre is related to the book of model letters: John Ayres's *The Trades-Man's Copybook or Apprentice's Companion* (1688) provides templates for penmanship, and William Mather's *The Young Man's Companion* (1695) and George Fisher's guide contain 'familiar letters'. Richardson's interest in the model letter and the letter of advice points to his engagement with the letter-manual and its subgenre, the letter-compendium (comprising model letters rather than compositional advice). The *Familiar Letters* was influential within the compendium subgenre: Katherine Hornbeak notes that 82 per cent of Richardson's material was appropriated by successors.[8] The letter-manual was a derivative form, and Richardson's text is no exception: many of his epistles share titles or subjects with earlier models, particularly John Hill's *Young Secretary's Guide* (1687). Interestingly, in 1730 John Clarke and Allington Wilde, Richardson's brother-in-law, purchased the quires of Hill's text, and although Richardson himself never printed Hill, it is tempting to speculate that his interest in Hill may have been piqued through this connection.[9] At any rate, there are some close echoes between them. Both feature, for example, very similar standard letters of consolation to an imprisoned friend, which dwell on the friend's 'noble mind' (Richardson) or 'Noble and Generous ... Soul' (Hill).[10] Each urges the platitudinous argument that 'You see all around you ... unhappy Objects reduced to the same Distress' (Richardson) or that 'such Casualties and Chances frequently befal Mankind' (Hill), and both invoke 'Fortune' or 'Fortune's Wheel'. Although Richardson does not plagiarise Hill, Hill certainly provided a source for the *Familiar Letters*. More generally, Richardson's manual is written within the genre's norms, sharing with popular guides such as Thomas Goodman's *The Experienc'd Secretary* (1699) a grounding in a commercial London milieu.

Richardson is distinguished, though, by his theorisation of the didactic impulse. Letter-manuals stemmed from a time-honoured European pedagogical tradition including commonplace and courtesy books, but generally speaking, books of model letters published before Richardson present themselves as providing materials for copying, rather than as fundamentally impinging upon the extradiegetic ethics of the manual's user. Hill, Goodman, and slightly later writers such as Henry Scougal (*The Compleat English Secretary*, 1714) do not justify their utility as *moral* guides. By contrast, Richardson proposes 'not only [to direct] the requisite style and forms' of correspondence, but also models for 'how to think and act justly and prudently, in the common concerns of human life'. His preface suggests that his letters will 'inculcate the Principles of *Virtue* and *Benevolence* ... describe *properly*, and recommend *strongly*, the Social and Relative Duties; and ... place them in such *practical* Lights, that the Letters may serve for Rules to Think and Act by, as well as Forms to Write after' (*EW*, pp. 323–4). In this way, Richardson helps to inaugurate a turn within the genre towards the idea that habitual epistolary composition, and even simply adapting others' compositions, could alter how letter-manual users thought. Comparably, John Tavernier, writing in 1759, believed that 'perspicuity' was a 'character of the thought' that could be developed through epistolary practice, and Charles Hallifax, also writing in the fifties, offered 'to instruct [Youth] how Wisdom and how Virtue dictate to them to act', with his letters providing 'Lessons ... for Behaviour in almost every Circumstance'.[11] In the *Familiar Letters*, then, Richardson develops a didacticism similar to that in his writing for apprentices: his text furnishes rules and forms, it describes and recommends, but its efficacy relies on engaging the reader, who is imagined not as having been stamped with indelible principles, but as thinking, acting, and writing independently.

The *Familiar Letters* offers another sidelight on Richardson's authorial practice. Its derivative nature can be considered as stemming partially from the old authorial method of *compilatio* and *ordinatio*, or the 'gathering and framing' of moral sayings or *sententiae* from the culture at large. Mary Thomas Crane notes the importance of 'gathering and framing' to a Protestant pedagogical practice, in which the mobilisation of moral commonplaces represented a powerful vehicle for establishing authority. Eve Tavor Bannet also argues that eighteenth-century letter-manuals were characterised by this model of authorship.[12] Richardson's assemblage and reuse of tropes in both the apprentice-guide and the letter-manual genres may be seen, then, as not merely derivative, but as participatory in a longstanding authorial method very different from that associated with novel-writing. As Christopher Flint argues above (pp. 119–20) with respect to assemblage as fundamental to Richardson's book-making, this method sheds light on his instructive and his novelistic work.

Richardson compulsively 'gathered' and reframed material, his own as much as other people's. *The Apprentice's Vade Mecum* reuses material from the letter to Thomas Richardson and from Richardson's 'Rules for this Chapel' for his apprentices, and also, as John Dussinger shows, ideas from Richardson's first publication, *The Infidel Convicted*. Equally, rhetoric from the *Vade Mecum* reappears in the *Seasonable Examination of the Pleas and Pretensions*.[13] One might add the development of the Andrews plot from *Familiar Letters* into *Pamela*, and the offshoots of *Six Original Letters* and 'The History of Mrs Beaumont' from *Familiar Letters* and *Grandison*, respectively. Richardson's interest in repackaging and extending material can, in part, be read as an industrious, apiary practice related to that tradition of gathering and framing material – often for instructional ends.

A good example is the 'Index Historical and Characteristical' appended to the third edition of *Grandison*. Richardson had long been interested in the index as a form of textual exegesis, as manifest in his provision of the substantial index to *The Negotiations of Sir Thomas Roe* (1740). The indices to his own novels represent not reference guides, but readings of the fictions: they treat the novels, presumably recently experienced by the reader, as moral mines from which nuggets can be selected and polished up for the reader, drawing out the correct sentiments from the text. For example, the index to *Grandison* frames the minor character Solomon Merceda as the 'worst of the three Intimates' of Sir Hargrave Pollexfen (*SCG*, VII.392). This phrasing is not taken from the main text, but rather provides a post-textual editorialising synthesis of ideas inherent in the novel. This shaping of the interpretative experience is comparable to the *Moral and Instructive Sentiments'* creation of a didactic voice, which John Dussinger identifies as that of 'the Compiler'.[14] The 'Index' and the *Sentiments* alike may be understood through the practice, common in Anglican moral writing, of using experience instrumentally, as material to be reshaped into useful 'reflections': a typical example is Jeremy Taylor's *Holy Dying* (1651), which Richardson knew well.

Indeed, the *Moral and Instructive Sentiments* participates on a grander scale in this commonplace book tradition of gathering and framing. The processes of *compilatio* and *ordinatio* occur in the novels themselves: at the end of *Clarissa*, Anna Howe records her friend's epigrammatic 'sentences' and 'sentiments'. Anna culls from the text of Clarissa's life a series of educative sayings, and we know that Belford will take Anna's letter as 'materials' for his own edifying text (*C*, VII.cv.381–2). This represents just one example of a general tendency of Richardson's characters to treat the virtuous protagonist's sayings as exempla to be extracted and repeated. The *Moral and Instructive Sentiments* extends a project inherent in the fictions, digesting and re-presenting multiple characters' utterances in aphoristic form. In this way, the authorial method that helps to structure Richardson's earliest didactic writings can also be seen as an element of his last novelistic endeavours.

In making this argument, it is important to note that far from representing a prescriptive or 'dry' didacticism – as Richardson himself
feared – the *Moral and Instructive Sentiments* participates in that dynamic
and open-ended pedagogy represented by the familiar metaphorics of
the chalked-out path (Richardson to Benjamin Kennicott, 26 November
1754). Ann Jessie Van Sant points out that rather than homogenising, the
drawing together of multiple *sententiae* creates instability, even cacophony,
'fragment[ing] the authority embedded in individual sentiments … pre-
venting the building of a single case'.[15] This articulates a recurrent principle
of Richardson's didacticism: the reader may be cajoled or lectured, but
ultimately, Richardson only proffers 'forms' that *may be* copied, paths that
may be followed. Where there is no choice, there can be no merit.

Richardson tended to disown his own didactic efforts. To Johannes
Stinstra, for example, he denied writing anything worthwhile before
Pamela (Richardson to Johannes Stinstra, 2 June 1753). Reading against the
grain, however – a practice with which Richardson always, at some level,
sympathised – it is possible to build a case for the central importance to
his pedagogic thought and to his novelistic practice of the rich traditions
of educational writing.

Notes

1 Samuel Richardson, *A Collection of the Moral and Instructive Sentiments,
  Maxims, Cautions, and Reflexions, Contained in the Histories of Pamela, Clarissa,
  and Sir Charles Grandison* (London, 1755), p. 150; Samuel Richardson, *Letters
  and Passages Restored from the Original Manuscripts of the History of Clarissa*
  (London, 1751), p. 116.
2 François de Salignac de la Mothe-Fénelon, *Instructions for the Education of a
  Daughter*, trans. George Hickes (London, 1721), pp. 21, 12–14.
3 Caleb Trenchfield, *A Cap of Gray Hairs for a Green Head; or, The Fathers Counsel
  to His Son, an Apprenctice in London* (London, 1688), p. 4.
4 See Alexander Pettit, 'General Introduction', in *EW*, pp. xxxi–xciv, especially
  pp. xxxix–xlix.
5 [Nicholas Zinzano], *The Servants Calling; With Some Advice to the Apprentice*
  (London, 1725), p. 4.
6 'Richard Burton' [Nathaniel Crouch], *The Apprentices Companion* (London,
  1681), pp. 1–2.
7 [Zinzano], *Servants Calling*, p. 64.
8 Katherine G. Hornbeak, *The Complete Letter-Writer in English, 1568–1800*, Smith
  College Studies in Modern Languages 15.3–4 (1934), p. 123.
9 Eve Tavor Bannet, 'Printed Epistolary Manuals and the Transatlantic Rescripting
  of Manuscript Culture', *Studies in Eighteenth-Century Culture*, 36 (2007), 13–32
  (p. 24).

10 John Hill, *The Young Secretary's Guide; or, A Speedy Help to Learning* (London, 1687), p. 87; compare *EW*, pp. 442–3.

11 [John Tavernier], *The Entertaining Correspondent* ... (London, 1759), p. 4; Charles Hallifax, *Familiar Letters on Various Subjects of Business and Amusement* (London, 1754), A2v.

12 Mary Thomas Crane, *Framing Authority: Sayings, Self, and Society in Sixteenth-Century England* (Princeton University Press, 1993), pp. 24–6; Eve Tavor Bannet, *Empire of Letters: Letter Manuals and Transatlantic Correspondence, 1680–1820* (Cambridge University Press, 2005), p. 6.

13 John A. Dussinger, '"Stealing in the great doctrines of Christianity": Samuel Richardson as Journalist', *Eighteenth-Century Fiction*, 15 (2003), 451–506; Pettit, 'General Introduction', pp. xxxiv–xxxv, lii.

14 John A. Dussinger, 'Introduction', in Samuel Richardson, *A Collection of the Moral and Instructive Sentiments*, in *Samuel Richardson's Published Commentary on 'Clarissa'*, eds. Florian Stuber and Margaret Anne Doody, 3 vols. (Pickering & Chatto, 1998), Vol. III, pp. vii–l (p. xxvii).

15 Ann Jessie Van Sant, 'Afterword', in Richardson, *The Moral and Instructive Sentiments*, pp. 411–37 (p. 427).

CHAPTER 20

The English Language

Carol Percy

In the eighteenth century, English and attitudes towards it were changing rapidly. Samuel Richardson's English had particularly ambiguous status because of his fiction's subject matter and his limited education. Since
he revised his texts constantly, Richardson presents an excellent subject
for exploring standardising practices and precepts. In turn, understanding something about the contexts within which he wrote can help us to
understand more about the texts as literature. This chapter will consider
three elements in Richardson's fiction: grammar, vocabulary, and the status
of the vernacular.

Grammars and *Pamela*

As Richardson began writing fiction, an ideology of correct English was
becoming more prominent. Especially after 1710, grammars and correct
grammar were publicised in fashionable periodicals such as the *Tatler*
and the *Spectator*. In the 1730s, the number of new grammars increased
remarkably.[1] Richardson's many revisions to *Pamela* reflect this climate of
linguistic prescriptivism. His revisions also reflect critics' reactions to a
social-climbing servant protagonist: he aimed to make Pamela and Mr B
worthy of each other. The most salient changes were lexical: for instance,
Pamela had deferentially made low *Curchees* to a seeming *Deboshee* in the
first edition, but in the second edition the unetymological spellings of
these words were consistently corrected. Richardson also moved in the direction of standardising grammar. For example, contractions, which had
been criticised by Swift, as well as mentioned in the *Spectator*, 135 (1711),
and which within a decade had been proscribed by some grammarians,
were expanded in both Pamela's and Mr B's speech. And *who* was corrected
to *whom* at least three times in Mr B's speech. However, these corrections were performed inconsistently, in both the second and subsequent

editions. For instance, the 'happy, happy, thrice happy *Pamela*' was 'at last, marry'd' not 'to who' but 'to whom' only by the fifth edition (*P*, p. 176).[2]

The inconsistency of Richardson's revisions might reflect his limited formal education. But some of his corrections seem to anticipate rules in contemporary grammar books. He sometimes replaced *you was* with *you were* when revising *Pamela*, before *you was* was first stigmatised in Robert Lowth's grammar (1762), and despite its increasingly frequent appearance in fiction of the 1740s and 1750s. Indeed, *you was* still persists in Richardson's later writing: examples remain in the sixth edition of *Pamela* (e.g. *P*, p. 184) and in the third edition of *Clarissa* (e.g. *C*, i.xxxiii.226),[3] and variation does not correlate with characters' social status. Richardson treated strong verb forms similarly: he sometimes corrected forms such as *wrote* to *written* a decade before they were first criticised in print, while continuing to use them in new work. Richardson's revisions suggest how some English standards were disseminated. Correct English was associated with knowledge of Latin; written rules were elusive, and other norms were forming. Richardson solicited the assistance of others as he composed and revised his work: his personal connections probably alerted him to certain variants that were not yet stigmatised in print.

Richardson's revisions to Pamela's grammar reflect the education and character that justify her social elevation. His revisions to the language of *Pamela*'s servants are not predictable: for instance, in the sixth edition he both expands and contracts Mrs Jewkes's verbs. Did he correct servants' language to dignify the text generally? Did servants ever style-shift? One error that persists in that edition of *Pamela* marks the confession of the double-dealing footman John Arnold: 'if ever there was a Rogue in the World, it is me' (*P*, p. 193); perhaps that variant marked Arnold's character as well as his class. Both Lovelace and Clarissa use the incorrect objective case with their close friends in moments of emotion, in examples retained in the third edition of *Clarissa*. Lovelace proclaims that 'there is now but one man in the world whom she can have – and that is *Me*' (third edition, v.xliii.350). The principled Clarissa errs when reporting Betty's account of her family's misrepresentation of her: perhaps channelling their grammar, she concludes 'It was ME in perfection!' (third edition, ii.xvi.97). We might infer that the case of the pronouns was a deliberate stylistic decision of Richardson's: Lovelace's '*Me*' appears in explicitly '*familiar writing*', and both characters elsewhere use the pronoun correctly (third edition, i.xliii.307; iii.ii.24, xlii.221; vii.lxxiv.283). As grammatical standards emerged, variation could be used for quite nuanced stylistic effects.

Barbara Strang admits the trickiness of identifying 'what belongs to the history of the language, and what to the artistry of a particular novelist' as she considers the rise of the continuous aspect and its use in fiction. Richardson's use of this construction is oddly prominent in *Pamela*, where it first appears on the second page: 'for I was sobbing and crying at her Pillow' (*P*, p. 2). The continuous aspect was used increasingly often and in more syntactic contexts, and it seems to have become obligatory when representing a subject's ongoing activity: such earlier variants as 'What do you read, my Lord?' were no longer grammatical. But in Strang's sampling of eighteenth-century fiction, the construction is restricted to animate subjects and certain activity verbs. Austen and Scott use the aspect more frequently in their later work. In Richardson, however, it appears more frequently in *Pamela* than in *Clarissa*: Pamela uses the construction at 'three times the norm for the period', while Clarissa uses it at 'less than the rate normal at the time', and in Strang's (admittedly restricted) sample less often than Mr Belford and Anna Howe. This construction and its social significance have received little attention from grammarians. But from these contrasts, Strang infers that attentive writers found it difficult to use this colloquial construction well. She also argues that Pamela's 'fondness' for the construction reflects her 'preoccupation' with writing about 'the activeness of her world', while the stylistically 'fastidious' Clarissa avoids a construction that in more general use was restricted to a few syntactic contexts and 'a handful of specific linking words'.[4] Literature has its own principles of linguistic variation, but Richardson and English can mutually illuminate each other.

Dictionaries and *Clarissa*

Richardson's contemporaries were also conscious of lexical standards: several criticisms of *Clarissa* were levelled at the 'new Words' he had coined.[5] Richardson is well represented in the *OED*, with his writing supplying first quotations for about 235 *OED* entries. Some of his neologisms denote (or address or judge) women and men, their emotions and behaviour, and their differences from each other; while his creativity may have reflected his lack of classical education, he used word-formation for characterisation and themes.[6] Using metalanguage, Clarissa observes the lexical adventurousness of Anna Howe, who reproved her for having '*modesty'd* away … opportunities' (*C*, IV.x.42). Male characters' classical neologisms can thematise masculinity and licentiousness: Lovelace explicitly prefers *somnivolences* to *opiates*, and uses the only instance of *concedence* in a text that is otherwise full of *concessions*. In what is the *OED*'s final citation for *pervicacy*, James Harlowe, Jr recalls his sister's accusations of pedantry when he labels her behaviour. Other hard words (though not neologisms) define an intelligent woman's restrictions in a patriarchal culture: Clarissa flags *immiscible* (*C*, III.li.255) and *compulsatorily* (VI.xiii.29) as her own.

Richardson's revisions suggest contemporary attitudes to vocabulary. *Pamela* was characterised by some dialect words: *Mort, tro'*, and *a Power of Money* remain in the sixth edition. But most of his revisions increased formality or social appropriateness; Richardson lacked first-hand experience of high life. *Pamela*'s *Squire* becomes *gentleman* or *Mr. B.*, for instance. Revisions to *Clarissa* are similar, although family and friends occasionally (and sometimes inappropriately) address *Clary* more intimately. Other revisions reflect developing lexical standards. Her family's *dependencies* upon Clarissa's good conduct become their *dependence*; in the third edition, *dependencies* continues to be used by Anna Howe (I.x.61), and *independency* (I.xiii.79) and *independence* (I.v.31) coexist. Emphasising key concepts, this lexical redundancy (or redundance) suggests less that Richardson was ignorant of standards than that some of them were not particularly fixed.

The anonymous 'Lover of virtue' who attacked *Sir Charles Grandison* in 1754 prophetically feared that Richardson's 'new-coin'd words and phrases' would be not only imitated by others but codified in dictionaries.[7] In 1755, almost 100 words from *Clarissa* appeared in Johnson's *Dictionary*. Johnson had explicitly excluded 'living authours' unless a word was needed, a work was excellent, or the author was a friend. Johnson's citations from Richardson demonstrate tensions between principles and practices and suggest some of his lexicographical methods.[8]

Of the words from *Clarissa* in Johnson's *Dictionary*, many denote 'moral sentiments' and behaviour and relationships. But words such as *devious*, *diffident*, and *domestick* were taken not directly from the novel but from the 'Ample' 'Collection of … Moral and Instructive Sentiments' appended to its third edition.[9] Here Johnson's dictionary (like *Clarissa*'s appendix) suggests the pedagogical potential of reference works. Johnson's dependence on this appendix also explains the appearance of some common words such as *give up, knock down, risk*, and *wrong*.

Since so many quotations can be traced to the 'Ample … Collection', the other words from *Clarissa* stand out as chosen or (mis)remembered by Johnson himself. Words such as *mensal, proleptically*, and *retributive* are illustrated only from *Clarissa* and demonstrate a dictionary's role in defining new or difficult words. Indeed, Richardson's use of *chuffily, disavowal*, and *modesty* as a verb are still first citations in *OED* entries. Clarissa's *immiscible* is among Johnson's few headwords lacking a quotation; Lovelace's *plication* is 'used somewhere in *Clarissa*'. And since Johnson's headword *compulsatively* does not occur in contemporary editions of *Clarissa*, he had probably misremembered *compulsatorily* and/or *compulsatory* (neither of which appears in his dictionary). Another word remembered by Johnson denoted a common theme in Richardson's fiction: *domesticate* is attributed by Johnson only to *Clarissa*. Finally, some other headwords demonstrate the dictionary's proscriptive function: *bumpkinly* is 'of uncertain etymology'; *proceeds*, as 'of an estate', is 'Not an imitable word, though much used in writings of commerce'; and Lovelace furnishes an ungrammatical example of '*Me* ... written for *I*'.[10] Not all of Johnson's quotations from Richardson were from *Clarissa*. *Pamela* furnishes a second example for *glisten* (verb) and the only examples for *key* – 'parts of a musical instrument' – and *romance* – 'to lie, to forge'.

Johnson's later additions to the dictionary suggest that he associated Richardson with quotidian and perhaps with low words. By the fourth edition, *Sir Charles Grandison* illustrates the second sense of *crow* ('to boast') and the headword *waistcoat*, though the latter is attributed only to 'Richardson'. And 'Richardson' has been added as the sole authority for sense 3 of *ear* – 'power of judging of harmony ... sense of hearing' – and for *latterly* – 'a low word lately hatched'. Richardson was criticised by David Garrick as an authority 'beneath the dignity' of the *Dictionary*, as reported by James Boswell in his *Life*.[11] But quotations from *Clarissa* positioned its author among the best authors: dictionaries have cultural as well as linguistic functions.

Sir Charles Grandison and the Vernacular

In *Sir Charles Grandison*, differences between the sexes and the difficulty of direct communication in a divided society are magnified by words such as *Femalities* (*SCG*, VII.340, index), perhaps especially when these words are explicitly attributed to an older man (uncle Selby), or, like *nun you up*, or *kittenish*, used by or about the wittily difficult Charlotte (V.ix.45, VI.li.311). And constraints on women's choices in life are focused by modal verbs, which contrast attitudes with reality and encode 'logical' reflection and 'social negotiation' in a 'curiously double register of meaning'.[12] For instance, Sir Charles presumes 'not to say what Clementina *will*, what she *can* do' (*SCG*, VI.v.17) and wonders 'whether there is any man that [his sister Charlotte] *can* or *does* prefer', since what even he deems her '*female circumambages*' (III.xvii.150) obscure her feelings. The novel also represents the possibility for such differences to be bridged. Despite his singular diction and his stereotypes of women, Selby is happily married, and even Charlotte is eventually *matronized* (VII.xxxix.190), having earlier come to appreciate one of her husband's *Femalities*: his enthusiasm for dancing at Sir Charles and Harriet's wedding (VI.liii.346). Indeed, for the protagonists, desire becomes reality in the speech act of *I will* (VI.lii.328). This simple assertion is anticipated by Harriet's 'Sir – I CAN – I DO' (VI.xxv.144) and Sir Charles's simpler 'How have I been, how am I, how shall I be, rewarded?' (VI.xxxi.212). The pedagogical atmosphere evoked by these verb conjugations reflects the text's broader engagement with debates about education, especially its contribution to gender differences and its (ir)relevance to adult life.

Charlotte intimates the incompatibility of women's and men's education, whether criticising a suitor's spelling (*SCG*, III.xvi.124) and her husband's grammar (V.x.54), or admitting that 'he spells pretty well, for a Lord' (IV.xxxiii.233). Of course the English language alone is not sufficient learning for any of the main characters. Their high social status is signalled by their knowledge of modern languages such as Italian, and their high moral status by their use of it to communicate rather than impress.[13] But the structure of *Sir Charles Grandison* questions the value of 'the learned languages' (I.xii.63): very early in the novel Harriet makes a case for the vernacular against an ineffective pedant, using Milton's *Paradise Lost* as her primary example (I.xiii.72–4). While the discussion also justifies a mother's classical learning (I.xiii.77), for much of the novel Richardson undermines the status of a classical education, the principal distinguisher of class and gender. Only near its conclusion is Harriet's attack on the classics authoritatively refuted – by her husband, after their marriage (VI.lv.364).[14]

Richardson's Influence

Richardson's English was criticised even by reviewers of other authors' works. In 1763, one writer in the *Monthly Review* uses Richardson's typographical techniques to contrast 'Mr. Richardson's *Femalities*' with the unaffected *Ladyism* of Lady Mary Wortley Montagu, another recently deceased letter-writer.[15] In 1765, the Revd John Entick was mocked for 'rank[ing]' '*Pamela Andrews*, or even *Sir Charles Grandison* ... with Shakespeare, Locke, &c' among 'our best authors' whose words were purportedly included in his *New Spelling Dictionary*. Richardson's marginal status is clear even for Entick: unlike Shakespeare and Milton, his name does not appear on the title page, and in the preface 'PAMELA' and

'GRANDISON' are mentioned rather than their author.[16] And the editor of his letters labelled his language as low: in her 1804 'Life', Anna Laetitia Barbauld explicitly linked Richardson's 'colloquial vulgarisms' with his vernacular education, shared with many men as well as women.[17]

Barbauld also claims, however, that the 'printer in Salisbury-court' had given 'one motive more to the rest of Europe, to learn the language of his country'.[18] Richardson's linguistic influence is tempting to trace. *Pamela* changed the pronunciation of the name, departing from classical accents,[19] and the novel probably popularised its punctuation for novelists conveying nuances of spoken and silent emotion and thought. Sarah Fielding used dashes in *David Simple* (1744), and in 1758 wrote to Richardson for printerly advice about capitalisation and punctuation.[20] Fielding then began to use an apostrophe in the preterite and participles of verbs such as *encourag'd*; Ingrid Tieken-Boon van Ostade attributes these spellings and Fielding's freer capitalisation to her imitating Richardson. Of course these spellings ending in *-'d* would become less common through the century: Richardson used them less frequently than his contemporaries, and in using them less often he may have copied Johnson, who had stopped using them before he met Richardson.[21] Tieken-Boon van Ostade also proposes that Johnson imitated Richardson. While contemporaries used the old-fashioned *I know not* primarily in their formal writing, Richardson preferred it even in letters. Johnson employed these distinctive *do*-less negative sentences in the very 'written' style of the *Rambler* (1750–2), to which he had asked Richardson to contribute.[22] Because of Richardson's limited education and social background, his fiction can indicate how standard English was codified and corrected from above. But the writing of this well-connected printer and popular author also shows how some norms may have spread from below.

Notes

1 Ingrid Tieken-Boon van Ostade, *The Bishop's Grammar: Robert Lowth and the Rise of Prescriptivism in English* (Oxford University Press, 2011), pp. 258–61.
2 Jarrod Hurlbert, 'Pamela: Or, Virtue Reworded: The Texts, Paratexts, and Revisions that Redefine Samuel Richardson's *Pamela*', PhD Dissertation (Marquette University, 2012), p. 40 and *passim*.
3 Shirley van Marter, 'Richardson's Revisions of *Clarissa* in the Second Edition', *Studies in Bibliography*, 26 (1973), 107–32 (p. 111).
4 Barbara M. H. Strang, 'Some Aspects of the History of the *BE+ING* Construction', in John Anderson (ed.), *Language Form and Linguistic*

Variation: Papers Dedicated to Angus McIntosh (John Benjamins, 1982), pp. 429–52.

5 Sarah Fielding, *Remarks on 'Clarissa'* (London, 1749), p. 12.

6 Donald L. Ball, 'Richardson's Resourceful Wordmaking', *South Atlantic Bulletin*, 41.4 (1976), 56–65, updated by the *OED Online* (March 2016).

7 Anon., *Critical Remarks on 'Sir Charles Grandison', 'Clarissa' and 'Pamela'* (London, 1754), p. 4.

8 Lynda Mugglestone, *Samuel Johnson and the Journey into Words* (Oxford University Press, 2015), pp. 77–8; Samuel Johnson, *A Dictionary of the English Language*, 2nd edn, 2 vols. (London, 1755–6).

9 William R. Keast, 'The Two *Clarissa*s in Johnson's *Dictionary*', *Studies in Philology*, 54.3 (1957), 429–39.

10 *Ibid.*, 430–3.

11 Boswell, *Life of Johnson*, Vol. IV, p. 4.

12 Lynne Magnusson, 'A Play of Modals: Grammar and Potential Action in Early Shakespeare', *Shakespeare Survey*, 62 (2009), 69–80 (pp. 69, 73).

13 Michèle Cohen, *Fashioning Masculinity: National Identity and Language in the Eighteenth Century* (Routledge, 1996), p. 63.

14 Paul Stevens, 'Raphael's Condescension: *Paradise Lost*, Jane Austen, and the Secular Displacement of Grace', in Ann Coiro and Blair Hoxby (eds.), *Milton and the Long Restoration* (Oxford University Press, 2016), pp. 531–53.

15 Joe Bray, 'Attending to the *Minute*: Richardson's Revisions of Italics in *Pamela*', in Joe Bray, Miriam Handley, and Anne C. Henry (eds.), *Ma(r)king the Text: The Presentation of Meaning on the Literary Page* (Ashgate, 2000), pp. 105–19 (p. 115); *Monthly Review*, 29 (1763), 57–8. Ball, 'Richardson's Resourceful Wordmaking', p. 62; Carol Percy, *A Database of Linguistic and Stylistic Criticism in Eighteenth-Century Periodical Reviews* (31 October 2000), http://projects.chass.utoronto.ca/reviews/ (accessed 9 May 2017).

16 *Monthly Review*, 32 (1765), 469–71; John Entick, *The New Spelling Dictionary*, 2nd edn (London, 1766), p. vii.

17 Barbauld, *Correspondence*, Vol. I, p. xxxiii.

18 *Ibid.*, Vol. I, p. lii.

19 *Ibid.*, Vol. I, p. lxxviii; Keymer and Sabor, *'Pamela' in the Marketplace*, pp. 7–8.

20 Janine Barchas, 'Sarah Fielding's Dashing Style and Eighteenth-Century Print Culture', *ELH*, 63.3 (1996), 633–56 (pp. 649–51).

21 Ingrid Tieken-Boon van Ostade, 'Social Network Analysis and the Language of Sarah Fielding', *European Journal of English Studies*, 4.3 (2000), 291–302 (p. 299).

22 Ingrid Tieken-Boon van Ostade, 'Samuel Richardson's Role as Linguistic Innovator: A Sociolinguistic Analysis', in John Frankis and Ingrid Tieken-Boon van Ostade (eds.), *Language Usage and Description: Studies Presented to N. E. Osselton on the Occasion of His Retirement* (Rodopi, 1991), pp. 47–57 (pp. 51–3); Tieken-Boon van Ostade, *The Bishop's Grammar*, pp. 249–50.

CHAPTER 21

Salon Culture and Conversation

Markman Ellis

Although Samuel Richardson lived in a period that greatly valued conversation and sociability, he never went to a salon, and his own abilities as a conversationalist, according to those who knew him, were very limited.[1] The primary forms of his literary contribution – fictional letters and journals – do not constitute anything much like conversation. Furthermore, he did not contribute to the greater eighteenth-century debate on conversation theory, like the moral philosophers and essayists David Hume, the earl of Shaftesbury, and Joseph Addison. Nonetheless, Richardson's fiction makes a very telling analysis of the limits of eighteenth-century models of polite sociability and the performance of conversation.

Richardson and the Salon

The term 'salon' is derived from the French term referring to the principal reception room of a large private house. In the eighteenth century, the term described a form of sociability in which a prominent *philosophe*, often a woman, met with an invited group of women and men for intellectual discussions in a private home. The common features of the salon were inherent in their structure and organisation: they were regular, relatively exclusive, invitation-only gatherings organised for the purpose of conversation and intellectual exchange, at which distinctions of rank, class, and nationality were temporarily suspended. In this sense, the salon followed wider eighteenth-century patterns of associational sociability, such as those adopted in the coffee-house, the club, the debating society, or the Masonic lodge. A distinctive aspect of the salon was the role of women. The salon was centred on and organised by women, and inasmuch as they embodied the notion of polite conversation, women, or the idea of feminine manners, were central to salon society (Figure 21.1). Furthermore, historians of the salon in the French tradition have located conversation, debate, and politeness as one of its central enabling structures (or enabling fictions).

The open and egalitarian conversation of the salon has been compared with the strict rules of conversation at the royal court, where those of the highest status commanded the conversation, while those of lower status spoke only when addressed or in confirmation.

Though he never participated in a salon as such, Richardson did engage in a rudimentary form of coterie criticism in the composition of his novels. He encouraged the friendship of young women, engaging them in discussion about his work, both through their correspondence and in personal encounters. In both modes, Richardson invited criticism of his writing, especially his interlocutors' reaction to the language and actions of his fictional protagonists. By this method, he refined both his estimate of how a young woman might behave, and the language he used to describe that behaviour. Richardson consulted widely with both lettered and unlettered women, from the middle station to the wealthy elite, including Sarah Wescomb; Mary Prescott; Ann Allen; Elizabeth Carter; Catherine Talbot; Hester Mulso; Sarah Fielding; Frances Sheridan; Jane Collier; Charlotte Lennox; Mary Delany; Elizabeth, Lady Echlin; and Dorothy,

Figure 21.1 Jean François de Troy, *A Reading of Molière* (1728). Fitzwilliam Museum, Cambridge.

Lady Bradshaigh.[2] But he also consulted with male friends (Aaron Hill, John Duncombe, and Edward Young), and with young men (Thomas and Edward Mulso). This is a heterogeneous set: some are notably intellectual and literary, whereas others seem almost to be valued for their undereducated ordinariness.

Conceptualising these sociable meetings, Richardson's friend, the painter Susanna Highmore, sketched Richardson reading aloud to company in the grotto of his garden at North End in Fulham (see Figure 1.6, above, p. 14). She depicts Richardson reading from the manuscript of *Sir Charles Grandison* with a group of young friends, three women and three men. Although not a salon, it is a sociable encounter, in which Richardson invites the coterie criticism of his assembled guests; it is also something of a performance, in which the guests admire Richardson's work in progress. Anecdotal evidence suggests that Richardson enjoyed conversations praising his works, but took criticism badly.

The closest analogues in England to the French salon were the assemblies organised by Elizabeth Montagu and Elizabeth Vesey, although they flourished in the 1770s and 1780s, well after Richardson's death in 1761, and they were not called a 'salon' until the late nineteenth century. But there is some evidence that Montagu sponsored forms of intellectually directed sociability akin to a salon in the 1750s and 1760s, when Richardson was alive. In this period Montagu met with groups of her friends in an 'assembly' or a *conversazione*, a gathering of men and women for conversation, social entertainment, and amusement. Montagu's assemblies were large meetings of people in her grand house, with a concert of music and other entertainment. On 1 May 1760, for example, she organised an assembly with Anne Ellis to entertain over 100 people.[3] The distinctive quality of Montagu's assemblies, as Nicole Pohl and Betty Schellenberg have argued, was that they professed 'principles of polite sociability, a limited social mobility based on merit, and equality between the sexes based on rational friendship and intellectual exchange'.[4]

Richardson was curious about and supportive of the nascent Bluestockings, and was on good terms with some intellectual women, including Mulso, Carter, and Talbot. But he was not a participant in Bluestocking sociability, in a period when men such as Benjamin Stillingfleet, George Lyttelton, and William Pulteney were not only present, but central to its operation. Richardson was too vulgar (as a mechanic printer and 'obscurely situated' man of business); even worse, he seems to have been poor company. In a period of inveterate clubbing, and some assembling, Richardson was curiously unsocialised, preferring small-scale assemblies where he was the centre of a group of submissive women, male literary friends, or business acquaintances. His own 'salon' scenario, in the grotto at North End, proposed that his ideal conversation was between a dominant master and subservient subalterns: in this way he was decidedly not a *salonière*.

Conversation

Conversation was extensively theorised in the eighteenth century, the subject of debate in periodical essays in the *Spectator* tradition, and by moral philosophers such as David Hume and Adam Smith. The 'sociable Disposition' of conversation, Hume argued, brought 'Mankind together in Society, where every one displays his Thoughts and Observations in the best Manner he is able, and mutually gives and receives Information, as well as Pleasure'.[5] Hume and Smith argued that conversation, one of the sociable arts of common life, fulfilled an important role in the civilising process of social improvement, even though it was also closely associated with the domestic and ephemeral world of women. Conversation was one of the activities through which the polite had the liberty to encounter each other's opinions, by which means, in the words of the earl of Shaftesbury, 'We polish one another, and rub off our Corners and rough Sides by a sort of *amicable Collision*.'[6] Of Richardson's novels, *Sir Charles Grandison* comes closest to Hume's vision of conversation: Schellenberg has argued that the novel uses conversation with and between women to demonstrate how they may improve themselves in knowledge and manners.[7]

Perhaps the most famous phrase that associates Richardson and conversation is his idea of letter-writing as 'the converse of the pen'. In a letter to Sarah Wescomb, Richardson wrote that their correspondence

> is the cement of friendship: it is friendship avowed under hand and seal … more pure, yet more ardent, and less broken in upon, than personal conversation can be even amongst the most pure, because of the deliberation it allows, from the very preparation to, and action of writing … Who then shall decline the converse of the pen?

As more deliberate and assured, he argues, letter-writing was a more reliable basis for friendship than conversation. Reading Wescomb's letters, Richardson imagined how close he felt to her: 'I have you before me in person: I converse with you … I see you, I sit with you, I talk with you, I read to you, I stop to hear your sentiments' (27 August 1746). The 'converse of the pen', he concludes, might even be preferable to personal conversation.[8] Richardson takes the metaphor of correspondence as conversation about as far as it can go, so that correspondence is more intimate than conversation, distance closer than presence. But in doing so, Richardson also advertises one of his greatest technical challenges in his epistolary fiction writing: absence. As he says to Wescomb, 'a correspondence by letters' is only 'written on occasions of necessary absence' (27 August 1746). Conversation is dependent on forms of face-to-face socialising, with participants close enough to hear each other talk comfortably. But epistolary fiction separates characters so that they keep writing to each other. This is the first problem for conversation in the novel: epistolary fiction, to an important extent, is allergic to conversation.

Nonetheless, Richardson's novels suggest he was a very astute conversation analyst. For historians, conversation poses an important problem, as it usually does not produce written or durable evidence. Samuel Johnson distinguished proper conversation from talk: in the latter, 'nothing is discussed'.[9] Richardson understood this distinction, but his novels were interested in all forms of talk, including that elevated into conversation and discussion. In an epistolary novel such as *Clarissa* each letter is written from the first-person point of view, in a series of I-narrations undertaken by different characters. Each correspondent has a narrator-like role to advance and explain the story, and also to participate as a character within it. Despite this, the I-narration letters in *Clarissa* include a considerable quantity of reported direct speech. These constitute extended records of conversations, as if the novel were a machine for recording talk.

The word 'conversation' is freighted with extra significance in *Clarissa*. In the 'Preface' to the novel, Richardson says

> That the Letters on both Sides are written while the Hearts of the Writers must be supposed to be wholly engaged in their Subjects: The Events at the Time generally dubious: – So that they abound, not only with critical Situations; but with what may be called *instantaneous* Descriptions and Reflections; which may be brought home to the Breast of the youthful Reader.

This reflective self-examination is a characteristic aspect of Richardson's fiction. To this he adds, almost as an afterthought: 'As also, with affecting Conversations; many of them written in the Dialogue or Dramatic Way' (*C*, Preface, vi). As Richardson recognises, *Clarissa* is an innovative and extraordinarily extensive examination of the nature of conversation, with his thematic (or ideological) interest in conversation underpinned by a technical interest in how talk is recorded.

This poses the second problem of conversation in the novel. As readers immediately recognise, many of the letters, but most especially Clarissa's, are very impressive acts of memory, as she reproduces whole conversations, apparently word for word. This is of course a fictional conceit: Richardson uses the epistolary method to allow Clarissa to recollect extensive speaking events for verbatim narration at a later time. Such acts of memory may stretch credulity now, in an age of mechanical reproduction, but eighteenth-century culture believed that extended conversations might be reproduced from memory in this way. Boswell, in his *Life of Johnson*, recorded whole evenings of Johnson's discussion, and defended the pleasure and utility of an 'exact transcript of conversation'.[10] Especially notable feats of memory were performed by the reporters of parliamentary debates, who were not permitted to take notes in the chamber, but subsequently were able to recall several hours of speech-making.

This practice is not without its difficulties. Although Richardson's novels report conversations in various ways, using a range of modes of talk description, of varying degrees of concentration and detail, there is no direct, immediate, and transparent relationship between the conversation event and its *post hoc* recording. All sorts of speculations and reflections populate the gap between event and recording. Although in *Clarissa* Richardson strives to present conversation in a realist mode, there is no actual conversation event that has been recorded. But Richardson was interested in recording conversational habits.

Richardson in Conversation

Richardson's description of conversation in *Clarissa* is both varied and technically sophisticated. The preface's proposal that conversation was recorded 'in the dialogue or dramatic way' suggests a context in contemporary theatrical texts. Some encounters in the book are described as if a playtext, such as a scene in Volume VII in which Colonel Morden, Belford, and Lord M debate with Lovelace concerning his actions and intentions, using direct speech marked by their abbreviated names in the margin, without further interpolation by author or letter-writer (*C*, VII.xiii.89–102). But this mode, directly emulating dramatic writing, is rare in Richardson.

Richardson's mode of speech reporting varies according to fictional purpose. When Clarissa is reporting on her spoken encounters with Lovelace or Solmes, she uses a form of indirect speech reporting, expressing the content of the conversation without quoting the actual words of the speaker. An example is Clarissa's account of the conversation she has with

Lovelace on Saturday 18 March in the woodhouse at Harlowe Place (*C*, 1. xxxvi.236–49). Clarissa summarises Lovelace's speech, reproducing some of his language, but without direct quotation. Indirect speech restricts the reader's access to evidence of Lovelace's courting language, a polite and solicitous mode of discourse that threatens to cast him in an attractive light. This mode is common in *Sir Charles Grandison*, where Richardson tends to summarise conversation rather than report direct speech in the dramatic mode.

In the first two volumes of Clarissa, however, many letters between Clarissa and Anna describe conversations using reported direct speech, quoting the actual words of the speaker. Richardson uses this mode for Clarissa's battle (in Volume 1, Letters xvi–xxi) with her family concerning her right, as she sees it, to choose whom she will marry. The letters are an epic of conversational reporting: nearly fifty-five pages of the novel (in the first edition), almost 19,000 words of text, all supposedly written by Clarissa over two days. Of this, 14,600 words are direct reports of speech in conversation. In these talk events, reported speech is supplemented by Clarissa's reflections and interpolations. The distinction is indicated by typographical conventions developed by Richardson, albeit rather inconsistently applied. Richardson usually indicates turn-taking, the process by which people in a conversation allow each other to speak, by starting each speaker's contribution in a separate paragraph, with the moment of splicing indicated with a long dash. But this is not consistent: in some instances, there is no new paragraph and no long dash, and readers establish who is speaking only by inference.

Conversation analysis suggests that turn-taking is the heart of conversation, allowing one person to cease speaking and another to respond or take up the subject. But turn-taking is fraught with difficulty, as Clarissa shows, as she struggles to get her point of view across. She both interrupts and is interrupted frequently, each signalled by the long dash. Both Clarissa and her mother interrupt themselves too, reproducing, to some extent, the broken sentence patterns of direct speech – what analysts call 'self-initiated sentence repair'. Richardson makes some limited attempt to delineate the hesitant flow of speech by denoting pauses or gaps with dashes, cut-off sentences, italics, or exclamation marks. Italics are freely used, sometimes to indicate vocal stress, and at other times simply to advertise emotional extremity. In narrating conversation, Clarissa inserts reporting clauses describing cadence, context, or ascription to speaker. These reporting clauses offer interpolative information describing speech cadence ('she hesitated'), but they also record her own extra-linguistic body rhetoric (tears, blushes, sobs, breathing, fainting, and syncope).

The speech patterns in these directly reported conversations reiterate the wider battle between Clarissa and her family. Her mother insists on the family's argument, and indeed, she makes clear that she has no power but to do her husband's bidding. This is not a negotiation. Clarissa struggles to get her point of view across in the conversation, as signalled by her constant interruption, both of herself, and by her mother. Her interrupted conversation reiterates Terry Castle's suggestion that the novel presents a battle for different accounts of Clarissa, in which Clarissa struggles, and fails, to get her narrative of her self accepted by the family and the wider world.[11]

Conversation and salon culture are both embedded in the ideological formation of politeness. As eighteenth-century moral philosophers argue, conversation polishes and refines manners, and so contributes to the improvement of society. Richardson was deeply immersed in that polite and sociable culture, yet he was also a recalcitrant and rather awkward proponent of conversation. This is not a contradiction. In his novels, Richardson does not offer any extended writing addressing the topic of conversation, as do other moralists of the period. Rather, his novels show that conversation is as much the home of contention and discord as it is of polite refinement, and as such, Richardson is a highly significant theorist of conversation in mid-eighteenth-century Britain.

Notes

1 Eaves and Kimpel, *Biography*, pp. 518–41.
2 Elspeth Knights, '"Daring but to touch the hem of her garment": Women Reading *Clarissa*', *Women's Writing*, 7.2 (2000), 221–45.
3 Elizabeth Montagu to Elizabeth Carter, 1 May 1760, Huntington Library, MO3035.
4 Nicole Pohl and Betty A. Schellenberg, 'Introduction: A Bluestocking Historiography', in Nicole Pohl and Betty A. Schellenberg (eds.), *Reconsidering the Bluestockings* (Huntington Library, 2003), pp. 1–19 (pp. 2–4); see also Deborah Heller, 'Bluestocking Salons and the Public Sphere', *Eighteenth-Century Life*, 22.2 (1998), 59–82.
5 David Hume, 'Of Essay-Writing', in *Essays, Moral and Political, Vol.* II (Edinburgh, 1742), pp. 1–2.
6 Anthony Ashley Cooper, earl of Shaftesbury, *Characteristicks of Men, Manners, Opinions, Times* (1709), ed. Philip Ayres, 3 vols. (Clarendon Press, 1999), Vol. I, p. 39.

7 Betty A. Schellenberg, *The Conversational Circle: Re-Reading the English Novel,*
   1740–1775 (University Press of Kentucky, 1996).
8 Bruce Redford, *The Converse of the Pen: Acts of Intimacy in the Eighteenth-
   Century Familiar Letter* (University of Chicago Press, 1986).
9 Boswell, *Life of Johnson*, Vol. IV, p. 186.
10 *Ibid.*, Vol. V, pp. 414–15.
11 Terry Castle, *Clarissa's Ciphers: Meaning and Disruption in Richardson's 'Clarissa'*
   (Cornell University Press, 1982), pp. 24–35.

CHAPTER 22

The Visual Arts

Lynn Shepherd

We have become so used to the idea that Richardson is a 'dramatic novelist' that it comes as something of a surprise to find that his own correspondents hardly ever use analogies from the theatre to describe their response to his works.[1] Even the dramatic theorist Aaron Hill resorts to the pictorial, rather than the theatrical, to express how Richardson's novels 'paint the Features of the Soul, so speakingly!' (Aaron Hill to Richardson, 5 May 1748). And when Richardson describes his literary practice to Sarah Chapone on 11 January 1751 (one of the rare occasions on which he does so) he draws explicitly on the language of painting:

> You wonder Madam, that the same Hand which could draw a Pamela & Clarissa, could draw a Mr. B. & an odious Jewkes; a Lovelace, & a vile Sinclair – From the amiable Character of a good Person, it is not hard to draw a bad one. But tho' I have had Ideas of this or that Person before me in *parts* no one Person Man or Woman sat before me for the *Whole* of any of my Pictures.

Analogies between the 'sister arts' of literature and painting are as old as Horace's famous dictum in his *Ars poetica*, 'ut pictura poesis' (as is painting, so is poetry), and three of the giants of eighteenth-century English fiction sit remarkably comfortably within the hierarchy of styles that then governed painting: at one extreme, Henry Fielding's comparison of his art to that of a 'Comic History-Painter' in the preface to *Joseph Andrews*; at the other, Daniel Defoe's 'Dutch school' realism; with Richardson suspended between the two, drawing for his own aesthetic on the representational systems of portraiture.[2] It is not a mere accident of history that portrait-painting achieved an unprecedented popularity in England at exactly the same time that the novel was emerging as the newly dominant literary genre. For Richardson's contemporaries, the portrait and the novel were often seen as mutually enriching forms: the painter and art theorist Jonathan Richardson talked of 'reading' a picture and, as we have seen, Samuel Richardson's readers thought of his novels as 'active Pictures [that] glow ... with speaking Life, and thinking Woe'.[3] His novels are, in fact, one of the most compelling examples of the intersection of the verbal and the visual that the eighteenth century can provide. The idea of portraiture operates on a number of levels in a Richardson novel: portrait 'likenesses' such as Clarissa's 'whole-length picture, in the Vandyke taste' (*C*, III.liii.259) function as significant physical and symbolic items in the plot, but Richardson also draws on the conventions of contemporary portraiture to create an eighteenth-century version of 'spatial form' narrative. And as Jeffrey Smitten remarks, the two central preoccupations of spatial form narratives are likenesses of individuals and tableaux of societies.[4] Richardson uses portraiture to explore these interdependent themes: on the one hand, the intimate examination of the 'inmost recesses of [the] heart' (*C*, I.xxxvii.253), and on the other, an articulation of the complexities of social ties, and the relationships of power and affection within the family.

Richardson may or may not be the 'father of the novel', but he is, unquestionably, the first writer of English fiction to publish a novel in which the process of reading is modified, enhanced, and to some extent controlled by a lavish set of illustrations. As Peter Sabor observes, 'as early as December 1740, within a month of its first publication, Richardson was already thinking of *Pamela* in visual terms'.[5] With sales soaring, he started planning a second edition, to be embellished with frontispieces by Hogarth. When Aaron Hill writes to Richardson on 29 December 1740, he notes that 'the designs you have taken for frontispieces, seem to have been very judiciously chosen; upon pre-supposition that Mr. Hogarth is able (and if any-body is, it is he), to teach pictures to speak and to think'. However, when the second edition duly appeared, it was without frontispieces – an absence Richardson felt compelled to explain:

> We shall only add, That it was intended to prefix two neat Frontispieces to this Edition ... and one was actually finished for that Purpose; but ... the Engraving Part of that which was done (tho' no Expence was spared) having fallen very short of the Spirit of the Passages they were intended to represent, the Proprietors were advised to lay them aside. (*P*, p. 475)

Hogarth's designs have not survived, and even though we might lament that loss, it is clear Richardson himself did not. The heroine he revealingly referred to as 'my Girl' had divided readers into passionate Pamelists and equally fervent Anti-Pamelists, and it is possible that Hogarth (like his friend Fielding) was in the latter camp (Richardson to George Cheyne, 31 August 1741). If he saw – and illustrated – the *Shamela* rather than the paragon Richardson believed he had created, it is hardly a surprise that the commission was such a spectacular failure.

But the experience was not enough to put Richardson off the idea of illustration altogether. By 8 October 1741, he was writing to Ralph Allen about his plans to publish a new sixth edition of *Pamela*, which would contain both parts of *Pamela*, and 'have Cuts to it, done by the Best Hands'. The 'Best Hands' in question were Hubert Gravelot and Francis Hayman, who may well have been painting his conversation piece of Richardson and his family at around this time.[6] There would be seven 'cuts' in each of the first three volumes and eight in the last, making twenty-nine in total – an unprecedented number for a work of fiction. As his own printer, Richardson was able to exert a degree of control any author would envy – then or now – and the sixth edition was in every respect a splendid artefact: a 'collector's item' costing £1 4s, compared to the 6s price of the earlier two-volume editions, and designed to be handled and displayed, as much as read. The illustrations were a key element of that aesthetic appeal, but they had another, more covert purpose too. As a printer of other people's works, Richardson was acutely aware of the 'propaganda value' of illustrations. In his preface to the edition of *Aesop's Fables* he published in 1739 he noted the 'alluring Force which Cuts or Pictures, suited to the respective Subjects, have on the Minds of Children' (*EW*, p. 109). He would now apply that same 'alluring force' to 'rehabilitate' Pamela, by presenting her to the world in all her 'Beauty of Mind, and Loveliness of Person' (*P*, p. 326), and in the process force the reader's attention away from the sexual content of the novel which had caused so much controversy, focusing instead on the 'Instruction' the book was always intended to provide (Richardson to George Cheyne, 31 August 1741). As Richardson himself put it, his 'new species of writing' was designed to 'turn young people into a course of reading different from the pomp and parade of romance-writing, and … promote the cause of religion and virtue' (Richardson to Hill, *c.* 1 February 1741).

This is what explains the startling – and otherwise inexplicable – omission of any of the so-called 'warm scenes' from the Hayman and Gravelot illustrations. Indeed, it is impossible to get any sense of the story of *Pamela* from the images alone. Moreover, the illustrative approach adopted by Hayman and Gravelot cleverly exploits the style contemporary readers would have associated with the pictures they saw in 'romance-writing', such as that in John Watts's *Select Collection of Novels and Histories* (1729), which includes a frontispiece for *The Princess of Cleves* where the heroine's posture is echoed in Hayman's later image of Pamela in the woodhouse.[7]

Hayman and Gravelot take this illustrative style and relocate it to a contemporary English interior for the novel's first illustration (Figure 22.1).

In fact, images like these function in a very similar way to those in modern celebrity magazines, offering the reader a glimpse into a world of refined feeling and equally refined surroundings. Moreover, the specific stance Pamela is adopting in this image would be recognisable to contemporary readers as the 'courtsie' described by François Nivelon in his hugely

Figure 22.1 Francis Hayman and Hubert Gravelot, first illustration to Samuel Richardson, *Pamela; or, Virtue Rewarded*, 6th edn (1742) (Vol. 1, opposite p. 4).

popular text *The Rudiments of Genteel Behavior* (1737). Hayman engraved an image of the 'courtsie', and Pamela's stance exactly matches every gesture. It is a deliberate and hugely significant choice of pose because the 'courtsie' was a mode of behaviour reserved to the genteel, and between those of broadly equal rank. Thus, while it takes two volumes of text to bring Pamela to her 'exalted condition', this illustration is already positioning her as Mr B's equal and an entirely appropriate marriage partner as early as page 4.

As Thomas Keymer and Peter Sabor remind us in *The 'Pamela' Controversy*, the *Pamela* 'phenomenon' was as much a visual as a verbal one: from the images produced for the pirated versions that irritated Richardson so much to unofficial 'merchandise' such as fans and a waxworks display. There was also another significant set of illustrations, but these proved to be much more to Richardson's taste.

On 22 February 1744, Joseph Highmore placed an advertisement in the *London Daily Post and General Advertiser* for 'Twelve prints, by the best French Engravers, after his own Paintings, representing the most remarkable Adventures of *Pamela*. In which he has endeavour'd to comprehend her whole Story as well as to preserve a Connexion between the several Pictures.' A further advertisement appeared on 10 May, announcing that the original paintings were on view at Highmore's house in Lincoln's Inn Fields. Richardson lived close by at the time, and must have liked Highmore's version of his heroine, because the two men became firm friends. Unlike Hayman and Gravelot, Highmore was free to choose the subjects for his paintings, and as a result, his images convey a more accurate record of the story, including the notorious 'warm scenes'. The question we have to ask, then, is how Highmore's version of these scenes managed to satisfy Richardson. Part of the answer, no doubt, is the extraordinarily elegant Pamela Highmore depicts, and even if the sexual content is there, it must have passed muster as true to the 'Spirit of the Passages', by depicting 'all [Pamela's] Sufferings ... [and] the laudable Resistance she made'.[8]

Highmore was primarily a portraitist, and it is as a portraitist that he approaches *Pamela*. For example, his image of Pamela and Mr B in the summerhouse draws its power and subtlety from its exploitation of the conventions of contemporary marriage portraiture. A spectator's first impression would be of a 'promenade portrait': a young husband and his fashionably dressed wife in their elegant garden. But a more detailed examination reveals that this image is nothing of the kind – their hands are joined by force, not mutual affection, and the needlework that would usually symbolise the tranquil domesticity of the wifely role has been cast violently aside (Figure 22.2).

Between the first publication of *Pamela* and the writing of *Clarissa*, Richardson had a 'conversation piece' of his family painted by Hayman, had his book illustrated (also by Hayman), and saw how his new friend Joseph Highmore presented the same story. Both *Clarissa* and *Sir Charles Grandison* are informed by the insights that he gained, and show Richardson drawing on a 'painterly' understanding of the way stance, gesture, space, and position can be used to express feeling, capture character, and articulate relationships. Figure 22.3 thus illustrates a virtuous circle in which the visual enriches the verbal, and the resulting text then inspires a new image in its turn. This is Joseph Highmore's painting of 'the assembled Harlowes, the accusing Brother, and the accused Sister on her return from Miss Howe's, as represented at the beginning of vol. I' (Richardson to Lady Bradshaigh, January 1749). If we look first at the text that inspired

Figure 22.2 Joseph Highmore, *Pamela and Mr B in the Summerhouse* (*c.* 1744). Fitzwilliam Museum, Cambridge.

this image we can see from the typography that we are to read the scene like a picture – italicised figure by italicised figure.

> I was no sooner silent, than my *brother* swore … that, for his part, he would never be reconciled to that libertine …
>
> A man who had like to have been my brother's murderer, my *sister* said …
>
> My *papa*, with vehemence both of action and voice … told me, that I had met with too much indulgence …
>
> Very true, my *mamma* said …
>
> My uncle *Harlowe* said, he hoped his beloved niece only wanted to know her papa's will, to obey it.
>
> And my uncle *Antony*, in his rougher manner, that I would not give them reason to apprehend, that I thought my grandfather's favour to me had made me independent of them all … (*C*, 1.vii.40–1)

Again and again, Richardson presents the narrative of *Clarissa* in this way, one character then another: gesture, countenance, speech; gesture, countenance, speech. In the later scene at the tea-table, for example, the power

Figure 22.3 Joseph Highmore, *The Harlowe Family* (1747–8). Yale Center for British Art, Paul Mellon Collection.

within the family is externalised, as in a conversation piece, through position, place, and possession: through the placing of the individuals ('my papa sat half-aside in his elbow-chair, that his head might be turned from me'); through physical accessories ('she was pleased to take the canister in her own hand'); and through gesture and expression ('my sister sat swelling', 'my brother looked at me with scorn', 'my aunt … bending coldly') (*C*, I.viii.48). Highmore takes his cue from this painterly mode by 're-digesting' Richardson's literary conversation piece of the Harlowes back into a visual one. In the eighteenth century, painters of 'conversation pieces' often used a 'triangular' composition to represent the family, with the father facing us at the centre and apex, and the family grouped around him according to age, gender, and status. As this implies, such images present a not-so-covert narrative of inheritance and power, despite the overtly domesticated setting and props. Highmore is deliberately subverting these conventions in this image of the Harlowes. In fact, it is more like an 'altercation piece' than a conversation piece: not Mr Harlowe but James stands at the apex of this group, with his back towards us. The principal lines of this composition, like the lines of influence in the family, run from James's hand lifted in command, past the father and uncles, down to the women. The symbolically empty chair is Clarissa's, and it functions to separate her from the rest of the family, relegating her to the part of the picture space usually reserved for servants. The painting thus enacts James's assumption of control, both of the family and of the physical space of Harlowe Place.

When Clarissa elopes, her elimination from the 'family piece' is formally completed. James orders that her 'whole-length picture, in the Vandyke taste' is to be 'thrown into [her] closet, which will be nailed up, as if it were not a part of the house' (*C*, III.liii.259). Much later, after the rape, Clarissa begins to create her own 'family piece', in which gesture is an authentic representation of love, and the lines of affection are all the more real for having no basis in actual kinship:

> She was sitting in her elbow-chair, Mrs Lovick close by her, in another chair, with her left arm round her neck, supporting it, as it were; for it seems the lady had bid her do so, saying she had been a mother to her, and she would delight herself in thinking she was in her mamma's arms. (*C*, VII.liii.201)

After Clarissa's death, the final pages of the novel offer us a gallery of new conversation pieces: on the one side the broken Harlowes and ruined Lovelaces; on the other, the newly established Belford and Hickman dynasties, already 'happy in a hopeful race' (*C*, VII.lxix.237).

And so to *Sir Charles Grandison*, in which portraits – literal and meta-phorical – move to the foreground of the text. Actual 'likenesses' operate within the plot as objective correlatives of emotion, whether displayed in formal galleries; exchanged between lovers, relatives, and friends; or treasured as mementoes of the absent and the dead. At the same time, Richardson's use of portraiture to represent character and relationship is as pervasive here as it was in *Clarissa*. Indeed perhaps more so, because the central character – the nexus of most readers' problems with the novel – describes himself thus: 'I am a painter, madam: I love to draw lady's pictures' (*SCG*, iv.iv.22). Sir Charles is describing his 'sitting' with the haughty Lady Beauchamp here, but the same dynamic operates in his handling of Lady L, Emily, Charlotte, and Harriet. As painter of their 'pictures' Sir Charles dictates how they are positioned, how they look, and how others are to see them, by moving them – in effect – from one acceptable female portrait 'type' to another: from the marriage-able maiden displaying her talents at the needle, to the demure wife and happy mother. Harriet, in particular, begins the novel as a vivacious and '*saucy* girl', but under his influence is increasingly 'composed' into a suit-able incarnation of 'Lady Grandison', destined to take her place in the 'unbroken series of … pictures' in the family gallery (*SCG*, iv.xxxii.222, vii.vii.31).

Sir Charles's control of the people and spaces of the novel is as absolute as James Harlowe's at Harlowe Place. We have already explored how the con-temporary conversation piece used triangular compositions to represent the structures of power in the family; in *Sir Charles Grandison*, Richardson uses the same organisational principle to dramatise Sir Charles's composi-tion of his own circle, positioning him habitually at the apex of a group of three. Whether as mediator, arbitrator, adjudicator, or 'matrimony-promoter' (*SCG*, iv.xii.94), Sir Charles actively seeks out such intermedi-ary roles, and exploits the influence they confer. He is likewise a composer of his own 'conversation pieces': the scenic form of *Sir Charles Grandison* typically has a group of people coming together spontaneously, and then clustering, under Sir Charles's direction, into a more formal seated struc-ture, in which he literally directs the conversation, dictating who speaks to whom. Thus, while *Grandison* is ostensibly about a 'family of love', that family's underlying composition is still one of patriarchal authority and control – a control that is all the more insidious for being covert (*SCG*, i. xxvi.185). Sir Charles's may be a benevolent dictatorship, but it is a dicta-torship all the same.

Notes

1 For a contrasting view of the response to Richardson as 'dramatic novelist', see Darryl P. Domingo, below (pp. 205–6). The phrase originates with Mark Kinkead-Weekes's highly influential study *Samuel Richardson: Dramatic Novelist* (Methuen, 1973).

2 On Defoe, see Maximilian Novak, 'Picturing the Thing Itself, or Not: Defoe, Painting, Prose Fiction, and the Arts of Describing', *Eighteenth-Century Fiction*, 9 (1996), 1–20.

3 Jonathan Richardson, *The Science of a Connoisseur* (London, 1719), p. 38; Urania Johnson, from a poem addressed to Richardson as '*Clarissa*'s Painter', appended to a letter to Richardson, 5 April 1750.

4 Jeffrey R. Smitten, 'Introduction: Spatial Form and Narrative Theory', in Jeffrey R. Smitten and Ann Daghistany (eds.), *Spatial Form in Narrative* (Cornell University Press, 1981), pp. 15–34 (p. 25).

5 Thomas Keymer and Peter Sabor, 'Introduction', in Keymer and Sabor, *The 'Pamela' Controversy*, Vol. II, pp. xiii–xxix (p. xxiv).

6 See Lynn Shepherd, *'Clarissa's Painter: Portraiture, Illustration and Representation in the Novels of Samuel Richardson* (Oxford University Press, 2009), Chapter 2. See also Peter Sabor, above (p. 21), for a more detailed discussion of the place of this edition in the *Pamela* publishing history.

7 John Watts, *A Select Collection of Novels and Histories*, 6 vols. (London, 1729), Vol. II, p. 1.

8 Richardson, 'Preface', in *Pamela*, 2nd edn (London, 1741), pp. x–xiv (p. x).

CHAPTER 23

Theatre and Drama

Darryl P. Domingo

When Richardson described *Clarissa* as a 'Dramatic Narrative', he established one of the central critical paradigms through which his novels have
subsequently been discussed. His 'Postscript' to *Clarissa* was intended to
serve a more local purpose, vindicating the novel's tragic ending by contextualising it in contemporary dramatic criticism and, specifically, in Joseph
Addison's rejection of 'the *chimerical notion* of Poetical Justice'. Like Calista
in Nicholas Rowe's *The Fair Penitent* (1703) or the eponymous heroine
of Charles Johnson's *Cælia; or, The Perjur'd Lover* (1733), Clarissa dies in
order to 'raise Commiseration and Terror in the minds of the Audience'.
The exemplary 'Catastrophe' to the novel thus serves an important didactic function in reminding readers that virtue cannot always be rewarded
in a world where God has 'intermingled Good and Evil'. If a *'fortunate
Ending'* is suspect in a tragedy, such as 'the altered King Lear of Mr. Tate',
then it must be avoided in a novel self-consciously formed, as Richardson
explains, on both a 'Dramatic' and a 'Religious Plan'. No less than dramatists, novelists present audiences with examples to imitate or abhor and, in
so doing, inculcate moral lessons 'under the guise of an Amusement' (*C*,
Vol. VII, pp. 425–8, 'Postscript').

Dramatic Novelist

Richardson's conception of *Clarissa* as a dramatic narrative encouraged
early readers to evaluate all of his epistolary novels in terms borrowed from
the drama and theatre. Indeed, these readers seem to have assumed, along
with Denis Diderot, that '*Pamela, Clarissa*, and *Grandison* are three great
dramas!'[1] Richardson's contemporaries viewed his plots and characters
as having analogues in the English stage tradition, and they understood
the novel in letters as a genre that could approximate the immediacy of
actors and actresses reacting to one another in the moment and playing
to audiences in, as it were, a 'lively *present-tense* manner' (*C*, v.xxv.221).

Describing the effect of Richardson's '*epistolary correspondence*', Anna
Laetitia Barbauld argues that this narrative technique 'makes the whole
work dramatic, since all the characters speak in their own persons'.[2] Yet, as
in drama, the absence of a narrator to mediate the action made the epistolary novel liable to objection. The initial response to *Pamela* was dominated by debate over the heroine's questionable sincerity and her capacity
as an actress. In Henry Fielding's parodic version of the Pamela story,
Shamela is counselled by a mother who 'sold Oranges in the Play-House'
and who cautions that she has 'a very difficult Part to act'.[3] And in Eliza
Haywood's *Anti-Pamela* (1741), Syrena Tricksey is praised for exceeding
'the most experienc'd Actresses on the Stage, in a lively assuming all the different Passions that find Entrance in a Female Mind'.[4] Less cynical readers
celebrated Richardson for his representation of the interior life of his characters, notably comparing his work to that of William Shakespeare, who
was gradually being recognised in the middle of the eighteenth century as
England's greatest dramatist. John Hawkins called Richardson 'a writer
similar in genius to Shakespeare, as being acquainted with the inmost
recesses of the human heart', and David Garrick inscribed the flyleaf to
the first volume of his third-edition copy of *Clarissa* with the lines 'Of
Nature born, by Shakespeare got, / Clarissa, well I know thy lot.'[5] By the
early nineteenth century, Richardson was often praised as the 'Shakespeare
of Romance'.[6]

Garrick's arrival on the London theatrical scene roughly coincided with
the enormously successful publication of Richardson's first novel, and commentators regularly noted the parallels between the reception of *Pamela* and
the sensational public response to Garrick's debut in the title role of Colley
Cibber's adaptation of *Richard III* at Goodman's Fields in October 1741.
Joseph Warton remarked, in an 'epistolary satire' of 1742, that all the fashionable 'prattle' was now 'Of *Vauxhall, Garrick*, or *Pamela*', contextualising
the craze for actor and novelist in London's expanding commercial leisure
industry.[7] Within weeks of his debut on the London stage, and amidst a
rapid succession of editions of *Pamela*, Garrick appeared as Jack Smatter
in the first of the period's numerous theatrical adaptations of Richardson's
novels: Henry Giffard's *Pamela: A Comedy* (1741). Giffard turned much of
the pathos of the novel into broad farce and exploited the erotic energies
latent in the original. But even in poking fun at *Pamela*, Giffard's comedy demonstrated the undeniable theatrical possibilities of Richardson's
fiction. According to Thomas Keymer and Peter Sabor, Richardson's 'tale
of private servitude' was among the resources that enabled a new generation of actors, playwrights, and managers to 'revive theatrical culture' in

the wake of the Licensing Act of 1737.[8] Giffard's *Pamela* was performed eighteen times during the 1741–2 season at Goodman's Fields, and its success inspired several other theatrical adaptations, including a two-act burlesque entitled *Mock-Pamela* (1750); a 1742 ballad opera; and *Pamela; or, Virtue Triumphant* (1741), which was advertised as 'the genuine comedy of Pamela'.

In many ways, the best reason for viewing Richardson's novels as dramatic narratives is the frequency with which *Pamela*, *Clarissa*, and *Sir Charles Grandison* were adapted for the stage during the eighteenth century. Despite its massive length, *Clarissa* was awkwardly abridged and adapted into theatrical form on a number of occasions, such as in Robert Porrett's *Clarissa; or, The Fatal Seduction* (1788), a domestic tragedy significant for its audacity in interpolating spectacular twists into Richardson's plot and for having Clarissa's ghost warn Lovelace 'thy hour's at hand' moments before the climactic duel. Even *Sir Charles Grandison* was loosely adapted by Jane Austen, who seems to have collaborated with her niece Anna on a dramatic burlesque to be performed by her family at Steventon Rectory (*c.* 1791–1800).[9] Not only did Richardson's novels provide subject matter for the stage, but they became a touchstone for dramatists keen to satirise the very fashion for novels. The quixotic heroine of George Colman's *Polly Honeycombe, A Dramatic Novel* (1760) is an avid reader of Richardson, and her naïve desire for a lover who 'writes as well as Bob Lovelace' implies much about the perceived impact of fiction on young women, as well as the dangerous appeal of the charismatic stage rakes upon whom the character of Lovelace was modelled.[10] By drawing attention to the convergence of stage and page, promoter and parodist alike suggest that Richardson's novels were as much a theatrical as a literary phenomenon.

Antitheatrical Polemicist

The conspicuously theatrical response of early readers to *Pamela*, *Clarissa*, and *Sir Charles Grandison* partially explains the tendency among more recent readers to characterise Richardson as a 'dramatic novelist'.[11] Several generations of critics have explored the complex formal and thematic intersections between Richardson's novels and plays as different in tone as William Wycherley's *The Country Wife* (1675) and William Congreve's *The Mourning Bride* (1697). Analysing Richardson's dramatic sense, critics have illustrated the various ways in which the novels reproduce in narrative prose the dynamic effects of theatrical representation. Such readings, however, have always been difficult to reconcile with Richardson's well-known ambivalence towards the drama, and his professed distrust of the London stage in his published works and correspondence. Richardson's description of *Clarissa* as a 'Dramatic Narrative' signifies a critical paradox, in that the novelist spent much of his literary career as an ardent opponent of the theatre. Among the 'strong Reasons' Richardson offers 'against Plays' in his earliest known work, *The Apprentice's Vade Mecum* (1734), is his warning of 'their deplorable Depravity at this Time, which is greater than ever was known'. 'A good Dramatick Writer', he asserts, 'is a Character that this Age knows nothing of; and I would be glad to name the Person living who is fit to be made an exception to this general Censure' (*EW*, p. 20). Richardson acknowledges the didactic potential of plays and goes so far as to concede that 'under proper Regulations, the *Stage* may be made subservient to excellent Purposes, and be an useful Second to the *Pulpit* itself' (p. 19). Yet in the commercial theatres at Drury Lane, the Haymarket, Covent Garden, and the upstart Goodman's Fields, crass managers have pandered to the base desires of the public, mounting 'wicked Dumb Shew' and 'infamous Harlequin Mimicry', and introducing characters 'for nothing but to teach how to cozen, cheat, deceive, and cuckold'. 'These are the edifying Subjects that have given Delight to crouded Audiences', he laments, 'to the Disgrace both of the *British* Taste and Stage' (p. 21).

Although the vehemence of Richardson's account of the 'superlative Wickedness' of the Georgian stage recalls the tone and diction of seventeenth-century Puritan attacks on the falsity of representation, as well as the resurgence of antitheatrical polemic during the early eighteenth century, the *Vade Mecum* derived from a more local concern with the deleterious socio-political consequences of an expanding London theatre. Specifically, it was a response to the 'pernicious' incursion of non-patent playhouses such as Goodman's Fields into the centre of the city, where their performances might corrupt 'People of Industry' (p. 23). Far from being an orthodox indictment of the evils of playing, Richardson's work developed what Keymer calls 'a coherent rhetoric of civic antitheatricalism'.[12] This rhetoric can be mistaken for more mainstream antitheatricalism because Richardson illustrates the disruptive effects of the unlicensed stage through a critique of the aesthetic license that he believes characterises contemporary dramatic performances. In a second antitheatrical publication, *A Seasonable Examination of … Play-Houses* (1735), Richardson argues that the failure of the legislature to regulate the London theatres has led to irresponsible management and to the production of '*polite* Comedies' and 'modern fustian Tragedies' that flout the rules of decorum. And anticipating his treatment of 'Poetical Justice' in the postscript to *Clarissa*, he attacks the popularity of plays that revel in the intrigues of libertines who 'confound all Distinction of Right and Wrong'. 'Instruction', he concludes, is 'beneath the Scope of all the Plays that have hitherto been represented on the *British* Stage' (*EW*, pp. 73–5).

'Second to the *Pulpit*'

Richardson positions the 'Dramatic Narrative' as an alternative to the drama – a means through which to realise the potential of the stage on the fictional page. His virtuous, vicious, and 'mixed' characters are intended to be exemplary, and their conflicts in life and love provide the moral edification no longer found in the playhouse. When these characters actually read plays or attend the theatre, their varying responses allow Richardson to use the novelistic form to dramatise his perennial anxieties about the drama. After her first visits to the 'Play-house', Pamela writes two lengthy letters to Lady Davers expressing her disappointment with London's 'lively Exhibitions' (*PE*, p. 341). Pamela admits that she is initially 'affected' by a performance of Ambrose Philips's pseudo-classical tragedy *The Distressed Mother* (1712), compiling several passages that she deems 'sweetly moving, and nobly pathetic' (*PE*, p. 348). Yet in its vivid representation of 'the most rageful Extreme of sensual Passion', Pamela warns that the play sacrifices 'all Considerations of public Good and private Right' and is 'not so exemplary as one would wish' (345–6). She is even more startled by the play's bawdy epilogue, which she believes is 'calculated only to efface all the tender, all the virtuous Sentiments which the tragedy was design'd to raise' (pp. 353–4). She responds in a similar way to Richard Steele's sentimental comedy *The Tender Husband* (1705), which she is distressed to find wanting in 'Probability' and guilty of 'Wickedness for Wickedness sake!' (*PE*, pp. 355, 357). Echoing Richardson's remarks in his antitheatrical publications, Pamela writes that 'the Stage, by proper Regulations, might be a profitable Amusement', but that 'nothing more convinces one, than these Representations, of the Truth of the common Observation, That the best Things, corrupted, may prove the worst' (p. 341).

The attitudes of Richardson's characters towards the drama and theatre are exemplary in that they often function as a clue to the characters' motivations and a guide to the broader themes of the novels. In *Clarissa*, Richardson gestures towards a right reading by having his best characters voice concerns about the theatre and his worst characters exploit dramatic representation for nefarious purposes. As Lovelace attempts to win over Clarissa, he persuades her to accompany him to a performance of

Otway's *Venice Preserv'd* (1682), confiding to Belford that men of his cast
'love not any tragedies but those in which they themselves act the parts of
tyrants and executioners'. He is nonetheless willing to endure the play's
'serious and solemn reflections' out of a conviction that 'affecting entertainment' can lull the senses and wear away the defences of virtuous young
women: 'Whenever I have been able to prevail upon a girl to permit me to
attend her to a play, I have thought myself sure of her.' Not yet realising
the ominous identity between the 'woes' of Belvidera and her own, Clarissa
sees the play 'for the sake of the instruction, the warning, and the example'
(*C*, IV.xxi.97). In such an episode, contemporary drama threatens to pre-
cipitate in its audience the very tragic distress or comic folly it performs.
Just as he had done with his novelistic progenitors, Richardson encourages
readers to be suspicious of plays and sceptical about the influence of the
drama on his fiction.

At the same time, Richardson's novels ironically redeem the theatre
as a didactic medium precisely by employing dramatic material to good
thematic effect. Indeed, one way to reconcile Richardson's conflicting
careers as dramatic novelist and antitheatrical polemicist is to examine
the productive uses to which he puts allusions to, and quotations from,
plays in his novels. In *Sir Charles Grandison*, Richardson's characters routinely compare their circumstances to those of popular stage characters,
as when John Greville dismisses his rival for Harriet Byron as 'this Sir
Fopling' (*SCG*, I.xx.136), the archetypal fop in George Etherege's *The
Man of Mode* (1676). In *Clarissa*, dramatic allusions and quotations serve
as a vital index to character. Lovelace's letters are filled with verses drawn
from Restoration heroic tragedies and comedies of manners, and his identification with lines originally spoken by tyrants and rakes exposes both
his hyperbolic taste and his moral dubiousness. His first letter contains
quotations from six plays that alternately characterise him as a sincere or
vengeful lover, including a passage from Robert Howard's *The Vestal Virgin*
(1664) on the expedience of hypocrisy: '*He who seems virtuous does but act
a part; / And shews not his own nature, but his art*' (*C*, I.xxxi.194). Clarissa,
on the other hand, rejects social artifice and the 'theatrical air' with which
Lovelace and his disreputable companions speak, and she surprisingly
illustrates her antipathy towards such performances through lines from *A
Midsummer Night's Dream* that proscribe '*The rattling tongue / Of saucy and
audacious eloquence*' (*C*, III.lxiii.302, v. 50). In *Pamela*, dramatic quotations
are rare, given the heroine's humble background. But on heated occasions
Pamela recites dimly remembered lines from well-known plays, so that
Richardson might emphasise her innocence and simplicity. When Mr B

attempts to kiss Pamela for the first time, her shock is expressed through a garbled misquotation from *Hamlet*: 'Oh how I was terrify'd! I said, like as I had read in a Book a Night or two before, Angels, and Saints, and all the Host of Heaven, defend me!' (*P*, p. 29).[13]

Little is known about Richardson's play-going habits in London, but the 'familiar quotations' that punctuate his novels generally support the character he liked to draw of himself as a respectable middle-class trades-man with conventional literary tastes and a prudent distrust of the con-temporary stage. Most of the dramatic passages that he has his characters quote were part of the common stock of poetical 'beauties' with which any reasonably literate author would have been acquainted. In fact, the major-ity of Richardson's quotations appear to have been drawn, at second hand, from Edward Bysshe's *Art of English Poetry* (1702), a collection replete with exemplary passages from the famous plays of Shakespeare, Dryden, and Rowe, among others.[14] Richardson, however, was also able and willing to utilise oblique allusions to plays that were not part of the canon of English drama and that he could only have known at first hand. For instance, he has Belford express regret at his misdirected efforts to bandy wit 'like a ball' (*C*, iv.xlvii.269), echoing lines from Christopher Bullock's *Woman Is a Riddle* (1717), a belated comedy of manners that was revived at Goodman's Fields while Richardson was actively writing and revising *Clarissa*. And he has Anna Howe repeat spirited lines first uttered by Lady Bellair in Elizabeth Cooper's *The Rival Widows; or, Fair Libertine* (1735), a satiric comedy that Richardson probably printed.[15] Whether Richardson came to know such plays through his work as a printer or through his close associa-tion with theatrical arbiters such as Cibber, Aaron Hill, and Garrick, or whether he actually saw them performed on the London stage, his use of 'unfamiliar quotations' seems to reveal that the so-called 'dramatic novelist' had a broader appreciation for theatrical culture than is usually recognised. In assimilating the drama into the novel, Richardson created a new hybrid genre that appealed to the 'mixed multitude' by representing, as Lovelace says of theatre, 'the epitome of the world' (*C*, vi.lxxvii.285).

Notes

1 Denis Diderot, in Bueler, *'Clarissa': The Eighteenth-Century Response*, Vol. 1, p. 394.
2 *Ibid.*, p. 601.
3 Henry Fielding, *'The Journal of a Voyage to Lisbon', 'Shamela', and Occasional Writings*, eds. Martin C. Battestin, Sheridan W. Baker, Jr, and Hugh Amory (Clarendon Press, 2008), pp. 160–2.

4 Eliza Haywood, *Anti-Pamela*, in Keymer and Sabor, *The 'Pamela' Controversy*, Vol. III, pp. 5–285 (pp. 6–7).

5 John Hawkins and David Garrick, in Bueler, *'Clarissa': The Eighteenth-Century Response*, Vol. I, pp. 218 and 265 respectively.

6 Thomas Keymer, 'Shakespeare in the Novel', in Fiona Ritchie and Peter Sabor (eds.), *Shakespeare in the Eighteenth Century* (Cambridge University Press, 2012), pp. 118–40 (p. 126).

7 Joseph Warton, *Fashion: An Epistolary Satire to a Friend* (London, 1742), p. 6.

8 Keymer and Sabor, *'Pamela' in the Marketplace*, p. 114.

9 Jane Austen, *Later Manuscripts*, eds. Janet Todd and Linda Bree (Cambridge University Press, 2008), Appendix C, *'Sir Charles Grandison'*, pp. 556–72.

10 George Colman, *Polly Honeycombe, A Dramatic Novel*, in Bueler, *'Clarissa': The Eighteenth-Century Response*, Vol. II, p. 75.

11 Mark Kinkead-Weekes, *Samuel Richardson: Dramatic Novelist* (Methuen, 1973), pp. 395–461.

12 Keymer, *Richardson's 'Clarissa'*, p. 145.

13 Kate Rumbold, *Shakespeare and the Eighteenth-Century Novel: Cultures of Quotation from Samuel Richardson to Jane Austen* (Cambridge University Press, 2016), pp. 37–8.

14 Michael E. Connaughton, 'Richardson's Familiar Quotations: *Clarissa* and Bysshe's *Art of English Poetry*', *Philosophical Quarterly*, 60.2 (1981), 183–95.

15 Darryl P. Domingo, 'Richardson's Unfamiliar Quotations: *Clarissa* and Early Eighteenth-Century Comedy', *Review of English Studies*, 66.277 (2015), 936–53.

CHAPTER 24

Humour

Simon Dickie

They might not be the first things one thinks of, but Richardson clearly had a sense of humour, a fine sense of the ridiculous in people and situations, and great gifts as a comic writer. Impeccably timed comic incidents, quick witty dialogues, and brilliant descriptions of gesture and facial expression are vital parts of his art of contrast – the jostling of voices, tones, and genres that give such life to all his novels. Who could forget the stammering Mr Hickman or the randy widow Bevis in *Clarissa*, 'staring with eyes as big as eggs' (v.xii.109)? Who would do without the sequence of sharp-tongued ladies from Lady Davers to Anna Howe and the glorious Charlotte Grandison? While there have been critical discussions of some of this material (the debt to stage comedy, for example), much humour in Richardson's fiction is obscure or repugnant and demands explication. Cruel practical jokes, ridicule, violence, and gruesome forms of vengeance were still funny in early modern culture. Richardson, more consistently than scholars have acknowledged, engages with contemporary debates about the nature and acceptability of such humour. Most significantly, as we know, he takes on age-old misogynist humour – the endless jokes about women as carnal, deceitful, irrational beings, and rape as something they both needed and wanted.

Comic elements provide powerful contrasts in *Pamela* and would expand in every direction with *Sir Charles Grandison*, but they are surely at their grandest and most mysterious in *Clarissa*. In retrospect, this novel seems like one great struggle between comedy and tragedy. The opening letters, packed as they are with ominous suggestions, already show Richardson's gifts for social comedy. Arabella Harlowe will soon turn poisonous, but we first meet her as a comical ugly sister, fluttering at the possibility of marrying Lovelace: 'So handsome a man! – O her beloved Clary! … He was but *too* handsome a man for *her!* – Were she but as amiable as *somebody*, there would be a probability of *holding* his affections!' Along the way, this lively piece of reported speech shows us Clarissa's own sense of humour. 'She was

always thought comely', Arabella goes on, and 'let her tell me', comeliness
was more permanent than beauty. Her features were not *so* irregular, were
they? (*C*, 1.ii.7). A similar transformation from laughable to malevolent
occurs with other characters. Betty Barnes will be spiteful as Clarissa's gaoler,
but she enters the book as a trollopy chambermaid. The heroine's uncle
Antony is a miserly old bachelor, full of stale locutions. 'Mind that', he jabs
at Clarissa, 'that's the plain Dunstable of the matter, Miss!' (1.xxxii.214–23).
It makes perfect comic sense to match up uncle Antony with the greedy,
meddling Mrs Howe. 'That old preachment-making plump-hearted soul',
Anna calls him in her report of his unwelcome visits (1.x.59).

For his part, Lovelace is equally surrounded by fools, and ridiculing
them is one of his great talents. Much humour comes from his agents'
semi-literate letters, beginning with Joseph Leman (planted in Harlowe
Place and soon beginning his own shabby amour with Betty Barnes).
'Promising all dilligince and exsacknesse', Joseph signs off, 'I reste, *Your*
Honner's dewtifull sarvant' (III.iii.28). At the other end of the social spectrum, the family bore is Lovelace's gouty uncle Lord M ('podagra-man'),
with his proverbs and '*Wisdom of nations*' (III.lxxv.349, IV.xviii.83). '*It is a*
long lane that has no turning', he warns Lovelace. '*He that eats the King's*
goose shall be choked with his feathers' (IV.xxxii.182–8). In these contexts,
Clarissa and Lovelace seem like intellectual and moral equals, raised infinitely above the dolts and dimwits of this world, as destined for each other
as Mirabell and Millamant or Beatrice and Benedick. Readers are effectively invited to expect a comic courtship plot: the story of a rake reformed
by a beautiful and witty young woman, a story like that of Dorimant and
Harriet in George Etherege's *The Man of Mode* (1676).

The question of humour in *Clarissa* cannot be separated from the figure
of Lovelace, and the dangerous charm he exercised over characters and
readers alike. Modern readers understandably struggle to laugh along with
a rapist who destroys a virtuous young woman. Yet Richardson's contemporaries – especially the earliest readers of Volumes I–IV, who didn't yet
know where the plot was heading – thought him a brilliant and charming
wit. 'I cannot help being fond of Lovelace', Richardson's admirer Lady
Bradshaigh confessed early on. 'Why would you make him so wicked,
and yet so agreeable?' 'Never any thing equall'd the Humour of that Man'
(Lady Bradshaigh to Richardson, 10 October 1748, 6 January 1749). Henry
and Sarah Fielding both marvelled at the exalted wit in Lovelace's early
letters. After *Pamela*, Richardson was determined to use *Clarissa* to correct 'that dangerous, but too commonly received Notion, *That a Reformed*
Rake makes the best Husband' (*C*, Preface, viii). At the same time, the book's

moral complexity depended on Lovelace's at least seeming reformable and having sufficient qualities to attract the heroine (thus we are told that he is not an atheist or even a drinker, avoids obscenities in speech, and treats his tenants more decently than most (1.xl)). Yet somehow Richardson made him much too appealing, and the problem was compounded by the book's appearance in instalments. A full twelve months separated the first two volumes (December 1747) from the final three (December 1748). By then, too many readers had fallen for Lovelace and wished that Clarissa had married him.

Since rake-humourists were the acknowledged tricksters of early modern society, the mistake was easy to make. Rochester and his 'merry gang' of Restoration wits remained legendary in Richardson's age and provided a model for contemporary bold young men – those who pulled fops by the nose, seduced honest women, and competed with each other to enact the most daring public pranks. Richardson would have heard all the stories about John, duke of Montagu (1690–1749) and his cousin Charles Lennox, duke of Richmond (1701–50) – Clarissimo and Magnifico, as their friends called them. As a young man, Montagu amused friends by organising dinners of squinters or stutterers. He once took the aldermen of Windsor out on the Thames, only to sink the boat and compel them to wade back through the mud. Shortly before his death in 1750, Richmond perpetrated a hoax on Richardson himself, writing as John Cheale, King of Arms, to correct 'mistakes' in *Clarissa* (all too awed, Richardson followed the advice). In the theatre, meanwhile, the witty seducers of Restoration comedy held the stage, and scholars have noted the influence of Etherege's Dorimant (so clearly modelled on Rochester) and Wycherley's Horner (to whom Lovelace explicitly compares himself). In fiction, too, trickster rakes appeared in increasing numbers of rake biographies, episodic jestbooks, and minor comic novels in the mode of Tobias Smollett's *Peregrine Pickle* (1751).

In Lovelace, Richardson works almost systematically through the standard repertoire of rakish pranks. The disguises, bribed servants, secret letters, duplicate keys, and confusion at the garden gate were established tricks. Disguises for seduction purposes were prime devices in Restoration comedy: dressed as a parson, music teacher, or dancing master, the young lover got past the chaperones and jealous husbands. Lovelace can change his shape four times in one day, he boasts to the startled heroine (*C*, II. xxxix.272). He is Clarissa's brother, he announces at St Albans, carrying her away from a confounded rake (III.x.76). Pursuing Clarissa to Hampstead, he passes as a long-suffering husband in search of his skittish young wife

('Mother-spoilt, landlord! – Mother-spoilt!' (v.i.8)). Having borrowed a hooded cloak and practised his limp on the bowling green, he comes into her presence as a gouty old man, his voice disguised as a toothless mumble (v.i–ii).

Even as his heroine tires of life, Richardson pours everything into his villain – every conceivable trick, and pages of ecstatic description. With little apparent effort, Lovelace invents 'Mrs Fretchville' (an inconsolable widow who may rent her house); 'Captain Tomlinson' (an envoy from John Harlowe, come to propose a reconciliation); and endless messengers, decoys, and supporting characters. Forgery, he brags to Belford, was 'one of my earliest attainments' (IV.xliii.249), one that enables him to produce letters in the handwriting of Anna and Clarissa, and letters from Tomlinson and his relatives to convince the Hampstead ladies of his marriage (v.ii). None of these contrivances is funny to us, and the rape and death of the heroine will make them atrocious. In more purely comic genres, however, they led to happier consequences, as so many readers hoped they might for Clarissa.

Other parts of Lovelace's humour are no less opaque. In an overwhelmingly hierarchical society, it was pleasurable – and entertaining to others – for gentlemen and aristocrats to ridicule their inferiors. Rochester was famous for the 'agreeable Manner of his chiding his Servants', and contemporaries recognised him in Act I of *The Man of Mode*, where Dorimant abuses Foggy Nan the bloated orange woman ('How now double Tripe, what news do you bring?') and Tom the drunken shoemaker ('How now you drunken Sot?').[1] Lovelace is surrounded by stupid, ugly inferiors who invite similar treatment. 'Crow, Joseph, crow!', he writes to Joseph about his plan to set up an inn with Betty Barnes (which itself recalls the old aristocratic game of pairing up rustics and simpletons). Soon he would be master of his own dunghill, with his own servants to abuse (*C*, III. xlvi.236). More often than not, such rascals had to be beaten, violence being the only language they would understand. Lovelace routinely beats Will Summers, and the damage is an in-joke between them (looking for Clarissa in Hampstead, Will has to stuff a handkerchief in his mouth, lest she recognise 'the tethe which your Honner was plesed to bett out with your honner's fyste' (IV.lvi.356)).

Part of this comic arrogance was a right of revenge: everyone who gets in Lovelace's way must pay for it. Though plainly unchristian, revenge and retribution were complex phenomena in the eighteenth century. Classical sources and late chivalric codes of honour effectively demanded them, and Lovelace's vengeance comes in the grandiose rhetoric of heroic tragedy.

Equally important, literary satire was consistently imagined as a form of violent punishment, with the lash and cudgel as its enduring emblems. In his plans for Solmes, James Harlowe, and Betty Barnes, Lovelace may be telling the truth as a satirist. But he is also indulging his *Schadenfreude*, as in his fantasy of mutilating Mr Brand, the Harlowes' flunky clergyman ('I am incensed at the insolence of the young Levite. Thou wilt highly oblige me, if thou'lt find him out, and send me his ears in the next letter' (VI. cxvii.374)). Even Anna amuses herself with such fantasies. Send Betty to me, she jokes. Were women protected by the Coventry Act (a statute outlawing facial mutilations)? She would love to chop Betty's nose off. At the very least, she would send her home 'well soused in, and dragged thro', our deepest horsepond' (II.xxi.130).

These were all mainstream forms of humour. What so distinguishes Lovelace's versions is his linguistic energy. Lovelace bursts onto the scene, his dazzling first letters rising far above the meanness of James, Arabella, uncle Antony, and the dreadful Solmes (who can't even spell). Here, suddenly, was an endless flow of wit, full of belletristic quotations and word play. Richardson's contemporaries immediately appreciated the humorous extravagance of Lovelace's boasts. 'Stand by, and let me swell! – I am already as big as an elephant; and ten times wiser!', he writes to Belford, before adding an absurd detail that somehow strengthened the charm: 'have I not reason to snuff the moon with my proboscis?' (III.xxxvii.191). This now sounds puerile, but readers were amused by the banter and the bold part Lovelace played in the war of the sexes. In one of his giddiest letters, Lovelace glories that he will get Clarissa to London, and into Mrs Sinclair's house, while leaving her under the impression that she has chosen the place: 'I love, when I dig a pit, to have my prey tumble in with secure feet, and open eyes: Then a man can look down upon her, with an O-ho, charmer! how came you there!' (III.xxxiii.177). 'I wish I cou'd help laughing at him', Lady Bradshaigh wrote in her copy at this point. 'I often check myself, as if he cou'd see me.'[2] 'The sex love to be called cruel', Lovelace writes in the same letter. 'Many a time have I complained of cruelty, even in the act of yielding, because I knew it gratified their pride' (III.xxiii.176). 'Comical wickedness', wrote Lady Bradshaigh, amused by Lovelace's commentary on a standard form of amorous cross-talk.

This ingratiating wickedness is enhanced, particularly in the middle sections of the book, by persistent dramatic ironies. The heroine's credulity at Mrs Sinclair's goes far beyond the necessary juxtapositions of epistolary fiction. Consider the ipecacuanha trick. Feigning illness to test a heroine's love was a familiar comic device. Deeply inside the role, Richardson gives every detail in advance. 'I shall be very sick tomorrow', Lovelace tells Belford. A few grains of ipecacuanha, blood from a poulterer's shop, and he will vomit 'like a fury' (*C*, iv.xxxiv.198–200). There is plenty of time for comic extras like the disastrous attempt to train Dorcas:

> Come hither, you toad (sick as a devil at the instant); Let me see what a mixture of grief and surprise may be beat up together in thy pudden-face.
>   That won't do. That dropt jaw, and mouth distended into the long oval, is more upon the Horrible, than the Grievous.

It's hopeless, he concludes, you have no control over those cheek muscles. Just run up and down stairs until you're out of breath. That will have to do for a sigh (IV.xxxvi.205–7). In the very next letter, Clarissa expresses her concern at painful length. 'He took great care to have his illness concealed from me as long as it could … The poor man, from such high health so *suddenly* taken! – And so unprepared!' She is strangely confused by her feelings, while readers wonder if there may indeed be some hope for the man prepared to make himself so ill to verify her love (IV.xxxvii.209–10).

No wonder so many readers continued to hope for a happy ending. The dialogues in these volumes come strikingly close to the quick epigrammatic repartee of Congreve's *Way of the World* (1700) and similar plays. In self-conscious recognition of these contexts, Lovelace keeps imagining himself and Clarissa as characters in a play, a comedy called alternately *The Quarrelsome Lovers* and *The Polite Lovers* (*C*, iv.ii.10, xli.236). 'Is she not a match for me? *More* than a match?', Lovelace asks Belford. 'Does she not out-do me at every fair weapon?' (iii.xvi.101). Later we see him accompanying Clarissa to church, almost taking to heart the sermon on 2 Samuel 11 (iii.lxv.318). Such small reformations, along with increasing awe at Clarissa's spiritual grandeur, suggest that a reformed rake might indeed make the best husband.

Of course it was not to be, but it is remarkable how many readers put the book aside when Richardson disappointed them. While the first four volumes of *Clarissa* sold well, the first impression of volumes v–vii (3,000 copies) took a full two years to sell and at least a quarter of purchasers never completed their sets.[3] The fashionable world, as T. C. Duncan Eaves and Ben D. Kimpel put it, found *Clarissa* 'very moral and very long and was not inclined to welcome novels with unhappy endings'.[4] To modern readers, the length and unhappy ending are precisely the point. If the book didn't end tragically, it would never show the consequences of rakish mistreatment of women. A happy ending would obliterate all trauma. As Lovelace himself declares, 'is not *the catastrophe of every story that ends in wedlock accounted happy*, be the difficulties in the progress to it ever so great?' (*C*, v.xlviii.331). In its entirety, *Clarissa* poses a formidable challenge to this endlessly repeated story and the barely questioned male freedoms that lie behind it.

The book also offers an unexpectedly detailed commentary on eighteenth-century humour and its power to help bold, clever, handsome men get away with so much. Clarissa makes plain English retorts to every one of Lovelace's boasted witty talents. His fine speeches, with their grandiose allusions and extended metaphors, are just 'libertine froth'. His tricks and disguises – 'my master-strokes' – are just lies and wicked schemes (III.v.49–50, xiv.93–4; IV.xxxix.221; III.xx.127). What is witty about them, Clarissa asks Belford? Anyone can deceive the innocent if they give up all moral standards (VI.xlvi.177–8). The vengeance shows Clarissa, early on, the type of man she is dealing with (III.xx.127). Immediately after her dinner with Lovelace's friends, Clarissa sends Anna a withering analysis of their supposed wit. It was all 'frothy impertinence'. Lovelace might believe that they had avoided double entendres, but Clarissa hears talk 'not free enough to be openly censured, yet too indecent in its implication to come from well-bred persons' (III.lxvi.321–8). In a sign of his own reformation – and the importance Richardson attached to these distinctions – Belford later repeats Clarissa's opinions to Lovelace. He also reminds Lovelace of Clarissa's counter-definition of true wit (verbal agility rooted in virtue, as described by Abraham Cowley). What the rakes think of as wit, he concludes, is nothing but saying and doing 'bold and shocking' things with as much assurance as possible (IV.xlvii.266–72).

But this assurance – the mixture of bluster and ridicule – enabled the Lovelaces of this world to get away with anything. Just a few pages into Volume VII, Clarissa gives her reasons for declining to prosecute Lovelace for rape. A public trial would be disastrous, she tells the naïve Dr Lewin: she would be laughed at. Her tragic story would be displaced by Lovelace's comic one – the ancient and culturally more plausible story of a woman who at first consents and then cries rape. Lovelace would charm the women and be admired by the men. The more he offered to repair the damage by marriage, the more irrational and vindictive Clarissa would seem. Even his 'infamous methods' – the opiates conveyed in a foul-tasting mug of 'London milk' – would be 'bandied about, and jested profligately with'. Her experience could be properly reported only to a '*private* and *serious* audience' (VII.x.49). If nothing else, the length of *Clarissa* attests to the sheer tenacity of early modern assumptions about the accessibility of the female body, and the power of bluff male laughter to affirm them.

Only an exhaustive record of the schemes against her, and an exquisitely circumstantial record of her own mental states, could make readers think that Clarissa had not courted her fate.

Notes

1 John Dennis, *A Defence of Sir Fopling Flutter* (London, 1722), p. 19.
2 Marginalia transcribed by Peter Sabor, 'Appendix 1: Lady Bradshaigh's and Samuel Richardson's Commentary on *Clarissa*', in Peter Sabor (ed.), *Correspondence with Lady Bradshaigh and Lady Echlin*, CECSR, Vol. VII, p. 823.
3 Tom Keymer, 'Clarissa's Death, *Clarissa*'s Sale, and the Text of the Second Edition', *Review of English Studies*, n.s. 45.179 (1994), 389–96. See also Peter Sabor's chapter, above (p. 22).
4 Eaves and Kimpel, *Biography*, p. 306.

PART VI

Social Structures and Social Life

CHAPTER 25

Money and Economics

Edward Copeland

In Samuel Richardson's novels there are two clearly differentiated economies operating in Great Britain, neither one particularly friendly with the
other: a money-based merchant economy and a more prestigious land-
based economy of inherited, aristocratic wealth. But as Richard Price
observes in his history of *British Society, 1680–1880* (1999), these two differing economies are actually interdependent at all times. They are not really
'at war', says Price; the two simply 'bump up against' one another as they
press their separate values, both social and economic. The paradox of their
relationship at mid-eighteenth century, however, lies in the working fact
that although in Great Britain 'all the key departures had been achieved
from an agrarian-based economy to a manufacturing-based one', as Price
reports, the general assumption remained that 'land and agriculture ... set
the foundational limits to the conception and reality of domestic growth'.[1]

In Richardson's first novel, a perfect shower of gold descends on the
wedding breakfast of Pamela, a poor waiting maid, and her new husband,
a gentleman of great landed wealth. 'O How this dear, excellent Man
indulges me in everything!', exclaims the bride, overwhelmed by the generosity of her husband, first to her impoverished parents – 'and he gave me
Fifty Guineas, and bid me send them to you in my Pacquet, to pay your
Debts' – and then to herself and her fellow servants:

> to me he gave no less than One hundred Guineas more; and said, I would
> have you, my Dear, give Mrs. *Jewkes*, when you go away from hence, what
> you think fit, out of these, as from yourself! – Nay, good dear Sir, said I,
> let that be what you please. Give her, then, said he, Twenty Guineas, as
> a Compliment on your Nuptials. Give *Colbrand* Ten Guineas: Give the
> two Coachmen, Five Guineas each: to the two Maids at this House, Five
> Guineas each: Give *Abraham* Five Guineas. Give *Thomas* Five Guineas; and
> give the Gardeners, Grooms and Helpers, Twenty Guineas among them.
> (*P*, pp. 325–6)

Henry Fielding recreates the happy occasion in *Shamela*, his parody of Richardson's *Pamela*, with a rather different impression of such free-handedness. '[He] made me a Present of 100 Guineas', Shamela writes to her mother, a brothel-keeper in Covent Garden,

> which I gave away before Night to the Servants, twenty to one, and ten to another, and so on … The next Morning we rose earlier, and I asked him for another hundred Guineas, and he gave them me. I sent fifty to Parson *Williams*, and the rest I gave away, two Guineas to a Beggar, and three to a Man riding along the Road, and the rest to other People.[2]

Other than the fifty guineas to her lover – '*O Parson* Williams, *how little are all the Men in the World compared to thee*'[3] – the guineas Shamela presents to her fellow servants, 'twenty to one and ten to another, and so on', are exactly the sums named in Richardson's novel and, in fact, match the scale of real-life gifts presented to servants of wealthy gentry on grand occasions, a family wedding, or the heir's twenty-first birthday.[4] How is it, then, that Pamela's guineas are offered to the reader as responsible and respectable while Shamela's are the mark of uncontrolled excess?

It depends on which of the two economic systems you subscribe to. Samuel Richardson, a man of business, writes from his substantial position in London's merchant economy, a system that rewards prudence and rational choice with wealth and social elevation. Henry Fielding, born into the land-owning gentry for whom land and inheritance determine wealth and social status, celebrates a different set of values, with 'spontaneous generosity' and 'aristocratic nonchalance' construed as its distinguishing economic posture, most notably represented in his own *Tom Jones*.[5] Pamela's redistribution of Mr B's landed wealth is for Fielding an act of reckless interference, the sign of an economy run wild. 'What signifies having Money if one doth not spend it', proclaims Shamela – a cheeky usurpation of aristocratic *noblesse oblige* by his jumped-up prostitute.

In Richardson's *Pamela* the education of the heroine commences when she learns 'to write and cast Accompts at her "good Lady's" knee'. The cash-and-carry economy of good accounting exerts a powerful influence on her young imagination. When she receives 'Four golden Guineas, besides lesser Money' from her 'old Lady's Pocket when she dy'd', the customary legacy to a personal servant, she promptly hurries the guineas to her parents: 'I seal it up in one of the little Pill-boxes which my Lady had, wrapt close in Paper that it mayn't chink' (*P*, p. 10). When the much greater sum of 50 guineas must be sent, a marriage gift from Mr B, she cautions her parents to be on the watch for its arrival: 'I send them, wrapt up, Five

Guineas in a Parcel, in double Papers' (*P*, p. 326). Mr B, like Pamela, also considers money as cash in hand, only in larger amounts. When he and Pamela return as a married couple to Bedfordshire from Lincolnshire, Mr B searches his memory to account for whatever money he might now have about him: 'I took with me to *Lincolnshire*, said my Master, upwards of Six hundred Guineas … But I have not laid out above Two hundred and fifty of them, so Two hundred I left there in my Escritoire … and Two hundred I have brought with me.' He adds a little improvised parade of 'aristocratic nonchalance' to embellish the occasion – 'And I have Money, I know not what … in three Places here' – and then, 'pulling out his Purse', hands it to Pamela and says, 'Tell out, my Dear, Two hundred Guineas, and give me the rest. – I did so' (*P*, p. 426).

Pamela in Her Exalted Condition (1741), written to stem an unexpected flow of spurious continuations, features small gatherings of Pamela's high-born friends and her new relations with their conversations and concerns recorded in letters to and from the heroine, an experiment to be refined later in *Clarissa* and *Sir Charles Grandison*. Pamela's main task in the continuation is to bear the good tidings of a mercantile economy to the aristocracy. Nothing could please them more. The Countess of D, who visits Pamela with Mr B's sister Lady Davers, exclaims with wonder: 'For here they have been giving me such an Account of Mrs. *B*.'s Oeconomy, and Family Management, as has highly delighted me. I never knew the like … We shall have strange Reformations to make in our families, Lady *Davers*, when we go home, were we to follow so good an Example' (*PE*, p. 166).

The world of *Clarissa* reveals a far darker vision of the two economies that structure Richardson's novels. In *Clarissa* both of them appear in corrupted states, traps to ensnare the heroine in the toils of her own virtue. The novel begins at Harlowe Place, Clarissa's family home, amidst a great bustle brought on by the family's anticipation of a highly desirable addition to their fortune. The Harlowe family, formerly in trade, 'Wealthy in all its branches', but now living in the country with great holdings of land, hovers on the edge of a pronounced advancement in station. The fly in its ointment, however, is the last will and testament of the deceased Grandfather, who has left one of the family estates, the Grove, to the sole ownership of Clarissa, his favourite grandchild. The Grove, now legally hers, sits between two parcels of land possessed by a near neighbour, Mr Solmes, in a location that unfortunately for the heroine makes it a highly negotiable property. Brother James, the most ambitious spirit in the Harlowe family, argues that a marriage between Clarissa and Solmes could lead to marriage settlements extremely advantageous to the family.

The Harlowes could consolidate enough local land holdings to create a formidable county presence for themselves, an accession of property that would create openings to political power, profitable social alliances, and the distinct possibility of a title. They have every reason, according to their narrow way of thinking, to expect the youngest daughter, Clarissa, to agree to a union with Solmes. To them, nothing could seem more rational: 'three times as rich he came out to be, as any-body had thought him', as Clarissa's Aunt Hervey tells her (*C*, 1.xlv.316). Now is the moment, brother James argues, for the Harlowes to make their move for greater power and landed status.

Unfortunately for the ambitions of her family, Clarissa cannot abide Mr Solmes, who disgusts her in every way with 'his disagreeable person; his still more disagreeable manners; his low understanding' (*C*, 1.xx.137). Nevertheless, the Harlowes press on in full-throated pursuit of the marriage and their anticipation of its advantageous outcome. They confine Clarissa to her room, deny her contact with anyone sympathetic to her reservations, and at last threaten her with a forced marriage. Meanwhile, arrangements for the marriage ceremony proceed with great noise and excitement: 'He talks of laying out two or three thousand pounds in presents, child!', Arabella cries, at once celebrating and taunting her sister (*C*, 1.xlv.319).

At the same time, Lovelace, a handsome young aristocrat, pursues a secret correspondence with Clarissa, persuading her at length to meet him by the 'Summer House' just as the day of the intended marriage with Solmes approaches. Lovelace hopes to persuade Clarissa to seek the protection of his family, but suspecting that she wavers in her intention to leave home, he bribes a servant to frighten her at a signal when she arrives. Terrified by the servant's shouting, as Lovelace intends, Clarissa finds herself pressed into his 'chariot-and-six' (*C*, 11.l.339). Worse yet, the heroine discovers that she has been tricked from home with only 7 guineas, plus change, in her pocket and only the clothes she is wearing: 'I looked over my little stock of money; and found it to be no more than Seven guineas and some silver: The rest of my stock was but Fifty guineas … left in my escritoire.' 'What will Seven guineas do?', she cries (111.ii.18, xxxvii.195).

These 7 guineas and change haunt the novel as the reader recalculates again and again the amount the heroine has remaining in her tiny cache while she endures successive attacks of both economies: the mercantile (the Harlowes) and the aristocratic (Lovelace). Clarissa, however, has faith that her own notions of rational behaviour will govern her family. 'I am willing to hope … that friends will send me my little money, together with my cloaths', she says (*C*, 111.v.45). Anna Howe, her confidante and steady correspondent, has her own ideas about that: 'I don't think you'll have a shilling or a shilling's worth of your own from your relations, unless you extort it from them' (III.iv.41). Anna Howe is right.

Richardson, having shown Clarissa's family at their greediest, most self-interested, and mercantile worst, next proceeds to unleash the power of Lovelace's aristocratic economy on the heroine – its resources of present and future inheritances, as well the privileges of rank and social command that come along with great landed wealth. Like the mercantile Harlowes, however, Lovelace also has a wish to see Clarissa penniless: 'The greater her disappointment *from them*, the greater must be her dependence *on me*' (*C*, III.lvi.279). He gloats cheerfully over her isolation, remarking that she has 'not one friend in town but me' (IV.ix.55). He intends, as he tells his friend Belford, to force Clarissa 'to accept of Money and Raiment from me … Nothing more effectually brings down a proud spirit than a sense of lying under pecuniary obligations' – economic manipulation masquerading as aristocratic generosity (III.xxii.121–2).

When Clarissa makes her last escape from the London house where Lovelace has imprisoned her, her correspondence inevitably focuses on the final cash resource in her possession, the remainder of the 7 guineas she brought from Harlowe Place. All she has left, she tells her servant Dorcas, 'is but four guineas, and two of them I found lately wrapt up in a bit of Lace, designed for charitable use'. Dorcas, much perplexed, asks Clarissa the very question that drives the reader: 'What will you do for Cloaths, Madam? … What will you do for Money, Madam?' (*C*, VI.ii.6).

Clarissa oddly enough finds the answer in Covent Garden, no more than half a mile from her prison – a part of town made infamous by Hogarth's engravings of its poverty, drunkenness, and prostitution, but in Richardson's novel a very different place indeed. Richardson's Covent Garden depends upon the well-established literary traditions of the West and East ends of town (Figure 25.1). The West end carries a reputation for aristocratic pleasures, high-stakes gambling, duels, cockfights, opera, masquerades, and other costly aristocratic distractions. The East end is the home of the middle classes, small tradespeople, as well as great merchants and men of business – the City itself. Clarissa takes lodgings in the East, in King Street, Covent Garden, with a Mr and Mrs Smith who have a glove shop on the ground floor of the premises.[6] Here amongst 'honest and humane' tradesmen Clarissa finds the moral high ground from which she is able to heap the coals and ashes of forgiveness on her tormentors: on Lovelace's aristocratic corruption – 'Money he values not, but as a means to support his Pride and his Independence' – and on

Figure 25.1 Pieter Angillis, *Covent Garden* (1726). Yale Center for British Art, Paul Mellon
Collection.

the Harlowes' mercantile greed, which renders them 'too rich to be happy'
(*C*, IV.li.318, I.x.56).

At the conclusion of the novel, following the chaos of Lovelace's
unceasing deceptions and the implacable hostility of her family, it is
death, ironically, that introduces Clarissa to her role as an heiress possessing great financial power along with a desire to set it into action. In
her last will and testament she emerges as manager of a valuable estate, a
competent 'oeconomist' in her own right with a spirit of activity previously obscured by her family's malice and Lovelace's manic energy. In
this character Clarissa rewards and punishes exactly as she sees fit. 'And
now', she writes in her will, 'with regard to the worldly matters which
I shall die possessed of, as well as those which of right appertain to me,
either by the Will of my said Grandfather, or otherwise' – that is to say,
by all the rights denied to her by the Harlowes – 'Thus do I dispose of
them' (VIII.96–113, 'Will').

In the closing pages of the novel, Clarissa's excellence as an economist
becomes the most frequently offered witness to her abundant talents. Anna

Howe's eulogy of her late friend maintains that, 'notwithstanding all her acquirements, she was an excellent OECONOMIST and HOUSEWIFE' and 'the perfect mistress of the four principal rules of arithmetic', which, as she notes bitterly, 'was the only excellence of her innumerable ones, which she owed to her family; Whose narrowness, immensely rich, and immensely carking, put them upon indulging her in the turn she took to this part of knowledge' (viii.xlix.203, 206). Miss Howe directs her anger at the moral failings of the Harlowes, but reserves with knowing irony their mercantile 'arithmetic' as Clarissa's means to her greatest virtue – economic generosity to the poor and needy – a virtue she shares surprisingly with Lovelace himself, though morally limited in him by its origins in aristocratic impulse.

The pregnant implication of stern mercantile principles happily joined to aristocratic *noblesse oblige* furnishes the leading economic motif in Richardson's final novel, *Sir Charles Grandison*. Britain's sudden prosperity in the 'boom years' of 1750 to 1780, the national economy as it is reflected in *Sir Charles Grandison*, produced a vastly increased interaction of inherited land and ready cash in agriculture, urban real estate, mineral discoveries, manufacturing, and commerce.[7] Sir Charles's return to England from Italy on the death of his father, Sir Thomas, an old-style aristocrat with spendthrift habits and morals to match, sets him the task of restoring a programme of sound management for his newly inherited estates in England and in Ireland. Sir Charles renews his family's fortunes within the general expansion of the British economy. In doing so, his proven skills in accounting become the moving engine of the plot, largely through the liberally dispensed economic guidance he provides across a range of classes – lowly tradesmen; great merchants; wealthy gentry; and, on occasion, the higher aristocracy itself.

Nothing, it seems, is beneath the notice of Sir Charles. Marriage settlements, investments, inheritance, debt management, agricultural improvements, small commerce and grand – all command his attention. When his sister Lady G rallies him about the numerous petty irritations he will face as a Justice of the Peace, Sir Charles answers her with due sobriety: 'And surely men of consideration in the world owe it to their tenants, neighbours, and to those whose industry they are obliged for their affluence … to clear up and adjust, in half an hour' matters of an economic kind 'that would be of endless perplexity and entanglement to the parties concerned' (*SCG*, vii.lii.263). When he takes his seat in Parliament, which he plans to do as a landed gentleman of rank, he will join his fellow MPs who represent the 'monied interests' of commerce, trade, and banking, and who, as the historian Richard Price writes, could in these years 'rival the landed interest in ease of entry'.[8]

From the promotion of mercantile values in *Pamela* and its continuation, through an examination of the separate moral failures of the duelling economies in *Clarissa*, the arc of Richardson's writing career culminates in a union of the two in *Sir Charles Grandison*. Aristocratic liberality joins merchant probity in this final novel to produce a narrative uncannily predictive of the political storm lying in wait for the nation three-quarters-of-a-century later, with the Great Reform Bill of 1832. The economic issues that Sir Charles solves with such confident aplomb reappear in that stormy year, but as political melodrama set on the greater stage of national debate.

Notes

1 Richard Price, *British Society, 1680–1880: Dynamism, Containment and Change* (Cambridge University Press, 1999), pp. 12, 19, 21.
2 Henry Fielding, *'The Journal of a Voyage to Lisbon', 'Shamela', and Occasional Writings*, eds. Martin C. Battestin, Sheridan W. Baker, Jr, and Hugh Amory (Clarendon Press, 2008), pp. 184–5.
3 *Ibid.*, p. 177.
4 Tim Meldrum, 'Wages and Remuneration', in *Domestic Service and Gender, 1660–1750: Life and Work in the London Household* (Routledge, 2001), pp. 183–206. See also Pamela Sambrook, 'Conditions of Employment', in *Keeping Their Place: Domestic Service in the Country House, 1700–1920* (Sutton Publishing, 2005), pp. 29–47.
5 Mary Poovey, *A History of the Modern Fact: Problems of Knowledge in the Sciences of Wealth and Society* (University of Chicago Press, 1998), pp. 144–5.
6 Edward Copeland, 'Remapping London: *Clarissa* and the Woman in the Window', in Doody and Sabor, *Tercentenary Essays*, pp. 51–69.
7 Frank O'Gorman, *The Long Eighteenth Century: British Political and Social History, 1688–1832* (Arnold, 1997), p. 103.
8 Price, *British Society*, p. 73.

CHAPTER 26

The Law

Simon Stern

Richardson was engaged with the law in various ways during the course of his career: as a printer of bills and committee reports for the House of Commons (starting in 1733), as a printer of the *Commons Journals* (starting in 1742) and the *State Trials* series (1742), as a victim of corporate fraud (1731) and of what he characterised as literary piracy (1741–2, 1753), and as part owner of the exclusive patent to print law books (starting in 1760). Richardson's acquisition of the law patent came late in his career, but any of these other events might have informed his thinking about the law and legal modes of argument, and indeed scholars have explored numerous contexts in which his novels address legal issues including marriage, rape, inheritance, citizenship, copyright, and liability for accidents.

Another important legal dimension of his work – and one that has received less attention – involves the forensic mentality revealed in his novels, and that he displayed in defending them against critics. His characters often seem aware of their status as exemplars, as participants in the logic of the case, understood both as a unit of meaning and as an invitation to interpretation. The case is, as Conrad van Dijk observes, one of the primary 'forms through which law becomes legible', and one that differs from the exemplum because 'a case is offered up for judgment and interpretation, whereas an exemplum is simply meant to be imitated'.[1] This distinction nicely captures the ambivalence that Richardson displays when responding to critics, using language that moves between case and exemplum. The conception of the literary character as a kind of case recalls Henry Fielding's claim, in *Joseph Andrews*, to describe 'not an Individual, but a Species', and this is one of the formulations that Catherine Gallagher cites when observing that the novel form gives a 'special turn … [to] empiricist logic by invoking both a knowledge that *types* are induced from persons in the world and a further awareness that *characters* are deduced from types'.[2]

Because of Fielding's legislative pronouncements on the rules of the novelist's art (as well as his many references to legal doctrine), his work has often been associated with a forensic mentality; in what follows, I will suggest that similar resonances appear in Richardson's work. If, in Ian Watt's famous analogy, the novel's readers resemble jurors in 'want[ing] to know "all the particulars" of a given case',[3] many of Richardson's letter-writers resemble trial lawyers because of their efforts to yoke particular and plausible details to an interpretation that countermands the one their epistolary opponent seeks to advance. Richardson himself adopts the same approach, also cast in legal terms, as for example when he observes, in one of the 'hints' towards a preface for *Clarissa*, that 'the Probability of all Stories told, or of Narrations given, depends upon small Circumstances; as may be observed, that in all Tryals for Life and Property, the Merits of the Cause are more determinable by such [details], than by the greater Facts; which usually are so laid, and taken care of, as to seem to authenticate themselves'.[4] The careful citation of specific details would thus serve the novelist as aiding in a forensic defence, when he views his characters and his approach to fiction itself as being on trial.

The legal decision was increasingly becoming a print genre in the eighteenth century. The conventions that govern the genre today had barely started to take root (such as the practice of commencing with a recitation of the facts before turning to the legal analysis they support), but the reports of that era nevertheless assume that a case must be a case *of something* – such as an area of law, or a doctrine, or an exception to a doctrine. The case is at once specific and generic, and its specific features are adduced insofar as they illuminate its generic nature. Even a letter-writing manual can reflect this logic, by treating the occasion for the letter as an opportunity to supply a template proper for occasions like the one at hand. Thus Richardson explains in the preface to his *Familiar Letters* that he presents 'Arguments … [that are] *new* and *uncommon*' as model responses 'in a Variety of Cases', exposing among other things 'the Folly of a *litigious Spirit*' (*EW*, p. 325).

While the volume does not treat every occasion as an adversarial one, at several points Richardson captures the effect of a legal debate between opposing counsels by offering a series of mutually antagonistic letters, written in succession. Indeed, the language of the 'case' permeates the volume as a whole, frequently appearing in a quasi-forensic sense ('the strict Inquiry which … [this] Case demands'; 'I will … put the Case that you have no *Proof*'; 'I will suppose two Cases' (*EW*, pp. 354, 382, 466)). In these examples, Richardson seems to take it for granted that the letters can readily serve the exemplary purpose for which they are offered. By contrast, the tension between the individual and the general becomes more pronounced in some of his defences of his novels. Indeed, his tendency is usually to begin by imagining his characters as typical instances of some category, only to refer with increasing determination to their individual features, while still insisting that they serve a generic function.

Richardson is notable, among eighteenth-century novelists, for his sensitivity to the problems of expressly assigning his work to the category of the fictional. He proclaims, on the title page of *Pamela*, that the narrative has its 'foundation in truth and nature'. Explaining his ambivalence about the preface that William Warburton wrote for *Clarissa*, Richardson observes that by acknowledging the book's status openly as fiction, the preface risks compromising the exemplary potential associated with factual narratives:

> I could wish that the *Air* of Genuineness had been kept up, tho' I want not the letters to be *thought* genuine; only so far kept up, I mean, as that they should not prefatically be owned *not* to be genuine: and this for fear of weakening their influence where any of them are aimed to be exemplary, as well as to avoid hurting that kind of Historical Faith which Fiction itself is generally read with, tho' we know it to be Fiction. (Richardson to William Warburton, 19 April 1748)

Richardson's use of the double negative puts the novel in a murky area between fiction and truth, preserving the possibility of the letters' exemplary effect where they aim for that kind of influence, while refraining from an active affirmation of their historical accuracy.

By holding open this middle ground, Richardson aims for the imitative force of the exemplum, while effectively conceding that readers might instead engage with the novels by treating the characters as cases. The difficulty of opting for either alternative is evident in Richardson's response to the critics of *Pamela*. Although Pamela and her creator were charged with many offences, perhaps the most frequent objection was that the novel would encourage young women to aspire to 'marry up'. Richardson answers this charge in *Pamela in Her Exalted Condition*, when Mr B is asked whether he would have to consider himself responsible 'if this Practice of Gentlemen marrying their Mothers Waiting-maids … should come into Vogue' (*PE*, p. 219). He responds that 'those Persons who are afraid the Example should be taken, [and] those who are inclin'd to follow it, should take *all* the material Parts of it into their Consideration: Otherwise … the Precedent may be justly cleared' (*PE*, p. 221). The material parts, as he explains, include the following considerations: 'That the Object of [the gentleman's] Wish should be a Girl of exquisite Beauty (and that, not only in their blinded and partial Judgments, but in the Opinion of *every one* who sees her, Friend or Foe)'; 'that she be descended of honest and conscientious, tho' poor and obscure Parents; who ... [have] laid deep in the Girl's Mind the Foundations of Piety and Virtue'; that she have 'an humble, teachable Mind, fine natural Parts, a sprightly, yet inoffensive Wit, a Temper so excellent, and a Judgment so solid, as should promise ... that she would become an higher Station, and be respected in it' (*PE*, p. 221).

Richardson continues in this vein for several more paragraphs, adding among other details that the girl must possess 'an Attention, Assiduity, and Diligence almost peculiar to herself, at her Time of Life, insomuch as, at Fifteen or Sixteen years of Age, to be able to vie with any young Lady of Rank' (*PE*, p. 222). He finishes with a similarly detailed set of specifications for the would-be Mr B. To conclude, the reader must '*reflect* and *compare*, and take the Case *with all its Circumstances* together' (*PE*, p. 223). In listing these requirements, Richardson in effect asserts that Pamela is a unique paragon whose traits ('almost peculiar to herself') ensure that no else should be able to take the example. Whereas Richardson had announced, in *Pamela*'s subtitle ('*Virtue Rewarded*'), that the book was designed to promote 'the principles of virtue and religion', he now undercuts this exemplary thrust by doubting whether there is any reader capable of taking the example, in the sense of applying the 'Precedent' to herself.

It is apparent, since Richardson himself draws the analogy, that this model of reflecting, comparing, and taking cases with all their circumstances resembles the practice of limiting a doctrine's application by distinguishing prior judgments. The criticisms that Richardson sought to fend off were formulated cynically, in terms of self-advancement (treating the novel as a how-to-do-it guide for female connivers), and while they may not appear to target questions of plausibility, that issue remains essential to the accusations against Pamela. The critics treated her concern with her virtue as a convenient cover story, and insisted that her behaviour throughout bespeaks the mentality of a self-interested schemer. In short, they contested her veracity, insisting that no one would behave as Pamela does out of pure motives, and neither would a Mr B restrain himself and ultimately reward her with an offer of marriage. The less cynical version of the criticism was that *Pamela* misleadingly encourages young women to think they can rise socially by protecting their virtue, which is to say that the book portrays the world unrealistically. One critic, for example, objected that

Pamela's highly emotional and frequently self-abasing behaviour could be met with 'no where ... except amongst the *Pamelas* ... of [Richardson's] own making'.[5] Quoting this passage, Bernard Kreissman observes that in characterising the novel as 'unreal and unlifelike', the complaint typifies a widespread criticism of Richardson's so-called realism.[6]

Richardson's response in *Pamela in Her Exalted Condition* is that the portrayal is realistic enough, if the two persons involved are just like Pamela and Mr B. Is it reasonable for the young female reader to hope for Pamela's good fortune? Does *Pamela* offer a plausible picture of what happens in the world? Yes, if the young woman has the same background, personality, and physical appearance as Pamela. Richardson maintains that such a combination of traits would be extremely rare, but the novel's plot is no less plausible for that. While the subtitle seems to insist on the generic application of the book's lesson, Richardson's defence qualifies and modifies the lesson to the point where it seems that no reader could expect to be rewarded in the same fashion as Pamela. The difficulty of negotiating between the two positions is apparent from Richardson's refusal to abandon the subtitle in later editions, even after having qualified the book's lesson so emphatically.

The same difficulty resurfaces in the discussions between Richardson and his critics about *Clarissa*. Albrecht von Haller, a Swiss physiologist and philosopher of 'common sense', praised *Clarissa* but wondered 'whether probability is preserved' in some of the actions performed by Lovelace, the novel's aristocratic villain. Specifically, von Haller doubted that someone who is 'not deficient in understanding, and who expect[s] to be a peer of the realm', as Lovelace does, would risk 'expos[ing] himself to the persecution' of Clarissa's family by kidnapping her, drugging her, locking her in a brothel, and raping her. Richardson responded by appealing to worldly experience and Lovelace's character. It must be recalled, the author insists, that Lovelace is too far gone to take account of practical considerations: 'He defie[s] the laws of his country, as too many of his cast do'; he is so angry at the Harlowes for keeping him away that 'in one place [he] vows revenge upon [them], altho', for the sake of it, he were to become an exile from his native country for ever ... Are there not such men in all nations? ... Need we refer to public executions for crimes the most atrocious?'[7] The appeals to experience ring hollow, however, because ultimately they are grounded in Lovelace's unique characteristics.

Summarising this exchange, Robert Newsom observes that 'von Haller drew evidence from the real world ... [which] functions to determine the probabilities associated with a set of young men to which Lovelace belongs … while Richardson's evidence particularizes the individual case and so defines precisely which set Lovelace belongs to'. Once again, the treatment of a character as typical of a certain class, as an instance of a recognisable case, turns into a highly specific case whose features are not easily generalised. Such arguments, Newsom adds, almost inevitably end by specifying a unique instance: as Richardson continues to accumulate evidence from the novel, 'the set of real young men that determines the probability of Lovelace's behavior becomes ever smaller', while 'detail upon detail about the fictional Lovelace is added … Inevitably, the set of "real" young men becomes a set with only one member and the question ultimately posed is a circular one: How probable is it that a young man exactly like Lovelace would behave exactly like Lovelace?'[8] By implication, if the dialogue were to continue, Richardson's answers would soon turn into another version of the defence of *Pamela in Her Exalted Condition*.

The most significant difference between Richardson's responses to the criticisms of *Pamela* and of *Clarissa* is that in the latter case, Richardson speaks expressly in probabilistic terms – because von Haller had used that language in formulating his objections. In other respects, however, the arguments about the two novels are fundamentally similar. Both examples show that from the outset of the debate over the novel's ability to use made-up people and events to convey the truth about human personality, participants in this discussion were concerned with how generally applicable those representations needed to be, if readers were to rely on them as accurate pictures of behaviour likely to be encountered in the real world. Richardson's frequent resort to the language and methods of the trial lawyer, when pressed on these questions, suggests that he understood novelistic representation itself as a fundamentally forensic activity.

The same forensic mentality would reappear, displayed in a factual register, when Richardson criticised the Dublin booksellers who printed *Sir Charles Grandison* without authorisation. He initially outlined his grievances in *The Case of Samuel Richardson … with Regard to the Invasion of His Property* (dated 14 September 1753), which he followed up seven weeks later with a longer *Address to the Public*, recapitulating the whole affair in detail and reprinting his correspondence with George Faulkner. For present purposes, one of the most significant aspects of the *Address* involves the double-entry form in which one column quotes 'Mr. Faulkner's Defence' of his own conduct, while the column next to it gives the 'Genuine History of the Transaction'. The document's typographical form thus reproduces a pair of arguments for the defence and (implicitly) for the prosecution, while soliciting the reader's belief, or 'historical faith', in the novelist's version of the events.

In a series of gestures that once again raise questions about the logic of exemplarity, Richardson insists that the case stands for a much larger set of concerns – involving the need for legislation to 'secure to Authors the Benefit of their own Labours' (*Case*, p. 3), and the dangers posed by 'these Booksellers of Dublin, [who] think themselves intitled to prey upon the property of every other man in every nation round them'. For those reasons, he concludes, 'this Cause is the Cause of Literature, in general'.[9] At the same time, Richardson suggests that his case is unique: 'never was Work more the Property of any Man, than *this* is' (*Case*, p. 2), because Richardson, by combining the roles of author and printer, can lay claim at once to both the ideational and the material aspects of the published text. That unusual combination allows him to embody, in a single person, the different parts of the literary economy that piracy threatens, with the result that he takes for granted a unity of purpose otherwise rarely seen among the various participants in this economy. The underhanded conduct of the Dublin booksellers would indeed be an attack on the cause of literature in general – if all members of the industry were just like Richardson. Among historians of publishing and authorship, Richardson's *Case* has become famous as an illustration of an emerging view in which conceptions of authorial originality and literary property were interdependent. Reading the *Case* alongside some of Richardson's novelistic defences may cast some doubt on the force of that illustration, by highlighting the tensions between exemplarity and individuality that run through many of his cases.

Notes

1 Conrad van Dijk, *Gower and the Limits of the Law* (Brewer, 2013), pp. 16–17.
2 Henry Fielding, *'Joseph Andrews' and 'Shamela'*, ed. Douglas Brooks-Davies, rev. Thomas Keymer (Oxford University Press, 1999), p. 164; Catherine Gallagher, 'George Eliot: Immanent Victorian', *Representations*, 90.1 (2005), 61–74 (p. 62; emphasis added).
3 Ian Watt, *The Rise of the Novel* (University of California Press, 1957), 31.
4 Samuel Richardson, *'Clarissa': Preface, Hints of Prefaces and Postscripts*, ed. R. F. Brissenden (Augustan Reprint Society, 1964), p. 5.
5 Francis Plumer, *A Candid Examination of the History of Sir Charles Grandison*, 3rd edn (London, 1755), p. 11, quoted in Bernard Kreissman, *Pamela-Shamela: A Study of the Criticisms, Burlesques, Parodies, and Adaptations of Richardson's 'Pamela'* (University of Nebraska Press, 1960), p. 45.

6 Kreissman writes that Plumer's objection is just one example of '[a] damaging criticism … which provoked … much discussion'. Kreissman, *Pamela-Shamela*, p. 45.

7 Albrecht von Haller, 'An Account of *Clarissa* and Richardson's Reply', *Gentleman's Magazine*, 19 (June and July 1749), repr. in Ioan Williams (ed.), *Novel and Romance, 1700–1800: A Documentary Record* (Routledge and Kegan Paul, 1970), pp. 130–41 (pp. 130, 139–40 n. 7).

8 Robert Newsom, *A Probable Story: Probability and Play in Fiction* (Rutgers University Press, 1988), pp. 92–3.

9 Richardson, 'Samuel Richardson, "Address to the Public"', in Betty A. Schellenberg (ed.), *Correspondence Primarily on 'Sir Charles Grandison' (1750–1754)*, CECSR, Vol. x, pp. 101–29 (pp. 126, 128).

CHAPTER 27

Family

Toni Bowers

Family relationships take centre stage in Samuel Richardson's novels, as his protagonists struggle to negotiate domestic power hierarchies in ways consistent with Christian virtue. With virtuosic intricacy, Richardson makes palpable the uneasily mingled feelings, intentions, contradictions, uncertainties, and impasses inseparable from domestic relationships organised around patriarchy, the system of governance defined as 'rule by fathers'. In patriarchal families, authority belongs to fathers, husbands, eldest sons, and uncles, while younger males and females of all ages are expected to submit. Mothers are granted comparable parental authority only in exceptional cases, such as during the minority of fatherless sons or when they are widows with daughters only.

Like most of his contemporaries, Richardson considered patriarchal family organisation to be natural and God-given.[1] The domestic patriarch was understood to be a kind of small-scale monarch and a representative of God, with the prerogative to demand unquestioning obedience. Richardson's minute delineations of family life start from this assumption. In his novels, the difference between successful and unsuccessful families depends on how virtuously individuals inhabit their respective places in established domestic hierarchies.

At the same time, Richardson recognised the vulnerabilities of patriarchal systems of governance, and excelled at teasing them out in narrative. Repeatedly, his work stages scenes of patriarchal abuse, error, or abdication in families, making clear the dilemmas that result for domestic subordinates when patriarchal power is misused. What if a wife or daughter should find herself caught between the commands of her husband or father and the dictates of her conscience, religious beliefs, intelligence, desires, or well-being, for example? Through an ever-more-sophisticated use of the epistolary method – with its glacial accretions, overlapping voices, echoing reconsiderations, and psychological intimacy – Richardson became the eighteenth century's great delineator of such conundrums.

Readers have debated for centuries the degree to which Richardson's work achieves credible balance between the impulses to defend patriarchal family governance despite its potential for abuse and the impulse to revise the structure itself. Today, most readers tend to consider these impulses to be mutually exclusive, but they may not have looked that way during the eighteenth century. Indeed, readers of Richardson, then and now, are caught in a bind of their own, forced to confront their own reductive thinking habits when faced with an authorial agenda that seems at once traditionalist and reformist. In Richardson's representations of family relations, it becomes clear that these need not be utterly opposed ideological positions.

Defining 'Family'

In Richardson's day, 'family' was still often used in the now-archaic sense of 'household': everyone living in or associated closely with a powerful man's living establishment(s), including wife and children, servants and dependents, and even, for the illustrious, 'retinue' or 'entourage'. 'Family' could also mean 'clan' during the eighteenth century – a group of people not necessarily closely linked genetically but who shared some degree of blood relation that created strong mutual allegiances and obligations. The word could even mean something like what we now might call 'race' or 'ethnicity'. Yet 'family' could also point, as it usually does today, to what we call 'the nuclear family' or, alternatively, 'the extended family', a somewhat wider circle of blood relations and relatives by marriage than the nuclear unit, but not so large a circle as is suggested by 'kin'.

Richardson wrote his novels in the middle of the eighteenth century, when possible meanings of 'family' were shifting. Using 'family' to mean 'nuclear family' was a practice gaining dominance during Richardson's lifetime. Indeed, by the time of his death in 1761, 'family' very often (though still not always) meant what John Stuart Mill would confidently call it twenty-eight years later: 'The Group, which consists of a Father, Mother, and Children'.[2] Ruth Perry has traced the process by which 'family' was increasingly pointing to the new relational group established by marriage, rather than the ties of birth.[3] Because of the wide cultural saturation of Richardson's novels during the eighteenth century, and the profound investments readers made in their plots and characters, the novels helped to naturalise developments in the meanings of the word 'family'. (As an index to readers' emotional investments in Richardson's novels, consider that even into the twentieth century, parents were christening their real-life babies after his characters. The full name of the pioneering Red Cross nurse Clara Barton, born in 1821, was 'Clarissa Harlowe Barton', for instance; the twentieth-century novelist/editor Charles G. Finney was Charles Grandison Finney.)

In *Pamela*, Mr B assumes a fairly expansive, old-fashioned meaning of 'family' when he asks whether the protagonist is 'of any Use in the Family' (*P*, p. 25) – that is, his household. Sir Simon Darnford uses the word in a related way when he expresses a lack of interest in the story of Mr B's attempt to exploit Pamela sexually. 'I don't see any great injury will be done her', Sir Simon remarks; 'he hurts no family by this' (*P*, p. 124). 'Family' here does not mean 'nuclear family' but the reputation of a family name, the status of an aristocratic or privileged 'house' within the hierarchies of the British propertied classes. A similar use of the word appears in *Sir Charles Grandison*, when Harriet Byron comments on her suitor Mr Fowler: he is 'not inconsiderable in his family or fortune' (1.viii.35). These formulations unambiguously link 'family' with reputation and property. At other places in Richardson's corpus, however, the denotation of 'family' is not so clear. In *Clarissa*, references to the heroine's 'family' often seem to point to her parents and siblings, but at other times include her uncles, aunts, and cousins, too. 'Family', it seems, can mean more than one thing in Richardson's novels.

Who counted as part of a family during the eighteenth century? Once again, the answer is not simple. When 'household' is meant, even servants were 'family'. And because marriage was difficult to dissolve, relation by marriage was permanent: those today called 'in-laws', and often distanced from nuclear families in the case of divorce, were routinely considered to be fathers, mothers, brothers, or sisters in their own right, as if they were blood relatives.

Adopted and 'step' family members were numerous because though marriages were usually lifelong, lifespans were comparatively short. *Sir Charles Grandison*'s Harriet Byron exemplifies one type of grafted-on family member. Miss Byron starts the novel without living parents: initially raised by her grandparents, when the novel begins she is much like a daughter to her loving aunt and uncle, the Selbys. (Harriet is close, as well, to her 'cousins', the Reeveses.) *Pamela*'s Sally Goodwin is another example, but with this difference: Miss Goodwin is actually Mr B's biological child, born out of wedlock, and this 'illegitimate' status makes her at once an insider and always an outsider in the B family. Readers today are likely to find something disturbing in the supposed magnanimity with which Pamela adopts

Miss Goodwin into what might be considered the girl's own family – after which she continues to be called 'Miss Goodwin'.

Like many of his contemporaries, Richardson tends to understand grafted-on relations as vulnerable socially and economically. Harriet's family is one of the few harmonious ones in Richardson's work, yet even so her position is precarious, as one of her suitors notes:

> A girl of twenty; her fortune between ten and fifteen thousand pounds only; for her father's considerable estate, on his demise, for want of male heirs, went with the name; her grandmother's jointure not more than five hundred pounds a year. – And what though her uncle Selby has no children, and loves her, yet has he nephews and nieces of his own, whom he also loves; for this Harriet is his wife's niece. (*SCG*, 1.ii.7)

It was possible for step- or adopted children to enjoy the privileges of full-fledged family members, but there were limits to their security in a society built firmly on bloodlines and patriarchal inheritance.

Representing Family Relationships

Richardson's fictional families reveal much about the broader social organisation of eighteenth-century British society, including its economic class structures, competing ideological and creedal values, and the changing locations and roles of public authority. Representations of family life are never merely metaphors for something else in Richardson, but they nevertheless carry broad resonances for other kinds of power relations in eighteenth-century British society.

This is because family hierarchies built around the prerogatives of fathers were understood in eighteenth-century Britain to mirror, validate, and reinforce structures of power and subordination on public and even cosmic levels. Any depiction of family relations was understood to be simultaneously commenting on the polity's relation to the monarch and humanity's relation to God. In most eighteenth-century writing, including Richardson's fiction, children who resist the wishes of their parents, like wives who resist their husbands' wills, threaten the stability not only of individual families, but of order and justice.

So while Richardson's novels may seem narrowly domestic, 'merely' focused on family interactions, we should recognise that the domestic focus does not preclude participation in contemporary public affairs. On the contrary, Richardson's novels create expectations, achieve effects, and mount arguments far in excess of their domestic frames of reference. Readers from the eighteenth century to the present have disagreed about precisely what ideological values are being inculcated in Richardson's depictions of family life. But we can say for sure that his meticulously phrased, intricately staged representations of relations within and among families contain a world of ideological (including religious) suggestion clearly discernible to early readers, though not always obvious today. Representations of families are Richardson's crucible for explorations of resonant questions about the meanings and practical possibilities of virtue in a wider world of unevenly distributed power.

Take for example the apparently simple matter of family size in Richardson's novels. Pamela Andrews's family consists, when the novel opens, only of herself and her two aging parents. In Richardson, this kind of small, nuclear structure characterises poorer families more often than better-off families. There is a clear sense of the aloneness and vulnerability of nuclear families in a world with few social supports, and it is often lower-class characters who negotiate the world from within very small families.

More privileged characters, by contrast – Mr B, Robert Lovelace, Sir Charles Grandison, Clementina della Porretta, and others – enjoy networks of relations from whom communications, advice, visits, and inheritances – and, of course, obligations and annoyances – are regularly forthcoming. These more extended and complex family networks are indeed a constituent feature of economic privilege. Having more family also means being granted comparatively complex and rounded characterisation. Not every member of Richardson's most populous families is intricately delineated, of course; but virtually all characters who *are* intricately delineated have (or, in Pamela's and Anna Howe's cases, gain) comparatively large families. In this structural tendency we may perceive an unspoken assumption shared among better-off people in eighteenth-century Britain: the idea that the poor were less appropriate subjects for complex delineation – perhaps even less fully and richly human – than the rich. Pamela's rise from poverty to riches is at once an exception that proves this rule and not quite a real exception, since she was not actually born into poverty. She was, as Lady Brooks correctly guesses, 'better descended' (*P*, p. 49). In this and other particulars, Richardson took pains to tamp down the potentially radical implications of his story.

Richardson shares his culture's prejudice when he focuses his attention most steadily on privileged families and has less interest in depicting the less affluent. Yet it is worth observing that in his comparatively limited representations of poor and working families, he demonstrates the same central principle staged in his more varied and nuanced depictions of privileged families: that virtue is always constructed within existing relations of authority and subordination. That is simply how things are, in Richardson's work, and indeed how things should be for both individuals and families, whether they are materially well off or not. In all cases, the question is not how to achieve more equitable distributions of authority and choice within families, but how members of families might best – that is, most virtuously – inhabit preordained positions of prerogative and obedience.

So in *Pamela*, the impoverished Andrews family is represented as a Christian model precisely because the father exercises patriarchal authority so lovingly and virtuously that his will is never resisted, or even questioned, by his wife and daughter. By contrast, the family of the tenant farmer Pamela stays with overnight (one of few other economically disadvantaged families Richardson represents at any length) shows the resentment and dishonesty that emerge among subordinates when patriarchs operate tyrannically. The behaviour of each father, as well as the answering behaviour of each mother and daughter, distinguishes these two families according to a clearly implied thesis about how authority and submission ought to be exercised.

The argument extends beyond the walls of home, to each family's corporate identity in the larger world. The Andrewses and the farmer's family practise different ways of inhabiting their positions of social and economic dependence on B, and readers learn that when a landowner abuses his authority, there are different ways to respond, some more virtuous than others. Once again, the point is less to interrogate the legitimacy of the power dynamic that keeps B powerful and the others dependent than to anatomise how each family will deal with the fact of its social subordination to a patriarch who is misusing his authority. In families' corporate roles, just as in individuals' roles within families, virtue is inseparable from the careful negotiation of existing relations of power and obedience.

That thesis, posed in shorthand in representations of working families such as the Andrewses and B's tenant farmers, becomes immeasurably more nuanced and generative in Richardson's much more extended depictions of economically privileged families. Balancing acts between prerogative and obedience in the private families of landowners and aristocrats, about whose existences Richardson could have had little first-hand knowledge, turned out, paradoxically, to be his most fertile narrative ground, the place where he explored with unmatched subtlety precisely how virtue can be achieved or thwarted within patriarchal systems of governance.

Among Richardson's privileged families – that is, in general terms, families whose heads need not work for a living – there are many varieties. The specific economic and social circumstances of particular families, like the constraints faced by individuals within those families, are not identical. What is more, in his representations of privileged families, Richardson experiments with different modal and tonal registers, creating different kinds of power dynamics. We can see how this works by comparing *Clarissa*, a tragic representation of family dynamics, to *Sir Charles Grandison*, a largely comic vision.

In *Clarissa*, difficulties emerge when the heroine, hitherto a docile daughter and sister, resists the improper exercise of her parents' patriarchal authority. Final authority over Clarissa's choice of husband is, of course, her parents' prerogative. But the Harlowes abuse their authority in two important ways: by attempting to force Clarissa into a degrading marriage from motives of pride and greed; and by abrogating their rightful authority, making possible its usurpation by Clarissa's overweening brother – and even, to an extent, her sister. The Harlowes, in other words, are at once too aggressive and too passive in their exercise of parental authority, and their failings lead to irredeemable family chaos, a type of political disturbance.

In *Sir Charles Grandison*, Richardson's protagonist comes from a family that is not merely economically privileged, like the *nouveau riche* Harlowes, but of old wealth. For the first time in Richardson's corpus, furthermore, the eponymous protagonist is male and aristocratic – two positions of unanswerable patriarchal prerogative in eighteenth-century British society. Richardson sets out to show in *Grandison* how the virtuous exercise of patriarchal authority can create peaceful families not only among the poor (as in the case of the Andrewses in *Pamela*), but among the rich, as well.

The measured, generous means by which Sir Charles Grandison exercises patriarchal authority over the members of his family prevents problems rather than creating them, and produces comedy rather than tragedy. (Things only go wrong when people fail to listen to Sir Charles or to follow his example.) Remarkably, too, Sir Charles is not only a model patriarch but also a model subordinate: he gracefully negotiates a position of necessary obedience towards the family of the woman whose hand he seeks for most of the novel, Clementina della Porretta. Grandison's ultimate failure to win Clementina is not the result of any false step on his own part; it is the result of that family's poor management of its own patriarchal power dynamics.

By positioning the failed family as Roman Catholic and Italian, furthermore, Richardson is able to mount a critique of wrongly exercised patriarchal authority similar to the one he dramatised in *Clarissa*, while still creating an overall happy outcome. Clementina's male relatives are at fault, but the foundational error lies in Roman Catholicism itself, an institution that, for British Protestants like Richardson, epitomised the perversion of patriarchal authority.

In Richardson's novels, family relations are the test site for struggles over dominance and subordination within patriarchal systems of governance. Tyrannically exercised authority leaves no room for virtuous submission; subordinates who resist legitimate authority (Charlotte Grandison, for example) must learn to obey. Stable assignments of authority and submission are necessary within families, those little societies. The question is not whether all are created equal – they are not – but how inequality will be negotiated.

Notes

1 For the relation of these hierarchical beliefs to one-sex and two-sex models of sexual difference, see Kathleen M. Oliver, below (pp. 247–50).
2 John Stuart Mill, *Analysis of the Phenomena of the Human Mind*, 2 vols. (London, 1829), Vol. II, p. 176.
3 Ruth Perry, *Novel Relations: The Transformation of Kinship in English Literature and Culture, 1748–1818* (Cambridge University Press, 2004).

CHAPTER 28

Gender

Kathleen M. Oliver

Gender is a complex affair, in a constant pas de deux with sexuality, intimately related (and sometimes opposed) to the sexed body, and central to notions of personal identity and subjectivity. During the early eighteenth century, a new model of sexuality was introduced, with the female now identified as a separate biological organism, rather than an inferior version of the male. Both models existed concurrently, though the two-sex model would soon dominate; both arose discursively; both held political consequences. For millennia, the one-sex model allowed for an array of gendered possibilities, but with the (freeborn) male always the epitome of perfection, and thus alone considered deserving of political rights. Under this model, gender was rooted in the body – specifically, in bodily sexual difference(s). In contrast, the two-sex model insisted upon binarism, and it fostered the belief that the sexes were distinct and separate – indeed, that they were opposites. Under the two-sex model, sex was rooted in the body; biological (sexual) difference suggested inherent behavioural (gender) difference. This new model provoked disparate reactions: for some, it confirmed women's inferiority; for others, it spawned the belief that women might be equal to men, even superior to them in certain aspects.[1]

Further complicating matters, the Lockean claim that all knowledge is generated through the senses suggested that women held the same capacity for reason and the same potential for learning as men; yet this contention was countered by the argument that women's nerves – the central conduits for the senses – were more delicate, softer, finer, unable to endure the rigours of intense study or thought. An increase in consumerism (identified as a feminine activity), a significant rise in female literacy (principally affecting the middling to lower classes), more leisure time for women of the upper and middling stations (concomitant with nascent 'separate sphere' ideology), claims by Dissenting sects as to women's centrality in cultivating the family's religious life, and the burgeoning culture of sensibility – all contributed to and altered, in often conflicting ways, what

it meant to be feminine, particularly among the middling and upper stations. During this period, debate also arose regarding what it meant to be
masculine. Was it drinking, swearing, whoring, gaming, fighting, hunting,
bear-baiting, and the like? Was it courage, valour, strength? Or was it sensitivity to the plight of others, elegant manners, the cultivation of reason,
and tasteful consumerism, as the third earl of Shaftesbury suggested? And,
if the last, then how much of a good thing was too much, enervating and
emasculating the English male subject? Since the late seventeenth century,
the Society for the Reformation of Manners, as well as religious reformers,
the Crown, and Parliament had sought to refashion male manners, yet
traditional masculine pursuits continued unabated throughout the eighteenth century. And, of course, there were also individuals who didn't fit
neatly into the new two-sex, two-gender model.

Richardson's novels, then, were written at a time when the meaning of
sexual difference as we now know it was new, and when gender was under-
going significant alterations. Richardson's novels tackled these changes
head-on, by identifying, categorising, debating, and judging the various
modes for expressing gender, and in many ways they helped to validate
certain gender types – and invalidate others.

Richardson and Gender

Richardson 'writes' gender in two (occasionally conflicting) ways. He first
establishes (and subsequently returns to) what others think about a particular character, a technique principally utilised in order to guide readers in responding 'appropriately' to that character – that is, as Richardson
wishes them to respond. He also allows the character to perform gender
through words, airs, and manners, a method that breathes life into the
character and that should confirm readers in the earlier judgment, but frequently does not. This is because Richardson's complete immersion in his
major characters often allows their wit, humour, and vitality to subvert his
didactic intent; as he writes to Lady Bradshaigh on 14 February 1754, 'I am
all the while absorbed in the character. It is not fair to say – I, identically,
am any-where, while I keep within character.' What we *should* feel about
a character is not necessarily how we *do* feel, as Richardson learnt with
responses to Lovelace. Thus, inconsistencies exist between Richardson's
purported beliefs regarding gender and the representations of gender with
regard to specific characters within his novels, a point many scholars have
noted.[2] Nonetheless, Richardson does treat certain gendered groups in a
cohesive manner across his body of work.

Femininities

Evidence that Richardson subscribed to the two-sex model and that he viewed women as separate but not equal biological organisms may be seen in his final novel, *Sir Charles Grandison*. Attempting to explain why 'there is a natural inferiority in the faculties' of *most* women and 'a natural superiority' in men, Sir Charles offers the following: 'There is a difference ... *generally*, in the *constitution*, in the *temperament*, of the two Sexes, that gives to the one advantages which it denies to the other' (*SCG*, VI.lv.360). Women are different in '*constitution*' (sex) and '*temperament*' (gender). While Sir Charles agrees with Mrs Shirley that 'we are apt to consider the Sex *too much* as a species apart', he qualifies this view by noting:

> Yet it is my opinion, that both God and Nature have designed a very apparent difference in the minds of both, as well as in the peculiar beauties of their persons. Were it not so, their offices would be confounded, and the women would not perhaps so readily submit to those domestic ones in which it is their province to shine. (VI.lv.362–3)

Women's 'natural' subordination becomes akin to 'natural' class subordination. Sir Charles's lecture culminates with the following: 'When Sex ceases, inequality of Souls will cease' (VI.lv.365), implying that sexual inequality originated with humanity's fall, but that its continuing existence is authorised by religion and biology. Richardson's own correspondence speaks to the necessity of women's subordination: 'It is certain that the Woman's Subordination was laid upon her as a Punishment. And why? – Because *Adam was not deceived*, says the Apostle; *but the Woman being deceived, was in Transgression.*' He continues: 'Subordination ... is not a Punishment but to perverse or arrogant Spirits' (Richardson to Sarah Chapone, 2 March 1752).

Richardson does allow the feminist side of the debate to be heard, principally through the characters of Anna Howe and Charlotte Grandison. Anna rebels against the cultural insistence that women must marry: 'Upon my word, I most heartily despise that sex! ... to be cajoled, wire-drawn, and insnared, like silly birds, into a state of bondage or vile subordination: To be courted as princesses for a few weeks, in order to be treated as slaves for the rest of our lives' (*SCG*, I.xxvii.177). Charlotte Grandison is even more outspoken than Anna, convinced of the 'natural independency' (VI.lv.353) of women and arguing that, if educated properly, women would be the intellectual equals of men. Yet Richardson marries Anna and Charlotte to men 'of talents inferior' (II.ii.9) to their own. And, while Sir Charles acknowledges that for women 'there is a degree of knowledge very compatible with their duties ... and highly becoming them' (vi.lv.364), he cagily refuses to be specific, and he continues to insist on the superiority of the male sex, though he admits that exceptions exist. In this he reflects his creator, who compiled a list of thirty-six women whose intelligence he admired (Richardson to Frances Granger, 8 September 1750). However, while Richardson does not permit Anna or Charlotte to win their respective cases, he does allow them to argue vigorously, intelligently, and feelingly.

Richardson's ideal women, his heroines, are fictional embodiments of conduct-book ideology – a Richardson innovation – yet, contrary to expectation, they are not perfect. The heroines are modest, virtuous, and respectful; they rise early and retire late; they excel in the execution of domestic duties. Nonetheless, they are often rebellious; occasionally proud; and always scribbling with pen and paper, something frequently associated with 'masculine' women. They also display intelligence, rationality, and 'Steadiness of mind (a quality which the ill-bred and censorious deny to any of our sex)', as Clarissa remarks (C, I. xix.126). Yet Richardson also depicts these exemplars in ways that victimise them: Pamela is kidnapped, imprisoned, and threatened with rape; Clarissa is tricked into eloping, trapped in a bawdy house, and raped; Harriet is kidnapped. Further, both Pamela and Harriet cede authority to their respective spouses: Pamela puzzles over Mr B's forty-eight rules for a wife (P, pp. 412–14) and later submits – albeit unwillingly – to his command against breastfeeding (PE, pp. 309–16); Harriet blushes over a former act of assertiveness (SCG, vi.lv.357). Clarissa resists compromise – and dies. Caught between duty and inclination, Clementina goes mad. Thus, while Richardson must be praised for creating intelligent, strong-minded heroines, he nonetheless insists that women require rescuing and guidance.

Masculinities

A wide array of masculine characters appears in Richardson's works: the hyper-masculine male; the rake; the somewhat effeminate, often boring 'good man'; and the ideal man. Representing the hyper-masculine male – a model associated with harsh patriarchal domination of women – are 'these fierce, these masculine spirits' (C, I.v.29) the Harlowe men (father, brother, and uncles); 'that fierce and wrong-headed man' (SCG, iv.x.80) General della Porretta; and any number of sword-wielding hotheads who constantly challenge Sir Charles. A prime example is James Harlowe, Clarissa's brother, who possesses a 'natural imperiousness, and fierce and uncontrollable temper' (*C*, 1.i.2), believing 'it a proof of a *manly* spirit, to be an utter stranger to the gentle passions' (1.xxix.187). An 'ill-temper'd young man', young Harlowe acts the tyrant towards women. For Richardson, the hyper-masculine male registers as an insensitive bully.

At first glance, the rake appears a variant of the hyper-masculine male, engaged as he is in sexual conquest, drinking, brawling, and violence toward women. Rakes were 'the most egregious representatives of a male culture now being defined by its incompatibility with a new sense of public "decency"'.[3] For many of Richardson's contemporaries, however, libertinism was considered a form of luxury, which 'tends to enervate the Mind, and divert it from all Thought or Consideration, which does not relate to the sensual Appetite'.[4] The rake's licentiousness exposed him to venereal diseases, by which means 'he destroys his own genitals – thus causing real physical effeminacy'.[5] Richardson himself asserted that the 'rake is, must be, generally, in dress a coxcomb,' and 'must flatter, lie, laugh, sing, caper, be a monkey, and not a man' (Richardson to Lady Bradshaigh, 5 November 1750). All of Richardson's rakes show signs of effeminacy. It is true, as E. J. Clery notes, that unlike most libertines Lovelace 'does not drink or carouse or blaspheme or use bawdy language',[6] but he does dwell obsessively on seduction, self-identifies with the feminine, and claims intimate knowledge of the female mind; clearly, his rape of Clarissa must rank as an 'imperfect enjoyment'. Richardson literalises the effeminacy of the rake by clothing Mr B in the attire of the maidservant Nan, and, in *Sir Charles Grandison*, every rake is rendered metaphorically or literally impotent: Jeronymo, Merceda, and Bagenhall all suffer debilitating groin wounds; Sir Hargrave Pollexfen's facial disfigurement at the hands of Sir Charles signals his metaphoric castration.[7]

Richardson's 'good men', softened by manners, eager to please, display the feminine emotions of kindness, compassion, sympathy; their effeminacy is radically different from that of the rake, and, on the whole, it is viewed positively. Lovelace describes Mr Hickman as a 'precise fop of a fellow, as starch'd as his ruffles' (*C*, VI.liii.199), yet Hickman is nonetheless a 'good man' in that he is 'honest … humane and benevolent, tolerably generous'; 'sober; modest' (11.i.6), and, thus, considered a suitable match for Anna Howe. A similar version of the effeminate man becomes husband to Charlotte Grandison. Possessed of 'a good many *Femalities*', Lord G has been 'brought up to be idle and useless, as women generally are' (*SCG*, VI.liii.346); he proves fond of collecting china and seashells, loves to dance, and appears 'a little too finical in his dress' (ii.ii.9). Nonetheless, he is modest, kind, and openly admiring of his sharp-tongued spouse. The fact that Richardson pairs gentle, effeminate men with women of sharp, masculine intellect suggests a belief that opposites provide balance. For Richardson, possession of 'the gentle passions' remains a valuable attribute in any character, male or female.

The ideal man appears only once in Richardson's novels – in the form of Sir Charles Grandison. (At best, the reformed Mr B counts as half an ideal man.) Sir Charles embodies the Shaftesburian model of masculinity: he is stoic, rational, in control, yet sympathetic towards others, particularly those less fortunate. He is kind to animals, refusing to dock his horses' tails. He excels at swordplay and pistols, proves ready with his fists when necessary, and takes on 'Brescian bravoes' (SCG, iii.xx.175) with little ado – yet he avoids fighting whenever possible. His home represents the epitome of tasteful consumerism. He enjoys dancing, singing, conversing. He is manly, yet genteel, polite, refined. He weeps, but only under extremely affecting circumstances, and he is quick to wipe away the tears. And, while he enjoys the company of the female sex – indeed, respects and admires them – he nonetheless believes them unequal to men and in need of male protection, as noted earlier in this essay. As Sir Charles comments, 'we men should have power and right given us to protect and serve your Sex' (vi.lv.363). The ideal man, then, carefully treads the middle path of masculinity.

Gender Trouble

'Can there be characters more odious than those of a masculine woman, and an effeminate man?', asks Sir Charles (SCG, vi.lv.361). No gay men, no 'mollies', grace the pages of Richardson's novels – perhaps from reasons of propriety, perhaps because they pose no threat to the virtue of the heroines – yet women whom we would identify today as lesbians appear in every one of his novels, with the exception of *Pamela in Her Exalted Condition*. What are we to make of this 'gender trouble', to use Judith Butler's phraseology?[8]

Before the eighteenth century, there was no such thing as sexual identity, but only sexed bodies, sexual acts, and gendered behaviours; by the eighteenth century, however, sexual identity was in its nascent stages. For many, tribadism – as sexual activity between women was then termed – continued to be viewed as female appropriation of male behaviour, on a par with such activities as studying Greek, scolding one's husband, wearing masculine attire, asserting female equality, publishing, and act-ing in any number of 'unwomanly' ways. Notably, Sir Charles's pro-nouncement regarding the odiousness of 'a masculine woman' comes in answer to Charlotte's assertion that women, if educated properly, would be the intellectual equals of men. His rejoinder implies that a learned woman is a mannish woman; and, under the rubric of '*women*, whose minds seem to be cast in a masculine' mould, Sir Charles includes 'your Barnevelts ... and those married women who are so kind as to take their reins out of their husbands hands, in order to save the honest men trou-ble' (*SCG*, vi.lv.361). The three presumed tribades in Richardson's fic-tions – Jewkes, Sinclair, and Barnevelt – appropriate the behaviour of the rake in their amorous pursuit of women, as well as the behaviour of the hyper-masculine male, thrilling to the 'glory ... to be gain'd in the martial field' and denying the 'gentle passions' (*SCG*, i.xiv.82), includ-ing empathy for their own sex. On the one hand, then, there are *no* lesbians in Richardson's novels, only Amazons who ape masculine behav-iour or engage in masculine pursuits. The two-sex model accommodates the 'masculine woman' and 'effeminate male', but only by viewing these individuals as behaviourally aberrant – that is, as aberrant in terms of gender, not sexuality.

Yet, there *are* lesbians or Sapphics in Richardson's fictions. Mrs Jewkes kisses Pamela, squeezes her hand suggestively, and, when she offers to kiss Pamela again, provokes a complaint from Pamela of 'I don't like this Sort of Carriage, Mrs. *Jewkes*; it is not like two Persons of one Sex' (*P*, p. 100); Jewkes also actively participates in the attempted rape of Pamela. Clarissa questions if Mrs Sinclair, with her 'mannish airs', '*be* a woman!' (*C*, v.x.61), and Sinclair partakes in Clarissa's rape, so much so that Lovelace questions whether or not she, not he, raped Clarissa. And Miss Barnevelt declares that she views Harriet 'with the eye of a Lover' (*SCG*, i.x.54), smothers her with kisses, and clasps her in 'one of her mannish arms' (i.xiii.75). Readers are meant to view these women as *sexually* menacing, aligned with the sexually threatening rake and allowed physical access to women in ways that a man would not be. By focusing on tribades and loading them with every type of vice – as James Grantham Turner notes in the following chapter, in Richardson's fictions, 'once a woman has crossed over into the world of lechery she takes on every known perversion, so she may as well be a lesbian *and* a procuress' (p. 258) – Richardson rendered judgment on those whose sexuality deviates from the heterosexual norm, and, thus, perhaps, acted as midwife to the notion of sexual identity.

Notes

1 See Thomas Laqueur, *Making Sex: Body and Gender from the Greeks to Freud* (Harvard University Press, 1990).
2 For instance, Madeleine Kahn, *Narrative Transvestism: Rhetoric and Gender in the Eighteenth-Century English Novel* (Cornell University Press, 1991); Tassie Gwilliam, *Samuel Richardson's Fictions of Gender* (Stanford University Press, 1993); and Bonnie Latimer, *Making Gender, Culture, and the Self in the Fiction of Samuel Richardson: The Novel Individual* (Ashgate, 2013).
3 G. J. Barker-Benfield, *The Culture of Sensibility: Sex and Society in Eighteenth-Century Britain* (University of Chicago Press, 1992), p. 49.
4 Caleb D'Anvers, 'No. 51, Saturday, June 24, 1727', *The Craftsman*, 14 vols. (London: [1731]), Vol. II, p. 44.
5 Stephanie Koscak, 'Morbid Fantasies of the Sexual Marketplace: "Lascivious Appetites", Luxury and Lues Venerea in England, 1750–1800', *Michigan Feminist Studies*, 21 (Fall 2008), 85–129 (p. 106).
6 E. J. Clery, *The Feminization Debate in Eighteenth-Century England: Literature, Commerce and Luxury* (Palgrave Macmillan, 2004), p. 104.
7 See Tassie Gwilliam, *Samuel Richardson's Fictions of Gender* (Stanford University Press, 1993), pp. 122–33. For a parallel reading of the cultural function of the rake in relation to Richardson's Lovelace, see Simon Dickie, above (pp. 214–20); Heather Meek also discusses the physical fates of Richardson's rakes, below (pp. 265–8).
8 Judith Butler, *Gender Trouble: Feminism and the Subversion of Identity*, 2nd edn (Routledge, 1999).

CHAPTER 29

Sexuality

James Grantham Turner

In the 1980s Penguin Classics published for the first time affordable editions of both *Clarissa* and '*Fanny Hill*' (John Cleland's explicitly sexual *Memoirs of a Woman of Pleasure*). In the bookshop I held one in each hand, as I would later do when introducing a graduate seminar called '1748': in my left, the slender paperback that happens when a woman says YES, in my right, the massive brick of a novel generated when a woman says NO. Though one celebrates 'pleasure' and the other 'virtue', both novelists place sexuality at the core of prose fiction. Richardson's main theme, the heroine's struggle to preserve her chastity, had been central to romance novels from ancient Greece onward. But *Pamela, Clarissa,* and '*Fanny Hill*' emerge at a particular moment in the history of sexuality.

Simply put, Richardson occupies the troubled zone between Puritanism and Enlightenment. The middle-class Englishman congratulated himself on living in a liberal, accepting, and 'polite' culture, which reconciled 'Sex and Sensibility' and celebrated the joys of companionate marriage, 'perfect Esteem enlivened by Desire'.[1] This culture avoided the extremes of the previous century – the godly repression of the Puritan Revolution, followed by the frenetic debauchery of the Restoration – and the excesses of France, where rejection of Christianity by 'philosophers in the boudoir' supposedly led to 'all forms of lasciviousness' and 'the most shameful orgies'.[2] Cleland espouses *that* kind of Enlightenment, as does Denis Diderot (who ironically became Richardson's most fervent admirer). Richardson evokes this deplorable extreme in his rake characters: Mr B in *Pamela*, and Robert Lovelace, the nemesis of Clarissa. As elaborated by Simon Dickie above, Lovelace is modelled on notorious Restoration libertines such as the earl of Rochester, whose poems in praise of 'handsome ills' and 'mannerly obscenity' inspire Lovelace's perverse delight in 'glorious mischief'. To make matters worse, Lovelace spent many formative years 'at the French Court', imbibing absolutist politics and techniques of deceit and seduction (*C*, I. xxxi.203, II.xvi.101).

Richardson detested the sexual arrogance of aristocrats like Lovelace, yet he was accused of promoting it. One anonymous critic complains that in *Pamela* 'there are such *Scenes* of *Love*, and such *lewd Ideas*, as must fill the Youth that read them with *Sentiments* and *Desires* worse than ROCHESTER can' (Figure 29.1).[3] At the same time he was frequently caricatured as an old-fashioned Puritan, seething with prurience while proclaiming his own rectitude and rebuking the sins of others. Even Coleridge denounces him as 'hypocritical', 'canting', and (most relevant to this chapter) 'concupiscent!'[4] Unjust as this is as a general verdict on a sensitive and gifted novelist, there are moments in his puffs for *Pamela* that deserve such a rebuke: Richardson's preface, for example, defies logic by promising not to 'raise a *single Idea* throughout the Whole, that shall shock the exactest Purity, even in those tender Instances where the exactest Purity would be most apprehensive' (*P*, p. 3).

For the historian Randolph Trumbach, the growing acceptance of sanctioned sexuality led to sharper definitions of those who deviate from the

Figure 29.1 Joseph Highmore, *Pamela Fainting* (1743–44), oil on canvas, 635 × 762 mm, National Gallery of Victoria, Melbourne, Felton Bequest, 1921 (1114-3).

norm: the homosexual 'molly' and 'sapphist', or the sadomasochist (who appears among Fanny Hill's customers).[5] These were becoming permanent identities rather than occasional practices that the debauchee might try at pleasure. But should the rake himself, the full-time womaniser, be counted among these unalterable, irredeemable perverts? *Pamela* says NO: Mr B becomes a loving husband, renouncing libertinage and climbing down from some of his absolutist positions (despite the argument over Pamela's breastfeeding her own baby, as interpreted by Howard Weinbrot, below (pp. 312–13)). But *Clarissa* says YES.

Double Standards

The idyllic synthesis of esteem and desire, celebrated in the eventual marriage of Pamela to her reformed-rake husband, was actually riven with complications and contradictions. Other parts of Richardson's novels allow us to see the immense divides of class and gender, as well as the internal fissures within each character. In the first half of *Pamela* Richardson skewers B's casual assumption that he can molest and imprison a chambermaid at will, as well as the upper-crust neighbours who dismiss the affair as trivial because it 'hurts no Family' – as if the lower orders *had* no families (*P*, p. 124). Lovelace's idea of 'a youthful frolick' is to seduce a woman, refuse to marry her because she is a tradesman's daughter, and let her die in childbirth (summarised in *C*, iii.xlvi.232–3, restored in full in the third edition, iii.xliv.228–9). He fantasises about keeping Clarissa and her confidante Anna Howe in an Ottoman-style seraglio (iv.xxiv.133), or raping Anna and her mother on a boating trip (another passage struck out but triumphantly restored in the third edition, iv.xlii.254–61). After entertaining the idea in *Pamela* and its sequel that '*a Reform'd Rake makes the best Husband*' (*PE*, p. 585), that the double standard should be tolerated, and the husband's bastard welcomed into the family, Richardson refuses such a compromise in *Clarissa* – even though many readers begged for it.

The double standard meant that for women, though not for men, a single act of vaginal penetration was an absolute defining moment, despite the possibility of detachment from consent or even consciousness – as in the rape of Clarissa, who insists she is 'ruined', and literally starves herself to death to avoid the social death that awaited fallen women (in reality if not in Cleland's pornotopian fantasy). Pamela's lower-class father declares he would rather see her dead than become B's mistress, driving home Richardson's message that woman's 'honour' is universal and not just confined to the gentry. But *Clarissa* adds an unusual twist: Lovelace, the embodiment of 'French' libertinage and upper-class masculine privilege, oddly identifies with the female. To explain his drive to persecute and ruin Clarissa he recalls a 'maiden vow' that he made in his teens, to avenge himself on all women because a fashionable seductress conquered and abandoned him (*C*, iii.x.78). It was a custom in France for experienced ladies to 'initiate' attractive young men, as Richardson would know from reading the memoirs of Ninon de L'Enclos, but Lovelace failed to grasp this, and thus feels permanently ruined and outraged by women: 'Who, that has once trespassed [with 'this sex'], ever recovered his integrity?' (i.xxxiv.232).

The 'woman of pleasure' is banished from society into the other world of prostitution and 'kept mistresses' – a parallel universe, with its own ethos and its own network of safe houses. Proper women, and morally improving novelists, were not supposed to know this black-market sexual economy. Here is the dilemma for Richardson, who must create believable yet innocent heroines, while making the dangers they face as real as possible. Unsympathetic critics of *Pamela* assumed that the heroine must be a manipulative and 'knowing' whore, partly because of class prejudice and partly because Richardson himself makes her cannily aware of sexual implications and innuendos. She understands that the master wishes her to be 'quick' in bed (not merely in repartee); that the corrupt housekeeper Mrs Jewkes speaks 'like a vile *London* Prostitute', cracks lewd jokes about 'Planting *&c.*', and fondles her in a too-masculine way (*P*, pp. 65, 99–100, 123, 165). (Richardson assumes that once a woman has crossed over into the world of lechery she takes on every known perversion, so she may as well be a lesbian *and* a procuress.) As a consequence of these touches of sexual realism, hostile critics assumed that Pamela consciously flirts and displays her 'charms', inducing an uncontrollable sexual frenzy in both Mr B and the reader.[6] Richardson, to give him his due, did take rape and sexual harassment seriously, and most of the Anti-Pamelists failed to understand his sensitivity to encroachment and coercion. But how are we to interpret Pamela sewing her journal into her underwear 'about my Hips', knowing that Mr B will search her (*P*, pp. 120, 211, 216–18)?

Diderot praises Richardson because, unlike his French contemporaries, he presents everyday life rather than escapist or pornographic fantasies, but he exaggerates when he claims that the English author never 'seals himself up in the clandestine places of debauchery'.[7] In fact, those 'places' are the main setting of Richardson's first two novels and the main source of their claustrophobic feel. Mr B jokes about setting Pamela up in London 'Lodgings' (*P*, p. 64), then later shuts her in a lonely country house guarded by that vulgar bawd who sounds like a London prostitute; Lovelace imprisons Clarissa in a specially built secret house behind a respectable London façade, staffed by a team of whores who masquerade as respectable relatives – under the direction of 'Mother' Sinclair. His faith in the architecture of illicit sexuality is almost touching: when she resists his first advances, he threatens to 'humble her pretty pride' by abducting her to 'a proper place, and proper company about her' (*C*, III.xv.99) – meaning of course the *im*proper, Clelandesque brothel.

The architecture and landscape of *Sir Charles Grandison* is considerably more open, but the focus is still on erotic love. Here at last the novel feels free to explore the 'natural passions', a phrase that became the title of Margaret Anne Doody's essential study of Richardson (1974). But how natural are the passions that spring up within the Grandison circle? There is still an evil rake who stalks the heroine Harriet, and a suspiciously mannish lady who does something similar. Charlotte Grandison's love for her brother is so strong that it makes all other men seem worthless. We see the fervent embraces of Harriet and Sir Charles's fifteen-year-old ward Emily, while the more-than-brotherly love between Sir Charles and Clementina's crippled brother Jeronymo, an 'Italian' rather than a man or a woman (according to Richardson's own list of characters), has been sympathetically interpreted as homoerotic.[8] Even the perfect hero, the antidote to Lovelace, might be 'a Rake in his address, and a Saint in his heart' (*SCG*, VI.xxiv.135) – a final attempt to balance Enlightenment libertinism and Puritan integrity.

Ways of Saying It

Richardson and Cleland would both consider their approach to sex 'polite', in contrast to the vulgarity of lower-class bawdy and the deliberate obscenity of Rochester and his peers. But did *politesse* mean a reformation in manners and attitudes, or a merely verbal propriety masking a greater acceptance of illicit sex? Cleland, for example, set out to describe the genitalia with 'all the refinements of taste and delicacy', replacing the old dirty words with genteel images that associate sex with the arts of painting and writing: the vulva becomes a brushstroke finer than Guido Reni's, the penis a sublime 'object of terror and delight' or a 'velvet tip!', the memory of which causes Fanny's pen to drop from her hand. (Ironically, the same aesthetic-erotic language was shared by supporters and detractors of Richardson's attempted-rape scenes, described as paintings with 'strong colouring' and 'glowing' figures.) Even with this flood of metaphors, however, Fanny worries about boring repetition, and her pen always falls short of Pamela's and Clarissa's.[9]

The phrases used to denote sexual intercourse are highly revealing. Restoration poets such as Rochester used the four-letter words, while dramatists of that period developed a 'libertine sublime' vocabulary almost as explicit as Cleland's. Oedipus, for example, leaps into bed with Jocasta hurling defiance to the disapproving gods: 'Claspt in the Folds of Love, I'll act my Joys!' (The rakes *and* Clarissa both quote from this 'heroic' play by Nathaniel Lee and John Dryden, intriguingly.)[10] Another influential seventeenth-century dramatic libertine, Molière's Dom Juan, removes even the 'clasping' and the 'joys', and reduces the consummation of a long seduction to 'being the master, one time' only – after which 'there is nothing more to be said'.[11]

Pamela largely keeps to conventional terms, such as offering to be rude or undone, while in the 'exalted' sequel Lady Davers uses the dark euphemism 'still *worse*' for the idea that her brother Mr B had actually raped Pamela in the notorious scene where she is pinioned in bed by Mrs Jewkes (*PE*, p. 34). The most telling ways of denoting intercourse, however, come in *Clarissa*. Lovelace, like Dom Juan, confesses that 'I have ever had more pleasure in my Contrivances than in the End of them', consummation being 'the End' rather than a beginning (third edition, III.xliv.228). He makes 'the crowning act' sound like that of an assassin rather than a lover: he will penetrate her 'by the sap' (i.e. by secret military tunnels), he will 'strike the blow'. Lovelace not only captures Clarissa's private correspondence but equates the sex act with opening a letter clandestinely; even after Clarissa has escaped from his captivity he still daydreams about the moment when 'the seal would have yielded to the touch of my warm finger … and the folds, as other plications have done, open'd of themselves, to oblige my curiosity'. Richardson here comes close to Cleland, referring directly to the dilating, aroused vulva by means of an archly decorous simile. Yet after all this, Lovelace reveals that he despises sex itself as empty and meaningless – 'a vapour, a bubble!' (*C*, IV.xx.94; III.vi.59, xiii.91; VI. xlviii.190).[12]

How then do the heroine Clarissa and her pious author counter this evil rake's language? Though he uses the disapproving word *outrage* for the actual rape – performed by Lovelace on the drugged, inert body of Clarissa, certainly no Dom Juan-style conquest – Richardson still makes that assault the defining, essential moment, as Lovelace intended, though for opposite reasons: 'Clarissa has the greatest of Triumphs … *in*, and *after* the Outrage, and *because* of the Outrage' (Richardson to Lady Bradshaigh,

15 December 1748). Clarissa herself insists that she is 'ruined', and turns the common French phrase for orgasm, *la petite mort*, or 'the little death', into a full-blown psychological association of penetration and death. In a dream, Clarissa is stabbed by Lovelace and tumbled into a mass grave; in real life she turns knives and scissors on herself (like a modern Lucretia) or begs Lovelace to 'let thy pointed mercy enter!' (v.xxxvi.276). In her Will (read out to the whole family assembled round her coffin) she forbids any surgical opening of her body and imagines Lovelace 'viewing *her dead*, whom he ONCE before saw in a manner dead' (vii.[lxxxvi].298). The linkage of Eros and Thanatos came naturally, perhaps, to an author whose six sons all died in infancy.

Sex and Sensibility?

In the liberal regime of the mid-eighteenth century, the respectable language of virtuous 'sentiment' easily slid into scandalous eroticism, and vice versa. This posed a problem for Richardson, who aspired to lead the cult of sensibility by instructing the public in properly emotional responses to his own writing, valued precisely for its attention to the minutiae of feeling. He reprinted gushing fan letters, laying himself open to the wicked parodies of Henry Fielding and his ilk. Penetrating inward emotion and weeping over virtue in distress, when translated into 'glowing' rhetoric, sounded like sexual excitement. Parts of Fielding's satirical *Shamela* are little more than collages of phrases published by Richardson himself to puff *Pamela*. Parson Tickletext moans, 'Oh! I feel an Emotion even while I am relating this; Methinks I see *Pamela* at this Instant, with all the Pride of Ornament cast off!', directly citing the second edition preface. Fans marvelled that 'a poor Girl's little, innocent, Story' could move them so deeply and 'stretch' to such a length; *Shamela* simply changed this to 'a poor Girl's little, *&c*'. Pornographic mirror images of Pamela's career remind us that official definitions of female 'Virtue' focused exclusively on the vagina. Richardson agrees, but insists that a *poor* girl's '&c' should be as valuable as a Countess's.[13]

Under the aegis of sensibility Richardson's admirers use remarkably erotic, suggestive language. Edward Young praises him for 'div[ing] / In bosoms of the fair'.[14] Aaron Hill urges Richardson to change the title of *Clarissa* to *The Way of a Young Man with a Maid*, and frequently describes readers 'All on Fire' or 'filled with Tremblings!'. Hill even recommends *Pamela* as an aphrodisiac ('an enamouring *Philtre* for the Mind' that excites an uncontrollable '*Passion* for Virtue') more intense than anything 'the

Loose can *dream*' (Aaron Hill to Richardson, 5 November 1746, November 1741, 29 November 1748; *P*, pp. 471, 476). Sarah Fielding, novelist sister of the scornful Henry, becomes 'all sensation' as she too succumbs to *Clarissa*: 'my heart glows; I am overwhelmed.'[15]

These exchanges between Richardson and his readers develop into full-blown seduction scenes. He poses as a 'designing' seducer or quotes Lovelace as an authority on the corrupt sexuality of women. Correspondents such as Lady Bradshaigh responded in kind.[16] As each new volume is pressed upon her she cries, 'I cannot, indeed I cannot!' Richardson must be one of those perverts who 'delight in horror … rapes, ruin, and destruction'. After a night of weeping over *Clarissa*, 'what must I say to the Man who has so disappointed and given me so much Pain? Why that I admire him for the Pain he gives, it being an undoubted Proof of his Abilities' (*C*, v.xxvi.222; Lady Bradshaigh to Richardson, <17 November>, 10 October 1748, 6–11 January 1749; this passage was understandably censored by Anna Barbauld in her edition of Richardson's correspondence). After the rape, in early December 1748, Lady Bradshaigh declares, 'you now can go no farther' – echoing the very words that Lovelace uses to announce the Outrage itself.

Notes

1 The titles of two famous studies by Jean Hagstrum (1980, 1992); the latter title is taken from the Scottish poet James Thomson's 'Spring', in *The Seasons*.

2 Serge Rivière, 'Philosophical Liberty, Sexual Licence: The Ambiguity of Voltaire's Libertinage', in Peter Cryle and Lisa O'Connell (eds.), *Libertine Enlightenment: Sex, Liberty and Licence in the Eighteenth Century* (Palgrave Macmillan, 2004), pp. 75–91 (p. 77).

3 Anon., *Pamela Censured* (London, 1741), p. 25.

4 Samuel Taylor Coleridge, *Anima poetae: From the Unpublished Notebooks of Samuel Taylor Coleridge*, ed. Ernest Hartley Coleridge, 2 vols. (London, 1895), Vol. 1, p. 166.

5 Randolph Trumbach, *Sex and the Gender Revolution, Vol. 1: Heterosexuality and the Third Gender in Enlightenment London* (University of Chicago Press, 1998). See also Kathleen M. Oliver, above (pp. 252–3), regarding the cultural significance of Richardson's portrayals of 'deviant' sexuality.

6 See James Grantham Turner, 'Novel Panic: Picture and Performance in the Reception of Richardson's *Pamela*', *Representations*, 48 (1994), 70–96 (pp. 79–80).

7 Denis Diderot, 'Eloge de Richardson', *Œuvres*, ed. André Billy (Gallimard, 1946), pp. 1090–1.

8 David Robinson, 'Unravelling the "cord which ties good men to good men": Male Friendship in Richardson's Novels', in Doody and Sabor, *Tercentenary Essays*, pp. 179–87.

9 John Cleland, *Memoirs of a Woman of Pleasure*, ed. Peter Sabor (Oxford University Press, 1985), pp. 20, 73, 94, 183, and cf. p. 91.

10 John Dryden and Nathaniel Lee, *Oedipus: A Tragedy* (London, 1679), final lines of Act II; cf. *C*, v.xxx.239 ('Paper x'), VII.i.9–10.

11 *Dom Juan; ou, Le festin de pierre*, I.ii ('lorsqu'on en est maître une fois, il n'y a plus rien à dire').

12 The euphemism 'crowning act' is also used by Fanny Hill (Cleland, *Memoirs*, p. 81).

13 Henry Fielding, *'Joseph Andrews' and 'Shamela'*, ed. Douglas Brooks (Oxford University Press, 1970), p. 322, citing *P*, pp. 464, 466.

14 Edward Young, *Resignation* (1762), Part I, quoted in Pat Rogers, ' "A Young, a Richardson, or a Johnson": Lines of Cultural Force in the Age of Richardson', in Doody and Sabor, *Tercentenary Essays*, pp. 203–22 (p. 212).

15 Henry Fielding and Sarah Fielding, *The Correspondence of Henry and Sarah Fielding*, eds. Martin C. Battestin and Clive T. Probyn (Oxford University Press, 1993), p. 123.

16 See Simon Dickie's parallel discussion, above (pp. 214, 217), of Lady Bradshaigh's response to the rakish Lovelace.

CHAPTER 30

Medicine and Health

Heather Meek

In a letter to Samuel Richardson, the well-known physician George Cheyne writes, 'It is a surprize to me that you, who have printed 3 or 4 of my Books wherein all the Turns, Symptoms, Nature & Cause of nervous Disorders are narrated & accounted for, should seem to know as little of the Affair as if you had never seen them' (2 February 1742). Cheyne, it seems, had prescribed a restrictive vegetarian diet to cure Richardson's 'Hyp' (a nervous condition known variously in the eighteenth century as hypochondria, hysteria, nerves, spleen, or vapours), and Richardson had, evidently, questioned the efficacy of the treatment. Exasperated, Cheyne asks, 'Did you think it was a supernatural Cure of Distempers, Witchcraft, or Enchantment?'. From his correspondence with Cheyne we learn that Richardson's particular case included a complex entanglement of physical and mental symptoms, including 'Pain, Anxiety', 'Discouragement', 'Startings, Twitchings', 'Cramps', 'Catchings, Lowness', and 'Terrors' (Richardson to Cheyne, 6 June 1740; July 1742), so his expectations with respect to the diet may well have been unreasonably high. But his unwillingness to follow his doctor's advice uncritically may strike us as quite sensible. The doctor's treatment, after all, involved bleedings, vomits, medicines, and the aforementioned notorious 'low Diet' – a startlingly sparse regimen that Richardson, like many of Cheyne's patients, followed only 'timorously, grudgingly, and repineingly' (Richardson to Cheyne, 10 January 1742).

Richardson's willingness to challenge his doctor speaks both to his understanding of medical issues and to the nature of the doctor–patient relationship in the eighteenth century. The model of the naïve and ill-informed patient who conceded to the superior wisdom of a learned practising physician was not the norm in this period in history, when medicine had not yet been fully consolidated as a profession. Practitioners of medicine often shared their knowledge freely and confessed to their own shortcomings and vulnerabilities, while patients sometimes possessed considerable medical knowledge themselves, challenged diagnoses, and administered their own treatments. Cheyne, certainly, did not assume the role of all-knowing physician, and in one letter to Richardson insists that 'personal Experience [is] infinitely more secure than the most learned and penetrating Speculation' (14 July 1742). Richardson, for his part, possessed a medical savviness that Cheyne himself recognised and respected. The famous doctor solicited Richardson's advice not only as a printer, but also as one who could offer sound advice on the content and structure of his publications. In one letter, for instance, he asks Richardson, in reference to the draft of a medical treatise he is working on, for his '[honest] Opinion … of its Merit' (7 September 1737).

Cheyne showed good instincts in soliciting Richardson's opinion on medical matters. In addition to being a sufferer from a nervous affliction and an established printer whose work included medical texts, Richardson would soon prove himself to be a writer with a complex understanding of the medical issues of his day. Indeed, medical matters figure prominently in Richardson's fictional worlds. His novels abound with detailed and sophisticated descriptions of medical states, symptoms, diagnoses, and treatments, and in this way reflect the fluid movements between medicine and literature in a period when many men and women of letters – such as Anne Finch, Jane Barker, Laurence Sterne, Tobias Smollett, and Oliver Goldsmith – either practised medicine, or engaged deeply with medical ideas. The nervous condition that Cheyne wrote about and that Richardson suffered from strikes many of Richardson's characters, including the eponymous heroines of *Clarissa* and *Pamela*. Smallpox, a disease much feared in eighteenth-century London, afflicts both Pamela and her newborn son; and gout, an illness associated with class and privilege, but also with excruciating pain and fatal attacks, troubles a number of the patriarchs in Richardson's novels, including James Harlowe, Sr and Lord M of *Clarissa*, Sir Simon Darnford of *Pamela*, and Lord W of *Sir Charles Grandison*. Consumption is evoked less explicitly than the above conditions, but Belton, an immoral rake in Lovelace's circle, meets his end with 'distorted' face, 'sinking jaws', and 'rattles in the throat' (*C*, VII.vi.32), signs of one of the more hideous strains of this prevalent eighteenth-century disease. Richardson's novels frequently evoke commonplace (and sometimes primitive) medical treatments as well. Phlebotomy, or the drawing of blood from veins, is alluded to in several places: Mr B, suffering from a 'feverish Complaint', is 'blooded' (*P*, p. 235); Mrs Norton's attendants 'breathe a vein, to bring her to herself' when she learns of Clarissa's death (*C*, VII.lxvi.230); and

Clementina of *Sir Charles Grandison*, who has 'wounds of [the] mind' (*SCG*, VII.xxvi.124), eventually consents to being bled (III.xxvi.281). Another common eighteenth-century practice – amputation – surfaces when, in *Clarissa*, the French surgeons of Mrs Sinclair – who suffers from a festering leg wound and severe bruising – provide a detailed 'anatomical description of the leg and thigh' and suggest its removal (*C*, VII.lxxviii.262). Lovelace, memorably, takes ipecacuanha root, which induces 'violent retchings' in the villainous protagonist (*C*, IV.xxxvi.205). Cheyne, incidentally, prescribed a tincture of this root to Richardson as a vomit (Cheyne to Richardson, 9 August 1735).

The medical episodes that appear in Richardson's novels, far from being incidental, are central to his novelistic vision. They are woven into the fabric of his plots, and they are crucial to the development of his themes and characters. The novel of psychological realism, of which Richardson was one of the originators, depended upon the new science espoused by Cheyne and other medical men. The connections between body and mind that underpinned earlier, humoural theories remained in place in the new science, but they were elaborated upon in complex ways. Just as the blood moved through veins and heart, 'animal spirits', as they were known, travelled to and from the brain through a nervous system composed of an 'infinite Number and Variety of differing Channels and Pipes'.[1] This process was narrativised by novelists of sensibility such as Richardson, who, like eighteenth-century physicians, imbued the body with extreme sensitivity. George Rousseau argues that novelists such as Richardson 'were the posterity of two generations of thinkers who had increasingly "internalized" … the new science of man, leading thought about him from his eyes and his face to his nerves and brain, from what he looks like to what he feels, and from what he feels to what he knows'.[2]

In Richardson's fictions, states of the body – in sickness and in health – are intricately connected to states of mind; these states carry substantial metaphorical weight. This can be seen, for example, in Belford's description of Mrs Sinclair's sickly and decaying body on her deathbed. Her 'goggling' eyes, the violent movements of her lips and tongue, her convulsing chin, and her contracting forehead, as well as the puffs, heaves, and gasps she emits and her 'oaths and curses' of 'wild impatience' (*C*, VII.lxxviii.259), point to a nervous constitution that is severely disordered. These symptoms are in turn tied to a life of 'intemperance' and 'diffusive wickedness' (*C*, VII.lxxviii.260) that has disturbed and darkened her mind and soul. In the new science of Cheyne's medical model, Mrs Sinclair's unsettled mind could be diagnosed as the result not only of a physical state but of years of debauchery and 'Indiscretion' – of 'over-loading, bursting and cramming the *poor passive Machine*'.[3]

In a particularly clear instance of the new science and eighteenth-century medical culture making their way into Richardson's art, Cheyne's phrase turns up later, in the mouth of his protagonist Clarissa. '[W]hat a poor, passive machine is the body, when the mind is disorder'd', she declares in a letter to Anna Howe (*C*, ii.xxxi.180). As it is uttered by Clarissa, this phrase offers a slight variation of the process alluded to in Cheyne's treatise. For her, as for Richardson (who, like Cheyne, endorsed a fluid, two-directional mind–body model), the 'machine' suffers not merely from being 'overload[ed]' or abused, but also from being at the mercy of the fluctuations of the mind. Bodily dissipation has worn Mrs Sinclair's nerves, but Richardson implies that the opposite process has also occurred: her 'misfortune' has 'increased her flesh' because 'rage and violence' have 'swell[ed] her muscly features' (*C*, vii.lxxviii.258–9). Clarissa, too, experiences misfortune that weakens her body, but her decline carries radically different meanings in its moral import. Unlike that of Mrs Sinclair, Clarissa's moral integrity never falters, even in sickness, and neither does her outward physical perfection. As she nears death, the only visible symptom that Clarissa experiences is emaciation, and even with this she remains a 'lovely skeleton' (*C*, vii.i.14). Whatever Clarissa dies of – and there has been much speculation, from anorexia nervosa, to nervous sensibility, to consumption, to a combination of the above – it does not manifest itself in any of the gruesome physical symptoms we see in Sinclair or in Belton. She has no 'bodily pain – No numbnesses; no signs of immediate death'; her breath is 'tolerable' and her 'intellects free' (*C*, vii.xli.166). The wasting, grief, and occasional fits she experiences are suggestive of a nervous imbalance, but Clarissa's almost symptomless medical state serves to illustrate her moral perfection.

Thus, Richardson's fictions evoke contemporary medical models of the nervous system and the interconnections of mind and body as a way of further developing his characters and even placing them on a continuum of goodness and morality. An engagement with the medical thinking of his time in some instances also influences the structure of his work. In *Sir Charles Grandison*, Jeronymo's wound – like Mrs Sinclair's – is a moral signifier, which in this instance invites a judgment of the rake figure. The unhealed wound in fact surfaces at various points in the work, sometimes as a device that drives the plot and determines

the movements of the characters. Jeronymo's (and Clementina's) ill
health motivates Sir Charles's voyage to Italy halfway through the novel,
for example, and it causes Jeronymo himself, at the novel's end, to
remain in England, apart from his family, to try as a cure the English
baths. A more clear case of medical thinking exerting an influence on the
structure of Richardson's work is found in *Clarissa*, which could reasonably be described as an illness narrative, or, more precisely, as a morally
inflected narrative that tracks its protagonist's progress from health to
illness and finally to death. In adopting this trajectory, Richardson was
following the medical wisdom of his day, which accepted the redemp-
tive and spiritual elements of illness, healing, and death, even as these
processes were becoming increasingly secularised. Commenting upon
the proof-sheets of *Pamela in her Exalted Condition*, Cheyne suggested
that the narrative activity around 'a broken Leg, a disjointed Limb', or
'a dangerous Fever' could inspire 'religious and beautiful Sentiments',
and observed that death or an 'Epidemical Distemper' had the possibility of 'beget[ing] Attention in the Reader and call[ing] for Instruction'
(24 August 1741). Richardson resisted some of Cheyne's advice, but he
seems to have agreed with the doctor on the moral potential of literary
depictions of medical states.

In the sequel to *Pamela* and (to a lesser extent) in *Sir Charles Grandison*,
the moral import and the action are determined by experiences of preg-
nancy, childbirth, and the rearing of children. Indeed, these novels interrogate the construct of the female domestic ideal that was, by the 1740s,
becoming prevalent in medical literature. Pamela experiences not only the
blissful anticipation of motherhood while pregnant with her first child
but also protracted apprehension. She contemplates death by childbirth,
and calls herself a 'sad Coward' with a 'thousand Anxieties' (*PE*, p. 279).
The novel also takes up a heated debate on the value of breastfeeding – a
practice that William Cadogan would celebrate in his *Essay upon Nursing*
(1748) as 'best for every Child, and every Mother'.[4] In conversations with
Pamela, Mr B presents a commonplace but increasingly obsolete resistance to breastfeeding, especially when practised by women of the middle
and upper classes. He sees it as an 'Office beneath my *Pamela*' that risks
creating a situation in which a 'Son and Heir' could become a 'Rival' in
his wife's 'Affections' (*PE*, p. 312). Pamela, in contrast, views it as a '*natural*' and '*Divine* Duty' that provides significant immunological benefits,
and refers to it as 'the Custom, of old, of all the good Wives we read
of in Scripture' (*PE*, pp. 309–10). By the early 1750s, when *Sir Charles
Grandison* appeared, breastfeeding had been more fully embraced. One of

its male characters, Lord G, displays an attitude towards the practice that is similar to Pamela's and in pointed contrast to Mr B's. When he intrudes upon his wife Charlotte nursing her child, he is not horrified, as Charlotte had expected he would be, but rather transported into a state of 'rapture'. 'Never, never, never, saw I so delightful a sight!' he exclaims (*SCG*, VII.xliii.211). As these examples make clear, the fluctuating approaches to breastfeeding that appear in Richardson's fictions reflect the changing medical views of his day, and at the same time determine the narrative and moral trajectories of his novels.

Richardson's medical positions are sometimes as bold as they are nuanced, and this is certainly true of his treatment of the relationship between nervous affliction and gender. Though it was acknowledged by Cheyne and others that outside forces could incite nervous illness, older understandings lingered, and there remained a tendency to insist that women had inherently weak nerves and pliable constitutions that made them more susceptible to nervous conditions. Richardson provides many examples of female characters who experience nervous attacks, but they usually have good reasons for doing so that are unconnected to a naturally disordered constitution. Most notably, of course, both Pamela and Clarissa suffer explicitly from the mistreatment they experience at the hands of predatory men. Mr B's treatment of Pamela forces her to 'bewail [her] miserable hard Fate' (*P*, p. 91), suffer from 'Grief and Confusion' (p. 157), fall into fits (pp. 29, 59), and at one point contemplate suicide by throwing herself into a pond (p. 158). The circumstantial nature of her illness is made clear as she undergoes a complete and sudden recovery when released from her confinement and Mr B proves himself honourable (Richardson in this instance does draw on the very conventional notion that marriage effectively cured female hysteria). Because Clarissa is raped and her moral integrity remains forever doubtful, she, unlike Pamela, never fully recovers, but her suffering, something like Pamela's, is tied to social forces. Almost immediately following her rape, she descends into what appears to be outright madness, grows 'worse and worse in [her] head; now stupid, now raving, now senseless', and falls into 'fits upon fits' (*C*, VI.xxi.73). She recovers her senses, and her ensuing 'grief' is posited by both Clarissa and her doctors as the main cause of her nervous decline. In contrast to Clarissa, the male rogue Lovelace suffers from the kind of nervous disorder most often associated with women: his malady is imbued with mystery; it is caused in part by excessive passion, and it brings with it perversely sexualised manifestations. Following Clarissa's death, Lovelace describes his brain as 'all boiling like a caldron over a fiery furnace' (*C*, vii.lxxvi.254). Belford calls his friend a 'mad fellow' who wishes, shockingly, to have Clarissa 'opened and embalmed' (*C*, vii.lxxv.249).

Samuel Richardson's literary engagement with medical discourse, perhaps more than anything, reflects an embrace of uncertainty – or, more precisely, a rejection of certainty. His novels sometimes take up medical ideas in ways that reinforce the accepted medical wisdom of the day and thus prove wrong George Cheyne's assertion that he knew 'little of the Affair' of nervous disorders – or of many other medical conditions, for that matter. Richardson's respect for the medical profession is made clear in his correspondence with Cheyne and in his efforts to render the most current mechanical views of the body in narrative form. But Richardson also rewrites commonplace medical wisdom in his fiction, and in doing so questions definitive and sometimes limited understandings of illness. He seems to have recognised the value of a literary interrogation of medicine and the ways that fiction can be used to challenge medical practices that appear either counterintuitive or inhumane. Richardson's mistrust of the certainty inherent in some physicians' theories and practices led him to present a remarkably nuanced and ethical model of medicine. Even a figure as unsavoury and despicable as Mrs Sinclair, Richardson seems to suggest, should not be treated without compassion. Her surgeons want to amputate her leg – to have her 'lanced and quartered', Belford remarks disgustedly – just so that 'it might be a satisfaction to the patient's friends' that 'all was done that could be done' (*C*, vii. lxxviii.263). These men, as they '[run] over their terms of art', Belford writes, prove that 'all their science has penetrated their heads no farther than their mouths' (*C*, vii.lxxviii.262). Richardson the novelist rejected the cavalier strain of the new science as it sometimes manifested itself in eighteenth-century medical culture. In his work, science, and in particular medical science, is respected and challenged, and it is sometimes even harnessed to tell a good story.

Notes

1 George Cheyne, *The English Malady; or; A Treatise of Nervous Conditions of All Kinds* (London, 1733), p. 4.
2 George Rousseau, 'Nerves, Spirits, and Fibres: Towards Defining the Origins of Sensibility (1975)', in *Nervous Acts: Essays on Literature Culture and Sensibility* (Palgrave Macmillan, 2004), pp. 157–84 (p. 174).
3 Cheyne, *English Malady*, pp. 3–4. Marie E. McAllister has identified venereal disease references in the deathbed scenes of Sinclair and Belton, and suggests

that though this illness is rarely mentioned explicitly in *Clarissa*, its spectre looms large. See Marie E. McAllister, 'Pox Imagery in *Clarissa*', *The Eighteenth Century Novel*, 9 (2012), 1–24.

4 William Cadogan, *An Essay upon Nursing, and the Management of Children, from Their Birth to Three Years Age* (London, 1748), p. 14. In addition to the medical and moral significance discussed here, see Howard D. Weinbrot, below (pp. 312–13), for a political reading of the breastfeeding debate in *Pamela*.

CHAPTER 31

Death and Mourning Culture

Peter Walmsley

At Mrs Moore's in Hampstead, where he has hunted Clarissa down, Lovelace dips into a devotional tract, Jeremy Taylor's *Holy Living and Holy Dying* (1650–1), about which he makes this jaunty observation to Clarissa: 'This old divine affects, I see, a mighty flowery style upon a very solemn subject. But it puts me in mind of an ordinary country funeral, where the young women, in honour of a defunct companion, especially if she were a virgin, or *passed for such*, make a flower-bed of her coffin' (*C*, VI.xx.58). Lovelace's performance is far from convincing: he focuses on Taylor's fervent style to distract from the book's advice on sober living. Worse still, more than a little manic at the prospect of drugging and raping Clarissa that night, he reveals his fantasy of having Clarissa 'in a manner dead' (*C*, VII.lxxxvi.298). This small scene resonates outwards, evoking the novel's proto-Gothic entanglement of marriage and death: Lovelace unwittingly foreshadows Clarissa's own coffin with its load of flowers,[1] a coffin by which she asserts that despite the rape her spirit remains inviolate and that she is Christ's bride, not Lovelace's. While *Clarissa*'s domestic tragedy is a particularly focused and intricate meditation on death, all Richardson's writings reflect on the social, material, and spiritual ramifications of the end of life.

A Good Death

Taylor's *Holy Living* was one of a host of works of practical divinity that strove to teach how to live with death in view. The English Church's break from Rome in the sixteenth century entailed a considerable disruption of practices surrounding death. Purgatory was dismissed as extra-biblical, and with it went masses for the dead and prayers to the dead to intercede on behalf of the living, effectively banning a tradition of imaginative communion between earth and heaven. Death now entailed an immediate translation to eternal bliss or eternal damnation, but where theologians argued for an absolute divide between the earthly and eternal realms, popular imagination preferred a more porous border. The English retained a sense that the dead had a lively interest in the affairs of the living. Joseph Addison, inspired by *Paradise Lost*, proposes that 'all the Regions of Nature swarm with Spirits; and that we have Multitudes of Spectators on all our Actions'.[2]

Devotional writers urged their readers to understand death not as the moment of the separation of the soul and body, but as the ongoing condition of life from birth. Adam's first sin brought death into the world, and ever since we have had to live in 'a state of change and affliction'.[3] A place in heaven could not be earned, but was seen as a gift of Christ's loving intercession. Still, God expects each of us to live a holy life, which entails what William Law called 'a regular course of piety', including diligent Bible reading, heartfelt prayer, and attentive church-going.[4] The capstone to a good life was a good death, in which the dying departed this world in a display of faith. Above all, Christians must repent their sins, a process that ideally involved a habit of self-scrutiny in light of the Ten Commandments, a confession to God of all infractions, and an active programme of restitution and reform. Repentance was seen to be transformative; in Taylor's words it 'lifts up the sinner from the grave to life'.[5] This very potency meant that it was often postponed, a trump card to be played later in the game – most of Defoe's protagonists only consider repenting after lives of swingeing sinfulness. Taylor led a growing chorus of objections to deathbed repentances, arguing that the only way to prove to God that we can cast away sin is by living a reformed life.

Richardson was deeply engaged in debates about dying well. Apart from *Holy Living*, many other devotional tracts are mentioned in *Clarissa*, including Lewis Bayly's *Practice of Piety* (1689) and John Inett's *Guide to the Devout Christian* (1688–92). These pious intertexts urge us to read the novel as a dramatisation of their themes, and certainly Clarissa attains, at some length, a death that is patient, faithful, and even pedagogical, inspiring the many witnesses of her last days to reform. We watch her wean herself from this world: writing a will, forgiving those who have wronged her, and inviting the attendance of clergy. Articulate to the end, she makes good use of the authority granted the dying to offer 'a charming lecture … upon the hazards of a late repentance' (*C*, vii.liv.208), a point on which Richardson clearly sides with Taylor. Clarissa's heroic death is made possible by a life lived with eternity in mind: she rejects both Solmes and Lovelace for the dangers they pose to her moral health and hopes of heaven.

Clarissa's exemplary end is framed by two horrific deathbed scenes: the rake and murderer Tom Belton spends his last days haunted by the spectres of those he has wronged and unable to repent, while the bawd Mrs Sinclair dies 'foaming, raving, roaring', denying the inevitable with her last breath – 'I *will not*, I *cannot* die' (*C*, vii.lxxviii.260). Lovelace's defiant 'LET THIS EXPIATE' is a little more stylish, but just as absurd (*C*, vii. cxiii.415). In this, Richardson shows his interest in the psychology of the sinful. Lovelace and Belford confess that they believe in future rewards and punishments, but have been postponing repentance until incapacity makes their pleasures easier to forgo. Both are, however, studies in the self-deceptions of a sinful life; Lovelace, tellingly, is forever diverting himself from the prospect of death, and Belford concedes that while attendance on his dying uncle 'may have contributed to humanize me' (*C*, v.xxvii.225), it takes several more deathbeds to move him to penitence. Richardson wants us, as fellow witnesses to Clarissa's last hours, to follow Belford's path of introspection, sorrow, and reform.

Wills

If death was a moment for spiritual accounting, it was equally an opportunity for more worldly reckonings, as wealth flowed from one generation to the next. People of all estates made wills, and while they were legally free to devise their estates as they wished, they were constrained by convention – for example, a widow typically had a life's interest in a third of her husband's estate – or by pre-existing legal documents, such as marriage settlements or the wills of previous generations. Gentry capitalism, which sought economies of scale through the consolidation of real estate, gave a new economic incentive to time-honoured practices of primogeniture. Wills, so important to this process, were often perceived as vulnerable instruments: executors could be incompetent and heirs dissatisfied. Testators often included clauses encouraging peace among beneficiaries, and even disinheriting any who chose to litigate.

Eighteenth-century readers and novelists alike had a strong interest in how inheritances could effect surprising revolutions in a character's earthly prospects. Richardson's imaginative exploration of gentry capitalism from below is critical of that class's obsessions with land accumulation and the concentration of that wealth in a single male heir, often at the expense of siblings and family harmony. Significantly, Sir Charles Grandison freely shares his inheritance with his sisters, who had been cruelly stinted in their father's will. That said, Richardson's drama builds on the tensions between the individual as a bearer of wealth and the family's economic and affective claims on its members, tensions that were just as real for Richardson's own class of established tradesfolk as for the gentry. Part of what makes Richardson's protagonists, like Defoe's, so interesting is that they enjoy considerable wealth and the power that comes with it. But Richardson also warns that inheritances can be ruinous, not just in Clarissa's case, but in Belton's too – an unexpected legacy has derailed his plans to be a clergyman and subsidised a self-indulgence that proves fatal. For the Harlowes in particular, a will is a tool for exerting control over the next generation: that wills can be rewritten (and several do get rewritten) is a continual threat in *Clarissa*.

Wills were typically private documents in Richardson's day; that two actually appear in the text of *Clarissa* is in tune with its gratifying publication of the private. The first, Clarissa's grandfather's will, excites the curiosity of the neighbourhood for its extraordinary disregard for primogeniture, giving a house with substantial land outright to a youngest granddaughter. He clearly realises that such a gift is 'not strictly conformable to law' and will cause umbrage (*C*, 1.iv.29), and, indeed, Clarissa's Dairy-House becomes the Harlowes' obsession. Clarissa's grandfather's main justification is that the family is already vastly rich, and that the three Harlowe sons can compensate in their wills for this loving preference of one granddaughter. Richardson thus sets up a debate within the novel about the economics versus the ethics of inheritance, pitting 'the honour and interest of the family' (*C*, 1.xx.131) against the impulse to reward goodness and to distribute wealth more widely.

This debate is only brought to a close in the novel's final pages, where Clarissa's will, in some ways the climax of the novel, is printed in full. As eighteenth-century wills go, this document too is exceptional, not only because it is written by a young woman, but because it is so elaborate, striving to meet competing demands. On the one hand, Clarissa undoes her grandfather's will, returning her inheritance to the previous generation and rectifying his slights of his sons: the Dairy-House goes to her father, its pictures to uncle John, and its plate to uncle Anthony. On the other hand, like her grandfather she uses her will to express love and gratitude, with substantial bequests for Mrs Norton, Dolly Hervey, Anna Howe, and Hannah Burton. Finally, there is an impressive charity established in her Poor's Fund. Clarissa thus attains a balance between maintaining the material interest and peace of the family, and abetting Providence. If Clarissa's deathbed performance is meant to inspire imitation, so is her will: Richardson is asking us to make wills that do God's work in the world.

Violent Death

Death was understood to be God's province, but despite the sixth commandment the spectacle of people killing people was common enough in eighteenth-century Britain. The popular press reported details of battles abroad and violent crimes and executions at home as never before. Richardson was troubled by these trends, and in his *Familiar Letters* he includes a country gentleman's horrified description of the impiety and tumult that attended an execution at Tyburn (*EW*, p. 505). In his later fiction, however, Richardson comes to focus his reforming energies on two forms of violent death that enter private life: duelling and suicide.

For Lovelace, duelling is a sport almost as beloved as seduction: indeed, he muddles the two in describing his encounters with Clarissa – 'Does she not out-do me at every fair weapon?' (*C*, iii.xvi.100). All men of rank owned swords, and for rakes they were essential daily wear, but swordsmanship was in decline, so many duels in the eighteenth century were fought with pistols. Duelling was condemned from all quarters: Charles II strove to discourage it by proclamation and writers such as Jeremy Collier and Richard Steele laid the groundwork for Richardson's own campaign against the practice. Clarissa's troubles stem in large part from Lovelace's readiness to sort things out at sword point, particularly his humiliating besting of James Harlowe, Jr. Exchanges between men of spirit can too readily descend into insults and challenges, Richardson argues, and he gives an extended example in the jockeying between Lovelace and Colonel Morden in their first meeting, where their touchiness and bluster verge on the comic. Clarissa makes it clear to her brother and her cousin that to challenge Lovelace for his offence to the family would be both 'an usurpation of the Divine prerogative' and 'an insult upon magistracy' (*C*, vii. xciv.347).

Clarissa's reworking of masculinity, imagining herself 'a man of temper' (*C*, ii.x.56), becomes fully fleshed out in the magnanimous Sir Charles Grandison, who coolly declines Sir Hargrave Pollexfen's challenge. Their subsequent meeting lets Grandison show how to defuse a confrontation, by keeping calm, making gestures of friendship, and refusing to draw his sword. In duelling, a man forgets that he does not live for himself alone, a point underscored by Grandison's story of how his mother died from the shock of his father's being seriously wounded in a duel. Richardson redefines honour as self-control: 'the man, who can subdue his passion, and forgive a *real* injury, is an hero' (*SCG*, II.iv.47).

Suicide is the feminine counterpart of duelling in Richardson's fiction: his heroines, under the threat of rape, contemplate self-murder as an expression of their outrage and grief. Like duelling, suicide was a crime in eighteenth-century Britain – suicides could be denied the burial office and have their property confiscated – but often these penalties were circumvented, an expression of the emergent uncertainty about the practice. While suicide was deplored in sermons and devotional texts, Greek and Roman precedents meant that it could not be dismissed, like duelling, as a barbarous custom, and some writers, including John Donne and David Hume, made a case for the right to take one's own life. In *Pamela*, Richardson frames his naïve heroine's suicidal moment as a battle between Satan, who prompts her self-pity, and divine grace, which bids her hope. Pamela reminds herself that despair is a sin, that God would not ask her to suffer more than she can bear, and that if she were to drown herself she would inevitably be damned, since she would have no time to repent the sin. And she thinks, too, of the pain her death would cause her parents (*P*, p. 160). Similarly Clarissa, persecuted by both her family and Lovelace, longs for death, and in several pathetic scenes appears in the role of a modern Lucretia, threatening to stab herself to prove 'that my honour is dearer to me than my life' (*C*, IV.l.296). Like Pamela, she fights against despair and rejects 'so horrid a rashness' as suicide on Christian principle: 'I am His creature, not *my own*' (*C*, II. xxxvi.251).

Mourning

Mourning for lost loved ones was governed by conventions of public display, including set periods for the wearing of black mourning dress (a year for a spouse, six months for a parent). Funerals and monuments served to express a family's attachment to the departed and, sometimes, its affluence and social aspirations. Undertaking had emerged as a profession, supplying the full range of equipment needed for a funeral, including candlesticks, coffins, palls, and hearses. Wills frequently included gifts of money to family and friends to pay for mourning dress, gloves, and rings. Such rings were often valuable, and sometimes held a lock of the deceased's hair in crystal. After the Restoration, the rich might build a neoclassical family monument in the aisle of a parish church, while churchyard gravestones became the norm for the middling sorts.

These developments attracted charges of luxury. Richardson joins the chorus in his revisions to Defoe's *Complete English Tradesman* (1738), calling for sumptuary laws to constrain the 'growing extravagancies' and 'frightful gewgaws of funeral pomp', including dressing the dead in the latest fashions and ordering a hearse even if the church is just two doors away.[6] *Clarissa* offers lessons in balancing social expectations with prudence and piety. In his will, Tom Belton, for example, clearly overspends on mourning rings for his brother rakes, cheating his poor sister, a situation Belford manages to rectify. Clarissa can afford to be more generous, and is, but her funeral arrangements are not extravagant: her indulgences in an ornamented coffin and a funeral sermon are not for material display but to inspire religious reflection.

Attitudes to the emotions of the bereaved were shifting in Richardson's day, changes that can be followed in his writing. His early *Familiar Letters* ends with three sample condolence letters in which Richardson, following the advice in much devotional writing, seeks to moderate mourning. These letters warn against an excessive sorrow, which would seem to question God's dispensation, and encourage the use of 'Reason and Piety … to rebuke the Overflowings of your Grief' (*EW*, p. 523). In *Clarissa*, which appeared six years later, this stoicism takes second place to an expansive sorrow, modelled for us in the manly grief of Colonel Morden and Belford, but also in Anna Howe's heart-wrenching encounter with Clarissa's corpse. Richardson's many correspondents confirmed that they read these scenes through tears. In this light, Lovelace is damned for his incapacity to grieve – he knows only the forms, not the feelings, of bereavement. And in *Grandison* we are invited to weep with Lady L and Charlotte Grandison as they recount the death of their mother (*SCG*, ii.xii).

This extension of emotional range is no doubt partly owing to the literary vogue in works that indulged in a melancholy brooding over the grave: Richardson was friend and printer to Edward Young, author of *Night Thoughts* (1742–5), the most widely celebrated of the many graveyard poems of the moment. This proto-Gothic vein of writing reworks the *memento mori* tradition by giving the affective full rein. In turn *Clarissa*, with its many scenes of death, recounted nightmares, hunted heroine, and pervasive melancholy, is a more obvious precursor to the late-century Gothic fiction of Ann Radcliffe than Horace Walpole's *The Castle of Otranto* (1764) could ever be. Richardson's depiction of death charts the rise of both sentiment and Christian heroism: his deathbed scenes provide affective instruction, nurturing our sympathy and capacity for grief, but they also offer exemplary performances by great souls who can calmly face the journey from this world to the next.

Notes

1 Margaret Anne Doody, *A Natural Passion: A Study in the Novels of Samuel Richardson* (Clarendon Press, 1974), p. 155.
2 Joseph Addison, *The Spectator*, 12, ed. Donald F. Bond, 5 vols. (Clarendon Press, 1965), Vol. I, p. 54.
3 Jeremy Taylor, *Holy Living and Holy Dying*, ed. P. G. Stanwood, 2 vols. (Clarendon Press, 1989), Vol. II, p. 69.
4 William Law, *A Serious Call to a Devout and Holy Life* (London, 1729), p. 45.
5 Taylor, *Holy Living*, Vol. I, p. 245.
6 Daniel Defoe, *The Complete English Tradesman*, 4th edn, 2 vols. (London, 1738), Vol. II, p. 327.

CHAPTER 32

London

Linda Bree

I am in a new World ... and see such vast Piles of Building every-
where, and such a Concourse of People, and hear such a Rattling of
Coaches in the Day, that I hardly know what to make of it.

(*PE*, p. 303)

Pamela B's first impression of London owes quite a lot to her naïveté, but
it is consistent with the recorded opinions of many of those who visited
the capital in the mid-eighteenth century, in expressing bewildered amaze-
ment at the sheer size of an enormous conurbation, the number of people,
and the general noise and hubbub. London offered life on a scale quite
different from anything anyone could experience elsewhere in Britain. The
population of London is estimated to have been about 630,000 in 1715; by
1760 it had increased to nearly 750,000; and these numbers were further
swollen by the many who visited the metropolis when Parliament was sitting and the genteel social season was in full swing, or for seasonal work, or
simply for tourism. The next biggest English city was Bristol with 45,000
inhabitants.

London had been at the heart of national life for centuries: it housed
the court and Parliament, and was the centre of national and international
trade (Figure 32.1). England's road network converged on it: as early as 1705
scheduled stagecoaches linked the capital with 180 towns around the country. The River Thames offered unrivalled opportunities for international
travel and international trade; a growing mercantile and trading middle
class had increasing wealth to dispose of; and both the hard-working and
the idle poor had a range of options to try to make ends meet somehow.
London was the city of streets and parks, coffee-houses and clubs, theatres
and public spectacles, banks and moneylenders, shops and services. There
were unique opportunities to get on in life. There was also little redress
for the victimised or unfortunate; crime was rife, policing primitive, and
penalties brutal.

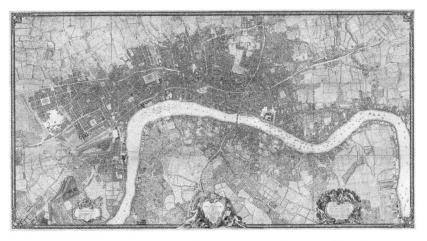

Figure 32.1 John Rocque, *London, Westminster and Southwark* (1746).

One of the reasons for the very wide range of people and activities in London was that in fact the 'metropolis' consisted of two cities. The City of London was the financial and mercantile centre: the Stock Exchange regulated the national finances; the docks offered facilities for the import and export of goods; administrative, industrial, and an ever-growing range of service activities were conducted out of overcrowded houses in the city's narrow streets. The City of Westminster – frequently called the West End since it was situated due west of the commercial city – accommodated the court (when it was in London) and Parliament; and they in turn attracted wealthy aristocrats and gentry who owned or rented London houses for the winter months when they were in residence for the parliamentary and social season. The West End and the City complemented each other, but there was a level of mutual antagonism too between the wealthy and leisured, whose income traditionally derived from the land, and those whose industrious endeavours were bringing a new kind of prosperity to the nation, no longer dependent on rural structures and traditions.

Samuel Richardson was very definitely a man of the City, although like many other City dwellers he was born elsewhere – in his case in the Derbyshire countryside 130 miles northwest of the capital. His father brought the family to London when Samuel was still a small child; by 1720 Samuel had embarked on his printing career and for the next forty years he carried on his business from various houses in and around Salisbury Court, between Fleet Street and the River Thames. These premises were very close to Temple Bar, the impressive structure that dominated the conjunction of Fleet Street and the Strand, the traditional dividing line between the City and the West End. But Richardson was never in any doubt as to which side of the Bar was home. He participated in City structures through his longstanding membership in the Company of Stationers, culminating in a term as Master of the Company in the mid-1750s. Moreover, he was active in the charitable activities that in the absence of effective state or parish assistance were essential to the survival of the most unfortunate in society: in 1754 he was elected as a governor of the Foundling Hospital founded a decade earlier by Thomas Coram, and later in the decade he contributed to the newly established Magdalen House for repentant 'fallen women'.

There was no doubt in Richardson's mind, either, about where he stood in the traditional antagonism between the two parts of the metropolis, the one devoted to business and the other – as he saw it – to leisure. Richardson's early published writings include strong criticism of the theatres – one of the main sources of leisure activity in London, with widespread appeal across the social divide – for distracting working men from their business: he argued that 'the Stage may be a tolerable Diversion to such as know not how to pass their Time', and pointed out that the very times of the performances were fixed to suit the leisured rather than the working day, while many modern plays were so far from sympathy with men of business that 'such persons are generally made the Dupes and Fools of the Hero of it' (*EW*, pp. 19, 20). Even much later in his career, when he had many acquaintances among the leisured elite, he wrote bitterly that 'upper life is low enough to despise the metropolis, which furnishes them with all their beloved luxury' (Richardson to Anne Dewes, 21 June 1752); and he commented that there was a bar between him and one of his genteel female acquaintances: 'Temple-bar – ladies who live near Hill-street, and Berkeley and Grosvenor squares, love not to pass this bar' (Richardson to Mary Delany, 14 March 1753).

Richardson was not very fond of exercise, but like many of those who lived in London he knew its topography intimately from walking its streets. He walked to business and social appointments, and he walked between five and six miles at the beginning and end of most weekends to reach his country villa in what is now Fulham. His path would have taken him through Temple Bar into the West End, along the Strand and through the parks and into the country, probably through the Knightsbridge turnpike, which features in Sir Hargrave Pollexfen's abduction of Harriet

Byron. Unsurprisingly in this context, his use of London in his fictions is detailed and precise, contributing significantly, in particular, to the air of realism that underpins the highly dramatic power of Clarissa's story. When Lovelace has Clarissa arrested outside St Paul's Church in Covent Garden 'at the door fronting Bedford-street' the desperate helplessness of her position is emphasised by the fact that all potential routes for escape – 'the three passages, to wit, that leading to Henrietta-street, that to King-street, and the fore-right one to Bedford-street' – are closed to her (*C*, vi.xl.137–8; see also Figure 25.1, above). Later, when Lovelace is desperate to hear news of Clarissa's last days he worries about missing the messenger 'as he might take either the Acton or the Hammersmith road; or … he might come thro' the Park or not'; his frantic riding 'backwards and forwards from the palace to the Gore' reflects a dilemma of real-life topography (*C*, vii. xliv.175).

In 1738 Richardson oversaw and printed the second edition of Daniel Defoe's *Tour thro' the Whole Island of Great Britain* including the wide-ranging and detailed description of London that occupied much of Volume ii, and that – unlike other parts of the *Tour* – was extensively recast for the new edition.[1] Defoe had died in 1731. As Pat Rogers has argued above (pp. 133–4), it is highly likely that Richardson was an active editor of the work, and it is reasonable therefore to regard the changes made for the new edition as reflecting Richardson's own knowledge and interests. Many minor adjustments provide more accurate information or offer a different opinion about London's topography, buildings, institutions, and social life: 'beautifying' City streets after the Great Fire is adjusted to 'widening'; 'Coffee, Tea, and Chocolate' are added to the concerns of the Excise Office; the Bridewell at Clerkenwell is 'adjoining to' rather than 'called' New Prison.[2] Notably, after an overall account of the size and scope of the twin Cities of London and Westminster that is carried forward more or less unchanged from the first edition, the rest of the section is completely restructured: where Defoe's descriptions are straightforwardly based on location ('Of the *Tower* and its Hamlets' … 'Of the Buildings on *Southwark* side'), the second edition takes a more thematic and social approach, so that the narrative clusters around descriptions not only of markets and shipping but also of hospitals, churches, schools, and libraries. (Occasionally the editor of the second edition is actively indignant with Defoe on these grounds: 'What induc'd our Author to assert … That it was scarce worth while to give an Account of the STATUES in this City; for that they were neither many, nor very valuable; we cannot say; but the following brief Account of them will shew how much he was mistaken.')[3]

Richardson may have felt obliged to include information on the homes of the aristocracy and gentry because Defoe had deliberately omitted to do so ('I design a particular Account of all the Houses of the Nobility and Men of Quality ... in a Work by itself', he had written⁴). However, the inclusion of detailed descriptions of the residential squares of the West End and the charitable foundations being set up there, together with a substantial new section on churches, cumulatively tilt the account of London away from Defoe's original conception about the nature of the metropolis and the relationship between its two parts: indeed, Defoe's statement that if the City and the West End were to come into conflict the City would win is omitted completely in the second edition. Defoe argues that if the stockjobbers' activities can be stopped and trade brought under good regulation then he expects that people will stop crowding to London in large numbers for the purposes of financial investment, and 'the vast Concourse of People to *London*, will separate again and disperse as naturally, as they have now crouded hither';⁵ the second edition editor on the other hand clearly sees London's expansion as likely to continue into the foreseeable future: citing 'a wise Act of Parliament against Stock-jobbing', the narrative envisages instead that once men's minds are 'cured' from the fever of financial gaming they will again turn 'to promote the Arts of Navigation and Commerce, the very Soul and Vitals of this mercantile Island'.⁶

That 'wise Act of Parliament' was passed in 1733 and it is one of many instances that draw attention to just how much had been changing in London in the fifteen years between the first and second editions. Occasionally the two editors almost seem in dialogue about the capital city they both knew so well, as when Defoe comments on the Royal Mews that 'I do not wonder that they talk of pulling it down, contracting the Stables into less Room, and building a Square of good Houses there', and the second edition reports that the work has now begun: 'The principal Range at the upper End is already finish'd; and when the other Parts are completed, it will be one of the finest Things of its kind in *Europe*.'⁷ It is striking just how much building was going on in the metropolis, not only the new squares and houses, but the effects of Parliament's decision to build fifty new churches, many of them described in 1738 in glowing terms: 'a noble Pile of Building', 'a very beautiful Structure', 'a most beautiful Performance in all its Parts'.⁸ The overall impression of the London section of the 1738 *Tour* is of a metropolis immersed in rebuilding and expanding to satisfy the requirements of a growing nation in which the West End and the City are playing their interdependent parts.

It was shortly after his work on the *Tour* that Richardson published his first fictional narratives, and it is unsurprising that he included in *Familiar Letters*, among 'Letters Written to and for Particular Friends', a sequence of eleven letters in which a young woman describes her experience of visiting 'this great Town' of London (*EW*, p. 485). Her letters record her impressions of many of the sites familiar from tourist accounts of the period as well as from the *Tour*, from prominent buildings in the City – the Tower of London, St Paul's Cathedral, markets, and hospitals – to the great houses of the West End, where she finds the grand new squares and streets 'a Sight worthy of Admiration' (*EW*, p. 487). She comments on the city's open spaces, from Greenwich Park in the east to Hyde Park in the west, and she takes in both the theatres (where she is disturbed by the low morality on show both on the stage and in the audience) and the pleasure ground of Vauxhall, 'whither every body must go, or appear a sort of Monster in polite Company', despite the expense involved (*EW*, p. 492).

The young woman's concerns about the questionable morality and high cost of leisure activities in the great city, like her discomfort with public viewings of the insane inmates of the Bedlam hospital, are mild enough within an overall context of touristic impressions. Two other letters in the collection express more serious concerns about aspects of London. One is a letter from a gentleman disturbed at the regular public hangings that take place at Tyburn. The other is a letter whose narrative is neatly summarised in its title: 'A young Woman in Town to her Sister in the Country, recounting her narrow Escape from a Snare laid for her on her first Arrival, by a wicked Procuress', and whose verisimilitude is vouched for in a note at the end of the letter, confirming that 'This shocking Story is taken from the Mouth of the young Woman herself … and is Fact in every Circumstance' (*EW*, pp. 390–3).

When Richardson turns to writing full-length fictions it is this power of London to deceive and ensnare that he chooses to invoke. Although all three of his heroines are country girls who find themselves in London at an important point in their stories, there is in fact very little of 'tourist London' in his fictions. Pamela declares to her main correspondent, Lady Davers, that she need not write about London places and activities because Lady Davers already knows about them. Harriet, whose journey to London is the starting-point for the narrative of *Sir Charles Grandison*, promises 'a description of the persons and characters of the people I am likely to be conversant with in the London World' and writes that she is to be taken to 'a Masquerade, to a Ridotto: when the season comes, to

Ranelagh and Vauxhall: In the meantime to Balls, Routs, Drums and so-forth' (i.v.17, 23), but her abduction from the first of these entertainments intervenes and thereafter she avoids public diversions.

Clarissa's arrival in London is of a very different nature from the outset. The early letters from Harlowe Place figure London as a distant location, the offstage scene of Lovelace's rather generalised reported debaucheries, and the source of wedding clothes for Clarissa's projected union with Solmes. But as the situation between Clarissa and Lovelace becomes more fraught, London grows in prominence as offering a desir-able way out of the impasse in which Clarissa finds herself. Anna Howe advises Clarissa to get to London, and despite reservations – 'what might not my youth, my sex, an unacquaintedness with the ways of that great, wicked town, expose me to?' (C, ii.xxxv.240) – Clarissa is gradually per-suaded of the rightness of the advice. But ironically the very reasons for London's appeal to Clarissa and Anna – 'London, I am told, is the best hiding-place in the world' (ii.xxxiv.232) – are the same as those motivat-ing Lovelace in his determination to get Clarissa there. Clarissa interprets this metropolitan 'hiding-place' as enabling her to be 'independent ... and at liberty' (ii.xxxv.239) and Anna assumes that there, 'in the centre, you'll be in the way of hearing from every-body, and sending to any-body' (iii.xxxiv.180). Lovelace sees things very differently. For him – a man who knows London well; is at home in its social and public spaces; and can navigate its streets, squares, parks, alleys, and churches – the capital provides the conditions in which he can carry out his plan of deception on a large scale.

In a variant of the miserable situation in which Richardson's earlier 'young lady' found herself, Clarissa is deceived into thinking that the brothel to which she has been taken is a respectable lodging house. In an ironic inversion of Anna's assumptions, since Clarissa has been deceived about the street address of the house, she is ignorant about where she is, and at Lovelace's mercy about whom she can communicate with. All this treachery occurs at the heart of the genteel West End. When Clarissa escapes for the first time she goes north out of London's clutches to Hampstead; and when – after the rape changes everything – she no longer attempts to leave London, having been tainted by its corruption, she establishes her independence in Covent Garden, a liminal space between the West End and the City, in lodgings owned by a tradesman of modest means. Even in his fictions Richardson's sympathies are with the City rather than with the West End. Though Clarissa is buried back at Harlowe Place her coffin is ordered from Fleet Street.

Notes

1 See Daniel Defoe, *Tour thro' the Whole Island of Great Britain*, Vol. II, pp. 94–192 in the first edition (1724–6), pp. 73–190 in the second edition (1738).

2 Defoe, *Tour* (1724–6), Vol. II, pp. 112, 135, and 180; (1738), Vol. II, pp. 88, 95, and 119.

3 Defoe, *Tour* (1738), Vol. II, p. 161.

4 Defoe, *Tour* (1724), Vol. II, p. 178.

5 *Ibid.*, p. 130.

6 Defoe, *Tour* (1738), Vol. II, p. 106.

7 Defoe, *Tour* (1724), Vol. II, pp. 176–7; (1738), Vol. II, p. 109.

8 Defoe, *Tour* (1738), Vol. II, pp. 141–3.

CHAPTER 33

Sentiment and Sensibility

Katherine Binhammer

Samuel Richardson was both innovator and chronicler of the language of feeling in the second half of the eighteenth century, a language in which 'sentiment' and 'sensibility' form two sides of the 'sentimental' coin. 'Sentiment' registers a reflective mental feeling or moral sense, a thought derived from an emotional perception, whereas 'sensibility' signifies a physical responsiveness to 'exquisite' or 'acute' feeling and originates in the body, particularly its nerves and sensible organs. Richardson harnessed the full symbolic range of sentimental discourse to develop a new narrative form that represented these internal affective states; his fiction is the first in the genre of 'the sentimental novel'. Lady Bradshaigh illustrates Richardson's import as originator of, and authority on, the language of the heart in a letter that the *OED* cites as the earliest example of the term 'sentimental': 'Pray, Sir, give me leave to ask you … what, in your opinion, is the meaning of the word *sentimental,* so much in vogue amongst the polite?' (<Early November?> 1749). Boswell famously cites Samuel Johnson as preferring Richardson to Fielding with the observation that 'there is more knowledge of the heart in one letter of Richardson's, than in all *Tom Jones*'.[1]

The eighteenth century conferred great weight upon, and took considerable interest in, the new 'knowledge of the heart' (Thomas Edwards to Richardson, 29 January 1749). As a number of chapters in this volume demonstrate, investigations into the world of feeling, the passions, and moral sense were taken up across a range of subjects and methodologies, from moral philosophy to medical treatises to conduct books and, perhaps most significantly, within literature. When Johnson remarks of *Clarissa* that it is 'the first book in the world for the knowledge it displays of the human heart', he presumes that fiction is the genre best suited to revealing the heart's truths.[2] This assumption is largely a product of Richardson's innovative epistolary form; his focus on moral sentiments, especially virtue;

and his ability to capture spontaneous emotions in writing. Because sentiment and sensibility are ubiquitous terms both in Richardson's writings and within the general cultural context, they are best understood as elements of the same organism rather than as discrete and separate attributes. Below I trace three components of sentimental alchemy – moral sense, the human sensorium, and social virtue – to illustrate how Richardson's literary imagination participates in and develops the period's emotional chemistry.

Moral Sense: *Pamela* and Virtue in Distress

Informed by the empirical and materialist philosophies of the seventeenth century, moral philosophers in the early eighteenth proposed that humans have a sixth sense, a 'moral sense', that produces truth about the good in the same way that visual observation produces truth about the natural world. Attending to what they saw as the inability of Cartesian rationalism to address questions of morality, and vehemently rejecting Hobbes's egoistic nihilism, philosophers such as Anthony Ashley Cooper, third earl of Shaftesbury, and Francis Hutcheson proposed that humans possess an innate understanding of virtue. Shaftesbury's *Characteristicks of Men, Manners, Opinions, Times* (1711) argues that reason alone does not motivate all human actions and that our passions and affections often cause spontaneous acts of virtue: we stop to help the stranger in need, we shed involuntary sympathetic tears at the sight of suffering, we are naturally drawn to beauty. Moral sense theorists have been categorised as optimists in that they believed the sense of right and wrong to be universal among human beings. David Hume and Adam Smith later developed this moral philosophy, focusing on the human capacity for sympathy as the grounds for a universal morality.

Hutcheson and Shaftesbury both spoke of a '*sensus communis*', or a common feeling that bound humanity together; this natural benevolence, while universal, can best be perfected within civilised societies such as Britain through a cultivation of moral sentiments. Through a study of good taste, moral reading, and an appreciation of exemplary conduct one can strengthen and refine one's sentiments. Richardson can be seen as a pedagogue in the field, interested in the moral education of his readership, especially through the use of exemplary characters. This didactic intent informs *A Collection of the Moral and Instructive Sentiments, Maxims, Cautions, and Reflexions, Contained in the Histories*

of Pamela, Clarissa, and Sir Charles Grandison (1755), a book of excerpts
of the important moral sentiments Richardson thought readers should
garner from his novels. Containing headings such as 'passions', 'pity',
and 'prudence', Richardson included short passages that, denuded of any
dramatic effect, read as Christian platitudes. *A Collection* provides an
excellent negative example of why sentimental discourse is liveliest in
narrative form.

What better character to illustrate universal moral virtue than a poor,
uneducated servant girl who is preyed upon by the sinful desires of her
rich master? Pamela's innate sense of what is right and virtuous endures the
extreme trial of Mr B's assaults and financial bribes to emerge untainted
by worldly concerns. Her repeated proclamations that she would rather
die than lose her virtue and that her virtue is worth more than 'all the
Riches of the *Indies*' (*P*, p. 177) are heightened by the divide between her
poverty and Mr B's wealth. Virtue knows no class, the novel insists, and
is not an inborn aristocratic attribute but is universally accessible even to
the lowliest servant girl. In fact, much is made of Pamela's 'innocence' and
'beautiful simplicity' as if the guarantor of her virtue is that it is 'artless'
and spontaneously felt. 'Virtue in Distress' became the defining plot of the
literature of sentiment in part because such a narrative allowed virtue, a
static quality in its moral ideal, to have a story.

Richardson's representation of 'natural' and 'undressed' virtue suc-
ceeds in large part because of his innovative use of the epistolary form.
His 'writing to the moment' stylistically mimics the spontaneous and
virtuous emotions Pamela feels, its immediacy producing the narrative effect of truthful confession. 'I wrote my heart', Pamela attests,
'and that is not deceitful' (*P*, p. 213). The heart in *Pamela*, as in all
Richardson's novels, speaks a truth that reason and philosophy cannot.
In the quest to capture the heart in motion, Richardson sought to elimi-
nate the space between experience and representation, life and writing,
internalised emotion and externalised text, an ontological experiment
doomed to fail but fascinating nonetheless for its desire to represent
interiorised subjectivity. Significantly, one of the most common modes
for representing the spontaneous affective life of characters was the rhetorical device of *occupatio*, or expressing one's emotions by stating that
'words cannot express' them. In *Pamela*, the heroine frequently faints,
sighs, and is rendered speechless as a way to demonstrate the intensity
of her feelings. The body within sentimental culture is imbued with an
expressive language such that blushing cheeks and throbbing breasts are
synecdoches for inner feelings.

The Human Sensorium: *Clarissa* and the Body of Sensibility

The language of sensibility framed the body's responsiveness as central to a person's capacity for 'fine feeling', with tears, throbs, and blushes demonstrating a 'delicate', 'acute', and 'exquisite' sensibility. Medical discourse sought a physiological basis for sensibility in the nervous system, literalising the language of the heart by connecting the body's organs with affective states. Influenced by seventeenth-century vitalism that understood living bodies as containing a vital 'spirit' or 'soul', and partly rooted in John Locke's sensationalist understanding of the self, medical treatises proposed a model of the human body as a sensorium in which the mind was not a separate organ but part of a larger network of nervous fluids and sensible tissues. Sensibility's association with intensified feeling and extreme bodily expressivity meant that it often veered into the territory of nervous disorders. This explains why medical treatises define the physiological nature of 'exquisite sensibility' through the symptomology of nervous diseases, readable in the titles of George Cheyne's *The English Malady; or, A Treatise of Nervous Diseases of All Kinds, as Spleen, Vapours, Lowness of Spirits, Hypochondriacal and Hysterical Distempers* (1733) and Robert Wyatt's *Observations on the Nature, Causes, and Cure of Those Disorders which are Commonly Called Nervous, Hypochondriac or Hysteric* (1768).

Dr Cheyne's medical writings were so popular that Samuel Richardson sought his professional advice, and the correspondence that followed blossomed into a lifelong friendship.[3] Both suffered from nervous disorders, and though the cause of Richardson's was possibly Parkinson's disease, Cheyne diagnosed himself in *The English Malady* as suffering from a melancholia that could be healed through diet and a bodily regime of moderation – one that he prescribed, unsuccessfully, to Richardson. Both Cheyne and Richardson, though in different discursive modes, developed a lexicon for describing the diseases of the heart, its palpitations, seizures, and enervations. In *Clarissa*, Richardson performs a literary heart surgery, opening up the organ for endless interpretations and staging a battle over 'knowledge of the heart' that Clarissa wins but at the cost of her life. Clarissa's moral and emotional response to the rape is written on her body as she slowly and painfully, yet exquisitely and soulfully, wastes away from a broken heart. As her 'Mad Papers' written in the rape's immediate aftermath attest, death becomes the panacea and friend to a sensitive body violated by the cruelty of an unfeeling world.

The sheer amount of space devoted to the description of Clarissa's wasting body (roughly one third of the text, between the rape and her death) is indicative of how sentimental discourse thrives in representing the suffering body, since such description allows for the delights of sympathetic identification, the pleasures of weeping for another's pain. There is a certain sadomasochism in sensibility's evocation of pitiful scenes of suffering, one that became a source of discomfort in the later eighteenth century, but in Richardson's moment the pathos was still fresh. *Clarissa* stages scenes that model the appropriate response to suffering in that the correspondents repeatedly sigh and weep over letters. Not only are the letters within the novel drenched in tears (Clarissa notes that her Mad Papers are 'blistered with … tears … which has made … [the] ink run here and there' (v.xxx.244)), but the novel itself provoked countless weeping feasts among its readers, a response in which Richardson seems to have taken great – if not sadistic – delight. 'I have shed a pint of tears', Lady Bradshaigh wrote to Richardson, 'and my heart is still bursting' (Lady Bradshaigh to Richardson, 6–11 January 1749). When he later teased her that he might kill off Sir Charles Grandison, Lady Bradshaigh replied 'You *love* to make one cry, you *love* to *kill* people' (Lady Bradshaigh to Richardson, 22 February 1754). What is true of Richardson's novels was also true of the larger cultural movement of sensibility: it lingered over distress in ways that potentially verged on the sensationalistic and pornographic.

Social Virtue: *Sir Charles Grandison* and the Good Man

In addition to moral philosophy and medical discourse, sentimentalism's genealogy branches into what is generally referred to as the bourgeois revolution, which included such major economic and social shifts as the rise of commercial capitalism, global trade, the explosion of print culture, the increase in the number of gentry or 'middling sort', the rise of consumer culture, and the emergence of a gendered domesticity. These large historical shifts brought on a crisis of moral and social value. Once wealth is displaced from land to capital, aristocratic birth no longer anchors concepts of virtue and, if blood and rank do not organise social relations, if strangers circulate anonymously within the new urban public sphere, on what basis are affective attachments formed? Sentimental culture with its meritocracy of feeling came to replace blood and tradition as providing a new way of calculating moral worth and of imagining social bonds. It promoted fellow feeling, polite manners, and good taste as the way to discriminate between friends and enemies, between good and bad people. In Richardson's friend Sarah Fielding's novel *The Adventures of David Simple*

(1744), the line between good and bad is easy to discern as it is drawn with money: those who value financial gain are morally bad characters, whereas those who sacrifice their finances in charity, such as David, are good men of feeling.[4] Charity became the marker of moral worth.

The man of feeling must illustrate his virtue not only by stopping on the street to hear the beggar's story and to drop a coin and a tear, but through large-scale philanthropic and humanitarian acts. Sentimental culture informs the late-eighteenth-century birth of the charitable organisation and the benevolent institution founded to help the sick, the poor, the orphaned, and the wayward: the Foundling Hospital for abandoned children, the Magdalen Hospital for the relief of penitent prostitutes, and the Lock Hospital for the treatment of venereal disease are examples of such institutions. The Society for the Discharge and Relief of Persons Imprisoned for Small Debts and the Marine Society were two of the many organisations founded to address the problems of crime and poverty. Sentimentalism's humanitarian impulse is evident in a wide range of social movements, from anti-slavery and abolition to animal rights and early feminist discourse.

Sensibility, with its sophisticated language of feeling, was most often explored in fiction through feminine subjects; in *Sir Charles Grandison*, Richardson develops the narrative range of the form by exploring what true sentiment looks like in a masculine subject eighteen years before Henry Mackenzie's *Man of Feeling* (1771). Charity and reform take centre stage when masculinity steers the representation of sentiment. Grandison is widely described both within the novel and by readers as a 'Good Man', and his goodness is visible through his benevolent acts; in fact, the novel as a whole stands as an allegory for the sentimental reform of aristocratic court culture in that Sir Charles inherits an estate corrupted by his libertine father who has squandered money on luxury and mistresses. Sir Charles puts the estate's accounts in order by spending money on the deserving poor, widows, and poor relations. His objects of charity include his father's mistress, Mrs Oldham, on whom he settles a small annuity even though other family members believe her immorality requires her disinheritance. Sir Charles shows pity, an important quality for the new man of feeling. Following the same theme of sympathy for fallen women, Richardson comes out as an early supporter of the Magdalen movement when he has Sir Charles describe his scheme for a 'Hospital for Female Penitents', a respite 'for such unhappy women, as having been once drawn in, and betrayed by the perfidy of men, find themselves, by the cruelty of the world, and principally by that of their own Sex, unable to recover the path of virtue' (*SGC*, IV.xviii.142). To the man of feeling, the world is full of penitents and victims in need of reform.

The double signification of a 'Good Man' in the period – meaning both a morally upright man and a man who was 'good' for his debts, or a wealthy man – introduces a certain paradox into sentimental discourse in that the man of feeling was assumed to possess enough wealth that he could prove his goodness by giving it away. Robert Markley has called this 'the paradoxical impasse of sentimental morality', for when money remains the medium of exchange, 'the more you give, the more virtuous you become, although your actions leave you with less and therefore limit your capacity to keep on demonstrating your virtue'.[5] The economics of charity also has the paradoxical effect of disproving the sentimental precept, stated by Sir Charles, that 'Riches never made men happy' (V. xvii.98). The novel repeatedly proves otherwise, since Sir Charles spends most of his time buying happiness for other people. Over and over again, he confronts people in need without expectation of fortune and surprises them with gifts of money. Money, given away, becomes the mechanism through which Sir Charles's goodness is valued, which prompts the question of whether we can recognise the purity of moral sentiments outside the world of commerce.

The alchemy of sentiment and sensibility ultimately includes much magical thinking: it proposes that the truthfulness of the heart is readable through spontaneous emotional and physical responses, yet it believes feelings can be taught and refined; it asserts that virtue knows no class, and yet bourgeois polite manners and good taste mark its presence; it declares that words cannot express feeling, yet its communicative medium is linguistic; it rejects financial modes of value as it exchanges money for morality. Richardson's brilliance may be that he discovered the perfect balance of ingredients in his sentimental narrative concoctions of throbs and thoughts, tears and metaphors, hearts and words to produce a groundbreaking emotional mimeticism in his readers who, if their reports are to be believed, throbbed, cried, sighed, and fainted alongside Pamela, Clarissa, and Sir Charles.

Notes

1 Boswell, *Life of Johnson*, Vol. II, p. 174.
2 Samuel Johnson, *Johnsonian Miscellanies*, ed. George Birkbeck Hill, 2 vols. (Barnes and Noble, 1966), Vol. II, p. 251.
3 Their correspondence has recently been published in *Correspondence with George Cheyne and Aaron Hill*, eds. David E. Shuttleton and John A. Dussinger,

CECSR, Vol. 11 (2014). See also Heather Meek's account, above (pp. 266–70), of Cheyne's influence on Richardson.

4 Sarah Fielding, *The Adventures of David Simple*, ed. Peter Sabor (University Press of Kentucky, 1998).

5 Robert Markley, 'Sentimentality as Performance: Shaftesbury, Sterne, and the Theatrics of Virtue', in Felicity Nussbaum and Laura Brown (eds.), *The New Eighteenth Century: Theory, Politics, English Literature* (Methuen, 1987), pp. 210–30 (p. 230).

CHAPTER 34

Religion

E. Derek Taylor

In a pre-emptive nod to his twenty-first-century European and North American readers, Samuel Richardson was not a churchgoer as an adult, because, he explained to Lady Bradshaigh in late November of 1749, of a 'nervous malady' that prevented him from participating in large gatherings of any sort. Nevertheless, Richardson maintained professional and personal relationships with clergy (primarily Anglican) throughout his life, and all of his eponymous literary paragons – Pamela, Clarissa, and Sir Charles Grandison – seek out and value their opportunities to worship in public as orthodox members of the Church of England. Indeed, Richardson's father had initially planned on preparing his son for a career in the Church, but business losses made it impossible to supply young Samuel with the requisite education – 'He designed me for the Cloth', Richardson explained to Johannes Stinstra in a rare autobiographical remembrance; 'I was fond of his Choice' (2 June 1753). As evidenced by the legion – and often extended – scriptural references he carefully worked into his fiction, Richardson, like so many in his age, knew his Bible backwards and forwards.[1]

Like John Milton before him, Richardson wrote the great English Christian theodicy of his century. The extraordinarily long and complex *Clarissa; or, The History of a Young Lady*, in fact, is quite consciously patterned on the equally complex, if not quite so long, *Paradise Lost* (1667; 1674). Both the poem and the novel, in their respective ways, attempt to 'justifie the wayes of God to men' (line 26), and each goes out of its way to confront intractable problems faced by faithful Christians without ever quite giving way to easy platitudes (though each contains more than a few). And both authors, to be sure, knew something about intractable problems. By the time *Paradise Lost* was published, Milton had lost not only his eyesight, but two wives, two children, and a defining political struggle. By the time Richardson had finished his first novel, *Pamela; or, Virtue Rewarded*, the well-established printer had lost both his first wife and eight children – 'some of them', he lamented years later to Lady Bradshaigh, 'living to be delightful Pratlers, with all the Appearances of sound Health' (15 December 1748).

Milton was generous enough, from the perspective of modern scholarship, to compose a companion piece, *De Doctrina Christiana*, alongside his grand work of theologically infused poetry to explain his actual religious views; Richardson did no such thing. In a recent account of Richardson's (likely) printing of a document (probably) written by John Wesley (1703–91), founder of the then controversial Methodist movement, John Dussinger notes with restraint Richardson's 'habitual wariness of exposing his religious and political sympathies'.[2] A less measured Dussinger responds somewhat differently to the author's contradictory statements on the nature of Adam and Eve's fall: 'Will the real Samuel Richardson please stand up?'.[3] Such an exasperated question will come as no surprise to anyone familiar with Richardson's reluctance to fit himself conveniently into the boxes we would prefer him to occupy. Consider the following anecdote, as recounted by Murray L. Brown, of Richardson's biographers, T. C. Duncan Eaves and Ben D. Kimpel:

> On one of what must have been many research trips to London, Eaves took an opportunity to visit St Brides, the church where Richardson is interred … During the Blitz St Brides was severely damaged, and Richardson's sarcophagus was disturbed as well – to the point that it sustained extensive damage and was actually cracked open. At least one of these cracks, it seems, was sufficiently large to admit a hand, and not being able to resist the temptation, Eaves actually reached inside the sarcophagus and retrieved a small amount of material. He took up the dust … and placed it in an envelope, which he sent back to Kimpel in the States. An enclosed note read: 'Behold the true Richardson!'[4]

As Eaves and Kimpel clearly knew all too well, we simply do not know with certainty what Richardson believed about much.

If Shakespeare is the ultimate cipher, Richardson is not far behind, and not, as with Shakespeare, for lack of material. Richardson generated thousands of pages of text in the course of his life; this much would be true had he only been a novelist. But before he was a novelist, Richardson had established himself as a major English printer whose output, stretching from the 1720s to the 1760s, we have yet fully to comprehend. Furthermore, alongside his efforts as a printer and a novelist, Richardson developed into an insatiable correspondent; Anna Laetitia Barbauld's initial gathering of this material, the abbreviated *Life and Correspondence of Samuel Richardson* (1804), stretches to six volumes, and the Cambridge edition, in progress, will run to twelve. An abundance of evidence, however, is not the same thing as an abundance of clarity.

Richardson's interest in religious matters emerges early, in anonymous contributions to newspapers and various conduct tracts published in the 1720s, and continues late; at the heart of his final novel, *The History of Sir Charles Grandison*, is a romantic triangle between an avowedly orthodox Anglican hero and the two women he loves: one aggressively Catholic, the other safely Protestant. Before that, the author had first created Pamela Andrews, a servant heroine whose radical claim of equivalence to her aristocratic master rests firmly on theological grounding: 'O Sir!', she exclaims early in the novel, 'my Soul is of equal Importance with the Soul of a Princess; though my Quality is inferior to that of the meanest Slave' (*P*, p. 146). He then wrote *Clarissa*, which many have taken to be his masterpiece, and which the author himself described to Lady Bradshaigh as a 'Religious Novel' (26 October 1748). Clarissa's implacable suffering – abandoned by her cherished family, duped by her ostensible saviour, poisoned, raped, falsely imprisoned – could only be countenanced, contemporary readers understood, by a dramatic turn in the final volume – a *deus ex machina* conclusion that (as in Nahum Tate's 1681 version of *King Lear*), would salvage the happy ending the heroine so richly deserved. At which point Richardson allowed Clarissa slowly, meticulously, excruciatingly, to die – and for reasons, he insisted to Lady Bradshaigh, that have everything to do with 'the Christian System' (15 December 1748). To conclude the novel with his heroine alive, he maintained, would not only postpone the inevitable outcome of what he wished to be a true human story – worse, leaving his 'Heroine short of Heaven' would vitiate the central argument, as he saw it, of his narrative: it logically follows from our shared human mortality that a genuinely happy ending is available *only* to faithful Christians.

Not that Richardson was eager to define precisely what constituted a faithful Christian. Milton went out of his way to court heresy – obliquely in his published essays and poems, directly in his personal credo, always in service to his desire to achieve a fully claimed and conscious faith. Richardson, to the contrary, seems to have found in his fiction space both to explore issues of faith with energetic uncertainty and to avoid saying too much about religious topics around which he otherwise thought it best to tread lightly.

What, for instance, were Richardson's thoughts on the Trinity, that central test of orthodoxy that Milton appears so eagerly to have failed? The word is used only once in the many volumes (of the new Cambridge edition) comprising Richardson's literary output – and as a recited part of a wedding ceremony, at that, and not in his self-described 'Religious

Novel'. When pressed by Lady Bradshaigh in 1753 to read Jonathan Swift's 'A Sermon on the Trinity', Richardson responded with hesitance: 'I have no notion of men's attempting to explain a mystery', he wrote. 'In short, I am afraid of raising doubts in my own mind, which I cannot, from the nature of the subject, lay' (2 June 1753). A similarly indecisive exchange occurred between the author and Sarah Chapone as she sought clarification on his views of the nature of Heaven. 'Do you think we shall know each other in the next Life?', Chapone asked in a letter of 9 December 1751. 'By many Hints, both in Pamela and Clarissa, you seem to hold that comfortable animating Opinion.' Richardson, as best we can tell, ignored the question – and, as Chapone 'hints' in her use of the word 'hints', his fiction, for all its references to a blissful afterlife, never fully commits either to a 'comfortable', social, 'modern view of heaven' or to a unitary, and solitary, version of heaven wherein 'friends, family, [and] change … are utterly unimportant'.⁵

Furthermore, although Richardson seems at times to be quite clear on the eternal fates warranted by his various good and bad characters – Clarissa dies with Jesus' name on her smiling lips, Lovelace consumed by a 'hell begun in [his] own mind' (*C*, VII.xlvii.184) – his final 'devilish' creation appears, just maybe, to achieve a measure of redemption. I am referring to Sir Hargrave Pollexfen, the Lovelace figure of *Sir Charles Grandison*, whose behaviour as death approaches is remarkable both for its Clarissa-like duration – it unfolds in fits and starts over nearly 400 pages – and for its gestures towards hard-earned salvation. 'Is there not hope that I have all my punishment in this life?', the ruined libertine asks the steadfastly good Sir Charles just prior to succumbing to the fruits of loose living; 'I am sure, it is very, *very* heavy' (*SCG*, VII.iv.14). 'Poor Sir Hargrave Pollexfen!' Harriet exclaims upon learning of her former assailant's painful last breaths: 'May he have met with mercy from the All-merciful!' (VII.lxi.298). Perhaps language such as this led Lady Bradshaigh to ask Richardson his opinion on David Hartley's universalist suggestion that, in the end, we all find salvation. 'I could hope that the Doctrine is true', Richardson replied, 'But dare not presume to decide (so fearful am I of weakening Foundations)' (30 May 1754).

Richardson had, in fact, printed the work in question – Hartley's *Observations on Man* appeared in 1749 – which tells us something important about how much we can expect to glean about the precise nature of Richardson's religious faith from his work as a printer. Scholars eager to pin Richardson down on the evidence provided by the output of his press are likely to find themselves engaged in a choose-your-own adventure story. Between 1746 and 1753, for instance, Richardson printed ten editions of James Hervey's *Meditations and Contemplations*, a personal statement of the Graveyard variety that, later in the century, William Blake loved. Should Richardson's commitment to keeping Hervey's text in print be taken as a sign of his concomitant commitment to Hervey's mystical brand of Christianity? Perhaps in keeping with the radical spiritualism of Jacob Boehme (1575–1624)? After all, Richardson also printed a work by Boehme's English disciple, William Law (1686–1761), in 1752. Here, however, is Richardson's comment on Hervey in a letter of 31 March 1750 to Lady Bradshaigh: 'a serious and good divine, of my acquaintance, sees [Hervey], as to his doctrines, too mystic; and I think him inclined to the enthusiastic part of Methodism'.

Whatever influence he exerted over the texts he printed, it was always in Richardson's professional interest to avoid ideological over-commitment. A case in point: despite his unremitting antipathy for the atheist David Hume (1711–1776) and the deist Henry St John, Viscount Bolingbroke (1678–1751) – 'I despise the one', he fumed in a letter to the Revd Peter Peckard, 'for his absurdities and contradictions of himself ...', and very much dislike the other, for his attempts to sap the foundations of our common Christianity' – Richardson advised Peckard to delete from his *Dissertation on Revelations* (1756) harsh comments directed at the two sceptics before moving to print (16 February 1656).

As eighteenth-century English Christians go, Richardson appears to have been generally open-minded. One of two handwritten 'prayers' included in his collected papers (the Forster Collection, held by the Victoria and Albert Museum) suggests that, at his most generous, Richardson inclined towards belief in a 'God of all Churches, who with unconfined / Unchanging Love embraces all Mankind'.[6] He respected Jews, as evidenced by his initial support for the Jewish Naturalisation Bill in 1753 – but not beyond the bounds of political pragmatism, as evidenced by his call for the bill to be repealed in light of the angry public backlash that ensued. His only Jewish character, Solomon Merceda, is drawn with relative (if not complete) even-handedness – a libertine Jew surrounded in the world of *Sir Charles Grandison* by equally immoral Christians.[7]

Richardson also found intellectual and emotional space for forms of Christianity that many of his contemporaries treated at best with suspicion, and at worst with paranoia. Pamela's piety had led to some embarrassment for the author – critics thought him 'too much a Methodist', he complained to George Cheyne in 1741. Rather than protect against charges of 'enthusiasm' in his next novel, however, Richardson instead doubled down by creating 'the beatified CLARISSA' (Richardson to Elizabeth Richardson, 1 December 1748), a protagonist whose rapturous final exchange of the world below for God above recalls the passionate theocentricism of figures admired by Wesley and his warm-hearted Methodist followers – such as John Norris of Bemerton (1657–1712), Mary Astell (1666–1731), and William Law.

Sir Charles Grandison too contains muted admiration for Methodism, though no one much noticed at the time owing to a more alarming religious development: Sir Charles nearly marries a Catholic foreigner, and even offers to raise any future daughters in her faith rather than his. Scores of Richardson's British readers were scandalised by Sir Charles's betrayal; as one anonymous correspondent put it in a letter of 11 January 1754,

> Sir Charles Grandison is a Charming Man! But some envious Demon, desirous to sully his Character, has spread a dark Cloud over his Excellencies, by supposing a true Englishman ... could take a zealous Papist, National irreconcilable Enemies! and by his Vows make her a Part of himself! wicked absurd Supposition! Always attended with uneasy Disputes. Could a true Protestant think of setting a part any Place in his House as an idolatrous Chappel? An undermining Priest! (the Nation, perhaps is on the Brink of Ruin with the number already here) always inflaming, always plotting.

As Patrick Mello reminds us, the legal strictures against Catholics in England in Richardson's day both reinforced and mirrored popular consensus.[8] Writing some thirty years before the violent anti-Catholic Gordon Riots that shook London in 1780 – and nearly eighty before the Roman Catholic Relief Act of 1829 – Richardson's refusal to revise away Sir Charles's concession to Clementina in later editions of *Sir Charles Grandison* is remarkable. Never, for that matter, did he adjust his hero's plans for the extra-textual future: the novel ends with Sir Charles and his Protestant bride promising 'in a twelvemonth' to visit their new, near, and dear Catholic friends in Italy.

Jews, Methodists, and even Catholics believed in *something*. Religious scepticism was another matter. Spread throughout Richardson's long list of printed books are scores of overtly Christian arguments, sermons, and histories, but one looks in vain for anything definitively irreligious. Even a pagan such as Epictetus, whose works, translated by Elizabeth Carter, Richardson published in 1758, had something to say for himself on this score. (Carter quipped that he may have been a 'better Christian' than Erasmus.)[9] So hostile to disbelief was Richardson that, like his friend Samuel Johnson (1709–1784), he seems to have been genuinely puzzled by the thought that such a thing as an atheist could truly exist; on the subject of atheism, we might say, Richardson was agnostic. While his earliest (and largely anonymous) writings, including *The Infidel Convicted* (1731) and *The Apprentice's Vade Mecum* (1733), comprise various standard arguments against noteworthy English sceptics such as Anthony Collins (1676–1729), John Toland (1670–1722), and Matthew Tindal (1657–1733), Richardson's own devilish characters are invariably posited as atheists only 'in *practice*' (*C*, v.lxii.377), not in conscience. One suspects that Richardson wished to believe that ostensibly avowed sceptics such as Hume were at bottom in agreement with his most satanic creation, Robert Lovelace, who insists that he and his crew of sensualists '[know] better than to be even *doubters*' (III.xlix.246). This might explain the disquieting satisfaction with which Richardson bid farewell to the 'quondam Peer' Bolingbroke upon the posthumous publication of the latter's *Works* in 1754: 'He seems to have been willing to frame a Religion to his Practices. Poor Man! He is not a Doubter now!' (Richardson to Thomas Edwards, 30 December 1754).

Over the past thirty years, Richardson has been described as having 'Puritan inclinations' (Angus Wilson), as tending towards mystical Gnosticism (Rosemary Bechler, Margaret Anne Doody), as embodying *via media* Anglicanism (T. C. Duncan Eaves and Ben D. Kimpel), and as presaging the onset of secularism (Florian Stuber, Patrick Mello). Perhaps this is only to be expected for someone equal parts reticent and ecumenical in matters of religion. But it would be a mistake to confuse Richardson's modesty as to the details of his faith with a lack of religious conviction; when, in a letter of 1 December 1748, the author directs his wife, Elizabeth, to the death of his own literary creation as exemplary of the end he trusts they too will finally reach – 'And may our last Scenes be closed as happily as [Clarissa's] last Scene is represented to have done!' (1 December 1748) – he is leaping with Kierkegaard over the abyss, not staring with Nietzsche into it. I might also suggest the following thought experiment: what would Richardson say to us, if we could reverse the flow of time, about our own clarity, consistency, and coherence in matters of politics, of family dynamics, of religion? Since we are already time-travelling, I propose we imagine him borrowing from T. S. Eliot, who was borrowing from Baudelaire: 'You! hypocrite lecteur! – mon semblable, – mon frère!'[10]

Notes

1 Of particular note in this regard are Pamela's clever interpolation (and reworking) of Psalm 137 (*P*, pp. 129–30 and 292–7) and Clarissa's various scriptural 'Meditations', which are spread throughout the novel and which Richardson gathered (and expanded) and then printed separately as *Meditations Collected from the Sacred Books* (1750) for distribution among friends.

2 John A. Dussinger, 'The Oxford Methodists (1733; 1738): The Purloined Letter of John Wesley at Samuel Richardson's Press', in Melvyn New and Gerard Reedy (eds.), *Theology and Literature in the Age of Johnson: Resisting Secularism* (University of Delaware and Rowman & Littlefield, 2012), pp. 27–48 (p. 38).

3 John A. Dussinger, '"Stealing in the great doctrines of Christianity": Samuel Richardson as Journalist', *Eighteenth-Century Fiction*, 15.3–4 (2003), 451–506 (p. 458 n. 15).

4 Murray L. Brown, 'T. C. Duncan Eaves, Ben D. Kimpel, and the Life: A Brief and Apologetic Memoir', *1650–1850: Ideas, Aesthetics, and Inquiries in the Early Modern Era*, 9 (2003), 327–37 (p. 334).

5 Colleen McDannell and Bernhard Lang, *Heaven: A History* (Yale University Press, 1988), pp. 183, 178. See also E. Derek Taylor, 'Samuel Richardson's *Clarissa* and the Problem of Heaven', in New and Reedy, *Theology and Literature*, pp. 71–89.

6 The poem is a setting by John Byrom of a passage from William Law's *Appeal to All that Doubt* (1742), p. 279.

7 On the 'deep rooted anxieties about the relationship between Jewishness and Englishness' that emerged during this debate and that informed Richardson's depiction of Merceda, see Bonnie Latimer, 'Samuel Richardson and the "Jew Bill" of 1753: A New Political Context for *Sir Charles Grandison*', *Review of English Studies*, 66.275 (2015), 520–539 (p. 526).

8 See Patrick Mello, '"Piety and Popishness": Tolerance and the Epistolary Reaction to Richardson's *Sir Charles Grandison*', *Eighteenth-Century Fiction*, 25.3 (2013), 511–31. See also Howard D. Weinbrot, below (pp. 314–15), for a discussion of the political significance of this religious open-mindedness.

9 Elizabeth Carter, *Memoirs of the Life of Mrs. Elizabeth Carter*, 2 vols. (1807), Vol. 1, p. 381.

10 T. S. Eliot, *The Waste Land*, line 76, in *Collected Poems 1909–1962* (Harcourt Brace Jovanovich, 1963).

CHAPTER 35

Social Hierarchy and Social Mobility

Karen Lipsedge

In the first two decades of the eighteenth century, Britain witnessed a rapid increase in its commercial wealth, resulting in what has been referred to as a 'stretching [of] the social fabric in its middle and upper sections'.[1] It was within the 'middling ranks' that the impact of this 'stretching' was most apparent. Social mobility between the 'middling' and upper ranks remained limited, and the upper ranks continued to exert the most political power, their status secured by land ownership and freedom from the necessity to labour for their livelihood. But as those in the 'middling ranks' began to have access to new wealth, and could imitate many of the sartorial and lifestyle symbols and privileges of those in the upper ranks, the traditional measures of status distinguishing these two social groups became increasingly blurred. The novels of Richardson provide a useful commentary on mid-eighteenth-century social hierarchy. Through his attention to the home and the domestic lives of the family, Richardson's novels also provide insight into the consequences of social mobility and the increased desire for luxury.

The ownership of a house was a symbol of and vehicle for expressing wealth, power, social status, and taste. Of equal significance was the organisation and domestic management of the home and its material culture. Consequently, the ability to own, decorate, and use a house appropriately and according to the latest demands of fashion and taste was as important for those with sufficient income in the 'middling ranks' as it was for those in the upper ranks. At the centre of each of Richardson's novels is property – as an indicator of status, as asset, as bargaining tool, and as home. In each novel, the protagonist's home or living space operates as a resplendent visual symbol in miniature of social hierarchy, with the 'structures of authority in the family and household management', as well as the use and organisation of domestic space, revealing as much about the social status and power of the inhabitants as material possessions, modes of behaviour, and domestic relationships.[2] Key domestic scenes at Mr B's

Bedfordshire estate, at Harlowe Place, and at Grandison-Hall demonstrate how Richardson employs the hierarchy and management of the household and the 'family' – that is, 'all those living in the same house' – to portray the consequences of social mobility.[3] These scenes also encourage the reader to question whether an emphasis on material culture as a measure of status impedes domestic order and the pursuit of prudential morality.

In *Pamela*, it is Pamela's late lady's dressing room to which Richardson devotes particular attention in those scenes set at the Bedfordshire estate. Pamela's change in role from lady's maid to carer of Mr B's linen at the start of the novel implies an alteration in her 'Place', both social and spatial, within her late lady's household (*P*, pp. 9, 36). The suggestion that this change will be beneficial is announced sartorially by Pamela's acquisition of an assortment of her late lady's attire, and architecturally by her freedom of access to and use of her late lady's dressing room (*P*, pp. 7–11, 15–18), a room associated more readily with the wealthy – and in which the mistress of the house would be guaranteed a degree of privacy. Pamela's access to it is as significant as her ability to wear her late lady's attire. It appears to connote an elevation in Pamela's status in the household. However, Richardson employs both dress and dressing room to emphasise the ambiguity of Pamela's 'Place'. This ambiguity is underlined by the dressing room's multiple functions; it is a place for reading, writing, and dressing in and, hence, referred to variously as a 'dressing room' and a 'closet'. At this time, a lady's dressing room was also associated with female sexuality, performance, and secrecy.

Pamela's late lady's dressing room could be read as an emblem of Pamela's intellectual freedom. But in Volume 1, Richardson also employs it as an architectural symbol of Pamela's ambiguous status within the household and of her sexual oppression. Pamela may now have the right to wear an assortment of her late lady's attire and to use her dressing room, but she does not have the same domestic status or right to privacy enjoyed previously by her late lady. Nor does she have control over her domestic space, or her body. Pamela is a servant and a member of the labouring classes, and thus remains at the whim of Mr B: her master, a wealthy country squire, and, following his mother's death, the owner of the household and the locus of domestic authority. Consequently, it is Mr B who determines how his late mother's dressing room is used and by whom. And, for Mr B, this dressing room operates as an interior space in which he can 'lay his Snares surer', and entrap both Pamela and her letters (*P*, p. 36).

Pamela's use of the 'bird in a cage' trope in Letter xvi to describe her sense of entrapment and fear prior to her appearance before her 'Judge' and master in the dressing room underlines the connection between her lack of domestic privacy and her lack of power and control over her domestic space, letters and body (*P*, p. 30). As she laments to her parents, 'At last he [Mr B] went up to the Closet, which was my good Lady's Dressing room; a Room I once lov'd, but then as much hated. Don't your Heart ake for me? I am sure mine flutter'd about like a Bird in a Cage new caught' (*P*, p. 31).

As a 'poor cast-off Servant Girl' whose master is a 'Batchelor' with 'Designs', the fact that Pamela lacks domestic privacy, power, and control appears inevitable (*P*, pp. 421, 14, 57). Throughout the novel, however, Richardson encourages the reader to question the inevitability of Pamela's fate – her loss of control over rooms, her body, and, potentially, her virtue. When Pamela is taken to Mr B's Lincolnshire estate, Richardson employs her access to and use of a closet to direct that questioning process. As with the dressing room at Mr B's Bedfordshire estate, Pamela uses this closet to read and write. But it is her additional use of the closet as a site for scholarly and religious activity that serves to distinguish it from her late lady's dressing room and its association with female sexuality and secrecy. Pamela's use of the closet as a site for her closet-duties reminds the reader that her virtue is unsullied and innate and thus deserves to be 'rewarded'. Accordingly, it is no coincidence that on Pamela's marriage to Mr B, Richardson alludes to Joel 2:16 and the closet's association with women and their preparation for marriage by depicting Pamela's prayer of gratitude in the closet at his Lincolnshire house (*P*, p. 324). Moreover, on their return to his Bedfordshire estate, Pamela writes that Mr B 'gave me Possession of my Lady's Dressing room ... &c. that were in her Apartments, and bid me call those Apartments mine. O give me, my good God, Humility and Gratitude!' (*P*, p. 431).

Mr B's quasi-ceremonial transference of his control over his late mother's dressing room to his new wife marks the point in the novel when the dressing room shifts from being an emblem of Pamela's ambiguous 'Place' in his household to representing her elevation from virtuous maid to mistress, and from the labouring classes to the upper ranks. It also marks when the dressing room changes from being a symbol of Pamela's sexual oppression to being one of her intellectual and spiritual freedom, and of her right to domestic status and privacy as Mr B's wife and domestic manager. As Richardson shows at the end of *Pamela*, and stresses in *Pamela in Her Exalted Condition*, Pamela's social and domestic elevation is beneficial for the household and the family. By aligning a change to Pamela's status with Mr B's transformation from rake to reformed rake and husband, Richardson also suggests that social mobility can facilitate domestic order and the pursuit of prudential morality.

The function of the private closet as an emblem for female virtue and a right to privacy is also evident in *Clarissa* (*C,* VII.cv.88). In *Clarissa,* as in *Pamela,* the heroine's right to a 'Place' of her own is central to the key domestic scenes at Harlowe Place. But Clarissa is neither a lady's maid nor a member of the labouring classes. She is the youngest daughter of the Harlowes: an upstart family, desperate to display their new-found status as extensive landowners. As 'the flower and ornament' of the Harlowe house, the '*mistress*-wheel of the family', and an exemplar of virtue and piety, Clarissa assumes that she will always have a place at the heart of the family and home (*C,* II.xxxi.191, III.xxxviii.197). When her virtue prevents her from agreeing to her parents' wishes to marry the 'odious' Solmes, Clarissa is removed from the centre of the family and made to enact the role of 'poor prisoner' in her own home (*C,* I.xvi.92, v.156). Richardson employs the representation of Clarissa's lesser parlour to highlight her loss of 'Place' at the heart of the family. He also employs the increasingly hostile treatment that Clarissa receives in her lesser parlour to underscore recurrent themes of the novel: divided families and the violation of space. The Harlowes' access to new wealth has led to a desire for luxury at the expense of morality and virtue, and resulted in disorder and disunity in a family once 'so happy and so united' (*C,* I.v.30).

Clarissa's lesser parlour dominates the first two volumes of the novel. It is located downstairs in the communal, social arena of Harlowe Place, and is 'next door' to Bella's lesser parlour. Originally, Bella's and Clarissa's parlours were a single room, 'separated in favour of us girls, for each to receive visitors in at her pleasure' (*C,* II.xxxi.180). Clarissa, however, uses her lesser parlour not as an informal entertaining room, but as a relatively private room for solitary and intellectual activities. Clarissa's lesser parlour is an anomaly, therefore. It is a relatively private room of her own that is situated in the main social part of Harlowe Place and at the centre of the house. This disjunction between location and function underlines the lesser parlour's significance for Clarissa. She can enjoy the relative privacy that this intimate room affords her, while still being a part of the social life of the family. Yet when Clarissa no longer complies with her family's wishes in Volume I, they deny her access to the lesser parlour (*C,* I.xxiv.153–5). In Volume II, they also violate the lesser parlour's symbolic function by using it as a setting for Clarissa and Solmes's 'interview' before the 'full *congregation*'. As a result, the Harlowes gradually transform what Betty mockingly refers to as Clarissa's 'own parlour' into an alien and uninviting room (*C,* II.xxxi.178). This alteration to her lesser parlour enables the Harlowes to reiterate the consequences of her refusal to marry Solmes.

Equally significant is what happens after each of the lesser parlour scenes. Clarissa's reduced access to both her parents and the communal domestic space downstairs in Volume I, for instance, first alerts her to her loss of status within the hierarchy of the family and household, and to her domestic and family exclusion. It is only at the 'interview' with Solmes that Clarissa becomes aware of how her emotional and physical dislocation from her family has affected her ownership of the lesser parlour. When Clarissa is 'permitted to go up to [her] own chamber' after the 'interview', she also discovers that her family have now turned their attention to her upstairs apartment. Even her closet – the one private place that Clarissa could still call her own – has been invaded (*C*, ii.xxxi.211–13).

Richardson's use of Clarissa's lesser parlour at Harlowe Place to signify her physical and psychological extrusion from her family is significant. In the eighteenth century, the domestic parlour was perceived as facilitating increased informality and sociability. Richardson, however, uses Clarissa's lesser parlour to highlight the absence of family harmony and reiterate how the Harlowes have replaced the conjugal value of love with the market economy of trade and exchange, thereby transforming both Clarissa and domestic space into commodities and assets for which the family bargain. Richardson's representation of the lesser parlour also enables him to underline the intimate relationship between morality and domestic order: an absence of both leads to a topsy-turvy and disordered family and home (*C*, ii.xxxiii.227).

The topsy-turvy nature of the family and domestic order is a recurring theme throughout *Clarissa*, underscoring the social and moral disorder at the heart of the novel, and the potentially dangerous consequences of social mobility and the access to new wealth. Social and moral disorder are also two recurring themes in *Sir Charles Grandison*. In contrast to *Clarissa*, however, in his third novel Richardson uses Grandison-Hall and Sir Charles to signify the beneficial consequences (both private and public) of domestic order and harmony. At the centre of Grandison-Hall is the baronet, Sir Charles – a model of masculinity and social order who is thoroughly enmeshed within domestic space and economy. Throughout the novel, Sir Charles is described variously as 'handsome', 'great and noble', and 'with a manly politeness' (*SCG*, i.xxvii.191, xxxvi.254). Hence, it seems only appropriate that he should be in possession of an equally 'venerable, large and convenient' 'family estate' (*SCG*, vi.xliv.277). In Volume vii, Richardson highlights the synonymous relationship between Grandison-Hall and Sir Charles, with the house and surrounding grounds symbolising Richardson's prototype of a domestic patriarch (*SCG*, vii.v.17–ix.47).

A man's authority in the home was founded not on his ownership alone, but also on his close involvement and investment in the daily life and 'things' of the home, as well as his command of the overall management of the household. The domestic patriarch's role as the principal manager of the household is often underlined in conduct and advice literature focusing on the well-being of the family, where household and family management tend to be presented as a 'joint endeavour', with the husband and wife assuming differing levels of domestic duties.[4] When Harriet becomes mistress of Grandison-Hall, Richardson highlights Harriet's and Sir Charles's differing levels of household duty to suggest that they conceive of 'housekeeping' as a 'shared' domestic practice from the start of their married life, and recognise its importance for maintaining order and harmony in the household. Yet Richardson also underscores that it is Sir Charles, as overseer and manager of domestic affairs and the everyday life of his estate, who is the locus of domestic authority and order at Grandison-Hall.

One strategy that Richardson uses to reiterate Sir Charles's domestic authority at Grandison-Hall is to highlight his hero's command and control over domestic sociability. Shortly after the small, intimate concert in the *'Music-parlour'* Sir Charles organises a larger domestic event for his 'neighbouring gentry' at Grandison-Hall, comprising a two-day-long series of 'entertainments, and the Ball' (*SCG*, vii.v.25–6, vi.27–35). Throughout the event Sir Charles oversees and controls the 'whole space' and 'every-body' (vii.vi.34). By making his household accessible as a site of sociability to all the neighbouring gentry, Richardson also stresses that Sir Charles's central role in the household is mirrored by his equally important role in the local community. As Harriet declares ecstatically to her family of readers: 'it is my wish … that you were present, and saw him, The Domestic Man, The chearful Friend, The kind Master, The enlivening Companion, The polite Neighbour, The tender Husband! Let nobody who sees Sir Charles Grandison at home, say, that the private station is not that of true happiness' (vii.vi.35).

Harriet's use of the term 'Domestic Man' underscores the connection between Sir Charles and the home, and its implications for a reading of Grandison-Hall and social and domestic hierarchy. For Harriet, Sir Charles's 'devotion to [his] home' is shown through his relationship to and responsibility for his 'family', his neighbours, and his local community. As land and property owner and baronet, Sir Charles, and his estate, Grandison-Hall, signify power and control. But, as Harriet makes clear, any tension between the private and the public is eradicated through Sir Charles's role as 'Domestic Man', which fuses together a man's public and private identity through his domestic engagements. As domestic patriarch, Sir Charles has dual but complementary responsibilities to those within and without his estate. Indeed, it is because of Sir Charles's complete control and command of the household and its inhabitants that he is able to unite his public and his private roles so harmoniously through the persona of 'Domestic Man'.

The image of the house dominates each of Richardson's novels. The attention he devotes to the home and the domestic lives of the family sheds light on mid-eighteenth-century social hierarchy, the consequences of social mobility, and the impact that the increased emphasis on the display of wealth had on domestic order and morality. In *Pamela*, Richardson uses the social and domestic elevation of Pamela from servant to wife and model domestic manager to highlight the private benefits of social mobility. In *Sir Charles Grandison*, he employs Sir Charles as 'Domestic Man' to show the benefits of domestic order and the obligations afforded by status, both to the family and to society. *Clarissa* also ends with domestic harmony and prosperity as symbolised by Belford's marriage (*C*, VII, conclusion, p. 422). But, reflecting Richardson's own moral concerns, disorder and the lack of morality of the Harlowe family dominate *Clarissa*, and shape a reading of Harlowe Place, Clarissa, and the novel.

Notes

1 Paul Langford, *A Polite and Commercial People: England 1727–1783* (Oxford University Press, 1992), p. 68.
2 Amanda Vickery, *Behind Closed Doors: At Home in Georgian England* (Yale University Press, 2009), p. 12.
3 Samuel Johnson, 'Family', in *A Dictionary of the English Language*, 2nd edn, 2 vols. (London, 1755–6). See also Toni Bowers's discussion of the notion of family, above (pp. 240–2).
4 Karen Harvey, *The Little Republic: Masculinity and Domestic Authority in Eighteenth-Century Britain* (Oxford University Press, 2012), pp. 32–3.

CHAPTER 36

Politics

Howard D. Weinbrot

Richardson long has been regarded as cautious in his political views and thereby encourages readers' speculation rather than certainty.[1] His early collaboration with the duke of Wharton's *True Briton* (1723) probably stemmed from the fledgling's need for business and his willingness to believe that Wharton was an 'Old Whig' opponent of Robert Walpole, rather than the Jacobite that he was.[2] Thereafter, Richardson soon became an official printer for the Whig governments, including Walpole's *Daily Gazetteer* from 1738 to 1746. He dealt with powerful members of the Walpole and other administrations on a regular basis, and corresponded with titled recipients such as Lady Bradshaigh and Lady Echlin, and men of letters such as Samuel Johnson, Aaron Hill, and Edward Young. With so varied an extended intellectual family, Richardson wisely judged prudence more appropriate than confrontation.

Or not, as the case may be. *Noscitur a socio* – you are known by the company you keep – suggests Richardson's political leaning. He long was a close friend of Arthur Onslow, Whig Member of Parliament from 1720 to 1761 and distinguished Speaker of the House from 1728 to 1761. Onslow supported both William of Orange's 1688 revolution and the Hanoverian succession, and adamantly protected the rights and privileges of the House of Commons. Samuel Johnson's *Debates in Parliament* (1741–4) describe Onslow as a man 'whose zeal for the present imperial house, and the prosperity of the nation, has been always acknowledged'. Onslow opposed the repatriation of the self-exiled Jacobite Henry St John, Viscount Bolingbroke as he then was, and also 'declared his abhorrence of persecuting any body on account of their opinions in religion'.[3] Like Onslow, the mature Richardson believed in dynastic loyalty, restraints upon monarchic power, national prosperity, and religious toleration, to which he added belief in progress. Richardson portrays much of this moderate agenda in key scenes in his novels in which domestic politics reflect national politics.

Samuel Johnson's sermon on Genesis 2:24 observes that in his culture the husband has more authority than the wife. Nonetheless, 'though obedience may be justly required, servility is not to be exacted; and though it may be lawful to exert authority … to govern and to tyrannize are very different, and … oppression will naturally provoke rebellion'.[4] Richardson makes this husband–wife–nation relationship central in *Pamela* and its sequel. In *Pamela*, Mr B demands Pamela's sexual obedience, and in Lincolnshire offers her and her parents financial security if she agrees to be his mistress. She already has refused dishonourable terms, 'were he not only my Master, but my King' (*P*, pp. 38, 64). She now again insists that like a noble Roman she can 'refuse the Bribes of the greatest Monarch' (*P*, p. 177). The frustrated Mr B provokes rebellion when he demands 'Silence! … You see, now you are in my Power! – You cannot get from me, nor help yourself' (*P*, p. 188). He is wrong. Pamela rejects his tyranny. Mr B finally recognises that if she is to become his sexual partner she must be his wife and life partner. He reforms, if only for the time being, asks to marry her, assures her that her practices of truth, virtue, wit, proper behaviour, and sweetness of person 'that itself might captivate a Monarch' are worth more than a large dowry (*P*, p. 310). Accordingly, 'The Word *Command* on my side, or *Obedience*, on hers, I would have blotted from my Vocabulary' (*P*, p. 409). Pamela redefines 'fortune', from inheritance and income to inner worth as expressed in action. She persuades Mr B to accept her related moral and political values – the Lockean freedom to defend herself from what she believes to be an attack upon her life.

Richardson shows Mr B's respect for those values in the larger political sphere – as in his political allegory of the English card game whist. The king is deservedly powerful in the game as in the nation 'because there is something sacred in the Character'. Whist, however, elevates practical politics above the vague 'something sacred'. The game pleases Mr B: 'by the Ace, I have always thought the Laws of the Land denoted; and, as the Ace is above the King or Queen, and wins them; I think the Law should be thought so too'. The former absolutist demonstrates his better political affiliation: 'May-be, I shall be deem'd a *Whig* for my Opinion' (*P*, p. 372). But once a Whig not always a Whig, it seems. In *Pamela in Her Exalted Condition* Mr B, as Pamela's social superior, again confuses governance with tyranny and again insists on destructive authority. Pamela longs to breastfeed her infant son Billy. Mr B forbids that bond as beneath their rank, reverts to his earlier rakish values, contemplates a polygamous marriage with a beautiful and wealthy widowed countess, and reminds Pamela of Old Testament marital customs. When Rachel was nursing her infant, Jacob 'the worthy Patriarch' visited his other wives. If Pamela nurses their child he too will find another 'wife' for sexual comfort: 'I will not think of any more Wives, till you convince me, by your Adherence to the Example given you by the Patriarch Wives, that I ought to follow those of the Patriarch Husbands' (*PE*, p. 313).

The next scene is one of the great moments in eighteenth-century fiction. Under James II the monarch governed the law. His abusive dispensing power allowed him to appoint to the judiciary those who would further his aims, give new and dangerous rights to his Catholic subjects, absolve them from oaths against the pope and transubstantiation, and perhaps even extirpate the Church of England and establish the Church of Rome. As Myles Stanhope wrote in 1754, James II's dispensing power 'put the whole Constitution out of Joint; and ... seemed to threaten the very Fundamentals of civil and religious Liberty'. Another commentator bluntly said that 'the *dispensing* Power ... is the same thing with Arbitrary Power'.[5] Pamela rejects Mr B's political and domestic abuse as she rejected his sexual abuse. He 'makes a body think a Wife should not have the least Will of her own. He sets up a dispensing Power, in short, altho' he knows, that that Doctrine once cost a Prince his Crown' (*PE*, p. 313). Pamela will take their child and move to her parents' home; she continues to respect Mr B, who may divorce her if he wishes, but she accepts neither his violation of her maternal role nor his violation of his marital oath to be faithful to her. He is stunned, realises that he indeed may lose his husband's crown, acknowledges Pamela's rightful roles as wife and mother, and abjures polygamy. Pamela teaches Mr B to govern, not to tyrannise, and thereby not to provoke rebellion.

Richardson has a related political problem in *Clarissa*. She deals with two kinds of tyranny, each again reflecting dark national politics. One is family politics as ordered by her oppressive father. Richardson's simple tactic guides the reader's response: Pamela's son was named Billy, a probable allusion to William of Orange, who replaced James II and excoriated his dispensing power. Both Clarissa's father and her brother are named James. Each tyrant requires complete obedience and each thinks Clarissa a traitor who resists proper demands. James and James, Jr act as one when Clarissa refuses to marry the offensive Mr Solmes: 'Son James, let the rebel be this moment carried away to my brother's – this very moment – She shall not stay one hour more under my roof!' Words such as 'command', 'Give up', and 'you must' follow (*C*, II.xxi.197–8).

Clarissa indeed rebels, but soon finds herself in even more hostile territory and with more hostile implications. Lovelace regards himself as

Caesar, Hannibal, an absolute monarch, and for the time being at least, an emperor. At one point he celebrates his own elevation and denigrates Clarissa with the commanding and degrading 'thou': 'If once thy emperor decrees thy fall, thou shalt greatly fall' (*C*, iii.vi.56). At another point he congratulates himself on his ability to raise or diminish his associates 'by virtue of my own imperial will' as based upon 'my own convenience. What a poor thing is a monarch to me!' (*C*, iv.i.5). Hannibal, Caesar, and European emperors cannot satisfy Lovelace's need for conquest. He soon fancies himself an Ottoman sultan contemplating his seraglio, with sobbing, broken Clarissa and Anna Howe at his disposal: 'And I their emperor, their then *acknowledged* emperor … Grand Signor like, uncertain to which I should first throw out my handkerchief' to select an enslaved woman as his nocturnal partner (*C*, iv.xxiv.133). Imperial Lovelace hopes that his dispensing power will subject the law and Clarissa to his radically unchristian desires.

Sir Charles Grandison is very different. 'The God of Nature intended not Human Nature for a vile and contemptible thing: And many are the instances, in every age, of those whom He enables, amidst all the frailties of mortality, to do it honour' (*SCG*, vii.303). So Richardson says in his defensive 'Concluding Note' to *Sir Charles Grandison*, which also quotes supporting remarks from Archbishop Tillotson's sermon 'Of the Divine Perfections' (vii.304–5). Richardson's title character dismisses the distant Jonathan Swift, the more immediate Lovelace, and the sexually profligate but triumphant Tom Jones. Richardson is defensive because several readers complained that Sir Charles was too good to be true, that he should never have sought to marry an Italian Catholic, raise their daughters as Catholic, and live outside his native land for much of his life.

Richardson designed Sir Charles as an honour to human nature, but more specifically as an honour to British human nature. That is a political statement sometimes camouflaged within a religious statement, as in Grandison's commitment to the Church of England by choice rather than by birth (*SCG*, iii.xxii.226). He also exemplifies the established Church's willingness to acknowledge Christian confessions other than its own as agents of salvation. The Lutheran Hanoverian accession to the throne enhanced this movement. In 1746 Robert Seagrave argued that from George I forward, 'Bigotry, has evidently lost Ground; and Liberty is more understood and esteemed daily.' Providence may have reserved for Britain the honour of bringing liberty 'to its Perfection'.[6] That is one reason Richardson allowed Sir Charles, nearly, to marry an Italian Catholic: he exemplified his country's liberal religion, which reflected its liberal politics.

In contrast, Richardson makes plain that the Catholic della Porrettas' religious zeal frustrates Sir Charles's British perfection. Clementina suffers a nervous breakdown at the thought of marrying a Protestant whom she and her family consider a heretic to be damned. Richardson saw the admirable Protestant Englishman as an extension of Christian generosity towards all in a shared communion. English readers who found that association unconvincing would nevertheless have responded comfortably to Sir Charles's attitudes toward commerce, the social order, and practical government.

Eighteenth-century nation-defining trade had theological support. As a result of the Fall, mankind was forced to earn its bread by the sweat of its collective brow – witness farming and fishing. God also designed individuals and nations to be sociable and connected, so that one nation supplied the wants and needs of another. Edward Young put it this way in his Pindaric *Imperium Pelagi* (1730): 'Heaven different growths to different lands imparts / That All may stand in Need of All' – and so that all, and especially Britain, profit.[7]

Both James, Sr and James, Jr in *Clarissa* try to escape from their commercial backgrounds for which Lovelace has contempt. In *Grandison* Mrs Reeves observes that 'A man can rise in a profession, and if he acquires wealth in a trade, can get above it, and be respected' (iv.xviii.140). In each case one must transcend commercial success to gain social success. Sir Charles disagrees. In 1745 Thomas Gordon insisted that the invading Young Pretender hated and would destroy 'Religion, Liberty, Trade'.[8] Sir Charles respects and educates those on his large estate, often with 'Husbandry and labour' for the lower classes. Providence provides different capacities for different purposes 'that all might become useful links of the same great chain'. Apply varied talents 'to Trade, to Mechanics', and then all will be useful and 'may be eminent in some way or other' (*SCG*, v.ii.16–17). Grandison as agent of that divinely ordained system preserves his estate and enriches his useful tenants, who in full employment 'grow into circumstances under him' (*SCG*, vii.viii.44).

This benevolence includes good sense, human decency, and *usufructus* – a form of stewardship that requires the Good and the Great to protect the wealth and land on which future generations rely. This conduct is a nationalist and political statement for the baronet who is so 'proud to be thought an Englishman' (*SCG*, iii.xxix.340) – and who brings the putative barbarian Shakespeare to culturally dominant, francophone Europe (*SCG*, iii.xxii.226). Grandison as citizen of the world has deep British roots. He objects to the grandees' sartorial ostentation, which harms their nation: 'Shall any one pretend to true Patriotism, and not attempt to stem this torrent of Fashion, which impoverishes our own honest Countrymen, whilst it carries Wealth and Power to those whose National Religion and Interest are directly opposite to ours!'. Grandison blocks that destructive torrent: 'on a double Principle of Religion and Policy, he encourages the Trades-people, the Manufactures, the Servants of his own Country' (*SCG*, VII.[iii].422–3).

Sir Charles can indeed do something about national prosperity. His inherited title as baronet is below the peerage and thus allows him to join the House of Commons. He returns to Grandison-Hall and marries Harriet Byron, after which the local Freeholders and their wives encourage him to represent them: 'They wondered he was not in Parliament, till they heard how little a while he had been in England' (*SCG*, VI.liii.341). By the novel's final volume, Grandison contemplates that electoral option – not for a 'party', but for a constituency in which he has a '*natural*' interest. 'I shall be proud to be initiated into the service of the public' (*SCG*, VII. lii.264–5). We may reasonably assume that Sir Charles as MP would support the international trade that he had described from Italy and by which Britain prospered.

We also may reasonably assume that either as parliamentarian or civilian he would respect his monarch as a secular head of state but without a divine right. Sir Charles agrees that he and Harriet will be presented to the king to 'shew his duty to his Sovereign' (*SCG*, VII.iii.10) – in an act of deference in part because he admires his sovereign's 'integrity of heart … as much as he reveres his royal dignity' (*SCG*, VII.iv.16). These values imply constraints upon the subject's obedience; lack of integrity does not evoke deference. Grandison emphasises such limits. He acknowledges that he is most resistant when his authority is challenged: 'I would call myself a *Man*, to a Prince, who should unjustly hold me in contempt; and let him know that I looked upon *him* to be no more' than a man (*SCG*, III. xxviii.323–4). He tells an overbearing Italian aristocrat that 'Princes, tho' they are intitled by their rank to respect, are princes to him only as they act' (*SCG*, III.xxix.341).

These several consistent episodes suggest sensible conjectures regarding Richardson's politics. The printer-tradesman understood the day-to-day exchange of labour, its products, and the people who used them. He understood the circulation of money that was as important to the nation's health as the circulation of blood is to the individual's health. Commerce made him wealthy and aware of complex human exchange in a fallen world. In his novels the conduct he regards as normative is likely to accept limits based upon restraint as characters work within constitutional, secular, or providential order. The conduct he regards as unacceptable is likely to be absolutist or to require unwilling submission to improper standards. The first is exemplified in Mr B and the game of whist: the ace denotes the law, which is superior to the king and queen. The second is exemplified in Lovelace and his attempted control of Clarissa: 'If once thy emperor decrees thy fall, thou shalt greatly fall' (*C*, III.vi.56). Law requires Parliament's debate and approval. Imperial decrees require personal demands and powerless personal acceptance – which can also be dangerous to the un-British politician, such as James II, or the mimic grand signor, such as Lovelace. Both James and Lovelace die in foreign lands as a consequence of their foreign actions.

Richardson also demonstrates that resistance at even the ultimate price is possible and desirable. Pamela reminds Mr B of the dangers of tyrannical dispensing of power, and of her willingness to leave him with their child in hand. She defeats and elevates him. Clarissa reminds Lovelace that she prefers death rather than, again, unwillingly submitting to him. Richardson varies this theme by showing Clementina della Porretta's mistaken alternative: retreat into temporary madness rather than advance to love and sane religious moderation. Grandison reminds us of the obligations of power: to preserve, build, and extend generosity in religion, charity, social order, and mutually advantageous commerce. His world finally is ruled by beneficial power rooted in the constitution Mr B epitomises and Sir Charles exemplifies. The baronet reflects Richardson's belief in progress and the possibility of happiness in this world when human nature is uplifting rather than degrading. Perhaps it is best to align Richardson with Mr B on the moral and constitutional balance appropriate for Britain: 'May-be, I shall be deem'd a *Whig* for my Opinion' (*P*, p. 372).

Notes

1 John A. Dussinger, 'Masters and Servants: Political Discourse in Richardson's *A Collection of Moral Sentiments*', *Eighteenth-Century Fiction*, 5.3 (1993), 239–52 (p. 239).
2 For an opposing view of Richardson's early political alignments see Thomas Keymer, above (pp. 6–7).
3 Samuel Johnson, *Debates in Parliament*, in *The Yale Edition of the Works of Samuel Johnson*, eds. Thomas Kaminsky, Benjamin Beard Hoover, and O. M. Brack, Jr, 23 vols. (Yale University Press, 2012), Vols. XI–XIII (XII, p. 714); Onslow quoted in Philip Laundy, 'Arthur Onslow', *Oxford Dictionary of National Biography* (Oxford University Press, 2004), online edn.

4 Samuel Johnson, *Sermons*, in Johnson, *Yale Edition*, Vol. XIV (1978), eds. Jean Hagstrum and James Gray, p. 14.

5 Myles Stanhope, *The History of the Several Oppositions which Have Been Made in England, from the Restoration of King Charles the Second* (London, 1754), p. 135; Bartolomé de las Casas, *Liberty and Property, and No Pretender* (London, 1745), p. 45.

6 Robert Seagrave, *The True Protestant* (London, 1746), p. 43.

7 Edward Young, *Imperium Pelagi: A Naval Lyrick. Occasioned by His Majesty's Return, Sept. 1729* (London, 1730), p. 14.

8 [Thomas Gordon], *Four Letters Taken from the General Evening Post, Relating to the Present Rebellion* (London, 1745), p. 24.

CHAPTER 37

Nationalism

Lisa O'Connell

From the moment *Pamela* was first announced to the public, it was understood to belong to English culture. 'I doubt not Pamela will become the bright example and imitation of all the fashionable young ladies of Great Britain', declares Samuel Richardson's friend, William Webster, in the Tory *Weekly Miscellany*. For Webster, the book is special because of its power to solicit readerly identification ('there is no reading it without uncommon Concern and Emotion'), which is itself a result of its 'spirit of Truth and agreeable Simplicity'. This is why he urges Richardson to resist the temptation to make his text more rhetorically proper. Were Pamela's tale of 'Virtue and Honour' to be written in politer prose, he warns, this might 'disguise the Facts, mar the Reflections, and unnaturalize the Incidents, so as to be lost in a Multiplicity of fine idle Words and Phrases, and reduce our Sterling Substance into an empty Shadow, or rather *frenchify* our *English* Solidity into Froth and Whip-syllabub'.[1]

Webster was not alone in believing that the virtue that might 'mend the Age' took the form of a plain anti-French Englishness – or 'native simplicity' as he put it – which marked *Pamela* off from 'pernicious novels' in general. Indeed, his pre-publication puff is characteristic of the nationalist lexicon in which Richardson's fiction was first canonised. Walter Scott spelt out the terms of that process:

> Hitherto, romances had been written, generally speaking, in the old French taste, containing the protracted amours of princes and princesses, told in language coldly extravagant, and metaphysically absurd. In these wearisome performances there appeared not ... the slightest attempt to paint mankind as it exists in the ordinary walks of life – all was rant and bombast, stilt and buskin. It will be Richardson's eternal praise, did he merit no more, that he tore from his personages those painted vizards, which concealed, under a clumsy and affected disguise, every thing like the natural lineaments of the human countenance.[2]

Scott celebrates Richardson's realism as a departure from the romance tradition's 'rant and bombast'. Richardson, not his predecessors, is branded 'English'.

Scott's assertion that earlier works were 'in the old French taste' was misguided. English prose fiction writers before Richardson, most notably Delarivier Manley and Daniel Defoe, claimed to offer faithful depictions of the world (or rather of 'History') in contradistinction to flights of heroic 'Fancy'. We know, too, that Richardson became as much an international literary phenomenon as a local one. As Mary Helen McMurran (pp. 45–9) and Norbert Schürer (pp. 94–8) have detailed above, his works were widely translated and distributed across international publishing networks. And, if Pamela was a homebody – a servant-girl-cum-domestic-paragon – whose struggle against libertine desire was indeed celebrated (and ridiculed) as an English story as Webster had anticipated, Clarissa was quite the opposite. Her tragic virtue elicited the praise of contemporaries such as Denis Diderot, sealing the novel's transnational reputation.[3] Indeed, as postcolonial scholarship on the history of the novel has made clear, Richardson's fiction belongs to the currents of cross-cultural exchange that underpinned eighteenth-century writing more generally. Richardson himself seems to have understood this: *Sir Charles Grandison*'s story of an English gentleman returned from the Catholic Continent is nothing if not cosmopolitan.

This said, old literary-historical truisms about Richardson's centrality to *English* fiction – and, even more, to an *anglophone* account of the 'rise of the novel' understood in Ian Watt's terms – are not simply to be dismissed. His narratives do have a particular relation to the nation, and that is what makes it possible to align them to nationalism, even if we need to recontextualise their 'English solidity' (to use Webster's phrase) in light of the broader historical and geographical contexts in which ideas of national identity and culture were formed. To think like this is to draw on the scholarship of nationalism itself, which asks, forthrightly enough, what is nationalism? What are its modes and pre-formations? Did they exist in England in the eighteenth century? If so, in what forms, and to what extent, were they specifically English, British, or both? It is through such questions that we can more fully understand Richardson's relation to nationalism.

Eighteenth-Century English Nationalism

Scholarly discussion distinguishes among three kinds of nationalism that, however, flow into one another. The first is political. This is the idea that a people can be properly organised politically and socially only in and as an autonomous nation. Political nationalism has a specific problem in the English case, which is that, after 1707, the nation contained more than one people, in particular the English and the Scots, and in this sense took the form of a multi-national state. There is another problem with political nationalism that relates specifically to Richardson. It has often been regarded as a modern phenomenon tied to capitalism and industrialisation as they developed after about 1800, and also as a driver of nineteenth-century liberation movements. We can broadly accept this understanding by conceding that we do not meet fully fledged political nationalism in Richardson.

The next form of nationalism is often termed 'romantic' or cultural. In this instance, nations are not just vehicles for a people's autonomy and freedom but for cultures. Indeed, for romantic nationalism, cultures achieve their full development only when bound to a nation and vice versa. Often associated with Johann Gottfried Herder, and ascribed to various nineteenth-century irredentist political movements, this form of nationalism also emerges after Richardson's time. Arguably, however, a softer, 'civic' form of cultural nationalism is evident in mid-eighteenth-century England. This is a national identity based upon a collective history and embodied in particular images, myths, and concepts (such as English 'liberty'). This identity, albeit constituted by different elements, helps unite the polity into an 'imagined community', to use Benedict Anderson's famous term for emergent modern, print-based forms of cultural nationalism.[4]

It is in these terms that Gerald Newman has argued, for instance, that a nascent English cultural nationalism is invented by 'patriot' and oppositional writers and artists of the 1740s such as William Hogarth, Henry Fielding, Oliver Goldsmith, Samuel Johnson, and Tobias Smollett. They draw on the lexicon of the free-born Englishman and the 'ancient constitution' to protest against the corruption associated with the local Court Whig oligarchy, on the one hand, and with forms of luxury and effeminacy associated with French absolutism, on the other.[5] As was the case for Webster's puff of *Pamela* or Scott's chivalric image of Richardson, Englishness here is not just aligned with nature, sincerity, simplicity, and authenticity, but is defined against Frenchness in particular. It is notable that, in this period, 'Britishness', as such, does not form the basis of a national identity (although there is some debate among scholars on this point).[6] Indeed, it is not just that the cultural construction of nationhood is primarily a matter of Englishness defined in moral terms, but that such Englishness is also defined against the Scots and the Irish.

The third kind of nationalism is religious. This is especially important in the English case because of England's very specific confessional structure. Indeed, Liah Greenfield has argued that nationalism is invented in the English Reformation. She thinks of it as a result of Henry VIII's rejection of papal authority, and his creation of an Anglican nobility in the 1530s to administer both his state and his Church. This was a (new) nobility that could appeal neither to blood nor descent nor land and that, thus, appealed rather to what Greenfield calls a 'national sentiment'.[7] For the first time, being a member of a particular confession (Anglicanism) and nation (England) constituted an elite status in itself. Linda Colley puts an eighteenth-century spin on this account, arguing that once Scotland and England were united, Anglicanism could not itself easily be appealed to by the state because the Scottish people were mainly Presbyterian. And so, in the context of Britain's expanding global empire, a more abstract concept of 'Protestantism' became the key component of British national sentiment, in particular against French Catholicism, rival imperial powers, and native peoples.[8] But, to the degree that this happens, it is a shift that is incomplete in Richardson's lifetime.

Richardson and Nationalism

How, then, does Richardson connect to nationalism? The difficulty of answering that question is obvious, since neither his work nor his context neatly aligns to the theories or chronologies outlined above. The actual political forces or interests most relevant to him – the Court Whig interest, the High Church, and the patriot Country Party – were not nationalist at all. For all that, they did each claim to represent a 'national interest' on the basis of different inflections of Church, state, and nation.

The Court Whigs were engaged in building a state that could secure both oligarchic order and commercial interests, but they did so without appealing to English national sentiment directly, partly because – after 1714 – they were so closely tied to the German Hanovers. Their programme was primarily committed to centralised power and the rule of law through Parliament, and was not grounded in English ethnicity, or in traditions of faith, or even in common law. From this point of view, theirs was a state-building programme but not a nation-building one.

The High Church faction (a component of the Tory Party) organised itself in the interests of the Anglican Church, not of the nation or community as a whole. That was because they did not accept any extension of civil rights to Dissenters. Although they were conscious of how Anglicanism defined England's uniqueness, their appeal was to a theological 'middle way' between Roman Catholicism and the Reformed Church, and then also to Anglicanism's unique constitutional role in English government, but not to any nationalism per se.

The patriot 'Country' interest, whose chief ideologue was Henry St John, Lord Bolingbroke, was defined most of all by vigilance in locating threats to 'traditional' English liberties as mounted by oligarchic commercial or court interests. Despite the party's name, however, they were not nationalists either, partly because their political model was classical Republicanism modulated into the idea of the Patriot King. At least until 1745 they also were tinged by Jacobitism. The later transformation of patriotism into a nationalist conservatism has been much discussed by scholars, but David Armitage's contribution to this debate seems persuasive. He argues that Bolingbroke and his circle are best aligned with cosmopolitan stoicism and cannot be properly considered as belonging to the forms of conservatism developed after 1789 by Edmund Burke in which English traditions and lifeways became an avowed political value.[9]

This context matters because, although Richardson himself (unlike Fielding, Swift, or Defoe) was never a party writer, it is possible to see him as linked to High Church Toryism early in his career and then as accommodating to the Court Whigs by the time *Sir Charles Grandison* was published in the early 1750s. If Richardson's political affiliations shifted, however, his commitment to a High Church form of Anglicanism remained constant. The older scholarship that thinks of him as some kind of 'Puritan' is mistaken – there is no room even for Dissent in his fiction. Nor was he an ambiently 'Protestant' author but precisely an Anglican one. More specifically, his novels can be regarded as belonging to the High Church 'moral reformation' movement, which was mounted against the age's perceived moral and religious backsliding.

Richardson's political realignment across his career means that his novels connect to nationalism in two different ways at two different moments. The first is evident in *Pamela*, where he establishes a modern English variation of the marriage plot, and the second in *Sir Charles Grandison*, where he constructs modern gentlemanly virtue as a form of (post-Jacobite) cosmopolitan Anglicanism. Both these inventions are connected to his Anglicanism, and both are foundational to the subsequent development of the novel in distinctly English terms.

So to *Pamela*. The novel's all but revolutionary force is connected to its presenting a servant girl as a pious Christian soul. However, Pamela remains attached to the Anglican structures in place, and in particular that of the country estate and parish, which she is able to reform and strengthen by her moral and religious exemplarity. That is the point of her victory over Mr B, a free-thinking libertine. Richardson invents the modern English marriage plot in this affirmation of piety and virtue, which was itself in the service of an Anglican missionary effort.

How does this relate to nationalism? I would argue that here Richardson puts in place the essential elements of plot, setting, and character out of which an important tradition of English fiction can be built. *Pamela* unfolds as a triangle among a vicar (Mr Williams), a squire (Mr B), and a young woman (Pamela herself), set in a landed estate and a rural English parish. These are the basic components of the rural-based English marriage plot as it passes from Richardson via Fielding and Goldsmith through to Jane Austen and George Eliot, and becomes central to the novel genre's contribution to English cultural nationalism. In this way, *Pamela* prepares the way for an Englishness that is particularly connected not to metropolitan spaces, not to the commons, but to the oligarchical rural English parish.

Sir Charles Grandison presents a different case. Grandison himself is a rich landed gentleman who is first engaged to be married to Clementina della Porretta, a Catholic woman from the Bolognese aristocracy, before finding his true love in Harriet Byron, an Anglican English woman. These parallel courtship narratives enable the novel to balance Grandison's tolerant attitude towards Catholicism with his loyalty to the Church of England. However, the terms in which this balance works are complex, and involve an appeal to natural law rather than to nationalism as such. As Harriet puts it, 'human nature [is] the same in every country, allowing only for different customs' (*SCG*, i.xxxvi.259), which is a vernacular statement of the fundamental presupposition of the natural law theorist Samuel Pufendorf, who believed that marriages were universal in all societies and a primary instance of natural law at work. This principle of uniformity allows Grandison readily to join the community of Italian Catholics around Clementina without a trace of xenophobia. Yet the uniformity of human nature is tested by the breakdown of his engagement to her. In the end their marriage cannot happen because, in Clementina's view, the religious barriers are too strong. And so, the uniformity of human nature posited by natural law is transmuted into a roaming sympathetic imagination, the terms of which are suggested by Clementina, when, having decided that she cannot marry Grandison since he refuses to convert to Catholicism, she appeals for his friendship, asking him to become Catholic, not in fact, but in an act of sympathetic imagination that will allow him to become 'the friend of her *Soul*' (*SCG*, v.xxxiii.212).

Grandison's ability to remain Clementina's friend and mentor after their engagement collapses marks his full achievement as an English gentleman. On the basis of a shared humanity, he has remained true to his identity as an Anglican while retaining his enlightened capacity to communicate across a divide that is less natural or cultural than confessional. Grandison's refusal to convert marks the novel's affirmation of Anglicanism's definitive place in the English constitution. Indeed, the Anglican ideal that he embodies is characterised by its openness to the commerce of the wider world, whereas Clementina and her family (and, by implication Italian Catholics en bloc) cannot transcend creedal limits. In this way, Grandison's sympathetic Anglicanism provides the grounds for his benevolence and allows the novel to figure his union with Harriet as an expression of their shared humanity and simultaneously of their Englishness. This reading of the novel situates *Sir Charles Grandison* within a lineage of Anglican – and English – nationalism in particular, even if its Anglican cosmopolitanism was not as influential for English cultural nationalism as *Pamela*'s rural parish-based marriage plot turned out to be.

In sum, Richardson may not have been a political or cultural nationalist in the strictest sense, and he may not have been intentionally involved in creating or imagining Englishness as such. Nonetheless, his novels helped to create the building blocks out of which the English national imaginary would be constructed.

Notes

1 William Webster, *The Weekly Miscellany* (11 October 1740), in Keymer and Sabor, *The 'Pamela Controversy'*, Vol. 1, p. xliii.
2 Walter Scott, *Lives of the Eminent Novelists and Dramatists* (London, 1886), p. 398.
3 Mary Helen McMurran, *The Spread of Novels: Translation and Prose Fiction in the Eighteenth Century* (Princeton University Press, 2010), pp. 114–15.
4 Benedict Anderson, *Imagined Communities: Reflections on the Origins and Spread of Nationalism* (Verso, 1983).
5 Gerard Newman, *The Rise of English Nationalism: A Cultural History, 1740–1830* (Weidenfeld and Nicolson, 1987), pp. 66–77.

6 Krishan Kumar, *The Making of English National Identity* (Cambridge University Press, 2003), pp. 176–9.
7 Liah Greenfield, *Nationalism: Five Roads to Modernity* (Harvard University Press, 1992), p. 42.
8 Linda Colley, *Britons: Forging the Nation 1707–1837* (Yale University Press, 1992).
9 David Armitage, 'A Patriot for Whom? The Afterlives of Bolingbroke's Patriot King', *Journal of British Studies*, 36.4 (1997), 397–418.

Further Reading

OVERVIEWS AND GENERAL REFERENCES

Bannet, Eve Tavor, *Empire of Letters: Letter Manuals and Transatlantic Correspondence, 1680–1820* (Cambridge: Cambridge University Press, 2005).

Boswell, James, *Boswell's Life of Johnson*, eds. George Birkbeck Hill and L. F. Powell, 6 vols. (Oxford: Clarendon Press, 1934–50).

Brant, Clare, *Eighteenth-Century Letters and British Culture* (Basingstoke: Palgrave Macmillan, 2006).

Bueler, Lois, (ed.), *'Clarissa': The Eighteenth-Century Response, 1747–1804*, 2 vols. (New York: AMS Press, 2010).

Castle, Terry, *Clarissa's Ciphers: Meaning and Disruption in Richardson's 'Clarissa'* (Ithaca, NY: Cornell University Press, 1982).

Curran, Louise, *Samuel Richardson and the Art of Letter-Writing* (Cambridge: Cambridge University Press, 2016).

Doody, Margaret Anne, *A Natural Passion: A Study of the Novels of Samuel Richardson* (Oxford: Clarendon Press, 1974).

Doody, Margaret Anne, and Peter Sabor (eds.), *Samuel Richardson: Tercentenary Essays* (Cambridge: Cambridge University Press, 1989).

Dussinger, John A. '"Stealing in the great doctrines of Christianity": Samuel Richardson as Journalist', *Eighteenth-Century Fiction*, 15.3–4 (2003), 451–506.

Eaves, T. C. Duncan, and Ben D. Kimpel, *Samuel Richardson: A Biography* (Oxford: Clarendon Press, 1971).

Hannaford, Richard G., *Samuel Richardson: An Annotated Bibliography of Critical Studies* (New York: Garland Publishing, 1980).

Keymer, Thomas, and Peter Sabor, *Pamela in the Marketplace: Literary Controversy and Print Culture in Eighteenth-Century Britain and Ireland* (Cambridge: Cambridge University Press, 2005).

Keymer, Tom, *Richardson's 'Clarissa' and the Eighteenth-Century Reader* (Cambridge: Cambridge University Press, 1992).

Keymer, Tom, and Peter Sabor (eds.), *The 'Pamela' Controversy: Criticisms and Adaptations of Samuel Richardson's 'Pamela', 1740–1750*, 6 vols. (London: Pickering & Chatto, 2001).

Kinkead-Weekes, Mark, *Samuel Richardson: Dramatic Novelist* (London: Methuen, 1973).

Maslen, Keith, *Samuel Richardson of London, Printer: A Study of His Printing Based on Ornament Use and Printers' Accounts* (Dunedin: University of Otago, 2001).

Myer, Valerie Grosvenor (ed.), *Samuel Richardson: Passion and Prudence* (London: Vision, 1986).

Redford, Bruce, *The Converse of the Pen: Acts of Intimacy in the Eighteenth-Century Familiar Letter* (Chicago: University of Chicago Press, 1986).

Rivero, Albert J. (ed.), *New Essays on Samuel Richardson* (New York: St Martin's Press, 1996).

Sale, Jr, William Merritt, *Samuel Richardson: A Bibliographical Record of His Literary Career with Historical Notes* (New Haven: Yale University Press, 1936).

Samuel Richardson: Master Printer (Ithaca, NY: Cornell University Press, 1950).

Shepherd, Lynn, *'Clarissa's Painter: Portraiture, Illustration, and Representation in the Novels of Samuel Richardson* (Oxford: Oxford University Press, 2009).

Slattery, William C. (ed.), *The Richardson–Stinstra Correspondence, and Stinstra's Prefaces to 'Clarissa'* (London and Amsterdam: Feffer & Simons, 1969).

Smith, Sarah W. R., *Samuel Richardson: A Reference Guide* (Boston: G. K. Hall, 1984).

Suarez, Michael F., S. J., and Michael L. Turner (eds.), *The Cambridge History of the Book in Britain, Vol. v: 1695–1830* (Cambridge: Cambridge University Press, 2009).

Warner, William Beatty, *Licensing Entertainment: The Elevation of Novel Reading in Britain, 1684–1750* (Berkeley: University of California Press, 1998).

Whyman, Susan E., *The Pen and the People: English Letter Writers 1660–1800* (Oxford: Oxford University Press, 2009).

1 PORTRAYING THE LIFE

Aikins, Janet E. (ed.), 'Meditations on Eaves and Kimpel's Samuel Richardson: Transactionality among Literary Biography, Fictional Narrative, and the Lives of the Critics', special feature in *1650–1850: Ideas, Aesthetics, and Inquiries in the Early Modern Era*, 9 (2003), 269–362.

Conway, Alison, *Private Interests: Women, Portraiture, and the Visual Culture of the English Novel, 1709–1791* (Toronto: University of Toronto Press, 2001).

Dussinger, John A., 'Richardson, Samuel (bap. 1689, d. 1761)', *Oxford Dictionary of National Biography* (Oxford: Oxford University Press, 2004), online edn.

'Samuel Richardson's "Elegant Disquisitions": Anonymous Writing in the *True Briton* and Other Journals?', *Studies in Bibliography*, 53 (2000), 195–226.

Kerslake, John F., *Early Georgian Portraits, National Portrait Gallery*, 2 vols. (London: HMSO, 1977).

Keymer, Thomas, 'Parliamentary Printing, Paper Credit, and Corporate Fraud: A New Episode in Richardson's Early Career', *Eighteenth-Century Fiction*, 17.2 (2005), 183–206.

Mild, Warren, *Joseph Highmore of Holborn Row* (Ardmore, PA: Phyllis Mild, 1990).

Pointon, Marcia R., *Hanging the Head: Portraiture and Social Formation in Eighteenth-Century England* (New Haven: Yale University Press, 1993).

Shepherd, Lynn, 'Samuel Richardson and Eighteenth-Century Portraiture' (dissertation, University of Oxford, 2006).

Wendorf, Richard, *The Elements of Life: Biography and Portrait-Painting in Stuart and Georgian England* (Oxford: Clarendon Press, 1990).

2 PUBLICATION HISTORY

Brack, O M, Jr, '*Clarissa*'s Bibliography: Problems and Challenges', in Florian Stuber and Margaret Anne Doody (eds.), *Samuel Richardson's Published Commentary on Clarissa*, 3 vols. (London: Pickering & Chatto, 1998), Vol. II, pp. 305–24.

Dussinger, John A., 'Fabrications from Samuel Richardson's Press', *Papers of the Bibliographical Society of America*, 100.2 (2006), 259–79.

'Samuel Richardson's "Elegant Disquisitions": Anonymous Writing in the *True Briton* and Other Journals?', *Studies in Bibliography*, 53 (2000), 195–226.

Eaves, T. C. Duncan, and Ben D. Kimpel, 'Richardson's Revisions of *Pamela*', *Studies in Bibliography*, 20 (1967), 61–88.

Gaskell, Philip, *From Writer to Reader: Studies in Editorial Method* (Oxford: Clarendon Press, 1978).

Keymer, Tom, 'Assorted Versions of Assaulted Virgins; or, Textual Instability and Teaching', in Lisa Zunshine and Jocelyn Harris (eds.), *Approaches to Teaching the Novels of Samuel Richardson* (New York: Modern Language Association of America, 2006), pp. 24–31.

'*Clarissa*'s Death, *Clarissa*'s Sale, and the Text of the Second Edition', *Review of English Studies*, n.s. 45.179 (1994), 389–96.

Pierson, Robert C., 'The Revisions of Richardson's *Sir Charles Grandison*', *Studies in Bibliography*, 21 (1968), 163–89.

Van Marter, Shirley, 'Richardson's Revisions of *Clarissa* in the Second Edition', *Studies in Bibliography*, 26 (1973), 107–32.

'Richardson's Revisions of *Clarissa* in the Third and Fourth Editions', *Studies in Bibliography*, 28 (1975), 119–52.

Zach, Wolfgang, 'Mrs Aubin and Richardson's Earliest Literary Manifesto (1739)', *English Studies*, 62.3 (1981), 271–85.

3 CORRESPONDENCE

Cook, Elizabeth Heckendorn, *Epistolary Bodies: Gender and Genre in the Eighteenth-Century Republic of Letters* (Stanford: Stanford University Press, 1996).

Dussinger, John A., 'Samuel Richardson's Manuscript Draft of *The Rambler* No. 97 (19 February 1751)', *Notes and Queries*, 57.1 (2010), 93–9.

How, James, *Epistolary Spaces: English Letter-Writing from the Foundation of the Post Office to Richardson's 'Clarissa'* (Aldershot: Ashgate, 2003).

Irving, William Henry, *The Providence of Wit in the English Letter Writers* (Durham, NC: Duke University Press, 1955).

McKenzie, Alan T., *Sent as a Gift: Eight Correspondences from the Eighteenth Century* (Athens: University of Georgia Press, 1993).

Sabor, Peter, '"The job I have perhaps rashly undertaken": Publishing the Complete Correspondence of Samuel Richardson', *Eighteenth-Century Life*, 35.1 (2011), 9–28.

Zirker, Malvin R., Jr, 'Richardson's Correspondence: The Personal Letter as Private Experience', in Howard Anderson, Philip B. Daghlian, and Irvin Ehrenpreis (eds.), *The Familiar Letter in the Eighteenth Century* (Lawrence, KS: University of Kansas Press, 1966), pp. 71–91.

4 EDITIONS

Carroll, John (ed.), *Selected Letters of Samuel Richardson* (Oxford: Oxford University Press, 1964).

Mangin, Edward, 'A Sketch of the Life and Writings of Samuel Richardson', in *The Works of Samuel Richardson*, 19 vols. (London, 1811), Vol. 1, pp. vii–xxviii.

McCarthy, William, 'What Did Anna Barbauld Do to Samuel Richardson's Correspondence? A Study of Her Editing', *Studies in Bibliography*, 54 (2001), 191–223.

McKenna, Ethel M. M., 'Introduction', in *The Novels of Samuel Richardson*, 20 vols. (London: Chapman & Hall, 1902), Vol. 1, pp. ix–xxxii.

Mullett, Charles F. (ed.), *The Letters of Doctor George Cheyne to Samuel Richardson (1733–1743)* (Columbia: University of Missouri Press, 1943).

Phelps, William Lyon, 'Samuel Richardson', in *The Novels of Samuel Richardson*, 19 vols. (New York: Croscup & Sterling, 1901–2), Vol. 1, pp. ix–lvi.

Richardson, Samuel, *The Shakespeare Head Edition of the Novels of Samuel Richardson*, 18 vols. (Oxford: Shakespeare Head, 1929–31).

Scott, Sir Walter, 'Prefatory Memoir to Richardson', in *The Novels of Samuel Richardson, Esq. viz. 'Pamela', 'Clarissa Harlowe', and 'Sir Charles Grandison'*, 3 vols. (London, 1824), Vol. 1, pp. i–xlviii.

Stephen, Leslie, 'Richardson's Novels', in *The Works of Samuel Richardson*, 12 vols. (London and Manchester, 1883), Vol. 1, pp. ix–lv.

Thomson, Clara L., *Samuel Richardson: A Biographical and Critical Study* (London: Horace Marshall, 1900).

Traill, H. D., 'Samuel Richardson', *Contemporary Review*, 44.4 (1883), 529–45.

5 CONTEMPORARY TRANSNATIONAL RECEPTION

Beebee, Thomas O., *Clarissa on the Continent: Translation and Seduction* (University Park: Pennsylvania State University Press, 1990).

Charles, Shelly, 'De la traduction au pastiche: *l'Histoire du chevalier Grandisson*', *Eighteenth-Century Fiction*, 13.1 (2000), 19–40.

Comparini, Lucie (ed.), *Pamela européenne: parcours d'une figure mythique dans l'Europe des Lumières* (Montpellier: Université Paul Valéry-Montpellier III, 2009).

Festa, Lynn, 'Sentimental Bonds and Revolutionary Characters: Richardson's *Pamela* in England and France', in Margaret Cohen and Carolyn Dever (eds.), *The Literary Channel: The Inter-National Invention of the Novel* (Princeton: Princeton University Press, 2002), pp. 73–105.

Krake, Astrid, ' "Translating to the moment" – Marketing and Anglomania: The First German Translation of Richardson's *Clarissa* (1747/1748)', in Stefanie Stockhorst (ed.), *Cultural Transfer through Translation: The Circulation of Enlightened Thought in Europe by Means of Translation* (Amsterdam: Rodopi, 2010), pp. 103–20.

McMurran, Mary Helen, *The Spread of Novels: Translation and Prose Fiction in the Eighteenth Century* (Princeton: Princeton University Press, 2010).

Pajares Infante, Eterio, 'Samuel Richardson's Presence and Absence in Spain', *Revista alicantina de estudios ingleses*, 7 (1994), 159–70.

Piva, Franco (ed.), *Les mémoires de Pamela, écrits par elle-même* (Fasano: Schena Editore, 2007).

Richardson, Samuel, *Lettres anglaises; ou, Histoire de Miss Clarissa Harlove*, trans. l'abbé Prévost, ed. Shelly Charles, 2 vols. (Paris: Desjonquères, 1999).

Slattery, William C., 'Samuel Richardson and the Netherlands: Early Reception of His Work', *Papers on English Language and Literature*, 1 (1965), 20–30.

Tennenhouse, Leonard, 'The Americanization of *Clarissa*', *Yale Journal of Criticism*, 11.1 (1998), 177–96.

6 REPUTATION

Aikins, Janet E., 'Picturing "Samuel Richardson": Francis Hayman and the Intersections of Word and Image', *Eighteenth-Century Fiction*, 14.3–4 (2002), 465–505.

Gamer, Michael, 'A Select Collection: Barbauld, Scott, and the Rise of the (Reprinted) Novel', in Jillian Heydt-Stevenson and Charlotte Sussman (eds.), *Recognizing the Romantic Novel: New Histories of British Fiction, 1780–1830* (Liverpool: Liverpool University Press, 2008), pp. 155–91.

Michie, Allen, *Richardson and Fielding: The Dynamics of a Critical Rivalry* (Lewisburg, PA: Bucknell University Press, 1999).

Price, Leah, *The Anthology and the Rise of the Novel: From Richardson to George Eliot* (Cambridge: Cambridge University Press, 2000).

Rain, D. C., 'Richardson's Character: A Case Study in an Author's Reputation', *English: Journal of the English Association*, 43.177 (1994), 193–208.

Simonova, Natasha, *Early Modern Authorship and Prose Continuations: Adaptation and Ownership from Sidney to Richardson* (Basingstoke: Palgrave Macmillan, 2015).

Warner, William Beatty, *Reading Clarissa: The Struggles of Interpretation* (New Haven: Yale University Press, 1979).

7 CRITICAL RECEPTION TO 1900

Bartolomeo, Joseph F., *A New Species of Criticism: Eighteenth-Century Discourse on the Novel* (Newark: University of Delaware Press, 1994).

Brophy, Elizabeth Bergen, *Samuel Richardson: The Triumph of Craft* (Knoxville: University of Tennessee Press, 1974).

Corman, Brian, *Women Novelists before Jane Austen: The Critics and Their Canons* (Toronto: University of Toronto Press, 2008).

Ingrassia, Catherine, *Authorship, Commerce, and Gender in Early Eighteenth-Century England: A Culture of Paper Credit* (Cambridge: Cambridge University Press, 1998).

Klancher, Jon P., *The Making of English Reading Audiences, 1790–1832* (Madison: University of Wisconsin Press, 1987).

Michie, Allen, *Richardson and Fielding: The Dynamics of a Critical Rivalry* (Lewisburg, PA: Bucknell University Press, 1999).

Ross, Trevor, *The Making of the English Literary Canon: From the Middle Ages to the Late Eighteenth Century* (Montreal: McGill-Queen's University Press, 1998).

Runge, Laura L., *Gender and Language in British Literary Criticism, 1660–1790* (Cambridge: Cambridge University Press, 1997).

Stephen, Leslie, 'Richardson's Novels', in John Charles Olmsted (ed.), *A Victorian Art of Fiction: Essays on the Novel in British Periodicals*, 3 vols. (New York: Garland, 1979), Vol. II, pp. 597–620.

8 CRITICAL RECEPTION SINCE 1900

Blewett, David (ed.), *Passion and Virtue: Essays on the Novels of Samuel Richardson* (Toronto: University of Toronto Press, 2001).

Brissenden, R. F., *Virtue in Distress: Studies in the Novel of Sentiment from Richardson to Sade* (London: Macmillan, 1974).

Eagleton, Terry, *The Rape of Clarissa: Writing, Sexuality and Class Struggle in Samuel Richardson* (Minneapolis: University of Minnesota Press, 1982).

Gwilliam, Tassie, *Samuel Richardson's Fictions of Gender* (Stanford: Stanford University Press, 1993).

Harris, Jocelyn, *Samuel Richardson* (Cambridge: Cambridge University Press, 1987).

Maslen, Keith, 'Samuel Richardson of London, Printer: Further Extending the Canon', *Script & Print*, 36.3 (2012), 133–54.

Watt, Ian, *The Rise of the Novel: Studies in Defoe, Richardson and Fielding* (Berkeley: University of California Press, 1957).

9 THE STATIONERS' COMPANY

Blagden, Cyprian, *The Stationers' Company: A History, 1403–1959* (London: George Allen & Unwin, 1960).

'The Stationers' Company in the Eighteenth Century', *Guildhall Miscellany*, 1.10 (1959), 36–53.

Blayney, Peter W. M., 'The Publication of Playbooks', in John D. Cox and David Scott Kastan (eds.), *A New History of Early English Drama* (New York: Columbia University Press, 1997), pp. 383–422.

The Stationers' Company and the Printers of London, 1501–1557, 2 vols. (Cambridge: Cambridge University Press, 2013).

Feather, John, 'The Book Trade in Politics: The Making of the Copyright Act of 1710', *Publishing History*, 8 (1980), 19–44.

Gadd, Ian Anders, '"Being like a field": Corporate Identity in the Stationers' Company 1557–1684' (dissertation, University of Oxford, 1999).

Gadd, Ian Anders, and Patrick Wallis, 'Reaching beyond the City Wall: London Guilds and National Regulation, 1500–1700', in S. R. Epstein and M. Prak (eds.), *Guilds, Innovation and the European Economy, 1400–1800* (Cambridge: Cambridge University Press, 2008), pp. 288–315.

(eds.), *Guilds, Society and Economy in London, 1450–1800* (London: Centre for Metropolitan History, 2002).

McKenzie, D. F. (ed.), *Stationers' Company Apprentices, 1701–1800* (Oxford: Oxford Bibliographical Society, 1978).

Saunders, Ann, 'The Stationers' Hall', in Robin Myers (ed.), *The Stationers' Company: A History of the Later Years 1800–2000* (London: Worshipful Company of Stationers and Newspaper Makers, 2001), pp. 151–73.

Turner, Michael L., 'Personnel within the London Book Trades: Evidence from the Stationers' Company', in Michael F. Suarez, S. J. and Michael L. Turner (eds.), *The Cambridge History of the Book in Britain, Vol. 1: 1695–1830* (Cambridge: Cambridge University Press, 2009), pp. 309–34.

10 TRANSNATIONAL PRINT TRADE RELATIONS

Beebee, Thomas O., *Clarissa on the Continent: Translation and Seduction* (University Park: Pennsylvania State University Press, 1990).

Cole, Richard C., *Irish Booksellers and English Writers, 1740–1800* (London: Mansell Publishing, 1986).

Fysh, Stephanie, *The Work(s) of Samuel Richardson* (Newark: University of Delaware Press, 1997).

Krake, Astrid, 'Der deutsche Richardson: Übersetzungsgeschichte als Beitrag zur Rezeptionsgeschichte', in Susanne Stark (ed.), *The Novel in Anglo-German Context: Cultural Cross-Currents and Affinities* (Amsterdam: Rodopi, 2000), pp. 23–35.

'"Translating to the Moment" – Marketing and Anglomania: The First German Translation of Richardson's *Clarissa* (1747/1748)', in Stefanie Stockhorst (ed.), *Cultural Transfer through Translation: The Circulation of Enlightened Thought in Europe by Means of Translation* (Amsterdam: Rodopi, 2010), pp. 103–20.

Lehmstedt, Mark, *'Ich bin nicht gewohnt, mit Künstlern zu dingen ...': Philipp Erasmus Reich und die Buchillustration im 18. Jahrhundert* (Leipzig: Deutsche Bücherei, 1989).

Philipp Erasmus Reich (1717–1787): Verleger der Aufklärung und Reformer des deutschen Buchhandels (Leipzig: Karl-Marx-Universität Leipzig, 1989).

Rosenstrauch, Hazel, *Buchhandelsmanufaktur und Aufklärung: Die Reformen des Buchhändlers und Verlegers Ph. E. Reich (1717–1787)*. (Frankfurt am Main: Buchhändler-Vereinigung, 1986).

Sale, William Merritt, Jr, 'Sir Charles Grandison and the Dublin Pirates', *Yale University Library Gazette*, 7.4 (1933), 80–6.

Temple, Kathryn, 'Printing like a Post-Colonialist: The Irish Piracy of *Sir Charles Grandison*', *Novel: A Forum on Fiction*, 33.2 (2000), 157–74.

Velema, Wyger R. E., *Enlightenment and Conservatism in the Dutch Republic: The Political Thought of Elie Luzac (1721–1796)* (Assen: Van Gorcum, 1993).

Vliet, Rietje van, *Elie Luzac (1721–1796): Bookseller of the Enlightenment* (Enschede: AFdH Uitgevers, 2014).

11 AUTHORSHIP

Ezell, Margaret J. M., *Social Authorship and the Advent of Print* (Baltimore: Johns Hopkins University Press, 1999).

Gerrard, Christine, *Aaron Hill: The Muses' Projector, 1685–1750* (Oxford: Oxford University Press, 2003).

Rose, Mark, 'Copyright, Authors and Censorship', in Michael F. Suarez, S. J. and Michael L. Turner (eds.), *The Cambridge History of the Book in Britain, Vol. V: 1695–1830* (Cambridge: Cambridge University Press, 2009), pp. 118–31.

Schellenberg, Betty A., *Literary Coteries and the Making of Modern Print Culture, 1740–1790* (Cambridge: Cambridge University Press, 2016).

Siskin, Clifford, *The Work of Writing: Literature and Social Change in Britain, 1700–1830* (Baltimore: Johns Hopkins University Press, 1998).

Stephanson, Raymond, *The Yard of Wit: Male Creativity and Sexuality, 1650–1750* (Philadelphia: University of Pennsylvania Press, 2004).

Zionkowski, Linda, *Men's Work: Gender, Class, and the Professionalization of Poetry, 1660–1784* (New York: Palgrave Macmillan, 2001).

12 THE LITERARY MARKETPLACE

Brewer, John, *The Pleasures of the Imagination: English Culture in the Eighteenth Century* (New York: Farrar, Straus, & Giroux, 1997).

Ingrassia, Catherine, *Authorship, Commerce, and Gender in Early Eighteenth-Century England: A Culture of Paper Credit* (Cambridge: Cambridge University Press, 1998).

Keymer, Thomas, and Peter Sabor (eds.), *Richardson's Apparatus and Fielding's 'Shamela': Verse Responses*, Vol. 1 of *The Pamela Controversy: Criticisms and Adaptations of Samuel Richardson's 'Pamela', 1740–1750*, 6 vols. (London: Pickering & Chatto, 2001).

McKillop, Alan Dugald, *Samuel Richardson: Printer and Novelist* (Chapel Hill: University of North Carolina Press, 1936).

Raven, James, *The Business of Books: Booksellers and the English Book Trade, 1450–1850* (New Haven: Yale University Press, 2007).
Rivers, Isabel (ed.), *Books and Their Readers in Eighteenth-Century England* (Leicester: Leicester University Press, 1982).
  Books and Their Readers in Eighteenth-Century England: New Essays (London: Continuum, 2001).

13 THE MATERIAL BOOK

Barchas, Janine, *Graphic Design, Print Culture, and the Eighteenth-Century Novel* (Cambridge: Cambridge University Press, 2003).
Brewer, John, *The Pleasures of the Imagination: English Culture in the Eighteenth Century* (New York: Farrar, Straus, & Giroux, 1997).
Flint, Christopher, *The Appearance of Print in Eighteenth-Century Fiction* (Cambridge: Cambridge University Press, 2011).
Johns, Adrian, *The Nature of the Book: Print and Knowledge in the Making* (Chicago: University of Chicago Press, 1998).
Loewenstein, Joseph, *The Author's Due: Printing and the Prehistory of Copyright* (Chicago: University of Chicago Press, 2002).
McKitterick, David, *Print, Manuscript and the Search for Order, 1450–1830* (Cambridge: Cambridge University Press, 2003).
Sher, Richard, *The Enlightenment and the Book: Scottish Authors and Their Publishers in Eighteenth-Century Britain, Ireland, and America* (Chicago: University of Chicago Press, 2006).

14 EDITING

Battestin, Martin C., and Clive T. Probyn (eds.), *The Correspondence of Henry and Sarah Fielding* (Oxford: Clarendon Press, 1993).
Davies, Godfrey, 'Daniel Defoe's "A Tour thro' the Whole Island of Great Britain"', *Modern Philology*, 48.1 (1950), 21–36.
Dussinger, John A., 'Anna Meades, Samuel Richardson and Thomas Hull: The Making of *The History of Sir William Harrington*', in Albert J. Rivero (ed.), *New Essays on Samuel Richardson* (New York: St Martin's Press, 1996), pp. 177–92.
  'An Overlooked Aesop from Samuel Richardson's Press', *Notes and Queries*, 56.2 (2009), 239–43.
Eaves, T. C. Duncan, and Ben D. Kimpel, 'Richardson's Connection with *Sir William Harrington*', *Papers on Language and Literature*, 4.3 (1968), 276–87.
Keymer, Tom, 'Richardson's *Meditations*: Clarissa's *Clarissa*', in Margaret Anne Doody and Peter Sabor (eds.), *Samuel Richardson: Tercentenary Essays* (Cambridge: Cambridge University Press, 1989), pp. 89–109.
Nace, Nicholas D., 'Filling Blanks in the Richardson Circle: The Unsuccessful Mentorship of Urania Johnson', in Anthony W. Lee (ed.), *Mentoring in Eighteenth-Century British Literature and Culture* (Farnham: Ashgate, 2009), pp. 109–30.

'The Publication of Urania Johnson's "Unpublishable" *Almira*', *Papers of the Bibliographical Society of America*, 103.1 (2009), 5–18.

Pettit, Henry (ed.), *The Correspondence of Edward Young, 1683–1765* (Oxford: Clarendon Press, 1971).

Rogers, Pat, *The Text of Great Britain: Theme and Design in Defoe's 'Tour'* (Newark: University of Delaware Press, 1998).

15 READING AND READERS

Bannet, Eve Tavor, 'History of Reading: The Long Eighteenth Century', *Literature Compass*, 10.2 (2013), 122–33.

  Transatlantic Stories and the History of Reading, 1720–1810: Migrant Fictions (Cambridge: Cambridge University Press, 2011).

Colclough, Stephen, *Consuming Texts: Readers and Reading Communities, 1695–1870* (Basingstoke: Palgrave Macmillan, 2007).

Dussinger, John A. (ed.), *Correspondence with Sarah Wescomb, Frances Grainger and Laetitia Pilkington*, Vol. III of *The Cambridge Edition of the Correspondence of Samuel Richardson*, 12 vols. (Cambridge: Cambridge University Press, 2015).

Knights, Elspeth, '"Daring but to touch the hem of her garment": Women Reading *Clarissa*', *Women's Writing*, 7.2 (2000), 221–45.

O'Neill, Lindsay, *The Opened Letter: Networking in the Early Modern British World* (Philadelphia: University of Pennsylvania Press, 2015).

Raven, James, Helen Small, and Naomi Tadmor (eds.), *The Practice and Representation of Reading in England* (Cambridge: Cambridge University Press, 1996).

Rivers, Isabel (ed.), *Books and Their Readers in Eighteenth-Century England: New Essays* (London: Continuum, 2001).

Schellenberg, Betty A. (ed.), *Correspondence Primarily on 'Sir Charles Grandison'*, Vol. X of *The Cambridge Edition of the Correspondence of Samuel Richardson*, 12 vols. (Cambridge: Cambridge University Press, 2015).

Sharpe, Kevin, *Reading Revolutions: The Politics of Reading in Early Modern England* (New Haven: Yale University Press, 2000).

16 THE NOVEL

Bowers, Toni, *Force or Fraud: British Seduction Stories and the Problem of Resistance, 1660–1760* (Oxford: Oxford University Press, 2011).

Flint, Christopher, *Family Fictions: Narrative and Domestic Relations in Britain, 1688–1798* (Stanford: Stanford University Press, 1998).

Harris, Jocelyn, *Samuel Richardson* (Cambridge: Cambridge University Press, 1987).

Macpherson, Sandra, *Harm's Way: Tragic Responsibility and the Novel Form* (Baltimore: Johns Hopkins University Press, 2010).

Schellenberg, Betty A., *The Conversational Circle: Re-Reading the English Novel, 1740–1775* (Lexington: University Press of Kentucky, 1996).

Spacks, Patricia Meyer, *Desire and Truth: Functions of Plot in Eighteenth-Century English Novels* (Chicago: University of Chicago Press, 1990).

Wall, Cynthia S., *The Prose of Things: Transformations of Description in the Eighteenth Century* (Chicago: University of Chicago Press, 2006).

Zomchick, John P., *Family and the Law in Eighteenth-Century Fiction: The Public Conscience in the Private Sphere* (Cambridge: Cambridge University Press, 1993).

17 FABLES AND FAIRY-TALES

DeJean, Joan E., *Ancients against Moderns: Culture Wars and the Making of a 'Fin de Siècle'* (Chicago: University of Chicago Press, 1997).

The Essence of Style: How the French Invented High Fashion, Fine food, Chic Cafés, Style, Sophistication, and Glamour (New York: Free Press, 2005).

Mack, Robert L. (ed.), 'Introduction', in *Arabian Nights' Entertainments* (Oxford: Oxford University Press, 1995), pp. ix–xxiii.

'Introduction', in *Oriental Tales* (Oxford: Oxford University Press, 1992), pp. vii–xlix.

Mernissi, Fatima, *Scheherazade Goes West: Different Cultures, Different Harems* (New York: Washington Square Press, 2001).

Perrault, Charles, *Complete Fairy Tales in Verse and Prose; L'intégrale des contes en vers et en prose*, ed. and trans. Stanley Appelbaum (Mineola, NY: Dover Publications, 2002).

Warner, Marina, *Once upon a Time: A Short History of Fairy Tale* (Oxford: Oxford University Press, 2014).

Zipes, Jack, *The Irresistible Fairy Tale: The Cultural and Social History of a Genre* (Princeton: Princeton University Press, 2012).

18 LETTERS

Beebee, Thomas O., *Epistolary Fiction in Europe, 1500–1850* (Cambridge: Cambridge University Press, 1999).

Benstock, Shari, 'From Letters to Literature: *La carte postale* in the Epistolary Genre', *Genre*, 18.3 (1985), 257–95.

Bray, Bernard A., *L'art de la lettre amoureuse: des manuels aux romans (1550–1700)* (The Hague: Mouton, 1967).

Cook, Elizabeth Heckendorn, *Epistolary Bodies: Gender and Genre in the Eighteenth-Century Republic of Letters* (Stanford: Stanford University Press, 1996).

Day, Robert A., *Told in Letters: Epistolary Fiction before Richardson* (Ann Arbor: University of Michigan Press, 1966).

How, James, *Epistolary Spaces: English Letter Writing from the Foundation of the Post Office to Richardson's 'Clarissa'* (Aldershot: Ashgate, 2003).

Kauffman, Linda S., *Discourses of Desire: Gender, Genre, and Epistolary Fictions* (Ithaca, NY: Cornell University Press, 1986).

Myers, Victoria, 'Model Letters, Moral Living: Letter-Writing Manuals by Daniel Defoe and Samuel Richardson', *Huntington Library Quarterly*, 66.3–4 (2003), 373–91.

Singer, Godfrey F., *The Epistolary Novel: Its Origin, Development, Decline, and Residuary Influence* (Philadelphia: University of Pennsylvania Press, 1933).

Versini, Laurent, *Laclos et la tradition: essai sur les sources et la technique des 'Liaisons dangereuses'* (Paris: Klincksieck, 1968).

19 EDUCATIONAL WRITING

Allan, David, *Commonplace Books and Reading in Georgian England* (Cambridge: Cambridge University Press, 2010).

'Printed Epistolary Manuals and the Transatlantic Rescripting of Manuscript Culture', *Studies in Eighteenth-Century Culture*, 36 (2007), 13–32.

Crane, Mary Thomas, *Framing Authority: Sayings, Self, and Society in Sixteenth-Century England* (Princeton: Princeton University Press, 1993).

Dussinger, John A., 'Introduction', in *A Collection of the Moral and Instructive Sentiments, Maxims, Cautions, and Reflections, Contained in the Histories of Pamela, Clarissa, and Sir Charles Grandison, 1755*, in Florian Stuber and Margaret Anne Doody (eds.), *Samuel Richardson's Published Commentary on 'Clarissa'*, 3 vols. (London: Pickering & Chatto, 1998), Vol. III, pp. vii–l.

Hornbeak, Katherine G., *The Complete Letter-Writer in English, 1568–1800*, Smith College Studies in Modern Languages, 15.3–4 (1934).

Mitchell, Linda C., 'Entertainment and Instruction: Women's Roles in the English Epistolary Tradition', *Huntington Library Quarterly*, 66.3–4 (2003), 331–47.

Mitchell, Linda C., and Carol Poster (eds.), *Letter-Writing Manuals and Instruction from Antiquity to the Present: Historical and Bibliographic Studies* (Columbia: University of South Carolina Press, 2007).

Myers, Victoria, 'Model Letters, Moral Living: Letter-Writing Manuals by Daniel Defoe and Samuel Richardson', *Huntington Library Quarterly*, 66.3–4 (2003), 373–91.

Van Sant, Ann Jessie, 'Afterword', in *A Collection of the Moral and Instructive Sentiments, Maxims, Cautions, and Reflections, Contained in the Histories of Pamela, Clarissa, and Sir Charles Grandison, 1755*, in Florian Stuber and Margaret Anne Doody (eds.), *Samuel Richardson's Published Commentary on 'Clarissa'*, 3 vols. (London: Pickering & Chatto, 1998), Vol. III, pp. 411–37.

20 THE ENGLISH LANGUAGE

Ball, Donald L., 'Richardson's Resourceful Wordmaking', *South Atlantic Bulletin*, 41.4 (1976), 56–65.

Bray, Joe, *The Epistolary Novel: Representations of Consciousness* (London: Routledge, 2003).

Cohen, Michèle, *Fashioning Masculinity: National Identity and Language in the Eighteenth Century* (London: Routledge, 1996).

Eaves, T. C. Duncan, and Ben D. Kimpel, 'Richardson's Revisions of *Pamela*', *Studies in Bibliography*, 20 (1967), 61–88.

Hurlbert, Jarrod, 'Pamela; or; Virtue Reworded: The Texts, Paratexts, and Revisions that Redefine Samuel Richardson's *Pamela*' (dissertation, Marquette University, 2012).

Keast, William R., 'The Two *Clarissa*s in Johnson's *Dictionary*', *Studies in Philology*, 54.3 (1957), 429–39.

Pierson, Robert C., 'The Revisions of Richardson's *Sir Charles Grandison*', *Studies in Bibliography*, 21 (1968), 163–89.

Tieken-Boon van Ostade, Ingrid, *The Bishop's Grammar: Robert Lowth and the Rise of Prescriptivism in English* (Oxford: Oxford University Press, 2011).

'Samuel Richardson's Role as Linguistic Innovator: A Sociolinguistic Analysis', in John Frankis and Ingrid Tieken-Boon van Ostade (eds.), *Language Usage and Description: Studies Presented to N. E. Osselton on the Occasion of His Retirement* (Amsterdam: Rodopi, 1991), pp. 47–57.

Tucker, Susie I., 'Richardsonian Phrases', *Notes and Queries*, 13.12 (1966), 464–5.

Uhrström, Wilhelm P., *Studies on the Language of Samuel Richardson* (Uppsala: Almqvist & Wiksell, 1907).

Van Marter, Shirley, 'Richardson's Revisions of *Clarissa* in the Second Edition', *Studies in Bibliography*, 26 (1973), 107–32.

'Richardson's Revisions of *Clarissa* in the Third and Fourth Editions', *Studies in Bibliography*, 28 (1975), 199–52.

21 SALON CULTURE AND CONVERSATION

Ellis, Markman, '*Reading Practices in Elizabeth Montagu's Epistolary Network of the 1750s*', in Elizabeth Eger (ed.), *Bluestockings Displayed: Portraiture, Performance and Patronage, 1730–1830* (Cambridge: Cambridge University Press, 2013), pp. 213–32.

Goodman, Dena, *The Republic of Letters: A Cultural History of the French Enlightenment* (Ithaca, NY: Cornell University Press, 1994).

Heller, Deborah, '*Bluestocking Salons* and the Public Sphere', *Eighteenth-Century Life*, 22.2 (1998), 59–82.

Knights, Elspeth, '"Daring but to touch the hem of her garment": Women Reading *Clarissa*', *Women's Writing*, 7.2 (2000), 221–45.

Mylne, Vivienne, 'The Punctuation of Dialogue in Eighteenth-Century French and English Fiction', *Library*, 6.1 (1979), 43–61.

Page, Norman, *Speech in the English Novel*, 2nd edn (London: Macmillan, 1988).

Schellenberg, Betty A., *The Conversational Circle: Re-Reading the English Novel, 1740–1775* (Lexington: University Press of Kentucky, 1996).

Literary Coteries and the Making of Modern Print Culture, 1740–1790 (Cambridge: Cambridge University Press, 2016).

Seedhouse, Paul, 'Conversation Analysis', in Robert Bayley, Richard Cameron, and Ceil Lucas (eds.), *The Oxford Handbook of Sociolinguistics* (Oxford: Oxford University Press, 2013), pp. 91–110.

Speer, Susan A., and Elizabeth Stokoe (eds.), *Conversation and Gender* (Cambridge: Cambridge University Press, 2011).

22 THE VISUAL ARTS

Aikins, Janet E., 'Richardson's "Speaking Pictures"', in Margaret Anne Doody and Peter Sabor (eds.), *Samuel Richardson: Tercentenary Essays* (Cambridge: Cambridge University Press, 1989), pp. 146–66.

Barchas, Janine, *Graphic Design, Print Culture, and the Eighteenth-Century Novel* (Cambridge: Cambridge University Press, 2003).

Bray, Joe, *The Portrait in Fiction of the Romantic Period* (Abington: Routledge, 2016).

Conway, Alison, *Private Interests: Women, Portraiture, and the Visual Culture of the English Novel, 1709–1791* (Toronto: University of Toronto Press, 2001).

Eaves, T. C. Duncan, 'Graphic Illustration of the Novels of Samuel Richardson, 1740–1810', *Huntington Library Quarterly*, 14.4 (1951), 349–83.

Leppert, Richard, *Music and Image: Domesticity, Ideology, and Socio-Cultural Formation in Eighteenth-Century England* (Cambridge: Cambridge University Press, 1988).

Paulson, Ronald, *Emblem and Expression: Meaning in English Art of the Eighteenth Century* (London: Thames and Hudson, 1975).

Pointon, Marcia R., *Hanging the Head: Portraiture and Social Formation in Eighteenth-Century England* (New Haven: Yale University Press, 1993).

Smitten, Jeffrey R., 'Introduction: Spatial Form and Narrative Theory', in Jeffrey R. Smitten and Ann Daghistany (eds.), *Spatial Form in Narrative* (Ithaca, NY: Cornell University Press, 1981), pp. 15–34.

West, Shearer, 'The Public Nature of Private Life: The Conversation Piece and the Fragmented Family', *Journal for Eighteenth-Century Studies*, 18.2 (1995), 153–72.

23 THEATRE AND DRAMA

Aikins, Janet E., 'A Plot Discover'd; or, The Uses of *Venice Preserv'd* within *Clarissa*', *University of Toronto Quarterly*, 55.3 (1986), 219–34.

Connaughton, Michael E., 'Richardson's Familiar Quotations: *Clarissa* and Bysshe's *Art of English Poetry*', *Philological Quarterly*, 60.2 (1981), 183–95.

Domingo, Darryl P., 'Richardson's Unfamiliar Quotations: *Clarissa* and Early Eighteenth-Century Comedy', *Review of English Studies*, 66.277 (2015), 936–53.

Harris, Jocelyn, 'Richardson: Original or Learned Genius?', in Margaret Anne Doody and Peter Sabor (eds.), *Samuel Richardson: Tercentenary Essays* (Cambridge: Cambridge University Press, 1989), pp. 188–202.

Keymer, Thomas, 'Shakespeare in the Novel', in Fiona Ritchie and Peter Sabor (eds.), *Shakespeare in the Eighteenth Century* (Cambridge: Cambridge University Press, 2012), pp. 118–40.

Keymer, Thomas, and Peter Sabor (eds.), *Dramatic and Operatic Adaptations*, Vol. vi of *The Pamela Controversy: Criticisms and Adaptations of Samuel Richardson's 'Pamela', 1740–1750*, 6 vols. (London: Pickering & Chatto, 2001).

Konigsberg, Ira, *Samuel Richardson and the Dramatic Novel* (Lexington, KY: University Press of Kentucky, 1968).

Palmer, William J., 'Two Dramatists: Lovelace and Richardson in *Clarissa*,' *Studies in the Novel*, 5.1 (1973), 7–21.
Rumbold, Kate, *Shakespeare and the Eighteenth-Century Novel: Cultures of Quotation from Samuel Richardson to Jane Austen* (Cambridge: Cambridge University Press, 2015).

24 HUMOUR

Dickie, Simon, *Cruelty and Laughter: Forgotten Comic Literature and the Unsentimental Eighteenth Century* (Chicago: University of Chicago Press, 2011).
'Fielding's Rape Jokes', *Review of English Studies*, 61.251 (2010), 572–90.
'Tobias Smollett and the Ramble Novel', in Peter Garside and Karen O'Brien (eds.), *English and British Fiction 1750–1820, Vol. II of The Oxford History of the Novel in English*, 12 vols. (Oxford: Oxford University Press, 2015), pp. 92–108.
Domingo, Darryl P., 'Richardson's Unfamiliar Quotations: *Clarissa* and Early Eighteenth-Century Comedy', *Review of English Studies*, 66.277 (2015), 936–53.
Ferguson, Frances, 'Rape and the Rise of the Novel', *Representations*, 20.1 (1987), 88–112.
Hudson, Nicholas, 'Arts of Seduction and the Rhetoric of *Clarissa*', *Modern Language Quarterly*, 51.1 (1990), 25–43.
Mackie, Erin Skye, *Rakes, Highwaymen, and Pirates: The Making of the Modern Gentleman in the Eighteenth Century* (Baltimore: Johns Hopkins University Press, 2009).
Warner, William Beatty, *Reading 'Clarissa': The Struggles of Interpretation* (New Haven: Yale University Press, 1979).

25 MONEY AND ECONOMICS

Bank of England, 'A Brief History of Banknotes', www.bankofengland.co.uk.
Brophy, Elizabeth Bergen, *Samuel Richardson: The Triumph of Craft* (Knoxville: University of Tennessee Press, 1974).
Copeland, Edward, 'Remapping London: *Clarissa* and the Woman in the Window', in Margaret Anne Doody and Peter Sabor (eds.), *Samuel Richardson: Tercentenary Essays* (Cambridge: Cambridge University Press, 1989), pp. 51–69.
Ferguson, Niall, *The Cash Nexus: Money and Power in the Modern World, 1700–2000* (New York: Basic Books: 2001).
Mahony, Stephen, *Wealth or Poverty? Jane Austen's Novels Explored* (London: Robert Hale, 2016).
Meldrum, Tim, *Domestic Service and Gender, 1660–1750: Life and Work in the London Household* (Harlow: Pearson Education, 2000).
O'Gorman, Frank, *The Long Eighteenth Century: British Political and Social History, 1688–1832* (London: Arnold, 1997).

Poovey, Mary, *A History of the Modern Fact: Problems of Knowledge in the Sciences of Wealth and Society* (Chicago: University of Chicago Press, 1998).

Price, Richard. *British Society, 1680–1880: Dynamism, Containment and Change* (Cambridge: Cambridge University Press, 1999).

Sambrook, Pamela, *Keeping Their Place: Domestic Service in the Country House, 1700–1920* (Stroud: Sutton Publishing, 2005).

Thompson, James, *Models of Value: Eighteenth-Century Political Economy and the Novel* (Durham, NC: Duke University Press, 1996).

26 THE LAW

Ferguson, Frances, 'Rape and the Rise of the Novel', *Representations*, 20.1 (1987), 88–112.

Groom, Nick, 'Unoriginal Genius: Plagiarism and the Construction of "Romantic" Authorship', in Lionel Bently, Jennifer Davis, and Jane C. Ginsburg (eds.), *Copyright and Piracy: An Interdisciplinary Critique* (Cambridge: Cambridge University Press, 2010), pp. 271–99.

Keymer, Thomas, 'Parliamentary Printing, Paper Credit, and Corporate Fraud: A New Episode in Richardson's Early Career', *Eighteenth-Century Fiction*, 17.2 (2005), 183–206.

Kibbie, Ann Louise, 'The Estate, the Corpse, and the Letter: Posthumous Possession in *Clarissa*', *ELH*, 74.1 (2007), 117–43.

Latimer, Bonnie, 'Samuel Richardson and the "Jew Bill" of 1753: A New Political Context for *Sir Charles Grandison*', *Review of English Studies*, 66.275 (2015), 520–39.

Macpherson, Sandra, *Harm's Way: Tragic Responsibility and the Novel Form* (Baltimore: Johns Hopkins University Press, 2010).

Price, Leah, '*Sir Charles Grandison* and the Executor's Hand', *Eighteenth-Century Fiction*, 8.3 (1996), 329–42.

Schwarz, Joan I., 'Eighteenth-Century Abduction Law and *Clarissa*', in Carol Houlihan Flynn and Edward Copeland (eds.), *Clarissa and Her Readers: New Essays for the 'Clarissa' Project* (New York: AMS, 1999), pp. 269–308.

Soni, Vivasvan, 'The Trial Narrative in Richardson's *Pamela*: Suspending the Hermeneutic of Happiness', in *Mourning Happiness: Narrative and the Politics of Modernity* (Ithaca, NY: Cornell University Press, 2010), pp. 177–210.

Stern, Simon, 'Copyright, Originality, and the Public Domain in Eighteenth-Century England', in Reginald McGinnis (ed.), *Originality and Intellectual Property in the French and English Enlightenment* (London: Routledge, 2008), pp. 69–101.

Swan, Beth, 'Clarissa Harlowe, Pleasant Rawlins, and Eighteenth-Century Discourses of Law', *Eighteenth-Century Novel*, 1 (2001), 71–93.

Vermillion, Mary, '*Clarissa* and the Marriage Act', *Eighteenth-Century Fiction*, 9.4 (1997), 395–414.

Wagner, Ann K., 'Sexual Assault in the Shadow of the Law: Character and Proof in Samuel Richardson's *Clarissa*', *Law & Literature*, 25.2 (2013), 311–26.

27 FAMILY

Bowers, Toni, *Force or Fraud: British Seduction Stories and the Problem of Resistance, 1660–1760* (Oxford: Oxford University Press, 2011).

The Politics of Motherhood: British Writing and Culture, 1680–1760 (Cambridge: Cambridge University Press, 1996).

Dussinger, John A., 'Love and Consanguinity in Richardson's Novels', *Studies in English Literature, 1500–1900*, 24.3 (1984), pp. 513–26.

Francus, Marilyn, *Monstrous Motherhood: Eighteenth-Century Culture and the Ideology of Domesticity* (Baltimore: Johns Hopkins University Press, 2012).

McCrea, Brian, *Impotent Fathers: Patriarchy and Demographic Crisis in the Eighteenth-Century Novel* (Newark: University of Delaware Press, 1998).

Perry, Ruth, *Novel Relations: The Transformation of Kinship in English Literature and Culture, 1748–1818* (Cambridge: Cambridge University Press, 2004).

Schwarz, Joan I., 'Family Dynamics and Property Acquisitions in *Clarissa*', in John V. Knapp and Kenneth Womack (eds.), *Reading the Family Dance: Family Systems Therapy and Literary Study* (Newark: University of Delaware Press, 2003), pp. 111–34.

Stone, Lawrence, *Broken Lives: Separation and Divorce in England, 1660–1857* (Oxford: Oxford University Press, 1993).

The Family, Sex and Marriage in England, 1500–1800 (New York: Harper and Row, 1977).

Uncertain Unions: Marriage in England, 1660–1753 (Oxford: Oxford University Press, 1992).

Tadmor, Naomi, 'The Concept of the Household-Family in Eighteenth-Century England', *Past & Present*, 151 (1996), 111–40.

Thompson, Helen, *Ingenuous Subjection: Compliance and Power in the Eighteenth-Century Domestic Novel* (Philadelphia: University of Pennsylvania Press, 2005).

Trumbach, Randolph, *The Rise of the Egalitarian Family: Aristocratic Kinship and Domestic Relations in Eighteenth-Century England* (New York: Academic, 1978).

Zomchick, John P., *Family and the Law in Eighteenth-Century Fiction: The Public Conscience in the Private Sphere* (Cambridge: Cambridge University Press, 1993).

28 GENDER

Backscheider, Paula R., 'The Rise of Gender as Political Category', in Paula R. Backscheider (ed.), *Revising Women: Eighteenth-Century 'Women's Fiction' and Social Engagement* (Baltimore: Johns Hopkins University Press, 2000), pp. 31–57.

Barker-Benfield, G. J., *The Culture of Sensibility: Sex and Society in Eighteenth-Century Britain* (Chicago: University of Chicago Press, 1992).

Butler, Judith, *Gender Trouble: Feminism and the Subversion of Identity*, 2nd edn (London: Routledge, 1999).

Clery, E. J., *The Feminization Debate in Eighteenth-Century England: Literature, Commerce and Luxury* (Basingstoke: Palgrave Macmillan, 2004).

Gwilliam, Tassie, *Samuel Richardson's Fictions of Gender* (Stanford: Stanford University Press, 1993).

Kahn, Madeleine, *Narrative Transvestism: Rhetoric and Gender in the Eighteenth-Century English Novel* (Ithaca, NY: Cornell University Press, 1991).

Laqueur, Thomas, *Making Sex: Body and Gender from the Greeks to Freud* (Cambridge, MA: Harvard University Press, 1990).

Latimer, Bonnie, *Making Gender, Culture, and the Self in the Fiction of Samuel Richardson: The Novel Individual* (Farnham: Ashgate, 2012).

McMaster, Juliet, '*Sir Charles Grandison*: Richardson on Body and Character', in David Blewett (ed.), *Passion and Virtue: Essays on the Novels of Samuel Richardson* (Toronto: University of Toronto Press, 2001), pp. 246–67.

Roulston, Christine, *Virtue, Gender, and the Authentic Self in Eighteenth-Century Fiction: Richardson, Rousseau, and Laclos* (Gainesville: University Press of Florida, 1998).

29 SEXUALITY

Cryle, Peter, and Lisa O'Connell (eds.), *Libertine Enlightenment: Sex, Liberty and Licence in the Eighteenth Century* (Basingstoke: Palgrave Macmillan, 2004).

Eagleton, Terry, *The Rape of Clarissa: Writing, Sexuality and Class Struggle in Samuel Richardson* (Minneapolis: University of Minnesota Press, 1982).

Hagstrum, Jean H., *Sex and Sensibility: Ideal and Erotic Love from Milton to Mozart* (Chicago: University of Chicago Press, 1980).

Trumbach, Randolph, *Sex and the Gender Revolution, Vol. 1: Heterosexuality and the Third Gender in Enlightenment London* (Chicago: University of Chicago Press, 1998).

Turner, James Grantham, 'The Erotics of the Novel', in Paula A. Backscheider and Catherine Ingrassia (eds.), *A Companion to the Eighteenth-Century English Novel and Culture* (Oxford: Blackwell, 2005), pp. 214–34.

'Novel Panic: Picture and Performance in the Reception of Richardson's *Pamela*', *Representations*, 48 (1994), 70–96.

'Richardson and His Circle', in John Richetti (ed.), *The Columbia History of the British Novel* (New York: Columbia University Press, 1994), pp. 73–101.

30 MEDICINE AND HEALTH

Cheyne, George, *The English Malady; or, A Treatise of Nervous Conditions of All Kinds* (London, 1733).

Davies, Rebecca S., 'The Maternal Contradiction: Representing the Fictional Mother in Richardson's *Pamela II* (1741)', *Journal for Eighteenth-Century Studies*, 33.3 (2010), 381–97.

Guerrini, Anita, *Obesity and Depression in the Enlightenment: The Life and Times of George Cheyne* (Norman: University of Oklahoma Press, 2000).

Lawlor, Clark, ' "Long *Grief*, dark *Melancholy*, hopeless natural *Love*": *Clarissa*, Cheyne and Narratives of Body and Soul', *Gesnerus*, 63.1–2 (2006), 103–12.

McAllister, Marie E., 'Pox Imagery in *Clarissa*', *The Eighteenth Century Novel*, 9 (2012), 1–24.

McMaster, Juliet, 'The Body inside the Skin: The Medical Model of Character in the Eighteenth-Century Novel', *Eighteenth-Century Fiction*, 4.4 (1992), 277–300.

Rousseau, George S., 'Nerves, Spirits, and Fibres: Toward the Origins of Sensibility (1975)', in *Nervous Acts: Essays on Literature, Culture and Sensibility* (Basingstoke: Palgrave Macmillan, 2004), pp. 157–84.

Scheuer, J. L., and J. E. Bowman, 'The Health of the Novelist and Printer Samuel Richardson (1689–1761): A Correlation of Documentary and Skeletal Evidence', *Journal of the Royal Society of Medicine*, 87.6 (1994), 352–5.

Shapin, Steve, 'Trusting George Cheyne: Scientific Expertise, Common Sense, and Moral Authority in Early Eighteenth-Century Dietetic Medicine', *Bulletin of the History of Medicine*, 77.2 (2003), 263–97.

Shuttleton, David, '"Not the meanest part of my works and experience": Dr George Cheyne's Correspondence with Samuel Richardson', in Sophie Vasset (ed.), *Medicine and Narration in the Eighteenth Century* (Oxford: Voltaire Foundation, 2013), pp. 65–81.

'"Pamela's Library": Samuel Richardson and Dr. Cheyne's "Universal Cure"', *Eighteenth-Century Life*, 23.1 (1999), 59–79.

Stephanson, Raymond, 'Richardson's "Nerves": The Physiology of Sensibility in *Clarissa*', *Journal of the History of Ideas*, 49.2 (1998), 267–85.

31 DEATH AND MOURNING CULTURE

Almond, Philip C., *Heaven and Hell in Enlightenment England* (Cambridge: Cambridge University Press, 1994).

Andrew, Donna T., *Aristocratic Vice: The Attack on Duelling, Suicide, Adultery, and Gambling in Eighteenth-Century England* (New Haven: Yale University Press, 2013).

Ariès, Philippe, *The Hour of Our Death*, trans. Helen Weaver (New York: Alfred A. Knopf, 1981).

Western Attitudes toward Death: From the Middle Ages to the Present, trans. Patricia M. Ranum (Baltimore: Johns Hopkins University Press, 1974).

Cressy, David, *Birth, Marriage, and Death: Ritual, Religion, and the Life-Cycle in Tudor and Stuart England* (Oxford: Oxford University Press, 1997).

Gittings, Clare, *Death, Burial and the Individual in Early Modern England* (London: Croom Helm, 1984).

Gittings, Clare, and Peter C. Jupp (eds.), *Death in England: An Illustrated History* (Manchester: Manchester University Press, 1999).

Houlbrooke, Ralph, *Death, Religion and the Family in England, 1480–1750* (Oxford: Clarendon Press, 1998).

Zigarovich, Jolene (ed.), *Sex and Death in Eighteenth-Century Literature* (London: Taylor & Francis, 2013).

32 LONDON

Bucholz, Robert O., and Joseph P. Ward, *London: A Social and Cultural History, 1550–1750* (Cambridge: Cambridge University Press, 2012).

Copeland, Edward, 'Remapping London: *Clarissa* and the Woman in the Window', in Margaret Anne Doody and Peter Sabor (eds.), *Samuel Richardson: Tercentenary Essays* (Cambridge: Cambridge University Press, 1989), pp. 51–69.

Defoe, Daniel, *A Tour thro' the Whole Island of Great Britain*, 2nd edn (London, 1738).

Gatrell, Vic, *City of Laughter: Sex and Satire in Eighteenth-Century London* (London: Atlantic Books, 2006).

Hitchcock, Tim, and Robert Shoemaker, *London Lives: Poverty, Crime and the Making of a Modern City, 1690–1800* (Cambridge: Cambridge University Press, 2015).

O'Connell, Sheila, *London: 1753* (London: British Museum Press, 2003).

Porter, Roy, *London: A Social History* (London: Hamish Hamilton, 1994).

Summerson, John, *Georgian London*, ed. Howard Colvin (New Haven: Yale University Press, 2003).

33 SENTIMENT AND SENSIBILITY

Barker-Benfield, G. J., *The Culture of Sensibility: Sex and Society in Eighteenth-Century Britain* (Chicago: University of Chicago Press, 1992).

Brissenden, R. F., *Virtue in Distress: Studies in the Novel of Sentiment from Richardson to Sade* (London: Macmillan, 1974).

Chandler, James, *An Archaeology of Sympathy: The Sentimental Mode in Literature and Cinema* (Chicago: University of Chicago Press, 2013).

Ellis, Markman, *The Politics of Sensibility: Race, Gender and Commerce in the Sentimental Novel* (Cambridge: Cambridge University Press, 1996).

Markley, Robert, 'Sentimentality as Performance: Shaftesbury, Sterne, and the Theatrics of Virtue', in Felicity Nussbaum and Laura Brown (eds.), *The New Eighteenth Century: Theory, Politics, English Literature* (New York: Methuen, 1987), pp. 210–30.

Mullan, John, *Sentiment and Sociability: The Language of Feeling in the Eighteenth Century* (Oxford: Clarendon Press, 1988).

Nazar, Hina, *Enlightened Sentiments: Judgment and Autonomy in the Age of Sensibility* (New York: Fordham University Press, 2012).

Todd, Janet, *Sensibility: An Introduction* (London: Methuen, 1986).

Van Sant, Ann Jessie, *Eighteenth-Century Sensibility and the Novel: The Senses in Social Context* (Cambridge: Cambridge University Press, 1993).

34 RELIGION

Bechler, Rosemary, ' "Triall by what is contrary": Samuel Richardson and Christian Dialectic', in Valerie Grosvenor Myer (ed.), *Samuel Richardson: Passion and Prudence* (London: Vision, 1986), pp. 93–113.

Chaber, Lois, 'Christian Form and Anti-Feminism in *Clarissa*', *Eighteenth-Century Fiction*, 15.3–4 (2003), 507–37.

Damrosch, Leopold, Jr, *God's Plot and Man's Stories: Studies in the Fictional Imagination from Milton to Fielding* (Chicago: University of Chicago Press, 1985).

Doody, Margaret Anne, 'The Gnostic *Clarissa*', *Eighteenth-Century Fiction*, 11.1 (1998), 49–78.

Dussinger, John A., 'The Oxford Methodists (1733; 1738): The Purloined Letter of John Wesley at Samuel Richardson's Press', in Melvyn New and Gerard Reedy (eds.), *Theology and Literature in the Age of Johnson: Resisting Secularism* (Newark: University of Delaware Press, 2012), pp. 27–48.

Keymer, Tom, 'Richardson's *Meditations*: Clarissa's *Clarissa*', in Margaret Anne Doody and Peter Sabor (eds.), *Samuel Richardson: Tercentenary Essays* (Cambridge: Cambridge University Press, 1989), pp. 89–109.

Mello, Patrick, '"Piety and Popishness": Tolerance and the Epistolary Reaction to Richardson's *Sir Charles Grandison*', *Eighteenth-Century Fiction*, 25.3 (2013), 511–31.

Stuber, Florian, '*Clarissa*: A Religious Novel?', *Studies in the Literary Imagination*, 28:1 (1995), 105–24.

Taylor, E. Derek, *Reason and Religion in Clarissa: Samuel Richardson and 'The Famous Mr Norris, of Bemerton'* (Farnham: Ashgate, 2009).

'Samuel Richardson's *Clarissa* and the Problem of Heaven', in Melvyn New and Gerard Reedy (eds.), *Theology and Literature in the Age of Johnson* (Newark: University of Delaware Press, 2012), pp. 71–89.

Wilson, Angus, '*Clarissa*', in Valerie Grosvenor Myer (ed.), *Samuel Richardson: Passion and Prudence* (London: Vision, 1986), pp. 41–51.

Wolff, Cynthia G., *Samuel Richardson and the Eighteenth-Century Puritan Character* (Hamden, CT: Shoe String Press, 1972).

35 SOCIAL HIERARCHY AND SOCIAL MOBILITY

Harvey, Karen, *The Little Republic: Masculinity and Domestic Authority in Eighteenth-Century Britain* (Oxford: Oxford University Press, 2012).

Hunt, Margaret R., *The Middling Sort: Commerce, Gender, and the Family in England, 1680–1780* (Berkeley: University of California Press, 1996).

Johnson, Samuel, *A Dictionary of the English Language*, 2nd edn, 2 vols. (London, 1755–6).

Langford, Paul, *A Polite and Commercial People: England 1727–1783* (Oxford: Oxford University Press, 1992).

Lipsedge, Karen, *Domestic Space in Eighteenth-Century British Novels* (Basingstoke: Palgrave Macmillan, 2012).

Tristram, Philippa, *Living Space in Fact and Fiction* (London: Routledge, 1989).

Vickery, Amanda, *Behind Closed Doors: At Home in Georgian England* (New Haven: Yale University Press, 2009).

Wall, Cynthia S., *The Prose of Things: Transformations of Description in the Eighteenth Century* (Chicago: University of Chicago Press, 2006).

Watt, Ian, *The Rise of the Novel: Studies in Defoe, Richardson and Fielding* (Berkeley: University of California Press, 1957).

36 POLITICS

Casas, Bartolomé de las, *Liberty and Property, and No Pretender* (London, 1745).

Doody, Margaret Anne, 'Richardson's Politics', *Eighteenth-Century Fiction*, 2.2 (1990), 113–26.

Dussinger, John A., 'Masters and Servants: Political Discourse in Richardson's *A Collection of Moral Sentiments*', *Eighteenth-Century Fiction*, 5. 3 (1993), 239–52.

[Gordon, Thomas], *Four Letters Taken from the 'General Evening Post', Relating to the Present Rebellion* (London, 1745).

Hagstrum, Jean, and James Gray (eds.), *Sermons*, Vol. xiv of *The Yale Edition of the Works of Samuel Johnson*, 23 vols. (New Haven: Yale University Press, 1978).

Kaminsky, Thomas, Benjamin Beard Hoover, and O M Brack, Jr (eds.), *Debates in Parliament*, Vols. xi–xiii of *The Yale Edition of the Works of Samuel Johnson*, 23 vols. (New Haven: Yale University Press, 2012).

Laundy, Philip, 'Arthur Onslow', *Oxford Dictionary of National Biography* (Oxford: Oxford University Press, 2004), online edn.

Seagrave, Robert, *The True Protestant* (London, 1746).

Weinbrot, Howard D., 'Historical Criticism, the Reclamation of Codes, and Repairs to Literary History: The Examples of Fielding and Richardson', *Eighteenth-Century Life, 41.3* (2017), 57–88.

'Johnson's *Irene* and *Rasselas*, Richardson's *Pamela Exalted*: Contexts, Polygamy, and the Seraglio', *Age of Johnson*, 23 (2015), 89–140.

Young, Edward, *Imperium Pelagi. A Naval Lyrick: Occasioned by His Majesty's Return, Sept. 1729* (London, 1730).

37 NATIONALISM

Alryyes, Ala A., *Original Subjects: The Child, the Novel, and the Nation* (Cambridge, MA: Harvard University Press, 2001).

Anderson, Benedict, *Imagined Communities: Reflections on the Origin and Spread of Nationalism* (London: Verso, 1983).

Aravamudan, Srinivas, *Enlightenment Orientalism: Resisting the Rise of the Novel* (Chicago: University of Chicago Press, 2012).

Ballaster, Rosalind, *Fabulous Orients: Fictions of the East in England, 1682–1785* (Oxford: Oxford University Press, 2005).

Colley, Linda, *Britons: Forging the Nation, 1707–1837* (New Haven: Yale University Press, 1992).

Greenfield, Liah, *Nationalism: Five Roads to Modernity* (Cambridge, MA: Harvard University Press, 1992).

Kumar, Krishan, *The Making of English National Identity* (Cambridge: Cambridge University Press, 2003).

McMurran, Mary Helen, *The Spread of Novels: Translation and Prose Fiction in the Eighteenth Century* (Princeton: Princeton University Press, 2009).

Newman, Gerard, *The Rise of English Nationalism: A Cultural History, 1740–1830* (London: Weidenfeld and Nicolson, 1987).

Parrinder, Patrick, *Nation and Novel: The English Novel from Its Origins to the Present Day* (Oxford: Oxford University Press, 2006).

Index

Printed in Great Britain
by Amazon